ENGLISH G

HEADLIGHT

Lehrerfassung

5

W0382018

Vokabel Trainer

Cornelsen

Vokabeltrainer-App

Verfügbar für: iOS, Android und Windows Phone

Dieses Buch gibt es auch auf
www.scook.de

Es kann dort nach Bestätigung der Allgemeinen Geschäftsbedingungen genutzt werden.

Buchcode: oe357-gdsu3

Cornelsen

English G · Headlight · Band 5

Lehrerfassung

Im Auftrag des Verlages herausgegeben von
Wolfgang Biederstädt, Köln

Konzepterarbeitung von
Susan Abbey, Nenagh, Irland
Wolfgang Biederstädt, Köln
Frank Donoghue, Nenagh, Irland

Erarbeitet von
Marc Proulx, Berlin
Susan Abbey, Nenagh, Irland
Frank Donoghue, Nenagh, Irland

unter Mitarbeit von
Joachim Blombach, Herford
Annette Bondzio-Abbit, Bielefeld
Hartmut Bondzio, Bielefeld
Uta Franke, Leipzig
Martina Schroeder, Stedtlingen
Udo Wagner, Voerde
Herbert Willms, Herford

in Zusammenarbeit mit der Englischredaktion
Klaus Unger (Projektleitung); Jutta Seuren (koordinierende Redakteurin); Doreen Arnold; Cornelia Frisse, Irja Fröhling, Undine Griebel, Annegret Hauser, Mara Leibowitz, Kathrin Spiegelberg, Silvia Wiedemann, Olivia Wintgens; Stefanie Tamke (bildrechtliche Unterstützung)

Vokabelanhänge
Ingrid Raspe, Düsseldorf; Uwe Tröger

Beratende Mitwirkung
Simone Beattie, Aalen; Eugen Blumenstock, Loßburg; Peer Brändel, Gütersloh; Uwe Chormann, Einselthum; Matthew George, Frankfurt a. M.; Bernhard Hunger, Dettingen; Anke Husmann-Niemann, Osnabrück; Prof. Dr. Jörg-U. Keßler, Ludwigsburg; Sylvia Krautstein, Köln; Jörg Rademacher, Mannheim; Ulrike Rath, Aachen; Mirjam Schrade, Böblingen; Udo Wagner, Voerde

Layoutkonzept und technische Umsetzung
Klein & Halm Grafikdesign, Berlin

Umschlaggestaltung
Cornelsen Schulverlage Design unter Verwendung der Entwürfe von Klein & Halm Grafikdesign, Berlin und kleiner und bold, Berlin

www.cornelsen.de

Druck: Firmengruppe APPL, aprinta Druck, Wemding

1. Auflage, 1. Druck 2016
ISBN 978-3-06-032654-9

PEFC
PEFC/04-32-0928

PEFC zertifiziert
Dieses Produkt stammt aus nachhaltig bewirtschafteten Wäldern und kontrollierten Quellen.

www.pefc.de

Dein Englischbuch enthält folgende Teile:

Unit 1–4	Die vier Kapitel des Buches
Diff-Bank	Weitere Aufgaben – unterschiedlich schwer
Wordbank	Zusätzliche Wörter und Wendungen zu bestimmten Themen
Text file	Interessante Texte, passend zu den Units
Exam file	Aufgaben zur Vorbereitung auf die Abschlussprüfung
Language file	Zusammenfassung wichtiger Sprachregeln
Skills file	Beschreibung wichtiger Lern- und Arbeitstechniken
Vocabulary	Wörterverzeichnis zum Lernen der neuen Wörter
Dictionary	Alphabetisches Wörterverzeichnis (*English-German*)

Die Units bestehen aus diesen Teilen:

Lead-in	Einstieg in die neue Unit
Theme 1/Theme 2	Neue Themen mit vielen Aktivitäten und Übungen
Focus on language	Entdecken von Regeln und Üben wichtiger Strukturen
Text	Eine Geschichte zum Lesen
Skills training	Hören: *Listening* – Lesen: *Reading* – Sprechen: *Speaking* – Schreiben: *Writing* – Sprachmittlung: *Mediation* – Hör-/ Sehverstehen: *Viewing*
More Challenge	Aufgaben mit höherem Schwierigkeitsgrad
Stop! Check! Go!	Üben, Vertiefen, Lernfortschritte feststellen (Von der Lehrperson kannst du ein Lösungsblatt erhalten. Hörtexte findest du auf der Audio-CD im Workbook.)

In den Units findest du diese Symbole:

	Partnerarbeit / Gruppenarbeit
	Nur auf CD / Auf CD und im Schülerbuch
	Filme auf der DVD
	Leichtere Übungen
	Schwierigere Übungen
// p.104	Parallelaufgaben: die leichtere in der Unit – die schwierigere in der Diff-Bank
More help p.102	Hilfen zu einer Aufgabe in der Diff-Bank
More practice 3 p.104	Weitere Übungen in der Diff-Bank
More challenge 4 p.107	Weitere Übungen mit höherem Schwierigkeitsgrad

INHALT

	Lerninhalte	Your task (Lernaufgabe)	Texte
Unit 1 Life down under 	· Geografie und Sehenswürdigkeiten Australiens kennen lernen · über Besonderheiten von Land und Leuten sprechen · sich in Notfallsituationen verständigen · sich mit der Geschichte und Kultur der australischen Ureinwohner/innen befassen · Interessantes über Sydney und Melbourne erfahren · Zeitformen korrekt verwenden · eine Präsentation vorbereiten, halten und auswerten	**A presentation about Australia** selbstständig für eine Präsentation recherchieren, sie erstellen und vortragen; dazu Feedback geben und erhalten (p. 25) 	**Magazine articles** *Ban on climbing Uluru comes nearer* (p. 10) *Proud to be a new Australian* (p. 10) *Fighting bush fires between exams* (p. 11) *Australia's deadliest animals* (p. 11) *First Australians* (p. 15) **Website** *Royal Flying Doctor Service* (p. 12) **Teens' real life stories** *Living in the Kimberley* (p. 18) *I'm a mud racer* (p. 18) *Beach culture* (p. 18) *One day changed my life* (p. 18) **Text** *adapted from the novel* **Swerve** (pp. 20–23)
***MORE CHALLENGE** A different world	· eine Geschichte über einen japanischen Gastschüler in Tasmanien erschließen · mit idiomatischen Wendungen umgehen		**Text** *adapted from* **The Spare Room** (pp. 26–27) **Cartoons** *English idioms* (p. 28)
Unit 2 Respect 	· über *cyberbullying* sprechen und mögliche Auswege diskutieren · sich über den Umgang mit *peer pressure* austauschen · ein Experiment zum Thema Diskriminierung durchführen und reflektieren · berichten, was jemand gesagt hat · lernen und üben, wie Konversationen gelingen	**Do something!** in Gruppenarbeit ein Projekt gegen Diskriminierung erarbeiten und präsentieren (p. 39) 	**Magazine articles** *Jamaal – It doesn't have to be uncool* *Emily – It really hurt* (p. 34) **Newspaper report** *Player and his teammates say "enough"* (p. 37) **Text** *"Natasha's side of the story" and "Matt's side of the story", adapted from the novel* **Watching you, watching me** (pp. 43–47)
***MORE CHALLENGE** Living with disability	· zwei authentische Texte über das Leben mit Behinderungen erschließen · eigenes Verhalten reflektieren		**Blog entry** *The kid in a wheelchair* (p. 50) **Online article** *A fashion model and a role model* (p. 50)

Die hier (und auf S. 5–7) aufgeführten Angebote sind nicht obligatorisch abzuarbeiten. Die Auswahl der Übungen und Übungsteile richtet sich nach den Schwerpunkten des schulinternen Curriculums. *markiert optionale Angebote.

Kompetenzen	Sprache	Seite
Listening: advert *The Flying Doctors* (p. 12) conversations *Emergencies on the beach* (p. 13) radio interviews (p. 16) teens' audio stories for a competition (p. 18) **Speaking course (1) *Giving a presentation*** (pp. 24–25) discussion *Australia – a place to visit?* (p. 11) silent dialogue *Getting help* (p. 13) **Reading:** articles *What makes Oz special?* (pp. 10–11) *Tips from the RFDS website* (p. 12); *First Australians* (p. 15); *One country, two centres* (p. 17) **Writing:** Artikel *Tips for tourists in Australia* (p. 13) zusammenfassen, was man einem Text entnommen hat (p. 15) einen Artikel schreiben, wo man leben möchte (p. 17) **Mediation** (+ intercultural competence): Teile eines Songtexts analysieren und sprachmitteln (p. 14) **Viewing** (+ intercultural competence): *An Australian road trip* (p. 9); *The Burdekin Crew* (p. 14) *How to improve your presentations* (p. 24)	**Wortschatz** und **Strukturen** *describing places and activities; avoiding emergencies; getting help, talking about a difficult history; teens' everyday life in Australia; useful phrases for presentations* **using tenses correctly** revision: ***simple present***, ***simple past***, **going to-*future***, ***past progressive*** (p. 19) ***STOP! CHECK! GO!** (pp. 29–31) Üben und vertiefen; Lernfortschritte erkennen	8
Listening: dialogues *Fun with idioms* (p. 28) **Speaking:** das Leben in einer anderen Kultur erörtern (p. 27) **Reading:** *Akira's first morning, Being me in English* (pp. 26–27) **Mediation:** English and German idioms (p. 28)	**Wortschatz** und **Strukturen** *talking about cultural differences* **dealing with idioms** (p. 28)	26
Listening: dialogues *Come shopping with me!* (p. 36); *Guess what happened last night* (p. 40) **Speaking course (2) *Successful conversations*** (pp. 48–49) Auswege aus *cyberbullying*-Situationen diskutieren (p. 33) sprechen über rassistisches Verhalten (p. 37) role-plays *Why don't you go out with us?* (p. 36) *Badges – a group experiment* (p. 37) **Reading:** articles about peer pressure (p. 34) **Writing:** comment *Peer pressure is a big problem for teenagers* (p. 35) **Study skills:** einen Slogan erschließen (p. 38) **Viewing** (+ intercultural competence): *Friends ...* (pp. 32–33) *'What you say matters' by Brothablack* (p. 38) *Dos and don'ts in conversations* (p. 48)	**Wortschatz** und **Strukturen** *speculating about a conflict; giving advice; supporting an opinion with arguments; reflecting on feelings and interactions; planning and presenting a project; useful phrases for conversations* ***indirect speech* in statements, questions and commands** (pp. 40–42) ***STOP! CHECK! GO!** (pp. 53–55) Üben und vertiefen; Lernfortschritte erkennen	32
Listening: radio interviews *Do the right thing* (p. 51) **Reading:** blog entry; article (p. 50) **Speaking:** Reaktionen auf Texte verbalisieren und eigene Haltungen reflektieren (p. 51) eine Präsentation erstellen und vortragen (p. 51)	**Wortschatz** und **Strukturen** *talking about feelings and attitudes* ***participles* (-ing-*forms*) instead of subordinate clauses** (p. 52)	50

INHALT

	Lerninhalte	Your task (Lernaufgabe)	Texte
Unit 3 Looking forward 	· über *life skills* und die eigene Zukunft sprechen · persönliche Stärken, Schwächen und Vorlieben beschreiben · Stellenangebote verstehen · über den persönlichen Idealberuf sprechen · *CV* und *cover letter* verfassen lernen · sich mit Freiwilligendiensten befassen · Fragen formulieren und *question tags* verwenden · sich auf *job interviews* vorbereiten	**Who will get the job?** Bewerbungsgespräche durchführen und evaluieren (p. 73) 	**Quiz** *Are you ready for the real world?* (p. 56) **Adverts** *Internet job ads* (pp. 60–61) **Official documents** *CV* (p. 62) *Cover letter* (p. 63) **Website** *European Volunteer Network* (p. 64) **Online article** *Work and travel* (p. 65) Text *adapted from the short story* **Seashell Motel** (pp. 68–70)
***MORE CHALLENGE** Looking to the future	· kreatives Schreiben in unterschiedlichen Genres · *let/make* verwenden		**Example texts** (p. 75) a self-description, a story, a dialogue and a poem
Unit 4 Generation *like* 	· sagen, was man *cool* oder *uncool* findet · eigene digitale Gewohnheiten reflektieren · über Selbstdarstellungen sprechen (*profiles*, *selfies*, *tattoos*) · mit Werbestrategien umgehen lernen · sagen, was passiert wäre, wenn … · sich an Diskussionen beteiligen	**Cool talk** eine Präsentation zum Thema *What's (not) cool and why?* halten (p. 81) 	**Articles** *Being a screenager* (p. 82) *Your kind of profile picture?* (p. 84) *Are you ad-savvy?* (p. 86) *Hundreds of teenagers gatecrash party* (p. 88) Text *adapted from the novel* **Gamer** (pp. 90–94) **Book review** **Gamer** (p. 95)
***MORE CHALLENGE** Street art	· über Kunst im öffentlichen Raum sprechen · einen Film über Banksy kennen lernen · Sidewalk poetry		**Film review** *Exit through the gift shop* (p. 99)

PARTNER-B-Seiten	104
DIFF-BANK	107
*WORDBANK	136
*TEXT FILE	140
TF 1 Oz: Facts for visitors (Unit 1)	140
TF 2 Waiting for something to happen (Unit 2)	142
TF 3 Job description: Cleaner of the world's oceans (Unit 3, bilinguales Modul *geography*)	148
TF 4 Music in your life (Unit 4)	150
TF 5 Images in the media (Unit 4, bilinguales Modul *social studies*)	152
*EXAM FILE	154

SKILLS FILE		160
SF 1–5	STUDY AND LANGUAGE SKILLS	160
SF 6–7	LISTENING SKILLS AND READING COURSE	165
SF 8	SPEAKING COURSE	169
SF 9	WRITING COURSE	171
SF 10	DESCRIBING PHOTOS AND PICTURES	179
SF 11	VIEWING SKILLS	180
SF 12	MEDIATION SKILLS	181
LANGUAGE FILE		182
LF 1–2	TALKING ABOUT THE PRESENT	182
LF 3–7	TALKING ABOUT THE PAST	183
LF 8–9	TALKING ABOUT THE FUTURE	187
LF 10	Using tenses	187

Kompetenzen	Sprache	Seite
Listening: interviews *Ideas for the future* (p. 59) Erlebnisberichte *The experience of volunteering* (p. 65) **Speaking course (3) *Doing well in job interviews*** (pp. 72–73) über *life skills* sprechen (p. 57) sich selbst beschreiben und mit anderen über Stärken und Schwächen austauschen (p. 59) über geeignete Stellenangebote sprechen (p. 61) **Reading:** scanning; reading for details (job ads pp. 60–61) website (p. 64) **Writing:** *CV* und *cover letter* verfassen (pp. 62–63) Figurencharakterisierungen verfassen (p. 71) a diary entry (p. 71) **Viewing** (+ intercultural competence): *Strengths and weaknesses* (p. 58); *Interview stress* (p. 72)	**Wortschatz** und **Strukturen** *describing people and job requirements; structures and phrases for CVs and cover letters; characterization of literary figures; evaluating job interviews* revision: **question words, word order in questions** (p. 66) **question tags** (p. 67) ***subject and object questions*** (p. 125) ***questions with prepositions*** (p. 126) ***STOP! CHECK! GO!** (pp. 77–79) Üben und vertiefen; Lernfortschritte erkennen	56
Reading: a conversation about Volunteer programmes (p. 74) **Writing:** *creative writing* (p. 75); *writing a conversation* (p. 76)	**Wortschatz** und **Strukturen** ***let/make + object + infinitive*** (p. 76)	74
Listening: interviews *Teens react* (p. 80); *Digital habits* (p. 83) **Speaking course (4) *Taking part in discussions*** (pp. 96–97) role-play discussing different viewpoints (p. 83) **Reading:** reading for details and note-taking (pp. 82–83) finding the main points of a text (pp. 86–87) **Writing:** a written discussion *For and against tattoos* (p. 85) keeping an ad diary; writing an ad report (p. 87) *An email to the author* (p. 94) **Mediation:** talking about the ad industry (p. 87) **Viewing** (+ intercultural competence): *Shocking news!* (p. 96)	**Wortschatz** und **Strukturen** *talking about digital habits, describing photos, talking about advertising strategies, taking part in discussions, argumentative writing* ***conditional sentences type 3*** (p. 89) ***gerund (-ing-form) or to-infinitive*** (p. 129) ***STOP! CHECK! GO!** (pp. 101–103) Üben und vertiefen; Lernfortschritte erkennen	80
Listening: presentation *An outdoor art gallery* (p. 98) **Speaking:** *Talking about street art* (p. 98, 100) **Reading:** review *Exit through the gift shop* (p. 99) **Writing:** einen *film review* verfassen (p. 99) sidewalk poetry dichten (p. 100)	**Wortschatz** und **Strukturen** *describing and analysing street art and sidewalk poetry and giving one's personal reaction; reviewing a film*	98

LF 11–12	Word order (statements, questions)	188
LF 13–15	Questions	189
LF 16	The comparison of adjectives	191
LF 17–19	Adverbs	191
LF 20	Indirect speech	192
LF 21	Modal verbs and their substitutes	195
LF 22–24	Conditional sentences: types 1, 2, 3	196
LF 25–26	Relative clauses, *contact clauses	198
LF 27	Participle clauses instead of subclauses	199
LF 28	Reflexive pronouns	200
LF 29	The *-ing* form (gerund)	200
LF 30	The passive	202
LF 31	Question tags	203
LF 32	The definite and the indefinite article	203
LF 33	Countable and uncountable nouns	204
	GRAMMATICAL TERMS	204
	VOCABULARY	206
	DICTIONARY (English–German)	234
	ENGLISH SOUNDS · THE ENGLISH ALPHABET	265
	IRREGULAR VERBS	266
	LIST OF NAMES	268
	ENGLISH-SPEAKING COUNTRIES	269
	TYPICAL INSTRUCTIONS	270
	QUELLENVERZEICHNIS	271

Unit 1 Life down under

▸ KV 1 ▸ INKL pp. 8–9

A

B

Meeting kangaroos

C

Uluru - an important place for Aboriginal Australians in the outback

D

A °sheep station near Perth in Western Australia

1 Discovering the land down under

a) Think: What do you know about Australia's …

- landscapes?
- nicknames?
- cities?
- animals?
- people?
- climate?
- history?

The photos and the map on the °inside cover can help you.

▸ *Text °file 1, pp. 140–141*

b) Pair: Compare your answers and add to your information.

c) Share: Talk about your results in class.

▸ KV 1 ▸ INKL pp. 8–9

Christmas on the beach

Diving at the Great Barrier **Reef**

Sydney – not the capital, but Australia's biggest city

2 VIEWING An Australian **road trip**

Young people often make their own films about their road trips in Australia.

a) Watch this road trip film and add to your results from task 1. Make notes. Then compare with a partner.

b) Watch the film again. What activities and places do you see? Then make a list in class – name as many as you can. More help p. 107

– swimming in ...
– surfing ...

c) Talk about these questions in class:

– Would you like to do a road trip in Australia?
– Why (not)?
– Where would you like to go? Why?
– Who would you go with?
– What activities would you like to do?

More practice 1 p. 107 More challenge 1 p. 107

Articles from around Australia

1 °JIGSAW What makes Oz special?

a) Make groups of four. Each member of the group should read one of the articles (A – D).

b) Work alone. First make notes on what your article is about. Then °note down anything that makes Australia special.

c) Compare your notes with someone who has read the same article.

A

Ban on climbing Uluru comes nearer

Together with Sydney Harbour Bridge and the Great Barrier Reef, Uluru is probably the best-known tourist sight in Australia. 200,000 visitors travel there every year and at the moment they are allowed to climb the rock. But for how long?

Uluru is the name that the local Aboriginal people give to the rock. People travel over a thousand miles across the flat, empty landscape of central Australia to see it. Most visitors want to see the rock when the sun goes up, or in the evening as the sun goes down. That's because it changes colour and becomes burning red. Others want to climb it and to see the view from the top.

But Uluru is more than a tourist sight. For the local Anangu people Uluru is °sacred and they don't climb it. According to their law, only a few people are allowed to go up the rock at special times. That's why they politely ask visitors not to climb the rock.

In the past most visitors went up on the rock. Today more and more people decide not to do it, but still about one in five visitors climb the rock. How much longer will they be allowed to do it?

B

Proud to be a new Australian

My name is Nikki Li. I'm originally from Hong Kong, but I moved to Australia several years ago with my family. Since then I've felt more and more like I belong here. That's why I finally decided to make my life in Oz. Last year on Australia Day (26 January) I became a new Australian citizen. It was one of the biggest days of my life. I wasn't alone – I shared the excitement with thousands of other people from different countries.

When we first moved here it was tough for my brother and me. We really missed our friends and family. But we discovered there were lots of other Chinese people here and that made us feel at home. It took time to get used to all the new things, but now I love my life here in Sydney. I wouldn't want to live anywhere else. I'm so happy and proud to be an °Aussie.

I've learned that since the arrival of the British here in 1788, Australia has been a country of immigrants. About one quarter of the 23 million people in Australia are not originally from here. That compares with 13% in the US and 9% in the EU. When you walk around Sydney – or Melbourne or Perth – you really see and hear how diverse our culture is. I'm part of a continuing tradition!

▸ DFF 1.2 ▸ INKL pp. 10–11

C

Fighting bush fires between exams

By Jake Nolan

I was sitting in a history exam at my high school and I noticed that the sky outside was changing colour. When I heard the fire trucks go past, I knew it was a bush fire. I wanted to get out there as quickly as I could and help. It was finally time to do what I was trained for.

In the Blue Mountains north of Sydney, where we live, bush fires are always a danger when the weather gets hot and dry. Every year in Australia bush fires destroy houses and burn large areas of land.

That's why I decided to join the Rural Fire Service about three years ago. Two other friends – Mel Forbes and Serena Jones – joined with me. It wasn't normal for teens to join, but we did and we trained hard. This would be our first experience fighting a bush fire. We were in our final school exams, but we didn't think much about that. As a volunteer you have to be ready to go.

Volunteers fighting a bush fire in the Blue Mountains

I remember looking up at the mountain and seeing spots of red everywhere. About three hours later we were up on the mountain with our team. It was both exciting and scary. The hardest part was seeing the people who lost their houses. They have nothing now. When the worst was over, the °fire captain thanked us and said he was proud of us. I just wished we could do more.

D

Australia's deadliest animals

Australia is home to some of the most dangerous animals in the world. Sharks, spiders and snakes are the things people worry about most. But now experts at the Australian Museum in Sydney have made a list of dangerous animals °based on how deadly they are and how likely you are to meet them.

There are snakes, spiders and sharks on the list, but it may surprise you that at the top are – jellyfish. Bees are at number two on the list, which may also seem a bit surprising. But lots of people are allergic to bee stings. At number six on the list are salt water crocodiles, which are common in the north, including tourist hot spot Kakadu National Park.

But Australian expert Steve Backshall says that, yes, Australia has lots of dangerous animals, but there is very little chance that you'll meet them. "The most dangerous animals to humans are horses and honey bees," he says. No one should be worried about visiting Oz because of its wild animals, says Backshall. "Quite the opposite, it's a great reason to visit."

d) Go back to your group. Summarize your article for the group. Then tell them the special things about Australia that you noted down. Together choose the top three things that make Australia special for you and °rank them 1 to 3. °Report to the class. More practice 2 p. 107

2 SPEAKING Australia – a place to visit?

In your opinion, what are the things that make Australia interesting and different for visitors? Would you like to visit Oz? Think about these questions and make notes. Then discuss in class.

More practice 3 p. 108 More challenge 2 p. 108

▸ Workbook 2–3, p. 5

Emergencies in Oz

1 LISTENING The Flying Doctors

a) Look at the photo. Talk to a partner. What do you think the RFDS does?

The Royal Flying Doctor Service (RFDS)

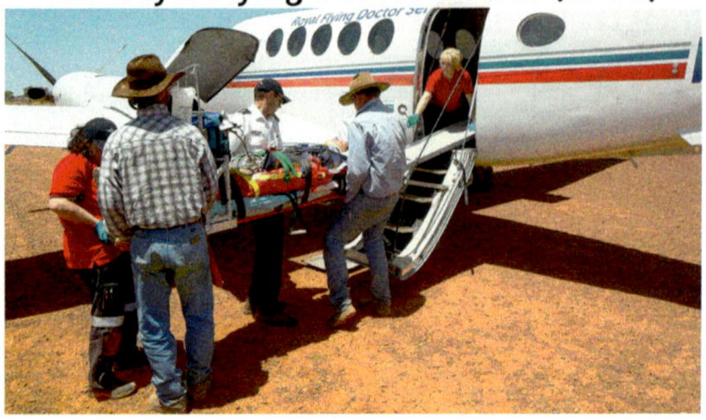

b) Now listen to the advert and make notes. (1.01)
- Where do the Flying Doctors work?
- Why are they important?
- What do they need? Why?

c) Listen to the advert again and note down any other main points. (1.01)
Summarize briefly what the advert is about. Give feedback on your partner's summary.

▸ *Skills file 9.4, p. 174*

2 READING Tips from the RFDS website

a) Scan the website. What situations do the Flying Doctors offer help with?

Royal Flying Doctor Service

Royal Flying Doctor Service

Outback travelling

The Australian outback is a great place to travel, but a lot of tourists get into trouble on their outback adventure. Here are some tips to help you to stay safe:
- Always bring lots of water with you – 10 litres per person, per day.
- If your car breaks down, never leave your vehicle in the heat. Use it for shade.
- If you get lost in the outback, go to high ground and light a small fire. At night, use your torch and your whistle.

Heat stress

If you suffer from heat stress and feel sick, this is what you should do:
- Get out of the sun and get into the shade.
- Cool down with wet towels.
- Drink lots of water.
- Call a doctor.

Snake bites

Australia has about 21 different dangerous snakes. If a snake bites you, here's some advice.
- Don't try to catch or kill the snake. It can bite again.
- Stay calm and don't move.
- Try to identify the snake, so the doctor can find an °anti-°venom more quickly.
- Get to a hospital or a doctor as soon as you can – or call the emergency services.

b) Read the text. Look at these situations and answer the questions.
1 You want to drive into the outback. What should you take with you?
2 You meet somebody hiking who is suffering from heat stress. How can you help him or her?
3 You get bitten by a snake. What should you do?

c) Think of other situations where people might need the help of the Royal Flying Doctor Service. Make notes. Then share your ideas in class.

More practice 4 p. 108

3 LISTENING Emergencies on the beach

1.02

a) Listen to conversations 1–3. Match them to these signs (A, B, C). More practice 5 p. 108

A

B

C

b) °Complete these sentences with the missing verbs. Then listen again and check. // p. 109

1 "G'day. I don't ... you should swim here. It's dangerous."
2 "If I were you, I'd ... between the flags. It's safer over there."
3 "G'day. Can you help us? My mate has ... his foot."
4 "It isn't bleeding, but I see some redness. Does it ... now?"
5 "I feel a bit sick and I ... a headache." Box: Voc., p. 208
6 "Let me ... your temperature. It's quite high and you ... a bit red."

! Some Australian phrases:
g'day – hello
°mate – friend
see ya later – goodbye
have a good one – have a good day
Aussie – Australian
bloody – very

c) Explain the signs to a partner in your own words. ▸ Skills file 6, p. 165

4 SPEAKING Getting help

a) °Silent dialogue: Decide who's partner A and who's partner B.
Partner A: Look at the picture. You're on a beach and your arm hurts. You see a lifeguard. Write the first line of your dialogue on a piece of paper. Then give it to B. Don't speak.
Partner B: You're a lifeguard on this beach. You see a young person with a problem. Try to help. Read what partner A wrote and write your answer. Give it to A. Don't speak. Continue like this.

b) When you've finished the silent dialogue, practise saying it with your partner.
▸ °Wordbank 1, p. 136

c) °Act your dialogue for the class.

5 WRITING Tips for tourists in Australia

▸ Skills file 9.1, pp. 171–172

a) Write an article (100–120 words) about how to avoid problems in Australia.
Begin like this: *Australia is a great country for a holiday. But you have to be very careful there ...*

b) **Reading circle:** Put all the articles on the wall. Read them and write comments.

► INKL pp. 14–15

My people

1 VIEWING The Burdekin Crew

The Burdekin Crew is a group of Aboriginal Australian high school kids from the town of Ayr. They wrote a song and made a video about who they are and where they're from.

a) Watch the video and look out for these symbols of Aboriginal culture.

A

body painting

B

the colours of the Aboriginal flag

C

traditional dance steps

b) Work in groups of three. Each student picks one question. Watch the video again and talk about your question.

1 What kind of music and dancing do they use? Do you like it?
2 What kind of place is Ayr?
3 What do you notice about the Burdekin Crew (how many, age, what clothes, etc.)?

c) **Discuss:** What's the message of the video? Give reasons for your answer.

A Life in a small town is boring.
B It's great to be Australian.
C Be proud of who you are.
D Things are difficult for young people.

2 Eyes wide open

a) °MEDIATION Pick one of these °verses (A or B) from the song. Explain the message in one or two sentences.

► *Skills file 12, p. 181*

A
Can you believe how far we've come?
The journey is long, but it has just begun.
Eyes wide open, walking into the sun,
Pride in my people, °roll as one.

B
Remember where you come from, °stay on track, look to the future, don't look back.
Stay positive, °stand tall like my °pop,
Burdekin from the bottom all the way to the top.

b) What things can you be proud of? Think and make notes. Then discuss in class.

3 'First Australians'

a) Skim this text and think of a heading for each paragraph. Compare your headings.

Aboriginal Australians have lived on this huge island continent for almost 50,000 years. They are often called 'Indigenous Australians' or sometimes 'First Australians' because they were the first people here. Aboriginal people lived along the coasts and inland in the bush. They had a special connection with nature and the land. They were mostly °nomadic – they moved around, gathered food, fished and hunted wild animals. But this life began to change in the late 1700s when Europeans came to Australia. Some of the early contact with Europeans was peaceful, but when the Europeans took Aboriginal lands to farm and to build towns, Aboriginal Australians fought hard to save their way of life. Many of them were killed or put in prison. Many others died from diseases that the Europeans brought to the continent. Their ancient lifestyle changed forever.

Today there are about 670,000 Indigenous Australians in Australia – less than 3 per cent of the total population (23.6 million). Some Indigenous Australians have taken on the modern Australian way of life. And some problems of the past have been corrected: the government has said sorry for the generation of Aboriginal children who were taken from their homes, and large areas of land have been given back to Aboriginal groups. But Indigenous Australians still face many problems. Many young people leave school early, are unemployed, have problems with alcohol. Many have bad health and don't live long. And lots of Indigenous Australians are very poor.

But Aboriginal culture is strong. It has no written language, so Aboriginal Australians tell their stories in dances and in 'dot paintings'. The painter uses a stick and makes thousands of dots in different colours. These stories are secret, so only Aboriginal people really understand them. But if you look at a painting long enough, you might see the stones, plants, trees, tracks and animals of the outback. Other things that you find in Aboriginal culture are °boomerangs and °didgeridoos. Boomerangs were used to hunt animals, to dig in the ground or as a knife. The didgeridoo is an instrument that makes a fantastic deep sound.

a didgeridoo

b) Which of these sentences best describes the first paragraph of the text?

- It talks about the beginning of Aboriginal culture and why it has continued for so long.
- It describes life for Aboriginal Australians before and after Europeans came to Australia.

c) Write °descriptions in one sentence for the other two paragraphs. More practice 6 p.109

d) WRITING Pick A or B and write a text (100–120 words). More help p.109

A I understand the song 'Eyes wide open' better now, for example ...

B I've learned some interesting things about Aboriginal Australians, for example ...

The coolest place on earth

Bondi Beach

1 LISTENING Sydney and Melbourne

a) What do the pictures tell you about Sydney and Melbourne? What else do you know about the two cities? Make notes. Compare your answers.

1.03 b) You're going to hear two interviews for an Australian radio programme. Copy the °table below. Then listen and complete the table (for questions 1–4 name at least three things).

	Brooke	Cody
1 What's a typical weekend for her/him?		
2 What's cool about Sydney/Melbourne?		
3 What's not so cool?		
4 What's a typical Sydneysider/ Melburnian like?		
5 Where would she/he prefer to live?		

Compare your answers.

Street art in Melbourne's lanes

One country, two centres

Sydney and Melbourne, Australia's two biggest cities, have much to offer in areas like arts and culture, sport, architecture, tourism and trade. They are also often listed among the most liveable cities in the world. Competition between the two is nearly as old as the cities themselves. Both grew from small colonies to busy port cities and state capitals that competed for trade. When the nation's capital was chosen, the two cities fought to be Australia's government centre. Because leaders couldn't agree, in the end Canberra was named the capital.
Competition between the cities is still strong – in sports like rugby and football, in the arts, in trade and in other areas. Some say the media make this competition seem bigger than it really is. Perhaps, but it's hard for Australia's two big cities not to look to each other when they do anything. And this can be good. Without the other, neither city would be as great as it is.

2 SPEAKING Sydney or Melbourne?

a) Think: Look at and listen to the information about Melbourne and Sydney again.
Which city is more interesting and attractive to you? Why? Make notes.

b) Pair: Compare your ideas.

c) Share: Talk about your ideas in class.

More challenge 3 | p. 110

3 WRITING The coolest place on earth

If you could live anywhere in the world, where would you live? In your view, what's the coolest place on earth and why? Write an article for the school magazine. ▸ *Skills file 9.1, pp. 171–172*

▸ INKL p. 19

1 A window on your life

a) These texts (A–D) were sent into a competition. Imagine you're part of the jury. Read the stories A and B. Then listen to C and D. Take notes about things you find °fascinating or unusual in the stories.

Give us a window on your life!
Enter our competition. Send us a short personal story about yourself, your hobby, family or area. The story must be real, and it must be short – about 200 words or 2 minutes of °audio or video.

A

Living in the Kimberley
by Aaron

This is probably the most remote place that you can live in Australia. My parents have a million-°acre cattle station, over 300 km from the nearest town. I do my school work on the computer with School of the Air. That means that I can be at home, and when school work is finished, I can do my jobs on the station, like feeding the cattle and horses, repairing fences, etc.

I don't have much contact with other kids, so I look forward to school camp in Broome. That happens once a year for a week. It's 700 km each way. But it's worth it.

In the dry season the weather is great here – that's from May to November. But in the wet season – from December to April – it rains a lot, and the roads are often closed. So by the end of October we have to order everything we need for the next six months. You have to think of everything – food, coffee, toothpaste, toilet paper – because if the roads are closed, you can't get any more.

Do we have a hard life here in the Kimberley? Sometimes, yes. But I don't want to live anywhere else.

B

I'm a mud racer *by Ella*

It was the day before my 16th birthday. I was so excited. The track was wet and the car was going everywhere. Then I hit the side, and my car turned over. At first I didn't know what happened. I was hanging upside down in my seat, and I was °freaking out.

Yes, I drive cars. I'm a mud racer. I'm a 16-year-old girl and I have an awesome car. It's white and it's got tractor tyres, and it's waterproof so it can go through a metre of mud. The idea is that two cars race around in a figure of eight and the fastest wins.

You might think I'm too young to drive, but in mud racing you can start from the age of 15. Dad did most of the work on the car when I started, but since then I've learned a lot about cars too. The best part is that dad gave me the car so now I'm going to stick with it and have as much fun as I can.

C 1.04

Beach culture
by Ava

A °dreamy day in the life of a teen who lives in a town on the coast ...

D 1.05

One day changed my life by Ethan

Sport came first for him – then something happened ...

b) Which story is the most fascinating? Discuss, then vote for your favourite.

More practice 7 p. 110

2 °REVISION Using tenses

Look at the FOCUS box and answer the questions.

FOCUS

1 In Text A, Aaron writes about his life and the things he does regularly. Which tense does he use?
▸ *Language files 1, p. 182; 3, p. 183*

2 In Text B, Ella writes about her hobby and she uses more than one tense.
a) In one paragraph she only uses the **simple present**. Which one? Why?
b) In the first paragraph she doesn't use the present tense. Why not?
c) In the last paragraph Ella uses different tenses. Find examples of something her dad did (**simple past**), something she has learned (**present perfect**) and something she plans to do (***going to*-future**).
▸ *Language files 3, p. 183; 5, p. 185; 8, p. 189*

3 Ella uses the **simple past** and the **past progressive** in paragraph 1. Find examples of both. Why does she use the **past progressive**?
▸ *Language files 3, p. 183; 4, p. 184*

▸ *Language file 10, p. 187*

3 An email from Broome

Aaron is writing to his parents from his school camp. Complete his email with the correct °form of the *simple present* and the *simple past*.

School camp ... (1 be) even better this year. Everybody ... (2 look) older and we all ... (3 know) each other now. ... (4 be) I shy last year? That's what people ... (5 tell) me this year. Well, I ... (6 not have) that problem any more. The classes ... (7 be) good this year too. ... you ... (8 remember) Mr Blake? He ... (9 be) our teacher last year. Everybody ... (10 like) him because he ... (11 tell) good jokes, but we ... (12 not learn) much. This year we ... (13 have) a different teacher, Ms Winslow, and she's great. She ... (14 know) a lot, but she ... (15 not talk) too much. That's the news! ... you ... (16 repair) the fences last week?

4 It was my 18th birthday

Niko from Melbourne sent this story into the competition. Complete the sentences with the correct form of the *simple past* or the *past progressive*.

1 It *was* (be) my 18th birthday and I *was travelling* (travel) with my mate Simon in the outback.
2 On the first day we ... (cross) a deep river.
3 We ... (be) a bit worried because it ... (not feel) safe. But it was ok.
4 The next day we ... (come) to another river. Two tourists ... (wait) there.
5 We ... (not try) to cross because the water ... (move) so quickly. But we ... (not panic).
6 We ... (go back) to the first river, but that was too high by then. So we ... (decide) to make camp for the night.
7 When we ... (get up) the next morning, it ... (rain) hard. The river ... (be) even higher than the night before.
8 We ... (start) to panic when we saw that the water ... (get) closer and closer to our tent.

More practice 8 | p. 110

5 NOW YOU A window on your life

a) Decide what kind of personal story you would like to write. More help | p. 110

b) Write a text for the competition. You can put your text in your °DOSSIER.

▸ *Workbook 12–16, pp. 10–11*

1 TEXT

► INKL pp. 16–18

Swerve is a book about a boy who loves muscle cars, a grandfather who has never met his grandson, and a girl who is in danger. These three people do a trip together - into the heart of Australia. Here is some of their story.

The Holden Monaro – a °muscle car

1 Before you read

Skim the pictures and the headings. What do you learn about the three main characters and their journey?

► *Skills file 7.1, p. 166*

1.06

Swerve (adapted from the novel *Swerve* by Phillip Gwynne)

1 Sydney School

A skinny old guy with a long grey ponytail and a waistcoat turned up at the school gate one afternoon.

"Hugh," he said as I walked past.

"Yes," I said, wondering how he knew my name.

"I want to talk to you."

Stranger danger! Stranger danger! I thought. But there was something familiar about him. So I stopped.

"About what?"

"About you and me."

Stranger danger! Stranger danger! I thought.

"Your name is Hugh Twycross. You were born on the seventeenth of February. Your mother's name is Carol Hughes. She was born on the third of May ..."

I stopped. "How do you know all this stuff?"

"Because I'm your grandfather."

"No, you're not!"

"Your mother is my daughter."

"My mum's real father is dead."

"Then you're looking at a ghost, kiddo[1]!" he said to me.

He did look familiar. He had my mother's nose and chin – my nose and chin.

Hugh and Poppy

That night I told mum that her father had come to the school.

"My father is dead!" she said. "He's dead to me!"

I rang grandma.

"It's best if your mother explains," was all she could say.

Mum said that I should have nothing to do with the old man. She phoned the school. She phoned the police. But he wasn't threatening me, so there was nothing they could do.

Every day he came to the school. At first I ignored him. But on the third day I stopped and talked to him. Looking at him was like looking in a funny mirror. He was my grandfather – my 'Poppy'.

One day Poppy phoned me at school.

"How's your driving?" he asked.

"I'm learning," I said. "But it's difficult to get the hours of practice."

"I have an answer to the problem," Poppy said. "You can drive me to the Big Rock."

"You mean Uluru?" I asked.

"You got it – Uluru!"

2 Plans

I visited Poppy at his apartment. He had a map of Australia open on the table. "We're here," he said, pointing a finger at Sydney.

"And Uluru is here," he said, pointing at the centre of Australia.

---

[1] kiddo (*infml.*) ['kɪdəʊ] *Kleine/r*

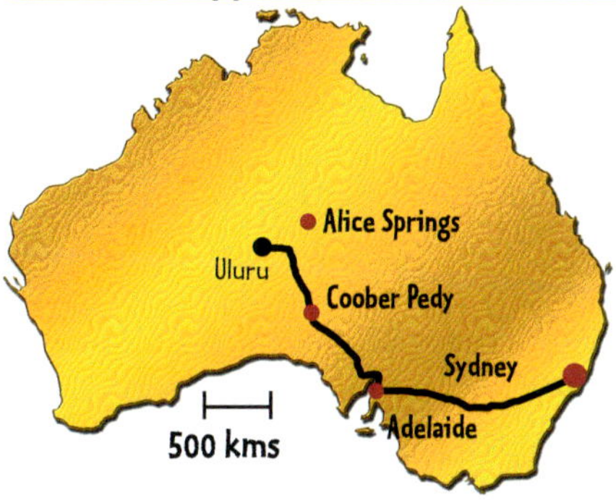

"Two thousand, eight hundred ks[2] away."

He looked at me. "It's a fair bloody hike[3]. So do you want to do it?"

"But why?" I asked.

"Because I always wanted to go there, and now is the time to do it. But I can't drive."

Then he said, "I'd like to show you something."

I followed him to an old garage behind the building.

"Are you ready?" he asked when he opened the door. There was a car in the garage, but it wasn't just any car. It was the best muscle car – a 1969 Holden Monaro. I had only seen pictures of these cars before.

Yellow and black stripes – it looked like a tiger. It looked amazing.

Box: Voc., p. 211

"Whose is this?" I asked. It was his.

"So are you up for it?" he asked.

I thought about my school, my music exam next week, my parents, my future …

Then I thought of driving 2800 ks to Uluru in a Holden HT Monaro GTS 350 V8.

"I'm up for it," I said.

3 The Million Star Motel

We were on the highway heading west towards the Blue Mountains. As the city's skyscrapers got smaller and smaller in the mirror, my excitement got bigger and bigger.

I looked over at Poppy and smiled. He smiled back at me.

It was getting dark and we drove onto a track. The Holden was fast, but it was old and not easy to drive.

"If you see a roo[4] on the road, don't swerve," Poppy said. "It's better to hit the roo than risk your life."

After an hour we came to a clearing. We stopped the car and got out beside a river – the Darling. Poppy opened the boot and took out cooking equipment, two camping chairs and two swags[5]. He put the swags – our beds – on the ground.

Then he made a fire and got the billy[6] to make tea. Poppy pointed to the sky.

"They call this the Million Star Motel."

at the Million Star Motel

4 South Australia

We were driving through the desert at 80 ks an hour. It was 415 ks to Port Augusta and 1700 to the Big Rock.

"Can't I go a bit faster?" I asked Poppy.

"No, you can't," Poppy answered.

A road train appeared behind us suddenly and wanted to overtake. So I pulled over to let it pass.

a road train

"Don't let them bully you," Poppy said.

There were also animals on the highway. This was the world's longest zoo. There were horses, cattle and sheep, kangaroos and °emus, and thousands of goats.

I saw a hooded figure standing by the road.

"Look, a hitchhiker," I said and I pulled over.

The hitchhiker was short, thin, wearing jeans and a hoodie with the hood up, hiding his face.

"Where are you going?" Poppy asked.

"Adelaide," he answered in a little voice. His name was Jimmy and he was from Broken Hill.

After about half an hour a big black car flew past us.

---

[2] k (Abkürzung, *infml.*) *Kilometer* [3] a fair bloody hike [feə blʌdi 'haɪk] *eine ganz schöne Strecke* [4] roo (*infml.*) [ruː] *Känguru*
[5] swag (AustE [swæg], infml) *Bettrolle* [6] billy ['bɪli] Kochgeschirr

"Hey," Poppy said. "What was that?"
"A Typhoon – with a four-litre °turbo-charged engine – very fast," I said.

a Typhoon – another muscle car

I noticed that the hitchhiker had sunk down in the seat.
We stopped at a roadhouse[7] for fuel.
"You hungry?" Poppy asked. – "A bit," I said.
"I'll stay here in the car," the hitchhiker said.

5 In the roadhouse

I ordered a cheese and tomato sandwich.
"Do you have any brown bread?" I asked the woman.
"It's all brown when you toast it, darl[8]" she said.
Poppy went to the toilet. A man and a woman came into the roadhouse. The man was short, but big – like a bodybuilder. The woman was kind of glamorous. They came to the counter.
"We're looking for our daughter," the woman said, taking out a photo.
"I haven't seen her," the woman behind the counter said.
"Can I have a look?" I asked. "I saw a hitchhiker this morning."
The glamorous woman showed me the photo – a girl about my age, blue hair, small face, big eyes.
"Have you seen her or not?" the bodybuilder asked.
"No, it was somebody else. A boy," I said.
The man and the woman talked to some truckies[9] at another table.
Poppy came back and we left the roadhouse.
I couldn't see the hitchhiker in our car.
"He's gone," I said to Poppy. But when I got into the car I could see he was asleep.
The bodybuilder and the glamorous woman came out of the roadhouse.

Bella

Suddenly I turned around to look at the hitchhiker. On his fingernails there was pink nail polish.
"Hey, your parents are looking for you," I said.
"They aren't my parents," she answered.
"Then why do they have your photo?" I asked.
"Please don't say anything. Those people, they're really dangerous," she said.
The couple got into their car – the Typhoon muscle car that had °rocketed past us earlier – and left.
"They've gone now," I said.
She sat up and pulled her hood back. Short messy hair. Nose stud. Big eyes. She said her name was Bella and she was seventeen.

6 At Yulara, near Uluru

Hugh, Poppy and Bella drive to Coober Pedy together. Hugh really likes Bella and he thinks that she likes him. But at Coober Pedy Bella meets another guy. She decides to travel to Uluru with him. Hugh is disappointed. Hugh and Poppy go on without Bella, and they arrive at a campground in Yulara, a small town near the Big Rock – Uluru.

I woke to the sound of my phone. It was Bella.
"Hello," I said. But there was no answer, just the sound of a car engine and voices.
Bella: "Where are we going?"
Bodybuilder: "To teach you a lesson."
We heard the sound of someone hitting someone else.
Bella screaming: "You °arsehole!"
It took me a while to understand what was happening. They had Bella. Her phone must be in her pocket and she had pressed 'redial' to call me.
Bella: "Help! We just passed *The Brain*. Please help!"
Then °the phone went dead.
"What's the problem?" Poppy asked.
"Bella's in trouble," I said, getting into the car.
"I'm coming," he said, jumping out of his swag.
"Where's *The Brain*?" I asked Poppy.
"It's at this end of the Big Rock," he said.
We drove out of Yulara campground to the Uluru road and I °put my foot down …

[7] roadhouse ['rəʊdhaʊs] *Raststätte* [8] darl (*infml.* [dɑːl], *kurz für* darling) *Liebling; freundliche Anrede, auch bei Unbekannten*
[9] truckie (AustE ['trʌki], *infml.*) *LKW-Fahrer/in*

2 The end of the story

1.07

a) What do you think happens next? Tell a partner. Then listen to the end and find out.

b) Which °version do you like better? Explain.

! The following tasks are on three different levels. Pick and complete one task for each °level.

3 True or false? Correct the false sentences.

1 Poppy was Hugh's grandfather. (part 1)
2 Hugh didn't want to go on the trip. (2)
3 They spent the night in a hotel. (3)
4 They stopped for a hitchhiker near Uluru. (4)
5 They left the hitchhiker at the roadhouse. (5)
6 Hugh was worried about Bella. (6)

4 What happened? Complete the sentences.

1 When Hugh first saw Poppy, he felt ... (1)
2 Hugh agreed to Poppy's plan after ... (2)
3 On the first day they drove to ... (3)
4 The hitchhiker told them ... (4)
5 The man and woman showed Hugh ... (5)
6 When Hugh understood the problem, he ... (6)

5 Summarizing ▸ *Skills file 9.4, p. 174*

What is the story about? Write a summary. You can put your summary in your DOSSIER.

More practice 9 p. 111

6 At the Million Star Motel

Look at the picture in part 3. Then do task a) or b).

a) Write a message from Hugh to his mum.

b) Write a dialogue between Poppy and Hugh.

7 An interesting character

a) Pick one of the characters in the story and write a description. Write about:

- what he / she looks like
- what he / she is like (his / her personality)
- what the other characters think of him / her
- if you like him / her and why (not)

Give reasons for your ideas. Use examples from the story.

b) Swap your description with other students. Do you agree with each other? What do you °agree about? What do you °disagree about?

8 A character network More help p. 112

Make a character network for the people in the text.

9 Hugh and Poppy

Describe the relationship between Hugh and Poppy. How did it change in the story?

At the beginning Hugh ... Then Poppy and Hugh ... In the end they ...

▸ *INKL pp. 20–21*

1 VIEWING How to improve your presentations

a) Watch part 1 – Oh no! A presentation for Friday!

1 Why does Tim want to do a good presentation?

2 How can the students help each other?

b) Watch part 2 – Practising the presentation.

Did you enjoy the presentation? Do you think Tim will impress Milly? Give reasons.

c) Look at the checklist with a partner.

- What things did Tim do well?
- What things could he do better?

Take notes. Watch part 2 again and check.

d) Watch part 3 – Feedback for Tim.

Do the group say the same things about Tim's presentation as you did? Explain.

e) Watch part 4 – Amy's presentation.

- First say what she did well.
- Then say where she could improve.

f) Watch part 5 – Feedback for Amy.

Do the group say the same things about her presentation as you did? ▸ *Skills file 8.1, p. 169*

More challenge 4 | p. 112

CHECKLIST: Preparing a presentation

Make your presentation interesting.

Don't copy from the internet or from books – use your own words.
Keep your notes *short*.
Start with an "attention getter".

Give your presentation a clear structure.

Use good phrases:
- for the introduction
- when you move from part to part
- at the end

Prepare your materials.

Make sure your visuals (photos, pictures, charts, etc.) are clear and interesting.
Make sure the audience can read them.
Check your equipment before you start.

Practise giving your presentation.

Don't just read from your notes – look up and speak freely.
Speak slowly and clearly.
Look at the audience and smile.
Ask for questions at the end.

2 NOW YOU What to work on?

a) You want to improve your own presentations. Choose three things from the checklist that you need to work on.

b) Share your lists. °Agree on a list of five things that you both need to work on. Talk about how you could work on them. These are the important things for your feedback on the other students' presentations.

! When you're giving feedback, be positive!

- First °pick out at least one good thing about the presentation – more if you can.
- Then pick out one thing that the presenter could do better.

3 YOUR TASK A presentation about Australia

Step 1: Choose your topic and do some research

a) You have to give a presentation about an aspect of Australia that °interests you. Look at the network. Choose a topic for your presentation.

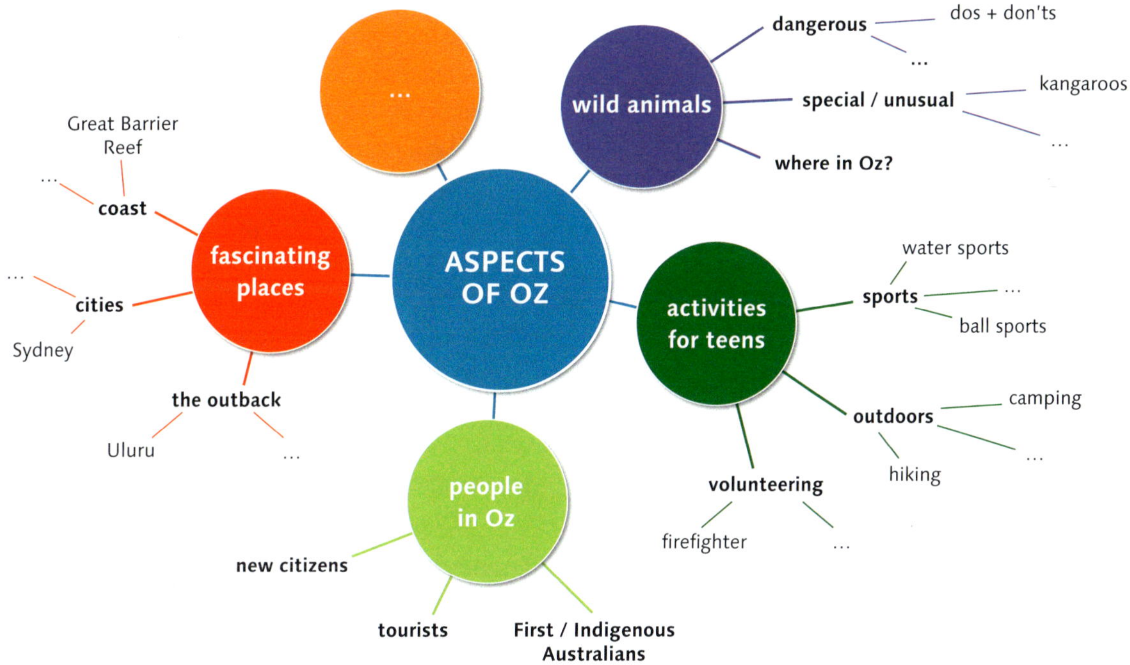

b) Make your own network for your topic. Do some °research and find out more.

> Use good websites and check on more than one site.
> ► Skills file 4, p. 163

Step 2: Prepare your notes and materials ► Skills file 8.1, p. 169

Step 3: Practise your presentation

Today I'm going to talk about … First … Next … Finally …	Now I'm going to explain / tell you about / …	I hope you enjoyed my presentation.
	Let's look at the screen.	Any questions?

Step 4: Give your presentation / Prepare your feedback

While listening, the other students prepare their feedback with a feedback sheet. More help p. 113

Step 5: Give each other feedback and learn from it

Think about how you can improve your presentation.

- The first part was great.
- I liked the part where you ...
- Try to speak more freely.
- Don't forget to look at the audience.

A different world

You'll find the new words from these pages listed on p. 230.

1 READING The °Spare Room

a) Read the blurb about the book. What kind of things do you think are new and different for Akira in Australia? Compare your ideas.

b) Imagine waking up on your first morning in a strange room, in a strange house, in a strange country. How would you feel? Now read the text below and find out how it was for Akira.

The *Spare Room*, by Kathryn Lomer, is about Akira, a 19-year-old Japanese boy who is in Tasmania (Australia) to learn English. He lives with the Moffat family – Alex, Jess and their daughters Angie and Daisy. Akira stays in their spare room. This is a journey into a world that is very different to Akira's own world. He has to deal with lots of things that are very new and strange for him.

1.08

I can still remember the strangeness of waking up in that room. The sounds around the house. A dog barking somewhere. Exotic bird calls. As I lay there I thought about how many mornings I'd woken up on my own futon at home ... and never thought about my °surroundings, what I could hear, smell.

I wondered what I should do first. What was appropriate – to go out to the kitchen for breakfast in my *yukata*? Did the family eat breakfast together? When did people °shower? Or perhaps they had °baths? I had noticed that the shower was above the °bathtub, which seemed strange. In Japan we have a bath in the evening after showering. So many questions about such a simple thing as getting out of bed and starting the day. I realized how much I would have to learn.

When I got to the kitchen, there was no one there. I looked around and found the kettle, filled it up and switched it on. I didn't know what else to do. I didn't want to go looking in the °cupboard for cups or tea. What kind of tea, °anyway? ... I sat down at the table, wondering what to do, and just as I did a growl came from under the table. I jumped. Under the table there was a little white dog! Next minute, Daisy burst into the room.
"*Ohaiyo-gozaimasu*!" she said.
"*Ohaiyo-gozaimasu*!" I answered.
She was so sweet, wanting to °put me at ease.
"But I want to speak English, Daisy," I said.
"Oh yes, I know. But just a little Japanese too. Please? For me? Pretty please?" she said.
Pretty please! I was lost. What did that mean? It was going to take me a long time to learn this language, I thought.

c) Answer these questions.

1 What things does Akira find different?
2 Describe what he doesn't know about Australia.
3 How comfortable does Akira feel? Explain with at least one example.
4 Name the Japanese words in the text. What do you think they mean?
5 How would you describe Akira? Explain.
6 Akira doesn't understand *'Pretty please'*. It's an °idiom. Explain what you think it means.

An **idiom** is a special phrase that can be difficult to understand. The meaning of the whole phrase is different from the meaning of the individual words.

2 READING Being me in English

a) What kind of problems do you face when you speak a foreign language? Make notes. Talk with a partner. Then read this extract in which Akira talks about communicating in a new language. Compare Akira's thoughts with your own.

1.09

When I arrived at the building where the language program was °run, there was the noise of many students from many countries all talking °at once. It was suddenly very exciting to be there. Chisuko °guided me to the right room and said she'd meet me later, at the morning break. Before she left me she added in English, "How's your host family?"

"Maybe normal," I answered.

I had no idea of what normal was in Australia. But °I suppose I did already have a feeling that this family was not quite normal. But 'maybe normal' were the only words I could find to say this in English. And that was something I discovered as I °went along. You often want to say something completely different, but you are °limited to the °vocabulary you know and you have to try to °construct something from the little that you have. A bit like trying to make a salad when you only have cooking vegetables, or trying to build a boat using only nails. There is a big °gap between what you think and what you say. It would be a long time before I felt that the real me, the one with ideas and opinions and funny stories to tell, could find his way out again. For a while that person was trapped inside a new language.

b) Which statement best summarizes Akira's ideas about communicating in a new language? Explain your choice.

- A You can never be yourself in a foreign language.
- B You can't say what you want to say, so you learn to say less.
- C You speak with the °few words you know until you get better at saying what you think.
- D You can be a different person and say things you wouldn't °normally say.

3 SPEAKING Living in another culture

a) What do you think you would or wouldn't like about living in another culture? Make a list of positive aspects. Then list things that might not be so positive – as many as you can.

b) Read out your lists and compare them. For Akira it's important to be able to speak the language of the other culture well. Talk about how important this is for you and why.

MORE CHALLENGE

4 LISTENING Fun with idioms

1.10

Akira hears lots of idioms, but he doesn't always understand them. Listen. Match each idiom (1–7) with the correct meaning (A–G).

1 I'm the °chief bottle-washer.
2 Can you give me a hand, please?
3 That should do the trick.
4 What's your °poison?
5 What's the damage?
6 I'm on cloud nine!
7 I'm like a fish out of water.

A I'm very happy.
B How much does that cost?
C That will be fine.
D I °feel uncomfortable.
E I need some help.
F I do all the jobs.
G What would you like to drink?

> It's important to understand idioms. But it's °risky to use them.
> ► *Skills file 2, p. 161*

5 MEDIATION More English idioms

a) What do you think the underlined idioms mean? Explain them in German.

1 How do you feel?
– I'm over the °moon!"

2 I'm going to pass my test.
– Yeah! Pigs might fly!

3 I know a good joke.
– I'm all ears!

4 Do you like my new phone?
– Wow! It's the bee's knees.

5 You're talking too fast.
Hold your horses!

6 How was the driving test?
– A piece of cake!

b) Can you think of idioms in German that match these English idioms?

6 MEDIATION German idioms

Explain these idioms to an English-speaking visitor.

1 Ich habe Schwein gehabt.
2 Ich verstehe nur Bahnhof.
3 Du hast nicht alle Tassen im Schrank!
4 Das Leben ist kein Ponyhof.
5 Das ist mir Wurst!
6 Ich habe die Nase voll.

> Say **when** you'd use these idioms, **who with** and **what they mean** in English.

► KV 5 ► DFF 1.3 ► DFF 1.7 ► INKL pp. 22–25

1 LISTENING

1.11

Planning a trip

Listen to Sophie (17) and Rani (18) from London. They want to see Australia, meet people and have fun.

a) Look at the pictures. Discuss which activity Sophie and Rani will choose and why.

b) Listen to the dialogue again and choose the correct endings for these sentences.

1 The turtles °lay their eggs …
- A in July.
- B all year.
- C between November and March.

2 Staying on Heron Island …
- A costs a lot of money.
- B °isn't allowed.
- C isn't expensive.

3 Sandboarding is …
- A a dangerous sport.
- B a sport for all ages.
- C a sport for young people.

4 The Ghan train journey goes …
- A from south to north.
- B from east to west.
- C from north to south.

5 Darwin is famous for …
- A a special °soft drink.
- B an unusual boat race.
- C a big parade.

6 The art in Kakadu is …
- A in a very old book.
- B °indoors, in an art gallery.
- C outdoors, on rocks.

2 LANGUAGE Rani's Oz travel blog

Sophie and Rani booked their trip to Australia and °off they went. Read Rani's blog and complete it with the correct forms of the verbs.

> Use the ***simple present***, ***simple past***, ***past progressive*** or **going to-*future***.

July 1st: Not a good start. We're still at the airport. When we … (1 arrive), the °pilots … (2 begin) to °strike. But we're lucky and in about an hour our plane for Australia … (3 be) ready for °take-off.

July 3rd: We … (4 arrive) at our hostel in Darwin early in the morning and … (5 meet) our tour guide, Tony, who … (6 wait) for us. Tomorrow we … (7 see) Aboriginal rock paintings in the Kakadu National Park. It's 10 pm now and we … (8 need) some sleep.

July 4th: It was amazing to see the ancient rock paintings. Even today, you can still … (9 find) traditional Aboriginal art all over Oz. While I … (10 enjoy) the art, Sophie … (11 chat) with the tour guide ;-))

July 6th: Yesterday we … (12 spend) a lazy day °sightseeing and shopping. Tonight we … (13 visit) Mindil Beach Sunset Market. The market … (14 start) at 5 pm every Thursday. It's famous for live music on the beach.

July 7th: When we … (15 have) breakfast and making plans for the day, Tony arrived and … (16 invite) us to Crocosaurus Cove. There we … (17 swim) with crocodiles – well, we were in a cage and the crocodiles were swimming all around us. It was an awesome experience – the highlight of an amazing first week in Oz.

► Language file 10, p. 187 More challenge 5 p. 113

▸ KV 6 ▸ DFF 1.2 ▸ INKL pp. 22–25

3 SPEAKING Talking about a picture

Partner B: Go to page 104. **Partner A:**

a) Describe to your partner what you can see in your picture. These questions can help you: Who? What? Where? When? Why?

▸ *Skills file 10, p. 179*

b) Listen to your partner.

c) Together find out what the pictures °have in common and what is different.

4 WRITING Slip, slop, slap, seek and slide

Ant (16) is from Australia. He's visiting Europe with his family. This is part of his travel blog.

Do they need a new health slogan in Germany?

Here in Germany you see a lot of people lying in the sun in the middle of the day. The problem is that they don't always protect their skin. That's not healthy! I think maybe it's because they think a °suntan is cool. In Australia skin °cancer is a big topic, so we always °cover our arms and shoulders, use °sunscreen, put on a hat, stay under a tree or an umbrella between 11 am and 3 pm and put on sunglasses. To help Australians to remember the rules, the government has a slogan. The slogan is "Slip, slop, slap, seek, slide". It means you should slip on a shirt, slop on sunscreen, slap on a hat, seek shade and slide on sunglasses.

I think there should be a similar slogan here in Germany too. What do you think of this idea?

a) Read Ant's post. Explain what "Slip, slop, slap, ..." means and why it's important.

b) Write a comment. If you agree with Ant, think of a good slogan for Germany. It can be in English or German. If it's in German, explain it in English.

More help p. 114

▸ *Skills file 9.1, pp. 171–172*

▸ KV 7 ▸ DFF 1.4 ▸ DFF 1.5 ▸ DFF 1.9 ▸ INKL pp. 22–25

5 MEDIATION Understanding signs and advice in Australia

a) Here are five signs that you can find at the beach and at the °roadside in Australia. Explain in German what they mean.

1

2

3

4

5

b) You've gone to a °pharmacy because your mother has been stung by a bee. Her hand is red and it hurts. Help her to talk to the °pharmacist.

Pharmacist G'day. What can I do for you?
Your mum Erkläre bitte, was passiert ist.
(1) You ...
Pharmacist Is she allergic to bee stings?
(2) You *Sie möchte wissen, ...*
Your mum Nein, bin ich nicht.
(3) You ...
Pharmacist Has she pulled out the sting?
(4) You ...
Your mum Ja, habe ich.
(5) You ...
Pharmacist Put this cream on the sting once or twice a day. Keep it away from your eyes, nose and mouth. It will feel better quickly, but it may be red for a few days. It will feel better if you put ice on it too. Use a towel between the ice and your skin – you shouldn't put the ice directly on your skin. And don't let the ice stay on the skin for longer than 20 minutes.
(6) You *Du sollst diese ... Sie darf nicht ...*
Du kannst ...
Pharmacist Your hand should be fine in two or three days. If it isn't better by then, you should see a doctor.
(7) You *Wenn es in ..., sollst du ...*
Your mum Thank you.

▸ Workbook My learner log, p. 17 and Revision, p. 12, p. 18

Unit 2 Respect

▸ INKL pp. 26–27

1

2

3

4

1 Six scenes from a film

Look at the six pictures. What do you think is happening? Who are these teens and where are they? What are they doing or saying or feeling?

2 VIEWING Friends ... (part 1)

a) Watch part 1 of the film. What did you guess right?

b) Watch part 1 again and finish these sentences:

1 We can see that the four teens are friends because ...
2 Perhaps Shaz is a bit jealous of Patrick because ...
3 When Patrick saw the messages, he ...
4 Patrick deleted the messages from his phone because ...
5 Patrick's dad knew something was wrong because ...

3 Watching the film with different eyes

a) Is the story in part 1 told

A chronologically?
B as a monologue?
C with monologues and flashbacks?

Explain your answer with examples from the film. ▸ *Skills file 11, p. 180*

b) Why do you think the story is told this way? What effect does it have? Discuss.

▸ DFF 2.1 ▸ INKL pp. 26–27

5

6

4 VIEWING Friends ... (part 2)

a) Before you watch, guess what will happen next.
Then share your ideas in groups of four. Which idea do you like best? Why?

b) Watch part 2 of the film.
Who said what?

1 "That's no big deal – everybody does it."
2 "We didn't think about how you were feeling."
3 "I hoped that the problem would just go away."
4 "I feel bad because I didn't say stop."

What do the statements tell us about each character?

Patrick

Shaz

Simone

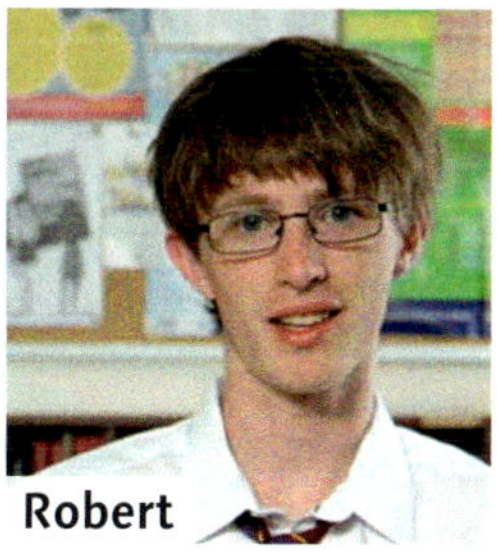
Robert

c) Now talk in class about these questions:

1 Do you think that it's a happy ending? Why (not)?
2 Can the four teens be friends again? Why (not)?
3 Explain the main message of the film.

5 NOW YOU About cyberbullying

What's the best way to deal with bullying that takes place through text messages, emails or social media? What advice would you give …

- to the victim?
- to the bystander (who sees the bullying)?
- to the bully?

If you think someone is bullying someone else, you should ...

If you get horrible messages, you should ...

Before you write a mean message, think about ...

More challenge 1 p. 114

▸ Workbook 1–2, p. 19

Dealing with peer pressure

1 Peer pressure

Your peers are people like you – your classmates, the people on your sports team, or members of your youth group. Because you're around your peers a lot, they influence you – it's normal. But when you feel that you should do something because other people are doing it – that's peer pressure.

Read what two teens wrote about peer pressure in a teen magazine.

With a partner, explain the two headings.

2.01

Jamaal – It doesn't have to be uncool

I go to school in a tough part of Brooklyn. A lot of kids here think it's not cool to be interested in school. When I take part in class and answer questions, those kids laugh at me. Or if they see me reading for fun, like in the school library, they tease me. I was reading a science fiction novel and this girl, Janine, walked past with a friend. Her eyes got all wide and she said, "What are you doin', man? Don't you have anybody to hang out with?" I smiled at her and just said, "It's a good book. You should read it." They looked at me like I was crazy and walked away. Some of my friends think that you're cool if you play basketball, dance, rap and go after girls. They think kids who read are boring or weak. Or that reading is a "white thing" – something black kids don't do if they want to be popular. I don't understand that. When I tell them school doesn't have to be uncool, they shake their heads or tell me I'm weird. When my mom talks about how important school is, I know she's right. She has always read a lot, and she has a good job that she likes. Still, sometimes in class I act like I'm not interested. I know it's stupid, but I don't want other kids to think I'm a geek.

Box: Voc., p. 213

2.01

Emily – It really hurt

When I first moved to Chicago with my family, it took a long time to meet people. Everybody at school had their group of friends, but I didn't know anybody. Then I met Claire in math class and we started having lunch and doing stuff together. We went shopping a lot – that was fun for a while. But then she began telling me that I needed to lose weight and that I wasn't attractive. Maybe it's what she thought, but it really hurt. And she weighed more than me! I got angry with her once when she said it in front of some people at school. They seemed to agree with her, but maybe just because she has a strong personality. Anyway, I had always felt okay about myself before I knew Claire. I started eating less – like a lot less. Even when I was hungry, I didn't eat. My parents were getting worried, but I was too embarrassed to talk to them about it. Two girls in my PE class, Sophie and Nuala, were nice to me and I started spending more time with them and less with Claire. They were in the school °glee club and they dragged me along one day to watch them practise. I saw all these kids singing and dancing and having a great time – it was amazing. I was shy at first, but then I joined. It was as if a light went on inside me. Things slowly got better after that.

▸ KV 8 ▸ KV 9 ▸ DFF 2.2 ▸ INKL pp. 28–29

2 READING Understanding the text

a) Answer these questions about Jamaal.
1 Why do some kids at Jamaal's school laugh at him?
2 What do some of Jamaal's friends think about reading?
3 How does Jamaal feel about school?
4 Describe in your own words the peer pressure that Jamaal feels.

b) Complete these sentences about Emily.
1 When she began at her new school, Emily ...
2 Emily's friendship with Claire changed when ...
3 Emily's parents worried about her because ...

c) Choose Emily or Jamaal and describe to a partner the positive influence that somebody has had on him or her. Explain why that influence has been important.

3 Perspectives on peers

Look at the two pictures and answer the questions.

a) What's happening in each picture? °Take turns describing the situations. ▸ Skills file 10, p. 179

b) Are these positive or negative examples of how peers can influence each other? Explain your answer.

c) Think of at least two more situations – one negative and one positive. Make notes. Then share with the class.

4 SPEAKING and WRITING "Peer pressure is a big problem for teenagers"

a) Do you think that peer groups have a positive or a negative influence on teens' lives?
Discuss the question in class.

b) Now write a comment (about 120 words) from your experience. Use your notes from task 3.

You can put your text in your DOSSIER.

▸ Skills file 9.1, pp. 171–172

Useful phrases:
- In my opinion, ...
- In my experience, ...
- I (definitely) think ...
- I (really) don't think ...
- On the one hand, ...
- On the other hand, ...
- Firstly, / Secondly, / ...
- For example, ...
- To sum up, ...

▸ Text file 2, pp. 142–147

5 LISTENING Come shopping with me!

2.02 **a)** Listen to part 1, then complete these sentences.

1 Megan is talking to Ava because ...
2 Megan wants Ava to ...

▸ Skills file 6, p. 165

b) Compare your answers to a). Then discuss: Do you think it was a good idea for Ava to say yes? Why (not)?

2.03 **c)** Listen to part 2, then complete these sentences.

1 Ollie thinks that Megan is ...
2 Ollie's advice to Ava is ...

d) Compare your answers to c). Then discuss: What should Ava say to Megan next time she sees her?

e) Look at the last picture and write your own version of that scene. Then °perform the dialogue for the class.

2.04 **f)** Listen to part 3 and find out what Ava does. Do you think she found a good solution to the problem? Do you like this version or your own better? Explain why.

6 ROLE-PLAY Why don't you go out with us?

a) Choose one of the role cards and think about what you can say.

Partner A

Your friend (partner B) hasn't gone out with you and your other friends lately. You begin.

- You ask why.
- He / she explains. You understand. You tell him / her: some people like to drink / okay not to drink.
- He / she explains further. You suggest: just the two of you go out.
- You have an idea: cinema. Together you decide which film.
- You ask where to meet.
- You agree. You finish and say goodbye.

Partner B

You haven't been out with your friends lately. One of them (partner A) wants to know why.

- You explain: don't like alcohol / some people in the group drink too much / not comfortable with that
- Your friend understands. You explain: feel silly / people say things / don't like it
- Your friend makes a suggestion. You agree.
- You agree with his / her idea (cinema). Together you decide which film.
- You suggest a meeting place.
- You finish and say goodbye.

b) Practise the dialogue. Swap roles. Then act the dialogue in front of the class.

More challenge 2 p. 114

▸ Workbook 3–6, pp. 20–21

▸ KV 10 A–C ▸ INKL pp. 30–31

How we see others

1 ACTIVITY Badges – a group experiment

a) Everybody gets a badge: red, green, blue, orange. Sit with your colour group. Read your role card on the page with your colour: 116 – 117 – 121 – 119.

b) Walk around and ask the question on your role card. Note the answers and the badge colour of your partners.

c) Sit in your colour group again and answer these questions:

1 How many green people, red people etc. did you talk to?
2 What interesting things did you learn?
3 Was everybody friendly and helpful?
4 Did everybody answer your question?
5 How did you feel? Explain why.

d) Make new groups of four with one of each colour in every group. Answer c) again.

e) Now talk about these questions in class:

1 Were there differences between people of different colours? Which ones?
2 How did you find the activity: fun / fair / frustrating / ...? Why?
3 What does this activity try to illustrate?

f) Give examples of discrimination in real life.

2 Racism and prejudice in football

a) Read this newspaper report. What does the writer mean by "enough"?

Player and his teammates say "enough"

Milan, Italy – Yesterday a football match between the Italian clubs AC Milan and Pro Patria ended when a black player and his teammates walked off the field after racist calls from fans.
The Ghanaian-German player, Kevin Prince Boateng, reacted when several fans made monkey sounds. It was the first time that a football team had ended a game because of racism.
"Shame that these things still happen," Mr Boateng said later.
Many players and fans have shown their support for Boateng. He said he hoped that his action would send a strong signal. Racism among football fans and players is nothing new in Europe and the UK. Mr Boateng said more action should be taken against racists: "They should be banned forever from the stadium."

b) A report answers the five questions *Who? What? When? Where? Why?* Find the answers to these questions in this report. Compare. ▸ *Skills file 9,2, p. 173* More practice 1 p. 115

c) Some people think this player reacted too strongly. What do you think? Discuss in class.

More practice 2 p. 115

► KV 11 ► INKL pp. 32–33

3 VIEWING 'What you say matters' by Brothablack

a) Look at the title of the song. Discuss: What do you think it's about? Then watch the video and compare.

b) Complete these sentences about the four scenes in the video. Then watch the video again and check your answers.

1 Kat thinks that Jane is good at maths because she looks ...

2 The two girls don't think that Sarah is Aboriginal because she looks too ...

3 The Aboriginal boy thinks that he should get on the bus first because the Aboriginal people came to Australia ...

4 One boy says that the other boy is fast only because he's ...

c) Think about this slogan from the song:
Face the racism, kick the racism.

1 Read the dictionary entries and pick the right meaning for *face* and for *kick*.
2 Say what the slogan means in German.

d) Find out what these phrases from the song mean. Check the new words in a dictionary.

1 You're not better than me, you're equal to me.
2 Stop the °negativity in your °vicinity.
3 Excuse me, your °ignorance is showing.
4 Stand up for °unity.

e) **Discuss:** What's the message of the video? Does the video work for you? Give reasons. More challenge 3 p. 116

face[1] /feɪs/ *Substantiv* Gesicht
face[2] *Verb*
1 (*einer Person / Sache*) gegenüber sein
2 vor etwas stehen
3 (*einer Sache*) entgegentreten
4 **Let's face it!** Machen wir uns nichts vor!

kick[1] /kɪk/ *Substantiv*
1 (*mit dem Fuß*) Tritt, Stoß
2 (*Sport*) Schuss, Kick
kick[2] *Verb*
1 (*mit dem Fuß*) treten
2 (*Sport*) schießen, kicken
3 (*Gewohnheit, Idee*) aufgeben, sich davon befreien

! Always look at **all** the words in an entry in the dictionary. Pick the best meaning.
► *Skills file 2, p. 161*

► Workbook 7–8, pp. 22–23

▸ KV 12 ▸ DFF 2.4 ▸ INKL pp. 32–33

4 YOUR TASK **Do something!**

No racism, discrimination or bullying in our schools! You can do something in your school. Here are some ideas.

Step 1: Pick a project Read through the four projects below and pick one. Find two or three other students who want to do the same project.

Step 2: Organize your project Meet in your groups and decide how much time you need for your project and who does what. Then work on your project.

Project A

Scenes of discrimination

1 Choose one scene or more from the film on p. 38 or think of a scene or some scenes (perhaps from your experience).

2 Write your own texts and dialogues for a short °play. Use your own words. More help p. 116

3 Check your texts with your group and with your teacher.

4 Learn your texts and practise your scene.

5 You can film your scene.

Project B

Immigrants' stories

1 Find people in your school or in your family who have come from other countries and who °are happy to talk about it.

2 Think of good questions and then interview the people. More help p. 117

3 Write short texts about these people's experiences. Add maps, flags, pictures, etc.

4 Ask the people to read your text – make sure they agree with it. Check with your teacher too.

Project C

A campaign

1 Collect lots of good English slogans for an anti-discrimination campaign.

Anti-bullying	Anti-racism
No place for bullying!	*Racism: °It stops with me!*

2 Then agree on your favourite slogans. Check your slogans with your teacher.

3 Make a poster, some badges and some postcards with your slogans.

Project D

Songs about discrimination

1 Find another song about discrimination, racism, bullying, etc. Or write your own song.

2 Pick out the important words and slogans. If they are new, first guess what they mean. Make notes and check in a dictionary.

3 Prepare to talk about your song and to explain it (including the difficult words). Put important parts of the text on the board.

4 Play or perform your song. You can film your °performance.

Step 3: Present your project

Project A: Act your scenes.

Project B/C: Put your stories, posters, etc. on the wall.

Project D: Present, explain and play your song.

▸ INKL p. 37

1 Guess what happened last night

2.05

a) Kai is telling his friend about what happened last night. Listen and answer these questions.

1 Who did Kai meet? 2 What did Big Dan want? 3 How did Emily get rid of Big Dan?

b) Listen again and complete the dialogue.

Josh: Hi Kai, so how did it go at the youth club last night?

Kai: Oh, not bad. I met this nice girl. Her name is Emily.

Josh: Sounds good. What did you say to her?

Kai: I asked her if she … 1 new.

Josh: And was she?

Kai: Yes. She said that this … 2 her first time at the club.

Josh: Ooooh … So then what happened?

Kai: I asked her what she … 3 of the music. She said that she liked it and that it … 4 her want to dance. So we danced together …

Josh: Wow, that's great!

Kai: … until Big Dan came over.

Josh: Hm, not so great. What did that bully want?

Kai: He asked Emily if she would dance with him. And she said yes.

Josh: Oh well. Did you get the next dance with her?

Kai: I wanted to, but Big Dan told me … 5 to be a pain. He told me to … 6 lost.

Josh: That sounds like Big Dan. What an idiot. So what did you do?

Kai: I told her that I enjoyed meeting her. Then I left. Later, outside the club, I turned around and she was right next to me. She said that Big Dan … 7 getting her coat for her.

Josh: Oh, no!

Kai: That's what I said. Then she told me she hadn't actually brought a coat. She asked me if I … 8 to walk her home. So we left together.

Josh: Oh, beautiful. °High five.

2 Indirect speech: statements

Look at the FOCUS box and answer the questions.

FOCUS

In both these sentences we find out what Emily said.

(A) She said, "This is my first time at the club." (B) She said that this was her first time at the club.

1 Which sentence ((A) or (B)) gives exactly the words that she said (= ***direct speech***)?

2 Which sentence ((A) or (B)) reports what she said (= ***indirect speech***)?

3 Write down the two sentences. Mark all the differences. What has changed?

4 Collect further examples of indirect speech from the dialogue in 1a).

▸ *Language file 20, p. 192–193*

▸ INKL p. 37

3 I didn't believe him

Dan told Emily a lot about himself. What did she tell her friend? Use the *simple past*.

1 I met this boy, Dan. He told me that he was …
2 He also said that …
3 He added that …
4 He told me that …
5 Then he said that …
6 Next he told me …
7 And finally he said that … But to be honest, I didn't believe anything he said.

More practice 3 p. 118

1 "I'm great at sport."
2 "I play in my school rugby team."
3 "I'm captain of the soccer team too."
4 "I can play six different instruments."
5 "My favourite instrument is the didgeridoo."
6 "My parents are famous actors."
7 "My dad lives in Hollywood."

4 Indirect speech: questions

FOCUS

1 What's different here? Complete the sentences below.
Ⓐ Kai asked Emily, "Are you new?" ➔ Ⓑ Kai asked Emily if she was new.
- A word has been added: …
- The word order has changed from verb + subject to …
- The direct question Ⓐ ends with a question mark. The indirect question Ⓑ ends with a …

2 Compare these examples:
Ⓒ I asked her, "What do you think of the music?" ➔ Ⓓ I asked her what she thought of the music.

▸ Language file 20, p. 193

5 Are you OK?

Eric had an accident and a woman stopped to help. What did he tell his dad?

1 "Do you need an ambulance?"
2 "Are you OK?"
3 "How do you feel?"
4 "Do you have a headache?"
5 "Can you move your leg?"
6 "Do you want some water?"

1 A woman asked me …
2 She wanted to know …
3 Then she asked …
…

6 Indirect speech: commands, requests, advice

FOCUS

Finish these sentences:
Emily asked Big Dan, "Can you get my coat for me, please?" ➔ Emily asked Big Dan to get …
Big Dan told Kai, "Don't be a pain." ➔ Big Dan told Kai not to …
Josh told Kai, "You should phone Emily." ➔ Josh told Kai to …

▸ Language file 20, p. 194

7 Good advice?

Josh is very nervous before his first date. He's reading his friends' advice. Complete the sentences.

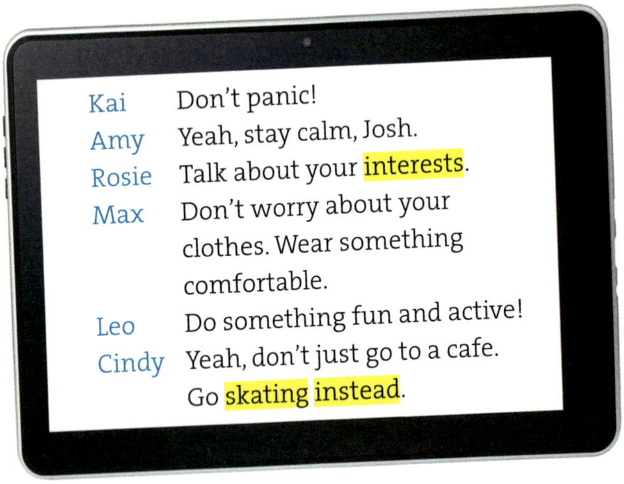

Kai told me ..., but I'm very nervous!
Amy told me ... Rosie told me ...
Max had some interesting advice. He ...
Leo had a good idea. He ...
Cindy agreed. She ...

8 More about indirect speech

a) Jessie wants to copy Tim's homework. But at their school you get into big trouble if you copy. He's telling his mum about it. What did Tim and Jessie say exactly (1–7)?

A girl at school talked to me yesterday. She told me that she had a problem. She asked me if I had done (1) my maths homework. I said I had finished (2) it the day before. She said that she hadn't started (3) hers. Then she asked me if she could copy (4) my homework.
I said that wasn't (5) a good idea. I also said that our teacher, Mrs Brown, would notice (6) and we both would get (7) into big trouble.

I have a problem. ... (1) you done your maths homework?

Yes, I ... (2) it yesterday.

Oh dear, I ... (3) started mine. ... (4) I copy your homework?

That ... (5) a good idea. Mrs Brown ... (6) notice. We both ... (7) get into big trouble.

b) How do the verbs change in indirect speech? Copy and complete this table.

▸ *Language file 20, p. 194* More practice 4 p. 118

direct speech	→	indirect speech
simple present	→	*simple past*
simple past	→	...
present perfect	→	
will		
can		

▸ Workbook 9–12, pp. 24–25

▸ KV 13 ▸ INKL pp. 34–36

Watching you, watching me

This story has two sides – a boy's side and a girl's side. You're going to read extracts from both sides of the story.

1 While you read

Think about these questions. Then compare answers.

1 Who is Natasha?
2 Where does she live?
3 Who does she live with?
4 What's she interested in?
5 What does she think about the neighbour from across the road?

Natasha's side of the story … (adapted from the novel by Chloe Rayban)

2.06

1 

There it was again – that funny feeling. I turned around and looked back down the road. I could feel someone watching me. But where from? The street was empty – not even a car. I looked at number twenty-five.

It had been empty for a long time. Jamie and Gemma called it the spooky house because sometimes I had told ghost stories about it to keep them quiet.

Number twenty-five really did look spooky. It was a tall house. The windows were boarded up and there were lots of weeds in the front garden.

2 Later that evening Jamie was hiding behind a curtain because he had to go to bed. He called me.

"Tasha!" He ran and put his arms around me. "They're there," he said. "They're really there."

"What are where?"

"At number twenty-five – the spooks!"

"Don't be silly. There's no such thing as spooks."

"Come and look. There are lights in the house …"

He took me to the window and we waited in the darkness, staring out. I looked at number twenty-five. And then I froze. He was right. A small light was moving through the rooms. It was moving upstairs now …

"What are you two doing?" Mum pulled the curtains back and found us sitting there.

"We've found a spook," Jamie said.

"Tasha," mum said with a warning look.

"No, it isn't me this time. But there is someone or something in number twenty-five. See for yourself."

The three of us stood behind the curtain … and then mum said, "Squatters! I knew this would happen if that house was left empty like that." Then she went downstairs to find dad.

"What are squatters?" Jamie asked.

I put my arms around him.

"Squatters are people who haven't got houses of their own. So they find empty houses and they squat in them. They live there without paying any money."

3 Dad came through the door at that moment. He stared out of the window.

"It isn't spooks, it's squatters," Jamie said.

"I can't see a thing," he said.

► KV 13 ► INKL pp. 34–36

We stood there together.
"See ... there it is in the top room," I said.
"Yeah," dad said. "It must be a candle."
"Right, I'm going to phone the police," mum said.
"No, wait," dad said. "Let's think about this for a moment. It's probably some poor guy who sleeps in the street or something."
"Dad's right, Mum," I said. "There could be some poor old homeless guy in there ..."
"This is a respectable street. Families, children ... the last thing we need is squatters," she answered.
Then she looked at Jamie.
"Bed for you, Jamie. Look at the time!"
She went off with him.
"I was a squatter once," dad said.
"You? You were a squatter?" I said, surprised.
"Not for long. When I was a student. We had no money ..."
"So what do you think we should do?" I asked.
"I guess I should visit our new neighbour. Bring the phone in here and if you see a problem, ring 999. Oh ... and don't tell mum, OK?"

4_ I stood at the window with the phone in my hand. I had a sick feeling in my throat. What if there were violent people in number twenty-five?
I watched dad as he crossed the road.

He hammered on the front door. Nothing happened for a while. Dad hammered again – harder this time. Number twenty-five was quiet. Then I saw the light, and it was moving down through the house. I waited, expecting the *Incredible Hulk* to come out. But it didn't. Dad stood there. He was talking through the door.
I couldn't hear what he was saying. Then he shook his head and came back across the road.
I heard our door and I went down the stairs.
"He said that he had every right to be there. He told me I was an old busybody. And he told me to °piss off!"
I wanted to laugh, but I didn't.
"What did he sound like?" I asked.
"Quite young."
"How young?"
"Hard to say – seventeen ... eighteen ..."

"What does he look like?" Gemma asked from the kitchen. My little sister loved romances, love stories ...
"I haven't met him yet. We talked through the door," dad said.
"Gemma, listen," I said. "This is like some tramp ... he probably smells."
"Hey Gem – bedtime. Off you go," dad said.

5_ Later that night, when I went up to bed, I opened my window as usual. I stared out of the window. The light was still there – in the top room now.
I just watched. Nothing was happening – the light was moving around.
"What's going on?" Gemma was beside me.
"Ssssh," I said. "Nothing."
"I guess he's cool," she said.
"What would you know?" I said.
Gemma was only nine. I was fourteen and I had never had a boyfriend.
Other girls at school had boyfriends – they teased me. But mum and dad were strict about pubs and clubs – parties too. It really wasn't fair.

► KV 13 ► INKL pp. 34–36

"Look, the light has gone out," Gemma said. After that I closed the curtains and went to bed. But I couldn't sleep for hours. I kept thinking of the squatter in number twenty-five – our mysterious new neighbour. Then I guess I fell asleep.

2 The other side of the story

Before you read Matt's side of the story, look at these questions. Based on what you know from Natasha's story, °speculate about the answers. Make notes.

1 Who is Matt?
2 Where does he live?
3 Who does he live with?
4 What's he interested in?
5 What's his connection with Natasha?

3 While you read

Think about the questions in task 2 while you read Matt's side of the story.
Then talk again and compare your answers with the story.

Matt's side of the story …

2.07

1 _

Number twenty-five was empty. I checked the address again. I didn't know it was going to be *this* bad. I opened the gate and fought my way through the weeds to the back door. There were lots of tools in the back garden.

2 _ When dad told me that we had to move to London for his job, I couldn't believe my luck. He thought my silence meant that I didn't want to go. He talked about how I'd soon make new friends and that we'd find a good school like my Stroud school. I just stopped him and said, "How soon can we move?" Dad found a school in London – West Thames College. There were girls and no uniforms. I started to imagine a school like you see in American college movies, where everyone sits on the grass and drives around in big old cars. So that's why I came up to London alone – to start at my new school.

3 _ Mum and dad had warned me about coming. They'd found out that the building work on the house wasn't finished and had decided to stay in Stroud for another few months. They'd wanted me to do another term at my school. But I was fed up with Stroud.
"Look, this summer my friends and I back-packed nearly across Europe. I think I'll be okay in a quiet London neighbourhood. Anyway," I argued, "I can keep an eye on the builders."
In the end they agreed that I could come to London alone.

London – it's a special place – it's full of life! You can feel that in the streets. You can see it in the faces of the people. You can hear it in the traffic noise. And when the lights come on at night, the city is magic, man!

4_ I went through the house – the hallway was full of boxes. I switched the light on, but nothing happened.

The building work wasn't finished downstairs ... up the stairs ... oops, one step missing! ... The bathroom was old. The two bedrooms on the first floor were big, but there were holes in the floors.
Up more stairs ... the top floor ... this was what I was waiting for – my floor! Two huge attic rooms ... I went back and forth between the two rooms. The back room was perfect for my music. I was so excited my heart was pounding. After our small house in Stroud this was like a palace.
I went into the front room, took a board off the window and looked out. The view! I looked down Frenshaw Avenue. I could see the tops of the trees ... cars ... and the city of London. And if I listened carefully I could hear it too – the sound of the city. I looked back into our street. Hey, look at that! A girl ... she looked nice. She stopped and turned around. Then she crossed the road and disappeared. I hoped she wasn't just visiting ...

5_ I went to the bathroom to have a shower. There was no hot water, so it was a very cold shower. Oh no – I had forgotten to bring the towel ...
That's when some crazy guy started to hammer on the front door.
"OK, OK, OK!" I shouted down.
I took a candle and went down the stairs ... oh! – I forgot the missing step.
"What do you want?" I shouted through the door.
"I saw your light. Look, you can't do this!"
"What?"
"You can't just move into this house like this."
"Look. I have every right to be here." Cold air was blowing in under the door. I tried to get warm by jumping up and down.

"I don't want to have to call the police."
This old busybody thought that I was a tramp or a squatter or something, destroying his comfortable life in this nice little neighbourhood ...
"Look, you old busybody! Why don't you get lost?"
"Well, I'm giving you a warning ..."
I was really cold and I just wanted him to go away.
"Yeah right! Go on, piss off!"

6_ I went back upstairs. After I'd dried myself, I sat in the window and looked out at the city again. Then I saw the window of the attic room in the house on the other side of the street. The curtains moved ... it was that girl again. She was opening the window ... and then she was closing the curtains. Oh no, please don't go ... but the curtains closed.

4 Paragraph headings

a) Match the headings (A–E) to the five parts of Natasha's story.

A Dad the detective
B An interesting new neighbour
C Dad the squatter
D Jamie sees a ghost
E Somebody is watching

b) Do the same for Matt's story. Watch out: two of the headings don't fit!

A I love London
B The girl across the street
C An unusual builder
D A new home, a new school
E Number 25 – an empty old house
F Going through the house
G Who's watching me?
H My horrible neighbour

5 Talking about the text

More help p. 119

a) Choose one side of the story – Natasha's or Matt's – and answer the questions.

1 *The **characters***: Who is the story about?

2 *The **setting***: Where does the story happen?

3 *The **plot***: Say what happens in the story – in a few sentences.

4 *The **mood***: How do you feel when you read this story? Why?

▸ *Skills file 7.7, p. 168*

b) Now find a partner who chose the other side of the story. Compare your answers. Do you agree with your partner's answers? Say why (not).

More practice 5 p. 120

6 Different perspectives

a) °Form groups of three or four. Look at lines 82–91 in Natasha's side of the story and lines 72–94 in Matt's side. Both characters describe the same event from their points of view. Discuss: What was each character thinking or feeling? Why did he or she feel this way?

b) Discuss the effect of telling the story twice from separate points of view. How does the reader experience the story differently? What are some advantages and disadvantages of telling the story this way?

7 SPEAKING and WRITING A book worth reading?

a) Discuss: How did you like the story? Did you like the way it's told from different perspectives? What did and didn't you like? Would you like to read the book? Vote in class.

b) Write a review of the story. In about 100 words, write about the plot, the setting, your favourite characters, the mood of the story and the structure of the book. Mention the things that you find good or not so good.

▸ *Skills file 9.8, p. 178* More help p. 120 More challenge 4 p. 120

2 SPEAKING COURSE (2) Successful conversations

► *INKL pp. 38–39*

1 VIEWING Dos and don'ts in conversations

a) Watch part 1 of the film.
What does Jan say about saying hello in English and German?
Do you agree with what he says about saying hello in German?

b) Watch part 2 of the film and spot Jan's mistakes. Make notes.
Compare your notes. Have you spotted all the mistakes?
What do Jan and Sarah think of each other? Why?

c) Before you watch part 3 of the film, think of useful tips for someone who is going to Great Britain on an exchange.
Agree on your top three tips.

! Look at the box below for ideas. Careful! Some of these are good tips. Others are not helpful.

- Only speak when you're spoken to!
- When people ask you questions, say as much as you can.
- Be careful. Don't make too many mistakes.
- Don't worry about making mistakes.
- Try to sound as English as you can.
- It's OK to sound German. The important thing is to talk!
- Be polite. Use words like *please*, *thank you* and *sorry* often.
- …

d) Watch part 3 with no °sound.
What do you think Jan and Sarah say this time?
Discuss in class and collect your suggestions on the board.

e) Watch part 3 again, this time with sound.
Compare your suggestions from d) with what Jan and Sarah say in the film.

f) Compare Jan and Sarah's tips with your tips from c).
Would you change any of your tips now?

2 NOW YOU Your conversation, step by step

A

B

C

Step 1: Starting off

a) How can you start the conversation? Choose a suitable phrase from the box for each scene or come up with your own ideas.

> Excuse me, is this seat free?
> Hi, I love your T-shirt / shoes / ...
> Hello. How are you?
> ...

b) How would you introduce yourself? There are some ideas in the box.

> I'm ..., by the way.
> My name is ... and I'm from ...
> Pleased to meet you.
> ...

Step 2: Keep the conversation going

a) Think of at least two things you could say to each of the people in the scenes above.

b) Compare your ideas. Then together think of at least two more things you could say.

> Where are you from?
> Do you like ...?
> Have you been to ...?
> I'm really enjoying my stay here.
> What class are you in?
> The weather is great today.
> ...

Step 3: A good ending

Choose phrases from the box for each scene, or come up with ideas of your own.

> It was really nice talking to you.
> See you around sometime.
> Have a good day!
> Bye. See you later.
> I hope we meet again.
> What are you doing tomorrow evening?
> ...

Step 4: Have a conversation

a) Pick one of the scenes A–C. Make a dialogue.

b) Perform your dialogues for the class. Give feedback. Did the people talk a lot? Did they sound friendly?

> **!** Be friendly. Smile!
> Listen carefully. Give full answers.
> If you don't know a word, paraphrase.
> ► *Skills file 8.2, p. 169*

More practice 6 p. 120

► *Workbook 17–20, pp. 28–30*

Living with disability

You'll find the new words from these pages listed on p. 231.

1 READING Two opinions

a) Britain and Jack both have to cope with disability. Compare their experiences and their feelings, and give examples from the texts (line numbers). ▸ *Skills file 7.4, p. 167*

'The kid in a wheelchair' *by Britain R.*

My life is happy and normal, but it isn't always easy, because of my disability. I have difficulty walking because I have a disease called muscular dystrophy, and over the years it has got worse.

When I was very young, I could still °keep up with my peers, although it took me longer to do some things. During °elementary school, however, things like standing and climbing stairs became difficult. Seeing other kids ride bikes or play sports, I had to accept that I would never be like those kids. By °middle school, I needed to use a wheelchair. My older brothers traveled °abroad with a student program, but I couldn't. More recently, I wasn't allowed to get a driver's license or a job.

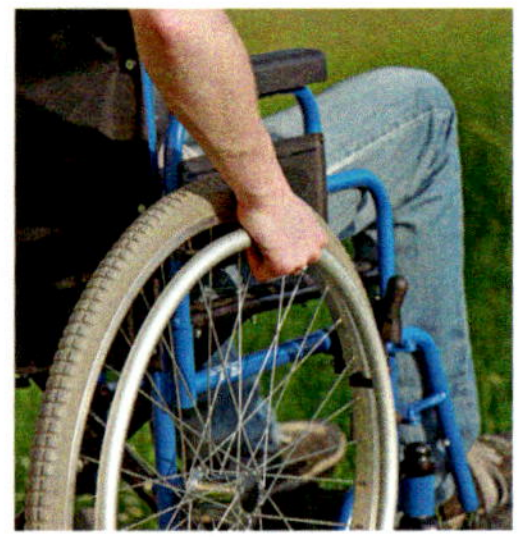

Believe me, there is prejudice against people with disabilities. I have been °called names like "cripple". For some people I'm "the kid in the wheelchair". They can't see °beyond my disability.

I have experienced many °hardships in my life because of my disability. I have also learned there are more important things in life than walking. Perhaps some °able-bodied people could learn from my experiences.

A fashion model and a role model

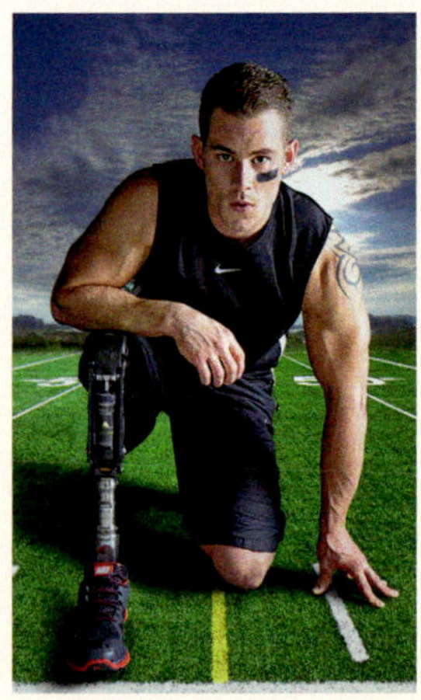

Jack Eyers is a personal trainer and has also worked as a fashion model, walking the catwalk at New York Fashion Week.

Eyers was born with a °rare °condition that meant that his right leg didn't grow °properly, and at the age of 16 he chose to have the leg amputated. He doesn't try to hide his prosthetic leg, °displaying it proudly and preferring to wear shorts °rather than trousers.

Being a sporty child, Eyers was frustrated by his disability – and by the °taunts of some of his classmates – but then he realized he could channel his frustration into weightlifting, boxing and, later, his career.

"If I had seen more disabled models when I was growing up, maybe I would have felt more confident about myself," °admits Eyers, who hopes he can now be as much a role model as a fashion model.

b) Do the following tasks.

1 Why do you think that Britain wrote his article? Discuss.
2 Explain how Jack can be a role model for disabled people and others.
3 Describe your response to the texts. How do they make you think about the way you react to people?

► *Skills file 7.5, p. 167*

2 WRITING A day in the life

a) Imagine a typical day in Britain's life. What's 'normal' and what isn't? Make notes. Then compare your ideas with those of another pair.

b) How is your daily life similar to Britain's? How is it different? What can you do that he can't do? Write about 120 words.

3 LISTENING Do the right thing

a) Think of a person at school, in your family or among your friends who has a disability. When you're with him or her, do you act differently? How?
Share with a partner.

2.08 **b)** Copy the table below. Then listen to the interview and complete the table.

disability	*dos*	*don'ts*
blind	*Ask someone before helping ...* ...	*Don't ...*
unable to walk	...	
all disabilities	...	

c) Compare your answers.
Choose two tips from each column and explain the reasons for them.

4 PROJECT A friendly school for all

a) Do a survey of all the places and things in your school (°doorways, stairs, signs, etc.) that are made for people with disabilities (e.g. blind people or people who can't walk). Make a list and describe how they help disabled people. Take photos too if you can. Identify any °barriers that your school still has and suggest how to get rid of them. Make notes.

b) Present your results in class.

5 LANGUAGE Understanding *participles* (*-ing*-forms)

a) Complete the FOCUS box.

FOCUS

In written texts ***participles* (*-ing*-forms)** can be used to say something in fewer words:

Example: Jack has worked as a fashion model, walking the catwalk ...
This is a short way of saying: ➔ ... and he has walked the catwalk

How could you replace the ***-ing*-forms *(participle)*** in this sentence?
'Being a sporty child, Eyers was frustrated by his disability.'

Ⓐ When he was ... Ⓑ Because he was ... Ⓒ Although he was ...

▸ *Language file 27, p. 199*

b) °Replace the ***participles*** in these sentences.
Use words like *and*, *while*, *because*, *when*.

1 Nellie got onto the boat, waving to her friends and family.
2 Sailing their small boat out to the starting line, Nellie and her partner prepared for the race.
3 Nellie saw the other boat crews and, knowing she was the only wheelchair user in the race, she felt the old fear again.
4 But when the race started she forgot about her fear, pulling in the sail.
5 Crossing the finish line later, she and her partner hugged and cheered.
6 "Now I know," Nellie thought, smiling at her mum and dad on the °dock, "I don't need legs to be a winner!"

6 LANGUAGE We're all good at something

Combine the sentences and replace the underlined words with ***participles***.

1 I was an energetic child. I enjoyed all kinds of sports, but I wasn't very good at them.
2 My parents °encouraged me. They thought it was good to do sport.
3 I joined a soccer club and went every week. I hoped that I would soon be in the team.
4 But the coach didn't pick me. She said I wasn't good enough.
5 I felt °rather fed up. I decided to look for a different sport.
6 I was walking through the park one day. I saw a game of tag rugby.
7 I joined in. I discovered to my surprise that I was good at it.

▸ KV 15 ▸ DFF 2.5 ▸ INKL pp. 40–43

1 LANGUAGE How to talk to your parents

a) O What exactly did Jay and her mum say? Complete the dialogue.

I said I wanted to meet Amy after school. Mum said it was a school night. She asked me how much homework I had. I told her that I didn't have very much.
Mum wanted to know where Amy lived. I said I didn't know. I told her we wanted to go to the mall. I asked her if she could °pick me up from there.
Mum asked if I had any money. I told her I didn't, but I reminded her that it was my birthday in ten days. Mum asked if I was serious. Then she said I couldn't go.

Jay	I ... to meet Amy after school.
Mum	But it'... a school night. How much homework ... you ...?
Jay	Oh, I ... ... very much.
Mum	Where ... Amy ...?
Jay	I ... know. We ... to go to the mall. ... you pick me up from there?
Mum	... you ... any money?
Jay	No, I .... But it'... my birthday in ten days.
Mum	... you serious? You ... go.

b) Two weeks later Jay wants to go to a concert, but she's afraid her parents will say no again. She has asked her friends for advice. Complete what she says.

Meg	Choose a good time to ask your parents.
Max	Stay calm and don't get angry.
Elli	Finish all your homework before you ask.
Tia	Tell them that you really want to go.
Meg	Don't ask for money for the tickets.
Max	You should use your birthday money.

1 Meg told me ...
2 Max told me ...
3 Elli ...
4 Tia ...
5 Meg ...
6 Max ...

c) What did Jay tell her friends about this discussion with her parents? Complete what she says.

Jay	Mum and Dad, can I talk to you about the concert? I really want to go.
Dad	Do you have any homework to do?
Jay	No, I don't. It's all finished.
Mum	How much do the tickets cost?
Jay	They are expensive, but I have the money from my birthday.
Dad	What time does the concert end?
Jay	Ten o'clock.
Dad	It's a bit late for a school night.
Mum	Yes, I don't want you to be tired at school.
Jay	It's just one night. But OK, I respect your opinion.
Mum	I really like your attitude, Jay.
Dad	I agree. You can go to the concert, Jay.

I asked my parents if I *could* (1) talk to them about the concert.
I told them I really ... (2).
Dad asked if I ... (3).
I ... (4).
Mum wanted to know how much the tickets ... (5).
I told them that they ... (6) but I ... (7).
Dad asked ... (8).
I said ten o'clock.
Dad said it ... (9).
And mum agreed with him. She ... (10).

I said it ... (11), but I ... (12).

Mum said ... (13).
Dad agreed and he said that ... (14)!
Wow! Great advice, guys!

More practice 7 p. 121

▸ *Language file 20, pp. 192–194*

▸ KV 15 ▸ DFF 2.2 ▸ DFF 2.6 ▸ INKL pp. 40–43

2 READING and WRITING Volunteering

Lily and Mike are volunteers. They've written about their work in texts A and B. Their notes for a presentation about the advantages of volunteering are in text C.

A

I'm Lily and I'm a volunteer lifeguard in LA. Every weekend our group meets and we learn about water safety and organizing beach games and competitions for hundreds of visitors. We're also taught first aid and °life-saving °techniques. Because a lifeguard has to be an excellent swimmer, I'm in a swimming program. The swimming has even helped me to do better in PE. And last month I became the leader of our school first aid crew.
What do I like most? I like °informing visitors about the safest places to swim and learning to use life-saving equipment. But I also enjoy just having fun with my friends on the beach. Also, this volunteer job keeps me fit.

B

My name is Mike and I'm at East High School. A friend asked me to volunteer to teach children with special needs how to swim. Doing this volunteer work once a week has made a big difference in my life. I've learned about the different °needs of all these children and how to help them to improve their skills. The highlight of every lesson is the water polo game we all play together. At school I used to have problems with keeping appointments and being on time. These children look forward to seeing us each week and I don't want them to be disappointed. Since I started, I've never been late or missed a lesson. It makes my °fellow students and me happy to help these kids to feel pride, improve their self-respect and have fun.

C

Volunteering has lots of advantages

1. You learn to communicate with people, to organize activities and to lead groups.
2. Volunteering teaches you time management skills.
3. Volunteers often do better at school.
4. Volunteering can help you to stay healthy.
5. You learn to be patient and to respect and understand other people.

a) ⭘ Find words or phrases that mean: //● p. 121

1 very good (text A)
2 team of people who work together (A)
3 things you need to rescue someone (A)
4 kids who have disabilities (B)
5 feel unhappy because something you hoped for doesn't happen (B)
6 organizing your own time (C)
7 able to deal with a difficult situation without getting fed up (C)
8 be polite and kind to others (C)

b) Match a final sentence to each text. (There's one more than you need.)

1 Everyone has the right to take part in sports activities, and that's why we think our work is important.
2 To sum up, volunteering – even if it's just once a week – can make a real difference to your life.
3 Volunteers need more help and support to do their important work.
4 I'm thinking of applying for a job as a professional rescue worker.

c) Write a comment for your school website. Do you agree or disagree with Lily and Mike? Give your opinion about volunteering.

▸ Skills files 9.1, pp. 171–172

▸ DFF 2.7 ▸ INKL pp. 40–43

3 LISTENING Friendly conversations

A

B

C

2.09 **a)** O Listen to dialogues 1–3 and match each dialogue with a picture (A–C). Say if the German student in each dialogue sounds friendly.

2.09 **b)** Listen again. Write down as many friendly and polite phrases as you can.

c) Write down three tips to help Robert from dialogue 3 to be more polite and friendly.

d) Complete the dialogue and help Robert to have a more friendly conversation with Amanda.

Robert ...
Amanda Oh! I'm sorry. I didn't see you. I haven't seen you before. Are you new?
Robert ...
Amanda Oh, cool, Germany? How interesting! I spent a week in Füssen last year. I was there with my °orchestra. It was beautiful.
Robert ...
Amanda Well, my next class is in a few minutes. What do you have next?
Robert ...
Amanda I'°m not really into maths and science. I like music and drama. What are your favourite subjects?
Robert ...
Amanda Well, OK, see you later. It was nice meeting you. Oh, by the way, I'm Amanda.
Robert ...

4 SPEAKING Role-play

Partner B: Go to page 104.
Partner A: Read your role card and prepare a role-play with your partner.
Start your conversation very politely. Don't forget to introduce yourselves to each other.

You've just arrived at Green Valley High School for an exchange programme. You're at a welcome party for exchange students. Maybe you can find somebody who can show you the most interesting places in town tomorrow?
You go over to the °buffet table to get a drink when you see somebody making eye contact with you. Keep a conversation going with him or her for at least three minutes.

▸ Workbook My learner log, p. 31 and Revision, p. 26, p. 32

Unit 3

Looking forward

► *INKL pp. 44–45*

1 QUIZ Are you ready for the real world?

In the near future your life will change. Perhaps you'll go to a new school or college. Perhaps you'll start training, or even start a job. And many of you will leave home.

a) What does being independent mean for you? Collect your ideas and make notes. Share your ideas with a partner.

b) Now do this magazine quiz and find out if you're ready for the real world.

1 If you had to make a meal, what would you do?

Ⓐ I'd cook pasta with tomato sauce. It's easy.
Ⓑ I'd look for a recipe, buy the ingredients and cook them.
Ⓒ I'd get a takeaway or order something online.

2 Imagine you had to do the shopping for a week. What would you do?

Ⓐ I'd probably buy lots of crisps and sweets, etc.
Ⓑ I'd go to the nearest supermarket and pick up the things that I see. Box: Voc., p. 216
Ⓒ I'd make a shopping list, go to cheap shops and buy only what I need.

3 What chores do you do at home?

Ⓐ I do some chores, e.g. I tidy up, set the table, etc. But I don't know how to use the washing machine and I hate using the vacuum cleaner.
Ⓑ I never do chores. That's for parents, brothers and sisters!
Ⓒ I use the dishwasher, the vacuum cleaner and the washing machine. Sometimes I iron my clothes.

4 Do you earn your own pocket money?

Ⓐ I have a part-time job, but I don't earn a lot of money.
Ⓑ Yes, I have a part–time job and I can buy my own stuff.
Ⓒ No! When I need money, I ask mum or dad, or my grandparents.

5 Do you manage your own money?

Ⓐ I budget – I plan how much I can spend on going out, hobbies, etc.
Ⓑ I often run out of money, so I have to borrow.
Ⓒ I try not to overspend. But I don't really budget. Box: Voc., p. 217

6 Do you save any money?

Ⓐ No. I like to enjoy my money.
Ⓑ Sometimes. But then I spend it!
Ⓒ Yes, I try to save a little every week.

► *INKL pp. 44–45*

7 Are you looking forward to living with other people?

Ⓐ I've never really thought about it. I think I'll miss home.

Ⓑ Yippee! I can't wait to leave home. It'll be party, party, party!

Ⓒ Yes, but we'll have to plan well, share the chores, clean often, etc.

8 Are you a responsible student?

Ⓐ I'm quite responsible. I do my school work, but I sometimes go to bed very late, especially at weekends.

Ⓑ I think I am. I work hard at school and I don't stay out late in term time.

Ⓒ Well … I like to go out a lot and to do things with friends, even in the week. I do my school work when I have time.

9 If you lost your bus ticket, what would you do?

Ⓐ I'd buy another one.

Ⓑ I'd go on the bus without a ticket.

Ⓒ I'd sit down and cry … or I'd phone home for help.

10 Are you good at making decisions?

Ⓐ I usually do the same thing as my friends.

Ⓑ Most of the time. Sometimes it's hard to decide.

Ⓒ Yes, but I sometimes get advice.

c) How did you answer the questions and what does it mean? Read the results on page 122.

2 Life skills

a) Think: When you leave home to live on your own, what do you need to know how to do? List six important life skills and the reasons why they're important. Look at the quiz for ideas and add your own ideas. More help p.122

b) Pair: Compare your lists and agree on the top five skills. Give reasons.

c) Share: Tell the class what you and your partner think. Give your reasons.

What are you like?

1 VIEWING Strengths and weaknesses

a) Watch the two scenes without sound and think about these questions:
1 What do you think is happening? **2** How do the figures seem to feel or react?

b) Read the statements below. Then watch the scenes with sound. Are they true or false?

1 This isn't the first time that Neil has been late for a match.
2 Neil says sorry and the coach says it's no problem.
3 Neil isn't allowed to play in the match.

Neil

4 Maggie is cross with Julie and talks to her rudely.
5 Maggie doesn't think that Julie's clothes are appropriate for her work experience.
6 Julie understands that Maggie is giving her some good advice.

Julie
Maggie

2 Describing people

a) Read the description of Neil. Then watch scene 1 again. Do you agree with the description? Copy the text and correct or change the things that you don't agree with.
The words in the box might help you.

*In scene 1 Neil is late for the football match.
He looks quite relaxed. He isn't sorry about being late and he isn't very polite to his coach. On the other hand, he's good at listening to the coach and he reacts well to criticism.*

confident • energetic • enthusiastic • helpful • polite • punctual • reliable • …

b) Now write a description of Julie (scene 2) in the same way.
Example: *Julie is a bit …, but towards the end she becomes more …*

c) WRITING Write a description of a friend or someone in your family.
Let them read it (or explain it in German). What would they describe differently?

► KV 16 ► INKL pp. 46–47

3 LISTENING Ideas for the future

2.10

a) You're going to hear five young people talking about their ideas for the future. Read the statements below. Then listen and choose the correct statement (A–F) for each person. (There is one more statement than you need.)

Example: *1 Charlotte: ... 2 Tom: ... 3 ...*

Charlotte

Tom

Max

Ruby

Summer

A I'm sporty and I like teamwork. I know what job I want to do.

B I like looking after people. I'd like to work with children or old people.

C I'm good at art. I'd like to study at university, but I don't know what job I want to do.

D I'd like to leave school and start work as soon as I can.

E I'm not very patient, so I can't imagine working with children.

F I'm good at finding solutions to problems. I like science.

b) Listen again. Add at least one more thing about each of the young people.

4 ACTIVITY Identity card

a) Make notes about yourself on a card like this. ► *Wordbank 2, p. 137*

What am I like? three adjectives to describe myself	**My strengths** at least two things I'm good at
My weaknesses one or two things I'm not so good at	**My hopes and plans** even if I don't have any real ideas for the future yet

b) Make appointments with three students. Tell each partner about yourself and get feedback.

c) Use your notes and feedback to write a text about yourself, your strengths and weaknesses, and your plans for the future. You can put your text in your DOSSIER.

I'm not so good at football, but I play the drums quite well and I'm quite good at ...

I haven't seen you play football, but I've heard you play the drums. Maybe you should focus more on music.

What's next?

1 Internet job adverts

Scan the job adverts and find as many jobs as you can. Compare your lists. More practice 1 p. 122

1

We are looking for an early years teaching assistant. If you
- have experience working with children under the age of five
- have excellent communication skills
- are a great team player

... then we would like to meet you!

APPLY NOW

Hours: Mon – Thu, 8 am to 5 pm
Salary: £60 per day

2

Elite Stylists, Liverpool

We are a leading make-up, fashion and hair stylist company for TV shows, fashion shows, film studios and °red carpet events. This is your chance to become a celebrity stylist, so start your new career now.
You should be energetic and reliable.

Full training on the job Box: Voc., p. 218
Salary: Up to °£20K, plus travel costs
Send us your CV and photo today.

3

LOLA Events Management

We need: bar staff • cooks • waiters

To work in our team, you must have some experience and excellent communication skills.
Pay: £6.75 to £10 per hour

We also need a trainee events manager
Do you enjoy planning, organizing and working with people?
Events managers organize all kinds of events. You will do our ten-week training programme to learn the skills you need.
Qualifications: °A Levels; work experience
Salary: £20 – £25,000 per year

Please apply now – we can't wait to meet you.

4

Jobs in Canada

If you are 18 to 30 years old, you can apply for a visa to live and work in Canada for up to one year.

Ski instructors: We are looking for qualified instructors who like to work with children. You have to be confident and enthusiastic. Other languages (especially French and German) are an advantage. Free accommodation and ski pass. Earn C$12 per hour.

Hotel workers: Work in a hotel in the ski season as a cleaner, receptionist or waiter. You have to be friendly, polite and helpful. Work 5 days per week and get 2 days free to ski and °snowboard. Earn C$10 per hour. No experience needed.

▸ KV 16 ▸ KV 17 ▸ DFF 3.2 ▸ INKL pp. 48–49

5

apprentice IT technician

Circle Square Health is a °non-profit organization that serves people with disabilities in Britain.

CSH

If you want on-the-job training as an IT technician, then become an apprentice in our IT department. You will learn as you help solve user problems on the 25 computers in our office and help take care of our day-to-day IT needs.

You need to:
- have a good knowledge of computers
- be a flexible thinker
- be enthusiastic and friendly

Salary: £21,000–27,000 per year
Apply now at Circle Square Health.

6

Ever thought of becoming a pilot?

You need to:
- be able to work shifts
- have good communication skills
- be calm at all times
- be fit
- be a team player
- be responsible

For more information, go to the LONDON CITY AIRPORT website.

2 Different jobs – different duties

a) Copy the table. **Partner A:** Look at the job ads 1–3 and complete the table. **Partner B:** Look at the job ads 4–6 and do the same.

job	qualifications or training?	skills and/or experience?	work alone or in a team?	inside or outside?	days or nights?	with people / kids / equipment/computers?
teaching assistant	experience	communication skills	team	…	…	…
hair stylist	training on job	…				
…						

b) Take turns asking questions to find out about your partner's jobs.

3 Advice for a suitable job

You're a job °counsellor and your partner has come to you for advice.

a) Think: Look at your partner's identity card. Then decide on the best job for your partner.

b) Pair: Explain your conclusions to your partner and give reasons. Does your partner agree or disagree? Discuss. Then swap roles.

c) Share: Share your results in class.

More practice 2 p. 123

4 Your ideal job

Imagine your ideal job. Do some research and write a text (150–180 words) about it. Explain why you think the job is right for you. More help p. 123 ▸ Wordbanks 3–4, pp. 138–139

Selling yourself

1 Paul's CV

a) Paul is applying for a job. Look at his CV, then look at the adverts on pages 60–61. Which job is he applying for?

b) Complete Paul's CV with the headings in the box.

Education • Key skills • Interests and achievements • Personal statement • References • Work experience

c) Choose three skills, interests or achievements from Paul's CV. Say why you think they're helpful for the job he is applying for.

Paul Schulz
Address: Goethestraße 37, 78467 Konstanz
Mobile: 0151 321 50717 Email: paulschulz23@gerlink.de

1) ...
I am a confident and enthusiastic student with good communication and social skills. I have some work experience and would like to experience other cultures and learn new skills.

2) ...
- Strong team member
- Friendly and polite
- Good organizational skills
- Good English and basic French

3) ...
2012 to present: Sophie-Scholl Gesamtschule, Konstanz
2008 to 2012: Gaisenthal Grundschule, Ulm

4) ...
Ski resort: ski hire shop assistant (part-time on weekends)
Summer camp: kids' group leader (3 weeks' work experience)

5) ...
I am interested in the outdoors and in winter sports. I have taken part in ski competitions and in summer I like hiking in the mountains.

6) ...
Dieter Lutz (English teacher)
Sophie-Scholl Gesamtschule

Monika Bold (manager)
Snowbird Ski Hire

2 NOW YOU Your CV

a) Write a CV for yourself like Paul's for one of the jobs on pages 60–61.
You can put it in your DOSSIER.

► Skills file 9.5, p. 175

> ! When you finish writing your text, use the spelling check tool on your computer to check your text.

b) Swap CVs with at least one partner. Give your partner feedback on his or her CV.
– Are there any mistakes?
– Is any information missing?
– Is the information appropriate for the job that your partner is applying for? More challenge 1 p. 123

3 Cover letters

Goethestraße 37
78467 Konstanz

Sports School Director
Sun Peaks Resort
1280 Alpine Road
Sun Peaks BC VOE 5NO
Canada

28th February 20..

Dear Sir / Madam

I am writing about the job of ski … (1) at your resort. I saw the … (2) on your website yesterday, February 27th and I would like to … (3) for this job.

I am a student and I worked part-time in the Snowbird ski … (4) shop for five months, where I helped customers with their ski equipment. I am also an experienced ski racer, so I think that I would be very … (5) for your job.

I am energetic and reliable. I am also healthy and … (6), and I enjoy working with people, especially … (7). I speak good English and I have a good … (8) of French too. I will finish school this spring, so I will be … (9) in the winter months – starting in November if possible.

I enclose my … (10) and I look forward to hearing from you.

Yours faithfully Box: Voc., p. 220

Paul Schulz

a) Complete Paul's cover letter with the words from the box.

advertisement • apply • available • children • CV • fit • hire • instructor • knowledge • suitable

b) Do you think that Paul is a good candidate for the job? Why (not)?

4 WRITING Now you

Look at the ad on the right. Imagine that you're applying for this job. Write a cover letter for yourself. Use ideas and language from Paul's letter in task 3. You can put it in your DOSSIER.

► *Skills file 9.6, p. 176* More practice 3 p. 124

Camp Swiss
Looking for group leaders

Are you a kind and enthusiastic person? Do you like children? Do you like the outdoors? We're looking for international group leaders for our summer programme starting 1st July.

Responsibilities: looking after and leading a group of campers (six to eight kids); supporting and helping your campers with all activities.

Requirements: You should be 17 to 25 years old, a team player, and speak good English. You should also have an open and positive attitude towards all cultures and languages.

Also an advantage: experience working with children; first-aid training; a strong interest in outdoor sports.

Location: Torgon, Switzerland   Please apply in English.

Into the world

1 READING Volunteer work

Scan the website and answer these questions:

1 In what areas of the world are the volunteer projects?
2 Who can be a volunteer?
3 How can a volunteer profit? Name three ways.
4 What kinds of work can you do?

European Volunteer Network

Getting started | Volunteer guide | Target countries | Volunteer specials | FAQ

Are you interested in being an international volunteer?
The **International Volunteer Programme** offers volunteer projects that give support to local communities in Europe, Africa, Asia and Latin America. Young volunteers who meet the qualifications listed below can do volunteer service for 2 to 12 months. The volunteer's costs for travel, food and accommodation are paid for by the International Volunteer Programme.

As an international volunteer you ...
- experience other cultures and meet new people
- help people in important ways
- learn about the problems that people in other parts of the world face
- discover abilities and learn new skills that you can add to your CV
- grow personally through new challenges and experiences

To qualify you need to ...
- be 18 years of age
- be a legal resident in Europe
- have a valid passport
- have a health certificate from a doctor
- have good language skills

Kinds of project work
- helping small children
- working on farms and nature reserves
- teaching in schools and training centres
- helping people with special needs
- assisting in rural hospitals
- building houses, schools, etc.

Some of our projects

Colombia: farm project
Help build an organic farm in a rural area close to a tropical rainforest. Live on the farm with the farmer's family.

Romania: projects street kids and disabled
Work with a small team of volunteers in a home for street children or help in a hospital for disabled people.

Ghana: football project
Teach village school children football and social skills through sport.

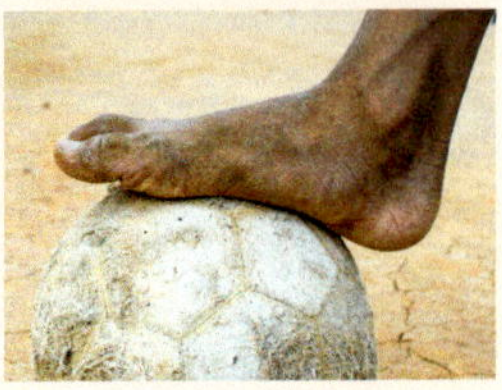

Nepal: water project
Live in a mountain village and help build a water system that brings fresh water to the village.

▸ KV 19 ▸ KV 20 ▸ DFF 3.5

2 The experience of volunteering

a) Choose one of the four projects described on page 64. Talk about what kinds of experiences – positive or negative – you think a volunteer could have on this project. Make notes. Then share your ideas in class. More help p.124

2.11 **b)** Copy the table. Then listen to four volunteers looking back on their experiences on the four projects. Complete the table. Compare and discuss your answers.

volunteer	project	positive experiences	negative experiences	tips / advice
Dominic				
...				

c) Would you like to be a volunteer? Why (not)? What kind of project would you choose?
More practice 4 p.124

3 Work and travel

Another way to get work experience and see the world is through a work and travel programme.

a) What do you already know about work and travel and how it is organized? Talk in small groups.

b) Read what Amanda wrote on a work and travel website about her experience. Where did she go and what kind of work did she do?

Hey, everybody, this is Amanda. Last year I spent an amazing ten months down under. There's so much I could say about my trip. I paid an organization to book my flight and my accommodation. They also organized my work visa and a job for me. I was glad I did it that way.
I arrived in Sydney and already had a place to stay and work – that was cool. Sydney wasn't easy at first. It's a great city, but it's huge and the public transport isn't very well organized.
Luckily the Aussies were always friendly and helpful.
I worked for a landscape gardener, taking care of people's gardens.
The pay wasn't great, but it was nice to work outdoors. After about four weeks I met a girl my age, Mel from South Africa, and we moved into a flat together with two other girls. Then the fun really started and I quickly made friends. After three months in Sydney I was ready for some travel.
Mel and I went on the road through the outback for five weeks and that was awesome.
We visited Uluru, went camping, did a camel trek and met some amazing people. Then I managed to get a job at a ski lift in Tasmania. I worked there for four months, and that gave me a chance to explore the island while making a little money. My biggest tip for anyone who is planning work and travel is: Don't plan too much – just take things as they come!

c) Think of five more questions about Amanda's work and travel experience. Make notes.

d) International volunteering or work and travel? Which do you find more attractive? First do a quick classroom survey to find out which is more popular. Then discuss reasons for the choices.

► INKL p. 55

1 Questions about Emma

a) Do you know why Emma Watson is famous? Skim the text and look at the photos to find out.

Facts about Emma

1 Emma Watson was ten years old when she played Hermione in the first Harry Potter film. That was in 2000.
2 Emma worked on the Harry Potter films for 10 years. She finished work on the last film in 2010.
3 In real life Emma is good friends with the actors who play Harry and Ron in the films.
4 Emma was born in Paris in 1990. She isn't French though! She's English. (She speaks French, but not very well.)
5 She moved to England with her mum and her younger brother when she was five.
6 The name of her first school in England is very appropriate for a Harry Potter actor. It was called the °Dragon School!
7 Since the end of the Harry Potter films Emma has done lots of things. She has acted in more films, and she has worked as a model. She loves fashion and many people admire her style.
8 She went to university in the US and studied English.
9 She's a great role model for young people. She gave a speech at the United Nations in New York about equal rights for women.
10 Who knows what Emma will do next? One thing is for sure. We will definitely hear more about her in the future!

b) Work in groups. Read the article. What questions do you think the interviewer asked to get this information? Write at least one question for each point in the article.

2.12 c) Then listen to an interviewer talking with a reporter about Emma. Which of the interviewer's questions are similar to yours?

2.12 d) Listen again. What other interesting or surprising questions does the interviewer ask?

2 REVISION Word order in questions

A Hollywood reporter has made notes for an interview with Daniel Radcliffe. What questions does she want to ask?

More practice 5 p. 124 | More challenge 2 p. 125 | ► Language files 11–12, pp. 188–189

Topics for interview

1 where he went to school
2 if he enjoyed school
3 where he met Emma for the first time
4 how long they have known each other
5 if he misses playing Harry Potter
6 what his next film role will be

► Workbook 12–13, p. 38

3 Question tags

a) Listen again to the interview in task 1 and complete these sentences. 2.12 // p.125

did she • isn't she (2x) • was it

1 - Okay. Emma was born in 1990 in Paris.
- In Paris? But she's British, ...?

2 - And the name of her school is interesting for someone who worked on Harry Potter films.
- Oh, let me guess. It wasn't the Hogwarts School, ...?

3 - I think that she's a great actor, ...?
- Yes, definitely.

4 - But she has also found time to go to university.
- What did she study? She didn't study magic, ...?

b) Complete the FOCUS box.

FOCUS

Question tags are used in speech when you want somebody to **agree with** or **confirm something**.

positive statement	+	negative question tag	But she's British, ... ?
negative statement	+	positive question tag	She didn't study magic, ... ?

▸ *Language file 31, p. 203*

c) Elias isn't sure that he heard some things in the interview correctly, so he's asking his classmates. Complete his sentences with the right question tag.

1 Emma was born in Britain, ...?
2 She has a brother, ...?
3 Her mother wasn't an actor, ...?
4 Emma went to acting school, ...?
5 She's finished her university studies, ...?
6 Emma is going to continue acting, ...?
7 She's done some work for the UN, ...?
8 She doesn't have a boyfriend, ...?

More practice 6 p.125

4 °PLACEMAT Great interviewers need great questions

Step 1: Work in groups of four. Draw a placemat like this on a big piece of paper. Who would you like to interview? Agree in your group.

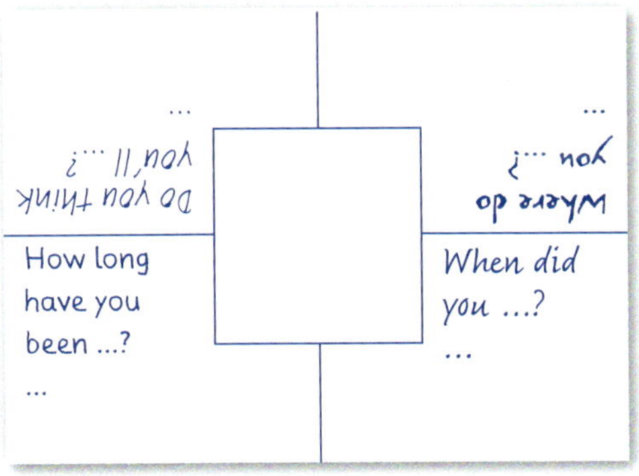

Step 2: Everybody writes questions in their part of the placemat that they would like to ask about the past, present and future – as many as they can.

Step 3: Read out all your ideas.

Step 4: Talk about the ideas. Agree on six questions and put them in the middle of the placemat.

I think a good question is "Where do you live now?" because ...

I think "How long have you ...?" is a more interesting question because ...

Step 5: Choose two people in your group to perform the interview for the class.

More challenge 3 p.126

▸ KV 21 ▸ KV 31 ▸ INKL pp. 52–54

1 Before you read: Look at the blurb

The blurb is the short text on the back cover of a book. It tells the reader what the story is about.

a) Read the blurb. How much does it tell you about the story? Think about the five *wh*-questions.

b) Compare. Then read the story.

'Seashell Motel' by Lois Metzger: Sixteen-year-old Cindy from New York pretends she's nineteen in order to work for the summer in a motel in Atlantic City. But she soon realizes that what she has done is far more complicated than to turn a six upside down ...

Seashell Motel (adapted from a short story by Lois Metzger)

2.13

Cindy Fisher, age sixteen, lied to get her summer job.

Before the summer, Mrs. Karpinsky, a teacher at Cindy's high school in New York City, told all the °tenth graders that a summer job was a good idea. She talked about jobs in neighborhood restaurants, bakeries, small offices and city parks. (Cindy had done those kinds of jobs before – boring!)

Then Mrs. Karpinsky mentioned the Seashell Motel down in Atlantic City, New Jersey. They were looking for a front desk clerk. Cindy immediately put up her hand and said, "I'll take that one."

Mrs. Karpinsky walked over to Cindy and handed her the application form. Then she looked at Cindy and said, "Sorry, you must be nineteen."

"I can do it," Cindy said.

"I'm sure you could, dear," the teacher said. "But for this job you have to live on your own in a strange city."

But Atlantic City's not strange, Cindy thought. When she was younger, she had gone there every summer with her family for two weeks. She remembered the beautiful boardwalk along the ocean. She loved going on the rides, eating candy and hearing the ocean all the time. In Atlantic City, the ocean seemed to be everywhere.

Cindy couldn't give the application form back to Mrs. Karpinsky.

"I'll give it to my older sister," she said. "She's nineteen."

"That's a fine idea," Mrs. Karpinsky said.

"Your baby sister is nineteen? Since when?" said Charlotte, a friend of Cindy's, who was sitting next to her. Cindy smiled. Box: Voc., p. 222

When she got home, Cindy told her parents that there was a new summer program at school and that lots of sixteen-year-old girls would be going to hotels all along the east coast.

"The teacher said that it would be good for me," she told them. Her parents looked impressed.

So Cindy filled out the application form and wrote down her age as '19', not '16'.

► KV 21 ► KV 31 ► INKL pp. 52–54

How easy, she thought. You just turn a six upside down!

---

2 Cindy read the Seashell Motel brochure on the bus to Atlantic City. 'Ocean view' it said, but when she got to the boardwalk there was no Seashell Motel there. Then she saw the sign for the motel – it was several blocks from the sea. As she walked along, she thought that the city seemed sadder than she remembered, with many stores closed.
Finally, on Arctic Avenue, there it was – the Seashell Motel. Only three storeys high, modern, unattractive, beige. No ocean view! Cindy couldn't even hear the waves.

Box: Voc., p. 222

At the front desk there was a young man with short brown hair, a blue jacket and a tie – about twenty-two years old.
"Welcome," he said and smiled. "A room for the weekend?"
"My name is Cynthia Fisher," Cindy said. Cynthia sounded much more mature, she thought.
"I'll be working here – with you, I guess."
"You look a little young," he said.
It's my clothes and my hair, Cindy thought. I have to look older. "I'm nineteen. This is actually my third job," she lied.
"Fine," he said. "I'm Tim Chamberlain. I'm studying hotel management in Louisiana."
Cindy heard his accent. She had never met a boy from the South before.
"Are you in college too?" he asked.
"High school ... I mean I finished high school last year ... now I'm at Queens College," she lied. I'll have to tell lies all summer, Cindy thought.

---

3 Cindy stood behind the front desk, her hair pulled back, in a white blouse, a dark blue skirt and pumps with heels. The make-up on her skin and the lipstick on her lips felt funny. Get used to it, she told herself.
Munny, the manager, was a tall, cheerful guy with curly brown hair.
"You can work the morning shift – from eight in the morning to four in the afternoon. Or the evening shift – from four in the afternoon until midnight. Or the graveyard shift – from midnight to eight."
There were also a couple of guys in the kitchen, two °bellhops and two ladies who did the cleaning. They were very sweet – but didn't speak much English.
Then there was Cal. He came to the motel every Thursday afternoon to fill up the drinks machine in the lobby. He had long dark hair, sea-green eyes and always wore a neon T-shirt. He was nice – he gave Cindy a couple of cans of *Orange* before he filled the machine.

He was sixteen and a half and lived in Atlantic City. Sometimes, when Cindy went to the beach in her time off, she imagined romantic walks with Cal.
And there were the guests. Cindy gave them their rooms, accepted their credit cards, answered their phone calls and sometimes made wake-up calls.
One night, when she was on the graveyard shift, Tim told her that the man in Room 111 wanted a wake-up call at 5 am.
"Good morning," Cindy said cheerfully on the phone.
"This is your °wake-up call."
"Are you crazy?" the man said and he slammed down the phone.
It was Tim's joke.
"You'll get me fired!" Cindy complained to Tim.
"Munny won't care. He likes a good joke," Tim answered.

---

4 One afternoon Cal gave Cindy three cans of *Orange* and said, "Hey Cynthia, want to go to the boardwalk tonight?"
"Yes, sure, that sounds like fun," she answered.
Later, when they were on the boardwalk, Cal asked Cindy, "Want to go to the Hall of Mirrors?"
It was dark in there and Cindy saw Cal and herself thousands of times in the mirrors. Cal took Cindy's hands and he wanted to kiss her,

but she pulled back. Cal liked Cynthia. But would he like Cindy? she thought. "I get it," he said, "I'm too young. Hey, it's OK, Cynthia." Cindy felt terrible. This Atlantic City summer was a bad idea. She hadn't just turned a number upside down, she had turned herself upside down! "Don't look so sad," Cal told her. "We can still take a walk together sometimes." "Let's just go," she said. Cindy wanted to leave the Hall of Mirrors, but she couldn't find the door. She felt trapped – trapped in her lies ...

5 The next week a hurricane hit Atlantic City. Cindy had never heard anything like it. She lay in her bed listening to the wind and the rain. Then the phone rang. It was Cal. "I'm downstairs," he said. "I thought you might like to go for a walk." "You mean now?" Cindy said, shocked. "Walk in the hurricane?" she asked. "You'll see, it's so beautiful," he said. "It's so crazy!" "I've lived here my whole life. I know what I'm doing," he said. Cindy wanted to go ... but did Cynthia? "Put on a swimsuit and sandals," Cal said. "I'll wait for you in the lobby." Down in the lobby Cal was wearing dark shorts and sandals. He took Cindy's hand. Outside the wind was much louder. They walked towards the boardwalk and they got very wet. The streets were flooded. It was dangerous, but Cindy felt calm and safe with Cal. At the boardwalk the sky and the sea were the same dark grey. You couldn't see where the sea ended and the sky began. "What do you think, Cynthia?" Cal said. "I told you the truth, didn't I?"

6 "Cal," Cindy suddenly said. "I haven't told you the truth. I'm not who you think I am." "You're not?" Cal said. "I'm only sixteen years old. So the way I dress, the way I act, the way I feel ... it's just one big lie!" Cindy could see that Cal was trying to understand this. Finally he smiled at her. "You're so brave. I'm sixteen and I've never been away from home – not even for a night," he said. "I don't feel brave, I just feel trapped. I told lies to the motel, I told lies to my parents and I told lies to you." "So you're brave, and also a little foolish. When will you tell your parents?" Cal asked. "I'll tell them everything, but not just yet," Cindy said. The hurricane was getting louder. "Let's go back," Cal said.

Back at the motel a window had broken and sea water was coming into the motel. Look! Cindy thought, the brochure wasn't lying, Seashell Motel does have an ocean view.

▸ KV 22 ▸ KV 31 ▸ INKL pp. 52–54

The following tasks are on three different levels. Pick and complete one task for each level.

2 Questions for you

a) **Partner A:** Look at parts 1–3 of the story and think of one question for each part. Make notes. **Partner B:** Look at parts 4–6 and do the same.

b) Take turns asking and answering the questions. Partner A begins.

3 Seashell in short

Copy the sentences and put them in the right order to make a summary of parts 1 to 3.

1 When she arrives at the motel, she meets Tim.
2 She has to get used to wearing make-up.
3 She applies for the job and lies about her age.
4 Cindy sees Cal every Thursday.
5 Cindy hears about a summer job in Atlantic City.
6 Atlantic City looks sadder than Cindy remembered it.

4 Sum it up

Write a short summary for parts 4 to 6 of the story. ▸ *Skills file 9.4, p. 174*

5 An interesting character 1

Copy this table and make notes about one of the characters in the story – Cindy, Tim or Cal. Use words and phrases from the story – and your own ideas.

NAME	FROM	AGE	PERSONALITY	APPEARANCE (hair, eyes, ...)	CLOTHES	WHAT HE/SHE DOES/LIKES
...	...	...	...	...	...	...

6 Cindy's diary

You're Cindy. Write a short diary entry for each of these times.

- after your day at school
- after you've arrived at the motel
- after your trip to the Hall of Mirrors
- after the hurricane

7 An interesting character 2

Write a characterization of Cindy, Tim or Cal. Write about the topics in the table in task 5. Use some of these words: kind, brave, honest, easy-going, funny, hard-working. And say what you think of him or her and why. ▸ *Skills file 7.7, p. 168* More challenge 4 p. 126

8 What happens next

How do you think the story continues? Make notes. Then write the last part or parts of the story.
Find another student who has written his or her own version. Swap texts and compare.

SPEAKING COURSE (3) Doing well in job interviews

▸ DFF 3.7 ▸ INKL pp. 56–57

1 VIEWING Interview stress

a) What do you need to think about when you're preparing for a job interview? Make a network.

b) Watch part 1 of the film. Do you think Mike has prepared well for the interview?
Can you add more ideas to your network in a)? Discuss.

c) Watch part 1 of the film again. Make a list of the mistakes that Mike makes.

d) Watch part 2 of the film. What things does Mike do better this time? ▸ *Skills file 8.3, p. 170*

e) What questions does the interviewer ask Mike? Watch part 2 again and write down as many questions as you can. More practice 7 p. 126

2 Body language

a) Look at these tips on body language in a job interview.
Why do you think each is important?

- Relax.
- Don't cross your arms in front of your chest.
- Don't shake hands too aggressively.
- Look interested.
- Don't sit or stand too close to the interviewer.
- Make eye contact.

b) Look at these pictures from the film.

part 1

part 1

part 2

part 2

Think: What's Mike doing wrong in part 1? How does he correct himself in part 2? Make notes.

Pair: Compare your notes. Make body language tips for the two situations. Give reasons.

Share: Read and compare your tips in class.

c) Watch the film again. What other dos and don'ts of body language can you notice? Make notes, then discuss.

3 YOUR TASK Who will get the job?

You're going to take part in an interview for a part-time job.

Step 1: Look at the advert

Think about these questions:

1 What skills are needed?
2 Why are you a good candidate?
3 Why do you want the job?
4 What questions can you ask?

More help p.127

Restaurant team member
in busy fast-food restaurant

Improve your service and teamwork skills in our restaurant. We're looking for very hard-working, enthusiastic individuals. Part-time or full-time work. Experience not necessary.

The ideal candidate has to:

- be able to work as part of a team
- speak clearly and listen carefully to guests and staff members
- have a professional, energetic and enthusiastic approach

If you like the sound of the job, please send your CV by email.

Step 2: Perform the interviews

Work in groups of at least three. Each member of the group will be interviewed for the job. The others will take turns to be the interviewer(s) or the assessor(s).

> Read the °instructions below together. Everybody must know what to do. Then perform and °assess the interviews.

The interviewers should talk like this:

Greet the candidate:	Hello, pleased to meet you. My name is ...
Ask at least three questions:	Can you describe yourself? What are your strengths and weaknesses? ...
You can also ask follow-up questions:	Can you give me an example? What exactly do you do?
At the end say:	Do you have any questions? Thank you for coming. We'll contact you soon.

The assessors need a copy of this form. They should make notes.

	very good	OK	needs work
1 How did the candidates present themselves? (e.g. handshake, body language, ...)			
2 How good / appropriate were their answers?			
3 Did they ask good questions?			

> Be as positive as you can when you're giving **feedback**.
> - First pick out one good thing in the performance – more if you can.
> - Then pick out one important thing that they could do better.

Step 3: Decide who should get the job

The assessors should use their notes to give feedback to the candidates. Decide in your groups who °performed best in the interview. Then tell the class who got the job and why. More help p.127 ▸ Wordbank 5, p. 139

Looking to the future

You'll find the new words from these pages listed on p. 232.

1 Going abroad

a) Three friends are having lunch together in the school canteen. Read and fill in the sentence parts with one or more words to complete their dialogue. There are different suitable answers.

Jessa: So, Lynn, what about the °overseas volunteer programme you applied for? ... (1) anything?

Lynn: Yes – didn't I tell you? They've chosen me! I just have to tell them if I ... (2).

Jessa: Wow, °congratulations! You ... (3), aren't you?

Lynn: Yes, I think so.

Clay: Do you really ... (4), Lynn? They might make you work in some horrible place somewhere. It could be really hard.

Lynn: They let me choose which project I wanted. So I ... (5) okay.

Jessa: You're planning to travel after your exams too, aren't you, Clay?

Clay: Yep. ... (6) Southern California for some fun in the sun. I ... (7) work and travel programme. I need an easy job that lets me surf and party a lot. It's just a shame that they make me pay for the flight.

Jessa: Oh, you poor thing. So, Lynn, what ... (8)?

Lynn: It's a project to °set up a youth club.

Clay: Working with wild, noisy kids? I ... (9) – not in a million years! While you're stressed, I'll be relaxing in Santa Monica.

Lynn: Actually, in the photos the kids ... (10). And they told me that people in the Philippines are ... (11).

Jessa: It's the tropical climate – it makes people slow down and relax.

Clay: The Philippines? Tropical?

Lynn: It's a lovely fishing village. °Palm trees, white °sandy beach. Look at these photos – the beach ... (12) except for a few surfers.

Clay: Let me see.

Jessa: Looks beautiful! You can ... (13) in your free time!

Clay: So, erm, what's this programme called again?

b) Compare your answers with a partner's. Together find other suitable answers.

2 WRITING Moving on

a) Pick one of the tasks below (A–D).

A
About me: Ten years from now

Look into the future and write about you and your life ten years from now. Start like this:

I'm a very different person now than when I was a teenager ten years ago. …

!
- You're writing about the future, but use the present tense – it's more exciting.
- Use your °imagination. Add interesting details about what you look like, your personality, your job, your family, your relationships, your feelings.

B
A story: The change

Continue this story:

When Andrew started his first job at the ice cream shop last Saturday, he had no idea that his life was going to change forever …

!
- Your story can be as long or as short as you like. But keep it simple.
- Write about only one setting.
- Use only one main character, but you can have °minor characters.
- Only one plot – one thing should happen.

C
A scene: The new °flatmate

Finish this scene:

Emma and Julia are in their first flat. They're very excited about it. But now they need a third person to share the flat, so they're °interviewing Justin.

Emma Hi Justin, I'm Emma.
Julia And I'm Julia.
Justin … Er … hi …
Emma And this is our flat …
Julia It's nice, isn't it?
Justin Yeah, but it looks very dark.
…

!
- Justin isn't very enthusiastic.
- But the girls really need a third flatmate, so make them sound really enthusiastic.
- You decide. Does Justin take the room?

D
A poem: You're nearly an adult

Read this poem from a parent to a teenager. Then write a response from a teenager to a parent.

You aren't a kid any more, are you?
You don't need your mummy, do you?
You can think for yourself, can't you?
You don't want my advice, do you?
You can stand on your own two feet,
can't you?
You're nearly an adult, aren't you?
But you still expect pocket money,
don't you?

!
- You don't have to take this poem seriously – your response can be funny.
- Think of the typical things a teenager says to parents.
- If you write a poem, it doesn't have to rhyme.

b) Swap your texts. Give each other feedback. Then read or perform some of your texts for the class.

MORE CHALLENGE

▸ *DFF 3.9*

3 LANGUAGE *let/make* + object + infinitive

a) Complete these sentences from the dialogue on p. 74.

1 They ... which project I wanted.
2 I need a job that ... a lot.
3 It's just a shame that they ... for the flight.
4 It's the tropical climate – it ... .

b) Complete the FOCUS box.

FOCUS

1 *let* + object + infinitive
In the sentence "They let me choose which project I wanted ...", Lynn was allowed to choose her project.
When *let* + object is followed by another verb, we use the infinitive without *to*.
Rephrase these sentences using *let*:
1 My parents don't mind if I watch TV on school nights. ➔ My parents ... TV on school nights.
2 His boss said he could start work later. ➔ His boss ...

2 *make* + object + infinitive
There are two possible meanings:
1. In the sentence "... they make me pay for the flight", Clay has to pay for the flight.
2. In the sentence "... it makes people slow down and relax", the hot climate leads people to slow down and relax.
When ***make* + object** is followed by another verb, we use the infinitive without *to*.
Rephrase these sentences using *make*:
1 Jon's parents told him to do his homework before going out. ➔ Jon's parents ...
2 The kids at the camp were fun and she laughed a lot. ➔ The kids ...

c) Here are more situations. Write the sentences with *let* or *make* + object + infinitive.

1 My dad said that I had to look for a summer job. *My dad ...*
2 At the camp you can take Saturdays off to go hiking. *The camp ...*
3 The restaurant owner gave us a choice of uniforms. *The restaurant owner ...*
4 The long hours were too much. I decided not to take the job. *The long hours ...*
5 Her boss says that she has to do a new training programme. ...
6 I can give you a few tips about writing CVs. ...

4 Summer camp

Marla and Andi both took summer jobs as camp counsellors. Now they're comparing their experiences. Marla liked her job, but Andi wasn't very happy with his. Write their dialogue. Write sentences with *let* and *make*. You can use the phrases in the box or make up your own.
Start like this:

Andi So, Marla, how was it at your camp?
Marla It was great. They let us ...

let
eat all we wanted • surf online in our free time • borrow the camp car • have a day off every week • ...

make
°work really long hours • write reports each week • get up early on Sundays • clean the buildings • ...

1 LANGUAGE Driving in Ireland p. 128

Michael (17), a German student in Dublin, is asking his friend Dylan about how to get a °learner licence. Pick the correct *question tags*.

are they • can't I • do I • haven't you • will I • won't they

1 I don't have to take a driving test, ...?
– No, but you have to take a °theory test.
2 OK. But then they'll give me a learner licence, ...?
– Well, no. You need to take an °eyesight test too.
3 Oh, right. And then I can practise driving on the °motorway, ...?
– No, I'm afraid not. Learner drivers aren't allowed on the motorway.
4 Hm. Learner drivers aren't allowed to drive fast either, ...?
– That's right. They can only go 72 kph.
5 But I won't have to have somebody in the car with me, ...?
– Actually, you will – somebody with a full driving licence.
6 Well, what about you? You've already got your full licence, ...?
– No, I haven't yet. I'm still a learner driver.

2 LISTENING Phoning about a job

River Tours, a river cruise company, needs someone to help international customers on their boats. Sarah Richter, a sixteen-year-old German teenager, is phoning about the job.

2.14 **a)** Listen to the dialogue and complete these phrases.

1 Can I ... a message? **2** I saw a ... on the internet. **3** I'll phone ... at 1:30. **4** ... welcome.

2.15 **b)** **Partner B:** Go to page 105.
Partner A: Listen to the dialogue between Sarah and Mr Thomson. Complete it. Talk to B to find out if your answers are correct.

S I'm very interested in the part-time job as a cruise assistant.
T Do you have any ... (1) experience?
S I've done two °work placements so far.
T That sounds ... (2). We need somebody to work at the weekends from ... (3) or from 4 pm to 10 pm.
S Working at the weekends is perfect for me.
T We can talk about more details in an interview. Can you come on ... (4)?
S Yes, that's fine. What do I need to bring?
T Can you bring ... (5), please?
S I'm looking forward to meeting you on Saturday.

c) Read your role card and °act out a dialogue with your partner.

Role card

Partner A
You're the manager of a coffee shop in an international holiday park. You need some °motivated part-time workers for your young team. Your mobile is ringing ...

1 Melde dich höflich. Frage den Anrufer, was du für ihn tun kannst.
3 Drücke Freude über sein Interesse aus. Frage, ob Arbeitserfahrung vorhanden ist.
5 Zeige dich erfreut. Deine Firma braucht jemanden, der freitagabends und samstags arbeiten kann.
7 Schlage ein Vorstellungsgespräch für nächsten Freitag, 16 Uhr vor.
9 Es soll ein Lebenslauf mitgebracht werden.
11 Verabschiede dich höflich.

Unit 4 Generation *like*

▸ KV 25 ▸ DFF 4.1 ▸ INKL pp. 62–63

A

B

C

D

E

H

F

G

1 What's cool and what's not?

a) **Think:** Pick three images that you like and three images that you dislike.

b) **Pair:** Explain your reactions.

c) **Share:** Which images got the most *likes* and the most *dislikes* in the class?

2 LISTENING Teens react

3.01

a) Copy this table. Listen to four teens talking and note down which five images (A–R) the teens are talking about.

b) Listen again. Note down if the teens think the things are cool (✓) or not (✗).

c) Compare their reactions with the reactions in class.

	1	2	3	4	5
Which picture?	B				
Amelia	✗				
Scarlett	✓				
Mohammed					
Thomas					

▸ KV 24 ▸ DFF 3.6 ▸ DFF 3.7 ▸ DFF 3.8 ▸ INKL pp. 58–61

1 LANGUAGE Driving in Ireland

// p. 128

Michael (17), a German student in Dublin, is asking his friend Dylan about how to get a °learner licence. Pick the correct *question tags*.

are they • can't I • do I • haven't you • will I • won't they

1 I don't have to take a driving test, ...?
– No, but you have to take a °theory test.
2 OK. But then they'll give me a learner licence, ...?
– Well, no. You need to take an °eyesight test too.
3 Oh, right. And then I can practise driving on the °motorway, ...?
– No, I'm afraid not. Learner drivers aren't allowed on the motorway.
4 Hm. Learner drivers aren't allowed to drive fast either, ...?
– That's right. They can only go 72 kph.
5 But I won't have to have somebody in the car with me, ...?
– Actually, you will – somebody with a full driving licence.
6 Well, what about you? You've already got your full licence, ...?
– No, I haven't yet. I'm still a learner driver.

2 LISTENING Phoning about a job

River Tours, a river cruise company, needs someone to help international customers on their boats. Sarah Richter, a sixteen-year-old German teenager, is phoning about the job.

2.14 **a)** Listen to the dialogue and complete these phrases.
1 Can I ... a message? 2 I saw a ... on the internet. 3 I'll phone ... at 1:30. 4 ... welcome.

2.15 **b)** **Partner B:** Go to page 105.
Partner A: Listen to the dialogue between Sarah and Mr Thomson. Complete it. Talk to B to find out if your answers are correct.

S I'm very interested in the part-time job as a cruise assistant.
T Do you have any ... (1) experience?
S I've done two °work placements so far.
T That sounds ... (2). We need somebody to work at the weekends from ... (3) or from 4 pm to 10 pm.
S Working at the weekends is perfect for me.
T We can talk about more details in an interview. Can you come on ... (4)?
S Yes, that's fine. What do I need to bring?
T Can you bring ... (5), please?
S I'm looking forward to meeting you on Saturday.

c) Read your role card and °act out a dialogue with your partner.

Role card

Partner A
You're the manager of a coffee shop in an international holiday park. You need some °motivated part-time workers for your young team. Your mobile is ringing ...
1 Melde dich höflich. Frage den Anrufer, was du für ihn tun kannst.
3 Drücke Freude über sein Interesse aus. Frage, ob Arbeitserfahrung vorhanden ist.
5 Zeige dich erfreut. Deine Firma braucht jemanden, der freitagabends und samstags arbeiten kann.
7 Schlage ein Vorstellungsgespräch für nächsten Freitag, 16 Uhr vor.
9 Es soll ein Lebenslauf mitgebracht werden.
11 Verabschiede dich höflich.

STOP! CHECK! GO!

► KV 24 ► DFF 3.4 ► INKL pp. 58–61

3 Writing a CV

Nele wants to do three weeks' work experience with a °travel agency where she can use her English. Read the advert and Nele's °biography and then write Nele's CV in English.

Work experience

At F&S TRAVEL we offer students work experience in our travel agency.

- You must be friendly and reliable and enjoy working in a team.
- You should be interested in travelling and should speak English well because we have a lot of international customers.
- Our opening hours are: Mon – Sat, 8 am – 9 pm

To apply, please send us your CV and cover letter in English.

Biography:

Nele was born in Stade on 12 Dec 2002.
She went to Grundschule Eickum (2008 – 2012). When her family moved to Hamburg she went to Otto-Hahn-Gesamtschule there. Now she is in year ten.
At school she likes languages best. She is also very good at geography, °politics and computer science and she likes learning new things.
Nele thinks she is a reliable and well-organized person. She likes talking to people, doing group work and has lots of friends. In her free-time Nele plays volleyball and likes reading. She is very interested in other countries. Nele often skypes with her English friends.
Last year she did three weeks' work experience in a hotel. For references please contact Nele's class teacher, Mrs Kurz, or the manager of Hotel Nordsee, Mr Rüttgers.

4 Completing a cover letter

a) Complete and *improve* Nele's cover letter using words and phrases from the box.

Stankeweg 3
22457 Hamburg

The Manager
F&S TRAVEL
Tomeustraße 54
22438 Hamburg

... (1)

Dear ... (2)
I would like to ... (3) for work experience with your company. I am in my last ... (4) at Otto-Hahn-Gesamtschule and I will leave school with Fachhochschulreife in June. My favourite ... (5) are English, German and French and I am also ... (6) in geography and computer science. I speak good English. *I'm* (7) a friendly, hard-working and reliable person and I like working with other people. I *don't* (8) mind working *Sats* (9) and in the evenings. Last year I did work experience at a hotel for *3* (10) weeks, where I welcomed people from all over the world. I really enjoyed helping and °advising people. *Here's* (11) my CV. *Write back soon* (12).

Yours *sincerely* (13)

Sir / Madam • interested • year • enthusiastic • apply • 20th March 20… • subjects • *faithfully* • *I am* • *on Saturdays* • *four* • *I am looking forward to hearing from you* • *I enclose* • *three* • *do not*

b) Write your own CV and cover letter to F&S TRAVEL.

► *Skills files 9.5–6, pp. 175–176*

▸ DFF 3.1 ▸ DFF 3.2 ▸ INKL pp. 58–61

5 READING Catherine Cook: A teenage °millionaire

It started when Catherine Cook, 15, and her brother David, 16, wanted to make more friends at their new high school in Skillman, New Jersey. They were looking at the school yearbook and complaining about the choice of photos. "David said 'What if we could choose our own photo?' and I said 'What if you could connect with other people online?' Then it just went from there," says Catherine. A business idea was born.

She turned to her older brother Geoff, who had already started two successful online businesses. He quickly °got involved in the project by helping to pay for the °start-up. In a short time they °launched MyYearbook, a social °networking website where friends can sign virtual yearbooks, swap photos, share information and play games. It's made for young people who go to the same school, or live in the same area, or are a similar age. After a few weeks MyYearbook had about 400 users. That number grew in only six years to 25 million users across the USA. The next step was to "°go global". Because yearbooks don't mean much outside the US, MyYearbook became MeetMe. Now the business is growing internationally.

A big part of Catherine's success has been the way her parents brought her up. They always wanted her to do things herself and to find her own way. And there was Geoff, who is 11 years older than Catherine. "I'd always looked up to my brother Geoff," she says. "I thought if he started a company, I could too." Geoff was more than an °investor. He gave Catherine advice and helped her with his experience. Catherine's own advice for anyone who wants to start something new: "Use all the °resources that are available to you. Never be scared of asking for advice. It's important to look for answers, but if you can't find them yourself, ask a friend for help."

a) Complete the sentences. Use four to six words.

1 Catherine and her brother David got interested in yearbooks because they ...
2 She and David went to ...
3 They noticed that their school yearbook ...

b) Are these statements true, false or not in the text?

1 The website can help people to meet people and make new friends.
2 Catherine and David's older brother Geoff went to the same school.
3 Geoff supported the project with money.
4 It took them many years to be successful.

c) How has Geoff been a good example to Catherine? Name two ways.

d) Complete each sentence with a phrase from the text (no more than seven words).

1 In Catherine's opinion you shouldn't be afraid of ...
2 Catherine says that if you can't find a solution, you should ...

6 SPEAKING Who has been important to you?

Say who has been an important influence on you in your life and explain why. More help p. 128

▸ Workbook My learner log, p. 45 and Revision, p. 40, p. 46

Unit 4

Generation *like*

▸ KV 25 ▸ DFF 4.1 ▸ INKL pp. 62–63

A

B

C

D

E

F

G

H

1 What's cool and what's not?

a) Think: Pick three images that you like and three images that you dislike.

b) Pair: Explain your reactions.

c) Share: Which images got the most *likes* and the most *dislikes* in the class?

2 LISTENING Teens react

3.01

a) Copy this table. Listen to four teens talking and note down which five images (A–R) the teens are talking about.

b) Listen again. Note down if the teens think the things are cool (✓) or not (✗).

c) Compare their reactions with the reactions in class.

	1	2	3	4	5
Which picture?	B				
Amelia	✗				
Scarlett	✓				
Mohammed					
Thomas					

▸ *INKL pp. 62–63*

I

J

K

L

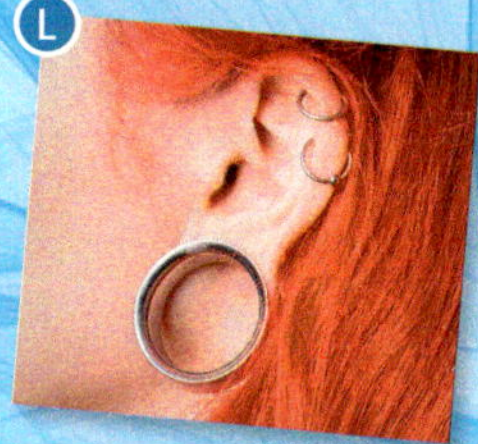

M

N

O

P

Q

R

3 YOUR TASK **Cool talk**

Step 1: Find a picture of something or someone that you both think is cool.

Step 2: Together prepare a three-minute talk about your picture.
- Say what the picture shows, and when and why you think the thing or person was popular.
- Say why you like the thing or person.
- Think of a reason why somebody might not think the thing or person is cool. Give your argument(s) against this opinion. Box: Voc., p. 223

Step 3: Do a quick survey in class with a show of hands: Who likes this thing or person? Who doesn't like it/him/her? Whose opinion was changed by your talk?

▸ *Workbook 1, p. 47*

▸ KV 26 ▸ INKL pp. 64–65

Screenagers

1 Before you read

What do you think a screenager is? Discuss this question and make notes. Then read the text and find out if you were right.

Being a screenager

Today's teenagers were born into the digital world, a world where screens are everywhere – TV screens, smartphone screens, tablet screens, laptop screens ... The average American teen spends 8.5 hours per day in front of a screen! In Britain it's a little less, about 7 hours per day. These screenagers don't look at only one screen – they usually multitask. They video-chat on their smartphone, play a game on their tablet and watch a programme on TV, all at the same time.

Not every teen is like this of course, and many have hobbies and interests away from their screens. But digital technology is part of every teen's world and the attraction of TV, video games and social media is strong. Most teens feel the pressure to do as their friends do. About 60% of teenagers today watch at least 20 hours of TV per week. About 94% of teenagers have social media accounts. So what are the pros and cons of being a screenager?

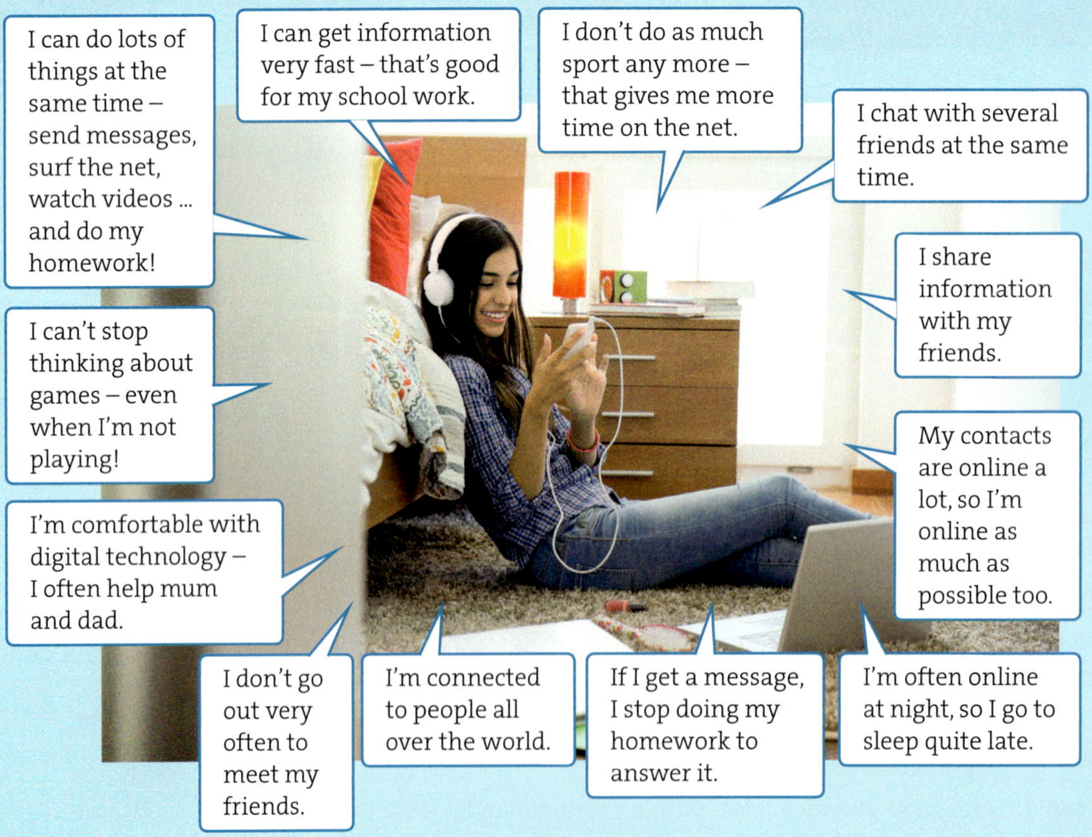

▸ KV 26 ▸ KV 27 ▸ DFF 4.2 ▸ INKL pp. 64–65

2 READING Working with the text

a) Copy this table and take notes from the text on p. 82.

pros of being a screenager	*cons of being a screenager*
– do lots of things at the same time	*– don't sleep enough*
– ...	*– ...*

b) Think of more pros and cons of your own and add them to your table.

c) Are you a screenager? Why (not)?

d) What do you think about the digital world of teenagers today? Write a comment.

3 LISTENING Digital habits

3.02

a) Some students are talking about digital habits. First read the tasks. Then listen and complete these sentences:

1 Kumar can't focus on his school work because ...
2 Oscar would like to ...
3 Devon isn't allowed to use her phone ...
4 Devon's mother complains that Devon ...
5 Mr Davis says that kids need to ...

b) Now read these questions. Then listen again and answer them.

1 Why does Kumar say that he's a drifter?
2 How does Oscar describe himself?
3 Why is Devon a 'social butterfly'?
4 What does Devon's mother miss?
5 What does Mr Davis say that most young people use computers for?

c) What are your digital habits? What does your digital day look like? Talk to a partner.

More challenge 1 p. 129

4 SPEAKING Role-play

Parents and teenagers often have different °viewpoints on the question of digital habits. **Partner A** takes the role of a parent. **Partner B** is a screenager. Go to p. 106.

a) **Partner A:** Prepare your role.

b) Act out your role-play with your partner. You begin.

c) Get feedback from the class. What was good / convincing / realistic? What could have been better?

More practice 1 p. 130 More challenge 2 p. 130

Partner A
- Your daughter or son spends over six hours per day in front of screens. You want to know why.
- You're not happy with the situation and you explain why. Think of at least two reasons.
- You want to discuss how your child could change her or his habits. Think of at least three suggestions.
- You try to convince her or him to agree with at least one of your suggestions.

▸ Text file 4, pp. 150–151 ▸ Workbook 2–4, p. 48

Perfect profiles

1 Profile pictures

a) Look at the article below. Which kind of profile picture do you like best? Why? What other kinds of profile pictures do you know? Compare ideas with a partner. More practice 2 p. 130

Your kind of profile picture?

If you use social media, then you probably have a profile picture. So which kind of picture do you prefer?

1 The standard profile picture
Many people just use a basic profile photo. But you could be more imaginative.

2 The group picture
Usually a group photo is taken somewhere cool and everyone in the photo looks extremely happy.

3 The action picture
Some people spend hours trying to take the perfect action photo.

4 The avatar profile picture
If you don't want to show your real face on your page, then this is perfect.

5 The arty picture
Some people love to be creative and do something different.

6 The 'here's some stuff that I like' picture
This could be anything at all: a place, your pet, your favourite food, a pair of shoes ...

b) Find a profile picture that you like, e.g. of a celebrity. Prepare a talk about it (1–2 mins.). First describe the picture. Then say why you like it and what it tells you about that person.

2 Putting yourself out there

When you put up information and photos on social media, the whole world can see them.

a) What kinds of profile pictures of yourself would you °happily put online? What kinds of pictures would make you feel uncomfortable? Explain why.

b) Make a list of dos and don'ts for putting up photos of yourself on social media.
Share your ideas in class and agree on the three most important dos and don'ts.

► KV 28 ► KV 29 ► KV 30 ► DFF 4.4 ► INKL pp. 66–67

3 Selfies: A written discussion

a) Which of these pictures would you call a selfie? Explain.

A

B

C

b) Put the paragraphs (A–D) into a °logical order. What words or phrases helped you decide?

A Why do some people hate selfies? Firstly, they say that the people who take them are vain. For example, people often use special apps to improve their photos and make themselves look good. Secondly, critics say that selfies can actually make you feel bad. For example, if you post your selfie on social media and nobody likes it, it can be depressing.

B Selfies are the photos that people take of themselves with their phones or tablets. Today everybody takes selfies – teenagers, adults, celebrities, presidents and astronauts. We post them on social media to show other people what we are like and what we're doing.

C To sum up, I think it's normal to take selfies. I definitely don't hate them. Like lots of famous people, I take them because they're fun!

D On the other hand, maybe the critics are too negative about selfies. Lots of artists have painted self-portraits over the years. They usually wanted to look good, and they definitely wanted people to look at their picture. In other words, selfies are modern-day self-portraits.

c) You could add these sentences to the text. Where do they °fit best? Compare.

So they feel that selfies are a bad idea.

Although the word selfie is new, self-portraits aren't.

Why should I? They make people smile.

They started around 2002 with the first camera phones.

More practice 3 p. 131

4 WRITING For and against tattoos

a) Collect ideas for a written discussion on this topic: "Tattoos – are they a good idea or not?" Make a plan, then write your text.

More help p. 131

b) Reading circle: Put your texts on the wall. Read other people's texts. Write positive comments on the texts you like best. Read out the most popular texts.

! A typical **written discussion** looks like this:

Paragraph **1**	introduction – describe the general topic
Paragraph **2**	arguments for (or against)
Paragraph **3**	arguments against (or for)
Paragraph **4**	conclusion – give your personal opinion

► Skills file 9.7, p. 177

► Workbook 5–7, p. 49

▸ INKL pp. 68–69

Targeting teens

1 SPEAKING You and ads

a) Talk about these questions.

- Where do you see ads?
- How many ads do you think you see in one day?
- What kind of ads get your attention? Why?

b) Scan the article and find out what coolhunters and teen vloggers do. Compare your answers.

Box: Voc., p. 225

Are you ad-savvy?

A **Do you know** why ads target teens? Firstly there are lots of teens, about 33 million in the USA. Teens have money. Teens want to be cool. Teens want to fit in. A teen can see up to 3000 ads in one day – on billboards, in shop windows, on buses and trains, on TV and in magazines, and of course on the internet. Ads that target teens are different to ads that target adults. For teens, you'll see ads for video games, clothes, fast food, music – all the things that are important to teens.

B **Do you know** that one in three teens who drink alcohol are influenced by ads? And most of the fast food ads target young people. So if we understand how ads work, we can reduce the dangers for teens.

C **Do you know** that advertisers understand that teens like to be cool? But what is cool? This changes all the time. So to find out what cool means, advertisers use '°coolhunters'. These are people who go out and meet teens. They look for new trends, different and interesting styles. Then the companies use this information to design the next products and make the next ads.

D **Do you know** that there are lots of tricks in ads? Here are some examples:

› Products often look amazing in ads, but not so good in real life.
› Models often have unnaturally perfect skin and teeth in ads.
› Ads repeat a product name many times, so that you remember it.
› They show beautiful people who are happy. And you want to be happy too.
› Ads use stars from films, music and sport. If they like the product, it must be good!
› They suggest that if you use the product you are 'cool'.
› They often use music – a jingle. When you hear the jingle again you think of the product.
› They hide the truth. For example, they don't tell you that there's lots of sugar in orange juice.

E **Do you know** that teen vloggers do advertising too? They tell the world what they like on the internet. The big ad companies watch this and if a vlogger has lots of followers, the ad companies get interested. They send free samples to the vlogger – things like shoes, clothes, make-up, etc. Then the vloggers talk about these products in their vlogs – that's advertising. So let's get ad-savvy!

Box: Voc., p. 225

▸ DFF 4.5 ▸ INKL pp. 68–69

2 READING The main point

a) Think: Find out the main point of each paragraph (A–E). Make notes.

▸ Skills file 7.3, p. 166

b) Pair: Compare your answers. Agree on one answer for each paragraph.

c) Share: Discuss your answers in class.

3 WORDS

Find words and phrases that mean:

1 be like other people (paragraph A)
2 big ads that you see in the street (A)
3 make less or smaller (B)
4 fashion (two possible answers) (C)
5 things that you buy (D)
6 say something again (D)
7 advertising music (D)
8 someone who does a video blog (E)
9 understand how ads work (E)

4 MEDIATION The ad industry

Jemand interessiert sich für den Artikel auf Seite 86. Erzähle – auf Deutsch:

1 ... warum Jugendliche besser über Werbung Bescheid wissen sollten.
2 ... warum viel Werbung auf Jugendliche abzielt.
3 ... welche Strategien in der Werbung verwendet werden (mindestens drei).
4 ... wie die Werbeindustrie herausfindet, was Jugendliche mögen.
5 ... welche Jugendlichen besonders interessant für die Werbeindustrie sind und warum.

▸ Skills file 12, p. 181 More practice 4 p. 132

5 ACTIVITY Get ad-savvy!

Pick one of these activities.

Your ad diary

a) Keep an ad diary for a day. Note down:
- How many ads do you see?
- Where do you see them?
- How do they target teens?
- Which ads do you find interesting?
- Do any ads make you want to buy something?
- Do any ads irritate you? Why?

b) Report about your ad diary to the class.

Ad report

a) First, collect ads. Cut them out of newspapers and magazines. You can take photos of billboards and posters. And you can take screenshots of internet ads too.

b) Next, find examples of the tricks in paragraph D on p 86.

c) Do a poster presentation for the class. Talk about the tricks you've found.

More practice 5 p. 132 More challenge 3 p. 132

▸ INKL p. 73

1 Social media: what can go wrong

a) Somebody wants to have a party and puts up an invitation on social media. What could go wrong? Talk with a partner. Then read the article.

Hundreds of teenagers gatecrash party

On Friday evening police were called to an address in north London. When they arrived, they found over 200 young people at the house. The owner of the house, Don Smith, wasn't there, and his 15-year-old daughter, Leah, couldn't control the situation.

Leah's father knew about the party. He had agreed that she could have a party for her 16th birthday with about 30 guests. Leah sent out an invitation on social media. That was the first mistake. She found out later that lots of people saw the invitation and decided to join the fun and gatecrash the party.

Then came the second mistake. Because everything seemed calm, Leah's father decided to go out for a while. After he left, the gatecrashers started to arrive, and Leah wasn't able to reach him on his phone. He had left it at home – another mistake. Leah said, "It was very scary. I didn't know the people. I didn't want them to come in, but they just pushed the door and walked in."

There was no damage in the house, but the party-goers left a lot of rubbish, and a few things were stolen, including Don Smith's smartphone. The next day Don and Leah had to do a big clean-up. Mr Smith wasn't cross with his daughter. "Poor Leah, it wasn't her fault. I should have stayed at home. But we've all learned a lesson about using social media. You have to be careful. We were lucky. If the neighbours hadn't phoned the police, things would have been different," he said.

b) Read the text and find the answers to these questions:

1 What was the problem at the party?
2 How had Leah invited her friends?
3 What were Mr Smith's two mistakes?
4 How did Leah's father react towards her?

c) Leah made several mistakes. What would you have done?

I would have ...
I wouldn't have ...

used social media / asked my dad to take his phone / let my dad leave / ...

d) If you had been Leah's dad, what would you have done?

I would have ...
I wouldn't have ...

helped Leah organise the party / left Leah alone in the house / ...

More practice 6 p. 132

2 *If I had …* (conditional sentences type 3)

Look at what Leah says. Then answer the questions in the FOCUS box.

After the party

If I had been more careful, everything would have been OK.

FOCUS

1 First think about the meaning of what Leah says: Was she careful? Was everything OK?

2 What verb form goes with 'If' here?

3 The other verb form has three parts. What are they?
? + ? + ***past participle***

► *Language file 24, p. 197*

3 Oh dear, what a shame!

a) Complete the sentences with the correct form of the verb in °brackets. p. 133

1 I was in trouble because I was late. If I … (send) mum a text message to let her know, she wouldn't have been cross.

2 My test results weren't great. If I had worked harder, I … (get) better marks.

3 I couldn't do my homework because I forgot my book. If I … (remember) my book, I would have done my homework.

4 I didn't tell my friend that I was going out. If I had known that she wanted to come, I … (phone) her.

5 I don't have enough money for a phone. If I … (work) in the holidays, I would have earned some.

b) Say how these situations could have been avoided.

1 I surfed the net last night until very late. I was tired at school this morning.
If I hadn't …

2 My sister put up a crazy photo of herself online. Her boss saw the photo and she lost her job.

3 Mel and Sue messaged so much that they didn't finish their homework on time.

4 Josh played video games before school. He forgot about the time and missed the bus.

More practice 7 p. 133

4 Poor me!

What is the person thinking? Use conditional 3.

1 If I … got up late, I wouldn't have missed …

2 If I … caught …, I … taken my bike.

3 If the car driver … suddenly opened the door, …

4 If I … crashed, …

5 … if I hadn't hurt myself.

6 …

1 Before you read

a) Discuss these questions:

1 Do you play computer games? If so, what kind of games?
2 What risks, if any, do you think there are with computer games?
3 What do you think the story below is about? Look at the pictures, headings and slogans.

b) Now read the text.

3.03

Gamer (adapted from the novel by Chris Bradford)

Part 1 Bread

I can't stop watching the fighters – Thunderbolt, the kickboxer and Destroy, the heavyweight boxer. Thunderbolt has just kicked Destroy in the teeth. Destroy puts his head down like a bull and runs at Thunderbolt. His huge fist catches Thunderbolt on the side of his face. Thunderbolt's whole body flies high into the air, then lands heavily in the centre of the arena. People shout and cheer. The game is over for Thunderbolt.

Then a big red and black logo comes onto the 3D screen: ***VK***.
A deep voice says,
"Virtual Kombat, so real that it hurts."
After that an ad comes on for *Synapse Drinks* – the company that sponsors Virtual Kombat. I try not to look. Adverts just make me want what I can't have.

Now the fight is over, the street kids turn away. They disappear into the lanes with the other rubbish that fills this city. Unwanted. Ignored. Forgotten. I'm one of them. I lost my parents to the killer virus of 2030. It killed millions.

The strange thing was that kids didn't get the virus. The doctors said that the kids might be spreading it. Some parents even dumped their own kids on the streets. Now there are thousands of us.

The whole world went crazy. Then the army took over with tough new laws. After that, people stopped going outside. The adults were still scared they might catch something. Most people escaped into life on the net. That's when ***VK*** first started:

"Virtual Kombat – the most realistic fighting game ever!"

That's what the ads say. Virtual Kombat is *the* number 1 game show in the world. Everyone watches or plays it. Huge street screens are everywhere in the city. On the screen in front of me there's a huge 3D picture of a *Zing* energy bar. I turn away – it's torture. Then I hear the ***VK*** jingle. The ad break is over and the ***VK*** logo returns. We see the highlights of today's fights and they show every horrible detail.

"Virtual Kombat. So real that it hurts!"

The only thing that hurts me at the moment is my stomach. I haven't eaten in days. VK helps me to forget that I'm hungry. When the show is on, you don't think about it so much. But when

▸ INKL pp. 70–72

it's over, the empty feeling in my stomach comes again.

I go up a narrow backstreet. There are big bins here, behind the restaurants where the rich and powerful people eat. They still go out – to the huge shopping malls in their big cars. If I'm lucky, I might find some food in the bins. Then I hear a voice. "Give it to me!"

In the shadows further up the lane I see two lads standing over a little girl and boy. The girl shakes her blond head and hugs a brown paper bag. The taller lad hits her hard in the face and pulls the bag from her. The girl doesn't cry. Street kids are tough.

"Leave my sis alone," shouts the boy as he steps between them. "Give that back. It's ours!"

"Finders keepers, losers weepers," the other lad says. He's short, with dark red hair. He pushes the boy to the ground and laughs as the kid hits his head on the pavement.

"You won't believe this, Juice," says the taller lad. "They have bread!"

Part 2 Street fighter

"Give me a bite, Stick," Juice says.

"No way." Stick holds the bag away.

"Ah, come on," Juice says. "The others won't know if a bit's gone."

While they're arguing, I creep up behind and grab the bread.

"Oi," Stick shouts, as he turns around. "That's ours!" he says.

"Finders keepers, losers weepers," I say. I'm not afraid. You can't be afraid in this city. Stick and Juice are just bullies who pick on smaller kids. So I'm not scared of them. But I'm taking a risk. It's still two against one.

"This was never yours," I say. "Now °zap off."

Juice looks worried and backs away. But Stick takes something long from his belt. He swings it wildly at my head. I drop the bread and jump forward to stop his attack. I catch his arm and force him to drop his weapon. Juice jumps on me from behind, but I hit him in the stomach and throw him over my shoulder onto the ground.

Stick pulls Juice to his feet. "Wait till Shark hears about this," Stick says. "He'll get you!"

I say nothing as they walk away. But inside I'm shouting at myself, "IDIOT!"

Shark is not someone you want to face. Not even for a bag of bread. He's bad news. But how could I know that his guys would be in this area?

As I pick up the bag from the ground, I feel weaker from the fight. I need food. The little boy and girl look cold and hungry. The slow rain never stops in this city. They hold each other close and stare at me. It's clear they're twins – blond hair, blue eyes. And they have a look of fear and sadness that breaks my heart.

"What are your names?" I ask.

"Mine's Tommy. My sis is Tammy," the boy says.

As hungry as I am, I give the little girl the bag of bread. "Well, this is yours, Tammy."

She says nothing, but she takes the bag and holds it close to her.

"Who are you?" whispers Tommy, his eyes wide with shock.

"Scott," I say.

"Where did you learn to fight like that?" Tommy asks.

"*Street fighter 7*."

I smile and think back to before the virus. I lived with my parents in a nice house on the south side of the city. I had some great video games and my dad and I were addicted to *Street fighter*. I used to try some of the fighting moves with him, but I never won. He was a very good fighter. We trained together every day. That training is one of the reasons I'm still here, when so many others aren't.

I focus again on here and now. Tammy opens the bag. Then she looks around the lane like a frightened mouse. Box: Voc., p. 228

"She doesn't say much, your sis," I say to Tommy. Tommy shakes his head. Tammy takes out a large piece of bread, gives half of it to Tommy and passes the bag to me. I look in the bag. She has left me more than half. I'm too hungry to even thank her. I eat it hungrily.

"This bread is fresh," I say with my mouth full.

"The cook always makes a little extra for us. It has extra vitamins in it," Tommy says.

I eat the bread quickly and I already begin to feel stronger. "That was great."

Tammy smiles for the first time. But suddenly her smile is gone.

"THERE HE IS!"

I turn around. Stick and Juice are standing at the end of the lane. They're pointing at me. This time they have the whole Shark gang with them. Shark himself is in front. He's wearing a black leather jacket. He grins at me and I see his broken teeth. No need to guess how he got his name. Shark takes out a knife. It's time to fight or run. I run.

Part 3 Roof escape

They run after me as I run down a narrow side street. I know this area of the city like the back of my hand and I take a short cut onto Main Street. I run between the cars, across the road and into a lane on the other side. But I can't get rid of Shark's gang.

They're closing on me fast. I can hear Shark's voice. I have to escape over the roofs. As I run around a corner, I see what I need. I jump onto a big bin and then with another jump my hands catch the bottom of a fire escape ladder and I pull myself up. I climb and climb until I get to the roof – 12 floors up. Far below me I see the city, the lights, the big screens, …

And I see Shark and the gang – they're still following me.

I run and jump to the roof of the next building. Without stopping, I run across to the next building. This time the jump is much bigger, but I do it anyway. Fear and the vitamins from the bread help me. I hit the roof hard and roll.

I sit up and see Shark. He's running towards me. I jump down to a lower roof.

▸ INKL pp. 70–72

Shark stays on the higher roof and we race side by side on different buildings. He's fast and I have to use all my skill to stay in front of him. Far below in the lanes I see his gang. They're watching me, hoping that I'll fall. Then I can't see Shark any more, and I think he's fallen. But then I see his leather jacket appear in front of me. I can't go forward, and Stick is behind me. My only escape now is the building to the right, but the roof is a long way down. Shark grins from ear to ear as he takes out his knife. I have no choice, I have to jump.
I run to the edge of the roof and throw myself through the air. For a few seconds the air seems to carry me as I fall. Then I crash onto the roof of the other building. I hurt my leg. In the next moment a shadow flies through the air and Shark lands next to me. He crashes into a TV dish. He's crazier than I am.
Pain shoots up my leg as I try to get away. I look around and Shark is back on his feet. He moves towards me. I'm hurt – and I have no way to escape. I see the flash of Shark's knife. "No hope for you now, pretty boy," he says, and points the knife at my face.

At that moment we hear the VK jingle. We both freeze. We know what that means. "I'll get you later," Shark says and he disappears.

Part 4 The *VK* truck

As I get to the square, I see I'm too late. Lots of street kids are standing around a big white truck with the VK logo on its side. The jingle stops. All the food has been given out and all the seats are full.
The VK truck is the only way to get off these streets. It's a mobile VK game station. If you're good enough, you can become a VK games tester. That means food every day, a bed, school – a chance of a normal life.
Even if they don't pick you, you still get free food. That makes a big difference on the streets. But I've missed my chance.
Shark hasn't. He has a seat and his gang are standing around him. As I move away, I hear my name.
I see Tommy. He has a seat. He waves at me to come over.
"Take my place," he says.
"What?" I say. "Are you crazy? Chances like this don't come every day."
Tommy looks at his sister, who is standing quietly beside me.
"I can't leave my sis, can I?" he says.
He gets off his seat.
"I was holding it for you, anyway," he says.
"Everybody ready to play?" a loud voice says.
There's no time to argue. I climb in as fast as I can. Just when I put on the headset, the game begins.

▸ KV 32 ▸ INKL pp. 70–72

! The following tasks are on three different levels. Pick and complete one task for each level.

2 Which part ...

- shows us what kind of person Scott is?
- gives information about street kids?
- gives some hope for Scott's future?
- describes an exciting race through the city?

3 True or false? Correct the false sentences.

1 A virus killed Scott's parents. (part 1)
2 Scott looks for food in shopping malls. (1)
3 Scott gets scared when Stick attacks him. (2)
4 Tammy gives Scott some bread. (2)
5 Scott hurts his leg on a fire escape. (3)
6 Tommy lets Scott take his seat. (4)

4 Information in the text

Complete the following sentences with information from the text.

1 In this story there are lots of street kids because ... (part 1, lines 22–29)
2 Not everybody is poor and hungry, for example ... (part 1, lines 54–57)
3 Scott can fight well because ... (part 2, lines 123–132)
4 Tammy and Tommy know that Scott is hungry, so ... (part 2, lines 137–141)
5 Scott is happy when he sees a fire escape ladder, because ... (part 3, lines 166–171)
6 If Scott becomes a games tester, he ... (part 4, lines 220–221)

5 Characters in the story

a) Make notes about two or more characters in the story under these headings:
name, age, personality, appearance, what you think of him/her

b) **Walk around:** Compare your notes with other students.

More practice 8 p. 133

6 WRITING An email to the author

Write an email (about 120 words) to the author of *Gamer*, Chris Bradford. Say what you think of ...

- the story and why you think that
- the main characters and why
- the setting and why
- the mood of the story and how it makes you feel
- gaming and why it can be bad and good

7 WRITING A story blurb

Write a blurb for this story. Include information about:

- the author
- the setting and time of the story
- the main characters
- what happens
- why it's a good story

More challenge 4 p. 134

! Look at the blurb in task 1 on page 68 in Unit 3.

▸ Workbook 15–18, p. 55

Gamer – a book review

1 Before reading

Think about what happens to Scott after part 4. Share and compare your ideas with another pair.

2 While reading

Read this online book review about *Gamer*. What does it tell you about the story that you didn't know before?

Gamer by Chris Bradford – *A review*

Box: Voc., p. 228

Gamer is an exciting novel that takes young readers into a dark fictional future world. The year is around 2030 and a terrible virus has killed millions of adults. But for some reason young people don't catch the virus. Many kids have lost their parents and are now living on the streets. The main character, Scott, is one of these kids. He searches hungrily for food in restaurant rubbish bins or, when there's no other way, he steals it. Scott is tough, but unlike many street kids he is still kind, and he helps others who can't protect themselves.

Virtual Kombat (VK) is a popular online game that is advertised everywhere on large video screens. For many kids it's their only chance of escaping life on the streets. Those who are chosen to be gamers get three meals a day and a bed to sleep in. When Scott is chosen it's a dream come true for him. He lives in an orphan home and all he has to do is play video games. He is introduced to other fighters that he will battle against in VK, and one of them, Kat-Anna or Kate, becomes his friend. From the other fighters he learns the tricks of the game. Scott's battle scores get better and better, but life in the orphan home begins to feel more like a prison than street life did. Then Kate mysteriously disappears and isn't seen again. It becomes clear to Scott that Virtual Kombat is more than just a game. Why do they need so many children to be gamers - and where do they all go?

The story has a strong plot with lots of surprises, the characterizations are well done and the action never stops. It's a book that young people will not want to put down. And you don't have to like video games to enjoy it.

3 After reading

a) How do the events that come after part 4 °compare with your own ideas from task 1? What does the review leave open?

b) Now that you know a bit more, what do you like about the story? What don't you like? Would you like to read the book? Discuss in small groups.

More challenge 5 p. 134

Taking part in discussions

Box: Voc., p. 229

1 VIEWING Shocking news!

a) First look at these scenes from the film. Take turns describing the scenes.
Talk about these questions:
- Where is the teenager? - What is he / she doing? - Why? - What is he or she thinking?

1

2
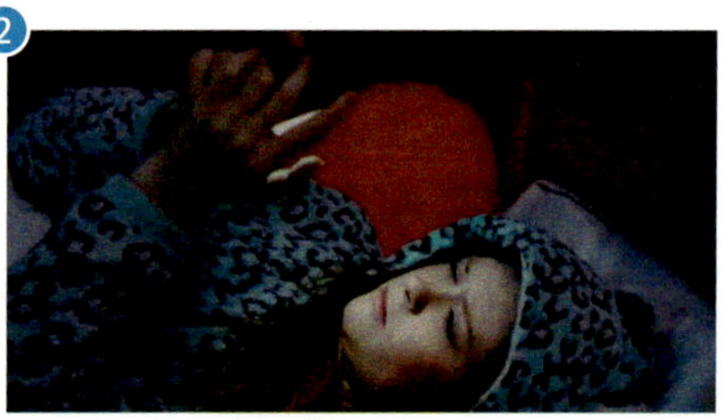

3
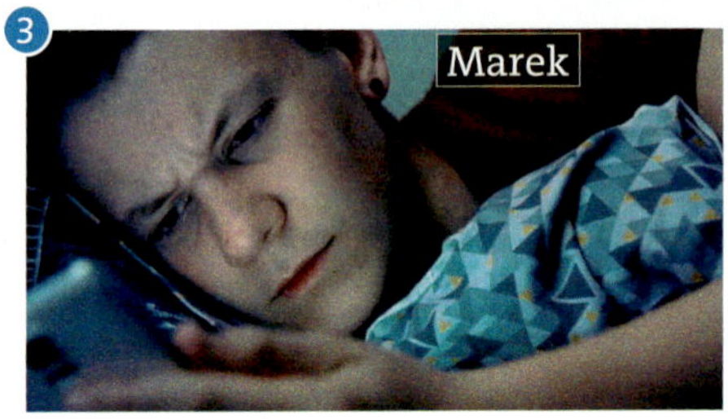

4

Now watch the film and compare your answers.

b) Here are some phrases from the film. Can you guess the missing words?

1 How can they do that? That's ... news!
2 Well, maybe it's ... that teenagers do too much 'vamping'.
3 Well actually, I don't think that's such a ... idea!
4 Sorry, I just can't agree ... that.
5 Yes, that's a ... point. Box: Voc., p. 229
6 In my opinion, ... has to be done.
7 Another ... is 'sleepy texting'.
8 It's true to ... that we can decide things for ourselves.
9 I see ... you mean.
10 You're right ... that.

c) Watch the film again and check your answers to b).
Note down more good phrases for discussions. More practice 9 p. 134

2 Expressing your opinion

a) Make six groups. Each group gets a statement from the box. Write it on a poster. Discuss your statement. Then write a short comment on it and put it on the wall.

b) Gallery walk: Move to other statements with your group. Discuss them and add your comments.

c) Return to your own statement and discuss all the comments.

1 Social media is dangerous – you have to be careful.
2 Digital technology is the best invention ever.
3 Phones shouldn't be allowed in teenagers' bedrooms at night.
4 Phones should be allowed in schools.
5 Gaming is great – it trains you for life.
6 Gaming is a waste of time – you don't learn anything.

3 NOW YOU Listen and speak

You're going to take part in a class discussion on this statement: "Video games are good for you." Or you can choose a different topic.

Step 1: Prepare your arguments More help p.134

a) Each group prepares a list of arguments. You will be either for the statement above, or against it, or not sure.

b) Choose at least three of your arguments. Think of examples and reasons to support them. Make notes.

Step 2: Take part in a discussion

a) Arrange the classroom like this. At least one person from each group should take part. The observers watch and make notes on a feedback sheet. More help p.135

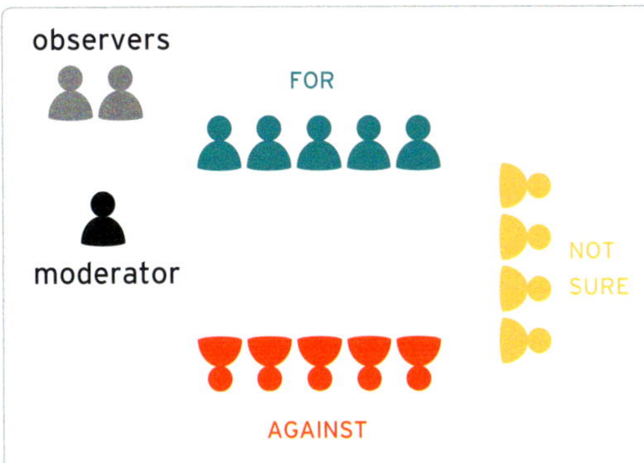

b) The moderator leads the discussion. If you want to speak, put up your hand. Everybody should speak at least once in the discussion.

1) Repeat in your own words what the last speaker said. You can check if you're not sure.

You said that ... / So you think that ...
Is that right?

2) Say if you agree or disagree. Speak respectfully.

I agree. / That's a good point / true.
I see what you mean but ...
I don't think you can say that.
Sorry, I don't agree with you because ...

3) Make your point. Give reasons and examples.

In my opinion, / I think / I feel / ...
That's why ... / For example, ...
Don't forget that ... /

c) During the discussion: If different speakers persuade you with their arguments, you can change sides in the classroom.

! Don't move when someone is speaking. Wait until they've finished. Observers shouldn't move. They just watch.

Step 3: Think about the discussion

Go back to your groups.

If you took part in the discussion:
What do you think you did / didn't do well?
Which were the strongest arguments?

If you watched the discussion:
Give feedback to your group member(s).
Which arguments persuaded you?

▸ Skills file 8.4, p. 171

Street art

! You'll find the new words from these pages listed on p. 232.

1 LISTENING An outdoor art gallery

a) Look at the pictures on this page. They're all examples of street art. How are they different from the kind of art that you'd find in a museum?

3.04 **b)** ´A girl is talking to her class about some street art she saw when she was visiting London.
Listen, then answer these questions:

1 What is special about the picture and the place where she saw it?
2 What does she think the artist wanted to say with the picture?
3 Do you agree with her °analysis? Explain.

Listen again if you need to.

2 SPEAKING Talking about street art

Make notes about one of these pictures. Give a short talk about it. Speak from your notes.
- First describe it, its °location, and the materials the artist used.
- Then talk about what the artist might be trying to say.
- Finally, give your personal °reaction to it.

▸ Skills files 8.1, p. 169; 10, p. 179

3 READING and WRITING A Banksy film

a) Read this review of a film about the famous British street artist, Banksy. Does it make you want to watch the film? Why (not)?

Exit through the °gift shop

by Michael A., Jr.

Some films about art are boring, but this one isn't. It's basically a documentary about street art, and you find out a lot about the street artists and how they work. But there's more to it than that.

First of all we meet the filmmaker, a crazy French guy living in Los Angeles. He's not a professional camera man. He just loves making films and he loves street art. So he follows the artists everywhere, and even climbs up to very dangerous places to film them as they quickly make their pictures before the police arrive. This part of the film is very °lively and interesting.

Then the French guy °gets lucky. He meets the British street artist Banksy, who is probably the most famous street artist of all. Some of his art has °sold for millions, but his identity is a secret. In the film we never see his face and his voice has been changed.

At that point the film changes. The French guy becomes a street artist himself, and the film is now all about him. °Incredibly, he becomes very successful, °even though he isn't really an artist. His art starts selling for huge °sums and things seem to go crazy.

Maybe that's the message of the film. Money is a bad influence on art. The title gives us a °hint. Art galleries and museums make people exit through their gift shops so that they spend money.

Personally I thought this film was brilliant. It was very interesting, but it was also very funny.

I think that Banksy's art is amazing. He is definitely a true artist, though I'm not so sure about the French guy. °In fact I'm not even sure if he's real. Maybe he's just a °made-up character. Nobody seems to be sure about that. But it doesn't matter. It's still a very °entertaining film.

b) Plan and write a review about a film that you've seen recently. You can use phrases from the review above.

! Before you write your review, **make notes** about the film.
- What kind of film is it?
- Where was it made?
- Who made it?
- Who is in it?
- What °aspects of the film are especially important (story, acting, music, setting, costumes, special effects)?

Also think about these questions:
- Does the film have a message?
- Did you enjoy the film? Why (not)?
- Would you °recommend it?

▸ *Skills file 9.8, p. 178*

4 READING and SPEAKING Sidewalk °poetry

Sidewalk poetry can be a short poem, a famous quote or a simple, funny or wise thought. Look at these examples that people actually wrote or painted on walls and in public spaces.

Now is our time

°Roses are red
°Violets are blue
You think this is
going to rhyme
But it's not gonna

An eye for an eye makes the whole world blind.

All in all
you're just
another °brick
in the wall.

All that we
See or seem
Is °but a dream
°Within a dream

Some people are so poor
All they have is money.

If you stare at this and stroke your chin you may appear °intelligent and °cultured.

This would be a nice place for a tree.

The EARTH without ART is just EH.

The hardest part is accepting how people change, and that alone changes everything.

Never °regret anything because at one time it was exactly what you wanted.

a) Think: Choose one or two texts that speak to you. Think about these questions:
- Are the texts just fun or do they have a deeper meaning?
- What do they make you think about or feel?
- What do you think the person who wrote them on a wall was feeling at the time?

Make notes.

b) Pair: Exchange and talk about your ideas.

c) Share: Discuss the value of sidewalk poetry. Some possible questions:
- Is it "just" graffiti or is it more?
- What's the difference between reading something like this in a book or magazine and reading it as graffiti on a wall?

5 NOW YOU WRITING Your message

a) Write your own sidewalk poetry. Think of a short message of no more than twenty words that you'd like to share. Write your text in large letters on a piece of paper or a poster. Then hang it on the classroom wall for a gallery walk.

b) Read the other texts and say which ones you like and why. Think about the questions in 4a.

▸ KV 33 ▸ DFF 4.6 ▸ DFF 4.7 ▸ INKL pp. 76–77

1 WORDS Media buddies

Media °buddies at a school in Bielefeld help younger students with digital media. Read the four texts. Choose the right words (A, B or C) for 1–8. Then put paragraphs A–D into the right order.

1 A book B certificate C smartphone
2 A training B chat C subject
3 A habits B advice C selfies
4 A support B avoid C post
5 A advantages B reasons C descriptions
6 A difficult B realistic C illegal
7 A arrive in B influence C accept
8 A details B mistakes C risks

A So, what do media buddies do? First they take part in a training course to improve their digital media skills. They get a ... (1) that confirms that they are experts in internet safety, computer °security or computer games. Communication skills ... (2) is part of the course. This helps them later to teach and advise other students. And students find it easier to accept ... (3) from their peers, not from parents or teachers.

B However, I think the advantages of media buddies are convincing. They can help people to ... (4) serious problems.

C Some teachers don't think media buddies are a good idea. Here are some of their ... (5). They argue that training takes too much time after school or at the weekend. Another argument is that the training costs a lot of money. °In addition, media buddies in schools can't deal with ... (6) internet activities – only the police can do that.

D Computers, smartphones and tablets ... (7) students' lives in many ways. But some young people °are not aware of the ... (8). That's why schools use digital media experts, or media buddies, to help with this problem.

2 LANGUAGE If I had known ...

a) Complete the conditional sentences in 1–4 with the right verb forms. // ● p. 135

1 I got a PC virus after downloading a game from the internet. If the media buddies hadn't helped me to get rid of it, my parents ... (take) away my PC.

2 A media buddy told me to change the settings of the app so that only some people can see my posts.
If I hadn't done that, my parents ... (see) all my conversations with my friends.

3 I found a website with lots of cool songs, I ... (be) in trouble for using an illegal music site if I had hadn't spoken to a media buddy first.

4 I'm a fool! I bought a new °gadget last week because of a cool ad. I ... (get) something much better for the same price if I had spoken to the media buddies.

b) Ratib, a media buddy, is talking with another student. Complete his sentences.

an antivirus programme • what you like best • something very quickly • the problem at once

1 If you had told your parents about the cyberbullying at once, they ... (do) ...
2 If you had sent me a screenshot, I ... (see) ...
3 I would have shown you a more interesting computer game if I ... (know) ...
4 Your PC wouldn't have crashed if you ... (install) ...

▸ KV 33 ▸ DFF 4.1 ▸ DFF 4.4 ▸ INKL pp. 76–77

3 LISTENING I can't live without my ...

3.05 You're going to listen to part of a radio programme. You'll hear it twice. While you're listening, complete tasks a) and b). Then listen again and complete tasks c) and d).

a) Listen and match the people (1–4) to their favourite gadgets (A–F).

1 Blake 2 Michelle 3 Jacob 4 Dana

A

game console

B

tablet

C

TV

D

smartphone

E

camera

F

laptop

b) Lynn's guests mention lots of things that they do with their smartphones. Name at least six of them.

c) Listen again and complete these sentences.

1 Blake says he usually texts his friends because it's easy and ...
2 Michelle likes her laptop more than her smartphone because she prefers ...
3 Jacob isn't a °couch potato because he plays ... and he ...
4 If Dana takes photos, she doesn't need a camera. She ...

d) Which sentence ending is correct?

Lynn McCarthy's radio show is about ...
- A a new survey on digital habits.
- B social networking.
- C teenagers' favourite digital gadgets.

4 WRITING One week without technology

For a reality show, *PQR Radio* is inviting 35 teenagers from all over the world to one week in a camp on a beautiful island. But the camp will be 100% technology-free.

Write an email to *PQR Radio* (150–200 words).
Say ...
- your name, age and where you are from
- how important your digital gadgets are to you (which ones you use most and what for)
- why you would like to take part in the camp
- what you can learn from a week without gadgets
- what activities you would like to do with the other young people at the camp

▸ *Skills file 9.3, p. 173*

▸ DFF 4.3 ▸ DFF 4.5 ▸ INKL pp. 76–77

5 SPEAKING Talking about a photo

Talk about the photo for 3–5 minutes. Ask your partner questions about his or her opinion. React, e.g. ask follow-up questions.

1. Describe what you see. What are the people doing?
2. What do they think about the situation?
3. What do you feel about this situation?
4. Describe another situation where mobile gadgets are a problem. Explain why.

6 MEDIATION Generation Z – a German article

Hilf deinem amerikanischen Freund, der nur etwas Deutsch kann, diesen Zeitungsartikel zu verstehen. Sage ihm, …

1 worum es generell in dem Artikel geht
2 wer zur Generation Z gehört
3 was ihre besonderen Merkmale sind
4 wie sie kommuniziert
5 wie sie lernt
6 was für sie im Leben wichtig ist

Generation Z
heißt der neue Trend

Als Generation Z wird die Generation bezeichnet, die in den späten 90ern auf die Welt kam. Typisch für sie ist vor allem, dass es die erste Generation ist, die vollkommen in einer digitalen Welt aufgewachsen ist. Mit vielfältigen Folgen. Nicht umsonst heißen sie im Englischen *digital natives.*

Mit Freunden wird über Facebook und Co. kommuniziert, aber man trifft sich nicht unbedingt in Vereinen oder mit den Freunden. Alles wird gepostet, geliked, kommentiert, aber nur digital. Die Welt der Generation Z ist noch digitaler als die ihrer Vorgänger, der Generation Y.

Die Angehörigen der Generation Z haben nicht mehr nur ein Leben, sondern viele: auf Instagram, Tumblr, Snapchat, Viner, ... Außerdem haben sie mit ihren 5000 bis 10.000 Followern auf Twitter einen riesigen Freundeskreis. Die Art, wie Lernen bei ihnen stattfindet, ist eine völlig andere: Wissen ist jederzeit und überall verfügbar und jeder User muss in der Lage sein, aus der Informationslawine das zu filtern,was in der jeweiligen Situation gerade wichtig ist.

Die Generation Z besteht auf einer klaren Trennung zwischen Beruflichem und Privatem. Freizeit und Familie sind wichtiger als die Arbeit. Sie ist – anders als die Generation vor ihr – nicht mehr teamorientiert, denn die meisten Menschen der Generation Z haben kein direktes Interesse an ihren unmittelbaren Mitmenschen. Wichtige Themen dieser Gruppe sind vor allem Umwelt und Fairness.

▸ Workbook My learner log, p. 59 and Revision, pp. 53–54, p. 60

PARTNER B

Unit 1

3 SPEAKING Talking about a picture ▸ Unit 1, p. 30

Partner B:

a) Describe to your partner what you can see in your picture. These questions can help you: Who? What? Where? When? Why? ▸ Skills file 10, p. 179

b) Listen to your partner.

c) Together find out what the pictures have in common and what is different.

Unit 2

4 SPEAKING Role-play ▸ Unit 2, p. 55

Partner B: Read your role card and prepare a role-play with your partner.
Start your conversation very politely. Don't forget to introduce yourselves to each other.

You're a student at Green Valley High School and you're at a welcome party for exchange students from Germany. The party is great: excellent food, cool music, some people are dancing. You're standing next to the buffet when you notice an interesting looking person coming over to get a drink.
Start a conversation to find out more about him or her.
Keep the conversation going for at least three minutes.

2 LISTENING Phoning about a job ▸ Unit 3, p. 77

2.15

b) Partner B: Listen to the dialogue between Sarah and Mr Thomson. Complete it. Talk to partner A to find out if your answers are correct.

S I'm very interested in the ... (A) as a cruise assistant.
T Do you have any work experience?
S I've done ... (B) work placements so far.
T That sounds really good. We need somebody to work at weekends from 10 am to 4 pm or from 4 pm to 10 pm.
S Working at the weekends is ... (C) for me.
T We can talk about more details in an interview. Can you come on Saturday at 10 am?
S Yes, that's fine. What do I ... (D) to bring?
T Can you bring your CV, please?
S I'm ... (E) on Saturday.

c) Read your role card and act out a dialogue with your partner.

Role card

Partner B

You need some extra money to buy a cool bike. An international holiday park has just opened nearby and they are offering °seasonal part-time jobs in their coffee shop. You're phoning about the job ad that you saw in the coffee shop window yesterday.

2 Stell dich höflich vor. Sage, dass du wegen des Stellenangebots als Kellner/in anrufst.
4 Letzten Sommer hast du ein Betriebspraktikum in einem griechischen Restaurant gemacht.
6 Sage, dass das perfekt ist und du gern freitagabends und samstags arbeiten kannst.
8 Nimm das Angebot erfreut an. Frage, was du zum Bewerbungsgespräch mitbringen sollst.
10 Bestätige, dass du die Unterlagen mitbringen wirst. Bedanke und verabschiede dich höflich.

Unit 4

4 SPEAKING **Role-play** ▸ Unit 4, p. 83

Partner B:

a) Prepare your role.

b) Act out your role-play with your partner.
Your partner begins.

c) Get feedback from the class.
What was good / convincing / realistic?
What could have been better?

Partner B
- Your mother or father wants to know why you spend so much time on your computer, smart phone, etc. Think of some convincing arguments.
- Your mother or father wants to discuss ways that you could change your habits. Think about how you want to react. Do you want to agree to make changes? What could those changes be? Or are you against any changes in your habits? If so, how do you want to say this?

More practice 1 SPEAKING **Young people together** ▸ Unit 4, p. 130

Partner B:

a) Look at the photo and think about these questions:
- What's happening?
- Where are the people?
- What are they doing?
- Do they know each other?
- Are they friends?

b) Listen to your partner.
Then describe your photo to him or her.
Compare the two photos.

c) Talk about these questions.
- How do you communicate with your friends?
- What kind of things do you and your friends do together? ▸ Skills file 10, p. 179

Unit 1

More help 2b An Australian road trip ► Unit 1, p. 9

Pick words from the two boxes and make phrases.

camping	jumping
climbing	running
cooking	sailing
cycling	skate-boarding
dancing	surfing
driving	swimming
diving	walking
	…

in a river	near a reef
beside a road	through a desert
in the sea	in a town
on rocks	in a forest
in the outback	…
on a track	
on a boat	
at a campsite	

More practice 1 More about the film ► Unit 1, p. 9

Watch the film again and make notes about these questions.
Then compare your notes.

1 What kind of music was used in the film? Did you like it? Explain why (not).
2 The film-maker uses °time lapse – that means that these parts are very fast.
- Why do you think time lapse is used?
- How does it make you feel?
- Do you like the °effect of time lapse? Why (not)?

More challenge 1 Your road trip film ► Unit 1, p. 9

a) What would you °include in a two-minute film about a road trip across Germany? Think about these questions. Then talk to a partner.
- Where would you make your film?
- What things would you show?
- What music would you use?
- When would you use time lapse (make parts of the film very fast)?

b) Write a plan for your film.

More practice 2 An Aussie network ► Unit 1, p. 11

Make an Australia vocabulary network. Find words and phrases in the articles on pages 10 and 11 to add to your network.

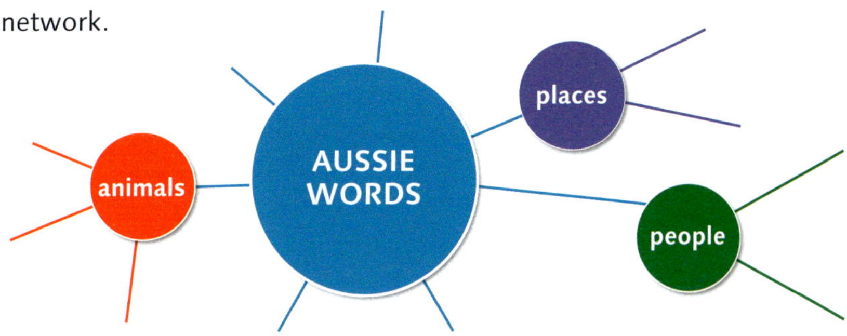

Unit 1

More practice 3 What have you learned about Oz?

► Unit 1, p. 11

Complete these sentences. Use information from the texts on pages 10 and 11.

1 The most popular places for tourists are ...
2 Some people decide not to climb Uluru because ...
3 Since the arrival of the British in 1788, ...
4 A quarter of the Australian population are ...
5 Australian teenagers who want to fight fires join ...
6 It's important to stop bush fires because ...
7 When people think of dangerous Australian animals, the first things they think of are ...
8 The most dangerous animal in Australia is ...

More challenge 2 Another point of view

► Unit 1, p. 11

Write a story from the perspective of one of these people:
- You're a tourist at Uluru. Do you decide to climb it or not?
- You're a new Australian. How do you spend the day after you become an Australian citizen?
- You're a teenage firefighter. You get a call to °go into action. How do you feel?
- You're swimming in the sea at a beach in Sydney. You see a shark. How do you feel? What do you do?

More practice 4 °In case of emergency ...

► Unit 1, p. 12

a) Put the words in the boxes together to make 'emergency phrases' – as many as you can.

break • call • cool • get (5x) • light • stay (2x) • use	a doctor • a small fire • calm and still • down (2x) • into the shade • into trouble • lost • out of the sun • safe • to a hospital • your torch and your whistle

b) Match these phrases with words or phrases from the text in task 2a on p. 12.

1 have problems (paragraph 1) *get into ...*
2 lose your way (1)
3 go under a tree (2)
4 make yourself feel cooler (2)
5 don't get excited (3)
6 °phone for an ambulance (3)

c) Use the phrases in a) and b) to make sentences – as many as you can.

If you get lost in the outback, ...

More practice 5 °Dealing with danger

► Unit 1, p. 13

Copy the table. Listen to the conversations again and complete the table.

	problem	advice
Text 1		
Text 2		
Text 3		

Compare your answers.

//● 3b Emergencies on the beach ▸ Unit 1, p. 13

Complete these sentences with the missing verbs. Then listen again and check.

1 "G'day. I don't ... you ... swim here. It's dangerous."
2 "If I ... you, I'd ... between the flags. It's safer over there."
3 "G'day. Can you ... us? My mate has ... his foot."
4 "It isn't bleeding, but I ... some redness. Does it ... now?"
5 "I ... a bit sick and I ... a headache."
6 "... me ... your temperature. It's quite high and you ... a bit red."

More practice 6 Understanding Aboriginal people ▸ Unit 1, p. 15

Read the text on p. 15 again and pick the correct answer.

1 Indigenous people came to Australia ...
 a) after the Europeans. c) at the same time as the Europeans.
 b) just before the Europeans. d) a long time before the Europeans.

2 Before Europeans came to Australia, the Indigenous way of life was mostly ...
 a) easy. b) nomadic. c) dramatic. d) fun.

3 Many Aboriginal Australians died from ...
 a) fighting against other Aboriginals. c) not enough food.
 b) diseases brought by Europeans. d) having to leave their land.

4 ... Aboriginal people have big problems today. a) No b) Many c) Some d) All

5 In Aboriginal paintings you see lots of ...
 a) kangaroos. b) dots. c) people. d) boomerangs.

6 According to the text, Indigenous Australians ...
 a) have lost their culture. c) now have a European culture.
 b) have their own special culture. d) don't care about culture.

More help 3d First Australians ▸ Unit 1, p. 15

Text A

You could write about any of these things:
- what's changed for Aboriginal people
- feeling positive about their future
- being proud of their culture
- not only remembering the difficult past
- being proud of where they come from
- ...

Text B

You could write about any of these things:

painting • flag • dance • proud • history • hunting • the Europeans • the land • diseases • school • jobs • health • money • ...

Unit 1

More challenge 3 **Competing cities** ▸ Unit 1, p. 17

Think of two other towns or cities that have a similar relationship.
List examples of how they compete with each other. Then share your results with the class.

More practice 7 **Who said it?** ▸ Unit 1, p. 18

°Match the sentences with the four kids (A) Aaron, (B) Ella, (C) Ava and (D) Ethan.
One sentence doesn't match any of them.

1 I like sport and music.
2 I don't mind living in a lonely place.
3 I like excitement.
4 I love living in a big city near the sea.
5 Where I live there are two seasons – not four.
6 I drive – but not on the road.
7 On Saturdays I like to go to the beach.
8 Something happened to me that made me change my hobby.
9 I don't think that living in a small town is boring.

More practice 8 **An interview** ▸ Unit 1, p. 19

You work for a radio station that is interviewing people who are taking part in the competition. You're preparing an interview with Niko about his experiences.

a) Read the text again and make questions with the simple past and the past progressive – as many as you can.

b) Ask your questions. Then swap roles. Try to answer the questions as Niko might answer them.

More help **5** **NOW YOU** **A window on your life** ▸ Unit 1, p. 19

Read the advert on page 16 again, and read or listen to the texts for more ideas.

1) Do you need ideas for your story?

> Ask yourself questions like this:
> Do you like the place where you live? Why (not)? (Think of Aaron in Text A.)
> What are you really interested in – a hobby, a sport, ...? (Think of Ella in Text B.)
> Do you want to write about a day in your life ? (Think of Ava in Text C.)
> Did something happen to you recently that changed your life? (Think of Ethan in Text D.)

2) Do you know how to structure your text?

> Look again at the texts for ideas and look at ▸ °Skills file 9.1, p. 171

3) Do you need a good first sentence?

Aaron, Ethan and Ella had good ones: Friday September 21st is the night that changed my life. It was the day before my 16th birthday. This is probably the most (remote / beautiful / interesting) place that you can live in ...

4) Do you need a good last sentence?

Ava and Aaron had good ones: Life here is sometimes hard, but I don't want to live anywhere else. Where I live is a really special place.

More practice 9 Work with the text ▸ Unit 1, p. 23

a) Look at **1 Sydney School**. Pick the right words and finish the sentences.

1 When Hugh first saw Poppy he was (A) excited (B) careful (C) scared.
2 Hugh's mum is Poppy's (A) daughter (B) sister (C) mother.
3 The police (A) arrested Poppy (B) came to the school (C) did nothing.
4 Hugh thought Poppy (A) didn't look like him (B) looked like him (C) looked funny.
5 Hugh (A) can't drive (B) doesn't like driving (C) is learning to drive.

b) Look at **2 Plans**.
Put the sentence parts together.

1 Poppy lived	to go to Uluru.
2 It's a long way from	a muscle car.
3 Poppy always wanted	in an apartment.
4 A Holden Monaro is	to drive Poppy.
5 Hugh agreed	Sydney to Uluru.

c) Look at **3 The Million Star Motel**.
What do you think? Finish these sentences.

1 Hugh felt excited when ...
2 Poppy looked happy because ...
3 Poppy told Hugh not to ...
4 At the Darling River Hugh and Poppy ...
5 The 'Million Star Motel' means ...

d) Look at **4 South Australia**.
Fill in the gaps with words from the text.

1 Poppy didn't want Hugh to drive ...
2 Hugh stopped the car to let a ... pass.
3 Another danger on the highway were ...
4 Hugh couldn't see Jimmy's face because ...
5 A Typhoon is a ...

e) Look at **5 In the roadhouse**.
Find and correct a mistake in each sentence.

1 Hugh ate a brown bread sandwich.
2 Hugh helped the people to find Bella.
3 When Hugh went back to the car, Jimmy was gone.
4 The people in the black car were nice.
5 The hitchhiker was a teen boy.

f) Look at **6 At Yulara, near Uluru**. Answer these questions.

1 How did Hugh know that Bella was in trouble?
2 Do you think that Hugh was a good friend? Why (not)?

Unit 1

More help 8 A character network ▸ Unit 1, p. 23

a) Copy and complete this character network for the story.

You can make notes about …

- the relationships between the characters (e.g. boyfriend / girlfriend; father / daughter; etc.)
- how the characters feel about each other (e.g. likes / doesn't like / hates / loves / is afraid of / …).

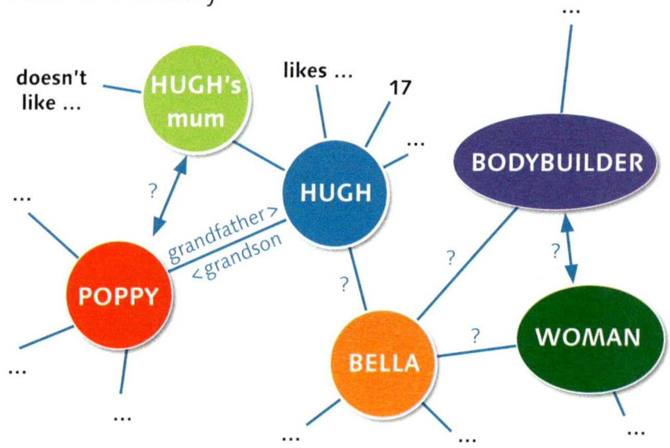

b) Pick words from this box and put them in your character network. If you don't know some words, check in a dictionary.

> big eyes • brave • caring • °cowardly • °dishonest • glamorous • grey hair • honest • helpful • loving • messy hair • mysterious • nice • old • ponytail • short • stupid • thin • terrible • (un)friendly • violent • young • …

More challenge 4 Getting Amy's presentation right ▸ Unit 1, p. 24

Try to improve Amy's presentation using her notes and visual materials (below). Follow these steps:

a) Watch part 5 again. Make notes about the things that Amy doesn't do so well.

b) Look at Amy's notes. Improve them. Add information (including visuals) that you feel °is missing.

Amy's notes

The history of Australia

I. First Europeans in Australia: – a lot of them °prisoners

II. England sent prisoners to Australia

When?
- *in 1788*
- *for the next 80 years*

Why?
- *English prisoners went to America until 1782.*
- *American War of Independence ended in 1783; America didn't accept any more prisoners.*
- *England had to find somewhere else to send their prisoners.*

III. °Transportation to New South Wales was the answer.

c) Then practise with a partner giving the presentation.

More help **3** YOUR TASK **A presentation about Australia** ▸ Unit 1, p. 25

Step 4: Give your presentation / Prepare your feedback ▸ Skills file 8.1, p. 169

While listening, prepare your feedback with a feedback sheet.

a) Copy this table:

important things for a presentation	very good	good	OK	needs work	notes
1					
2					
3					
4					
5					

b) Put the important things that you agreed on with your partner (in task 2 on page 24) in the first °column of your feedback sheet.

c) When you're listening, make notes on your feedback sheet like this:

important things for a presentation	very good	good	OK	needs work	notes
1 a clear structure		✓			intro – very clear middle – less clear
2 short notes			✓		a bit long
3 an interesting presentation	✓				very interesting!
4 speaking slowly and clearly			✓		clear, but a little too fast
5 using good phrases				✓	use more good phrases, e.g. for intro: "Now I'm going to talk about ...".

Unit 1 **Stop! Check! Go!**

More challenge 5 **Our trip to Oz** ▸ Unit 1, p. 29

After their trip to Australia, Sophie and Rani write an article about Oz for their school magazine. Think about their plans, their internet research and their blog, and write the article (about 150 words) from their perspective.

Unit 1 Stop! Check! Go!

More help 4b WRITING Slip, slop, slap, seek and slide

▸ Unit 1, p. 30

Some ideas for your comment:

- People like to lie in the sun when they're on holiday.
- People think that this looks beautiful / healthy / ...
- People don't understand the dangers of too much sun (e.g. skin cancer).
- Skin must get used to the sun slowly.
- More and more people like spending their holidays in hot countries.
- Skin cancer is the most common cancer among young people.
- Sun makes your skin look old at an early age.

Unit 2

More challenge 1 Letter from a student

▸ Unit 2, p. 33

Imagine you're Patrick. Write to a student magazine about your experience.

- Don't give your real name or the names of your friends or your school, etc.
- Write about the text messages, how you felt, and what happened after that.
- Do you think that you'll be friends again?
- What advice would you give other kids who are victims of cyberbullying?

More challenge 2 A °tricky problem

▸ Unit 2, p. 36

Read the situation below. Write a dialogue between the two friends. Perform it for the class.

There's a party on Friday night and everybody is going. You and your friend would like to go. Plus, if you don't go, everybody will say that you're losers.
But there's a problem.
Partner A: You're worried because you have a swimming competition on Saturday, and the trainer doesn't want swimmers to °have a late night.
Partner B: You're worried because you don't want to go to the party on your own.

Talk together and try to find a solution, so that you can both go to the party.

More practice 1 Report from London

▸ Unit 2, p. 37

a) Copy the table. Then look at the notes below for a newspaper report.
Find the answers to the five *wh*-questions (and *How?*) and put them in your table.

Who?	What?	When?	Where?	Why?	How?
…	…	Late Saturday evening	…	…	…

Regent's Park near Chester Road

stopped racist attack

Late Saturday evening

four theatre-goers

victim taken to hospital, doctors say he'll be fine

two skinheads passed Ghanaian man

three held men, fourth called police

chased man, began kicking him

"I'm very °thankful for what they did"

Police arrived, arrested men

four saw what was happening, fought attackers

b) Use the information in your table to write a short report.
- First structure your information.
- Add other words (e.g. linking words, adjectives, …) to make your sentences complete.
- Think of a good headline for the report.

! Remember that the reader should see quickly what the report is about. Start with the most important facts (the five *wh*-questions), then go on to more °detailed and background information.

▸ Skills file 9.2, p. 173

More practice 2 Sending a signal

▸ Unit 2, p. 37

a) Complete the sentences about what happened.
1 Some racist fans …
2 A black player …
3 The player's teammates …

b) Answer the questions.
4 What do other players and fans think about what Kevin Prince Boateng did?
5 What does Kevin Prince Boateng hope for?
6 What else could be done to deal with racism and prejudice in football?

Unit 2

1 ACTIVITY Badges – a group experiment ▸ Unit 2, p. 37

Role card

RED PEOPLE

Ask this question:

If you could visit any country, where would you go?

Tips:

- The blue people are the most important. Try to talk to all of them.
- The green people are nice and funny. Talk to two or three of them.
- The orange people aren't so important. So don't worry if you don't have time for them. Maybe just talk to one.
- Be polite to everybody.

More challenge 3 Your review ▸ Unit 2, p. 38

Write a review of the video "What you say matters". Write about:

- who sings the song
- the style of music
- the important lines / slogans of the song
- the different scenes of the video
- the message of the video
- what you (don't) like about the video and why

More help 4 Project A Scenes of discrimination ▸ Unit 2, p. 39

You can write a dialogue like this for the first scene.

We're in a classroom. The students are about 16 and they're sitting down. The teacher starts to give the students their tests and their results.

Teacher Here are your maths tests from last week. You have 79, Tom – that's good. And you have 61 – that's OK. Kat – only 55! You can do better. Jane – 98 – great work.

Jane smiles and takes her paper. Kat is sitting behind her. She doesn't look happy. She looks at Jane and whispers.

Kat You think you're so good! Of course you're the teacher's °favourite. ...

Jane looks ... Will she say something or ...? Then she gets up and walks ... She talks to ... She says ...

Jane ...

More help 4 Project B Immigrants' stories ▸ Unit 2, p. 39

Ask these questions. You can ask them in German or in your own language too.

- What country does your family come from?
- When did they come here?
- Do you visit your family's country?
- Can you speak the language?
- Do you like it there? What's special?
- What's different to Germany?
- Would you recommend it for holidays? Where should people go?

You can write texts like this:

Alex's family comes from ... They came to Germany ... ago.
The family left ... because they wanted a better life / because of the war ...
Alex and his family go back to ... every ...
They can't go back to ... at the moment because it's too dangerous / ...
It's very different to Germany – it's ...
...
Here's a map and some of Alex's photos. ...

1 ACTIVITY Badges – a group experiment ▸ Unit 2, p. 37

Role card

GREEN PEOPLE

Ask this question:

If you were an animal, which animal would you like to be?

Tips:

- The blue people are the most important. Try to talk to all of them.
- The orange people aren't so important. So don't worry if you don't have time for them. Maybe just talk to one.
- The red people are a bit stupid. Their question is stupid, too. Don't answer it and don't ask them any questions.
- Be polite to everybody (except the red people).

Unit 2

More practice 3 What were their exact words?

► Unit 2, p. 41

Complete the °speech bubbles.

1 The girl told Kai that her name was Emily.
2 He said that his name was Kai.
3 Kai told Emily that he often came to the club.
4 She told him that she didn't come very often.
5 She explained that she played soccer, and practice was usually on the same night.
6 He suggested that she should come to the talent show on Saturday night if she was free.
7 She thought that was a great idea.

1 ... name ... Emily.

4 I ... ... very often.
5 ... ... soccer, and practice ... usually on the same night.

7 ... ... a great idea.

2 ... name ... Kai.
3 ... often ... to the club.

6 ... should come to the talent show on Saturday night if ... ... free.

More practice 4 Tim and Jessie

► Unit 2, p. 42

Here Tim is reporting what he and Jessie said when they met again later. Complete his report.

Jessie	Do you have that homework for me?
Tim	Ah no, Jessie, I can't do that.
Jessie	Are you crazy? I copied from Julia last time and there wasn't a problem.
Tim	Well, I have thought about it, and I really don't feel comfortable with it.
Jessie	You're a pain.
Tim	I'll explain the homework if you like.
Jessie	I don't have time for that.

Jessie asked me if ...
I told her that ...
Jessie asked me if ...
She said that she ...
and there ...
I said that I ...
and I really ...
She told me that ...
I told her that ...
But she said that ...

1 ACTIVITY Badges – a group experiment ▸ Unit 2, p. 37

Role card

ORANGE PEOPLE

Ask this question:

If you could eat only one thing for lunch every day, what would that be?

Tips:

- The blue people are the most important. Try to talk to all of them.
- The green people are interesting. Talk to two or three of them.
- The red people aren't interesting. Don't answer their question and don't ask them any questions. Tell them you're too busy.
- Be polite to everybody (except the red people).

More help 5 Talking about the text ▸ Unit 2, p. 47

a) Choose one side of the story – Natasha's or Matt's – and answer the questions.

Natasha's side of the story

1 *The* ***characters***: Who is the story about?
- The main character in this story is ... She's ... It's also about ...

2 *The* ***setting***: Where does the story happen?
- The story happens in a street in ... We're in ... We also learn about ...

3 *The* ***plot***: Say what happens in the story – in a few sentences.
- First Natasha thinks that ... Then her brother sees ... He thinks it's ... Natasha's mum says that ... Natasha's dad goes ... Then ...

4 *The* ***mood***: How do you feel when you read this story? Why?
- I think that it's scary / funny / exciting / ... when ...

Matt's side of the story

1 *The* ***characters***: Who is the story about?
- The main character in this story is ... He's ... It's also about ...

2 *The* ***setting***: Where does the story happen?
- The story happens / takes place in ... We're in ... He's ...

3 *The* ***plot***: Say what happens in the story – in a few sentences.
- First Matt arrives ... When he goes ... He wants to have ..., but ... Then someone ... – it's ...

4 *The* ***mood***: How do you feel when you read this story? Why?
- I think that it's interesting / funny / exciting when ...

Unit 2

More practice 5 **The story continues** ▸ Unit 2, p. 47

Pick a) or b):

a) Imagine that Matt and Natasha meet in the street. Write a dialogue between the two.

b) Imagine that you're the writer – Chloe Rayban. Write the next °chapter of this story.

More help **7** **WRITING** **A book worth reading?** ▸ Unit 2, p. 47

Write a review of the story. In about 100 words, write about the plot, the setting, your favourite characters, the mood of the story and the structure of the book.

Here are some ideas:

First say something about the story in a few sentences. Use your ideas from 5 and from 6a).
Example: *Who is the story about? Do you have a favourite character? Where does the story happen? What happens? How do you feel when you read the story?*

°Comment on the structure of the book – the girl's story and the boy's story.
Example: *The book is unusual because you can read the boy's story or the girl's story.*
I think that's interesting / boring / fun / ... because ...

What else do you think is good or not so good about the story? Who do you think might enjoy it?
Example: *Personally I think the story is funny / interesting /...*
I really want to know what happens next / ...
I can recommend / wouldn't read this book because I'm (not) interested in the characters / the structure is interesting / boring / ...
I think that this book will be popular with girls/ boys/ anybody who likes ...

More challenge 4 **Different points of view** ▸ Unit 2, p. 47

Pick a) or b).

a) Look at Natasha's story, lines 18 to 49. Describe what happened from Jamie's point of view.

b) Look at Matt's story, lines 69 to 96. Describe what happened from the neighbour's point of view.

More practice 6 **Do it again!** ▸ Unit 2, p. 49

Pick another situation from page 49. Make another dialogue and practise it together. Then swap roles.

Unit 2 | Stop! Check! Go!

More practice 7 LANGUAGE How to talk to your parents

▸ Unit 2, p. 53

It's the morning after the concert. Jay is chatting online with her cousin. She tells him what her friends said after the concert. Write what Jay says to her cousin.

Max	I will always remember this concert.	1 Max said …
Meg	It was the best concert I have ever been to.	2 Meg said …
Tia	I've never been to a concert before.	3 Tia said …
Tia	Can one of you take a photo of me beside the poster?	4 Tia asked if one of us …
Elli	I've forgotten my phone!	5 Elli said …
Tia	Don't worry. I'll take some photos of you.	6 Tia told Elli … She said she …
Max	I started to °record the concert on it, but after about 30 minutes my phone died.	7 Max said that …

//● 2a READING and WRITING Volunteering

▸ Unit 2, p. 54

Find words or phrases that mean:

1 very good
2 team of people who work together
3 things you need to rescue someone
4 kids who have disabilities
5 feel unhappy because something you hoped for doesn't happen
6 organizing your own time
7 able to deal with a difficult situation without getting fed up
8 be polite and kind to others

1 ACTIVITY Badges – a group experiment

▸ Unit 2, p. 37

Role card

BLUE PEOPLE

Ask this question:

If you moved to a °desert island, what three things would you take with you?

Tips:

- You like blue people best. So talk to other blue people first.
- The orange people aren't so important. You can answer their question if you like, but don't ask your question.
- The green people aren't very interesting. You can talk to one or two, if you like.
- Forget the red people. Don't even look at them when they talk to you. Just walk away.
- You aren't very polite.

Unit 3

1 Your quiz results from pages 56–57

► Unit 3, p. 57

How did you answer the questions? Find out if you picked mostly answers with 3 points, 2 points or 1 point. Then read the results further below.

1	2	3	4	5	6	7	8	9	10
Ⓐ (2)	Ⓐ (1)	Ⓐ (2)	Ⓐ (2)	Ⓐ (3)	Ⓐ (1)	Ⓐ (2)	Ⓐ (2)	Ⓐ (3)	Ⓐ (1)
Ⓑ (3)	Ⓑ (2)	Ⓑ (1)	Ⓑ (3)	Ⓑ (1)	Ⓑ (2)	Ⓑ (1)	Ⓑ (3)	Ⓑ (1)	Ⓑ (2)
Ⓒ (1)	Ⓒ (3)	Ⓒ (3)	Ⓒ (1)	Ⓒ (2)	Ⓒ (3)	Ⓒ (3)	Ⓒ (1)	Ⓒ (2)	Ⓒ (3)

Mostly (3)
Great! You're ready for the real world. You manage your money well and you seem to have most of the life skills that you need to be independent. So get ready to enjoy the rest of your life.

Mostly (2)
You're quite independent, but you still need to learn a few important life skills before you leave home. Decide which skills are important for you and try to get some advice.

Mostly (1)
You know how to have fun, but you're not ready for the real world. You need to be more independent. Make plans to change. Learn one new skill every week.

More help 2a Life skills

► Unit 3, p. 57

These sentence structures and the skills listed in the box can help you.

- You should know how to …
- It's important to be able to …
- I think … is important because …

become a resident in a new city • buy a car • do chores • look for a flat • make decisions • manage your money • rent a flat • start a business • take out °insurance • …

More practice 1 Talking about jobs

► Unit 3, p. 60

a) Finish these sentences.

1 Someone who organizes events is …
2 Someone who helps with computers is …
3 Someone who flies planes is …
4 Bar staff are people who …
5 A ski instructor is someone who …
6 A stylist is …
7 A cleaner …
8 A receptionist …
9 A cook …
10 A waiter …

b) Think of five other jobs. Write questions about them.
Then read your questions to a partner. Can your partner guess what the job is? Even in German?
Example: *What do you call someone who works in a … / helps … / …?*

► Wordbank 3, p. 138

More practice 2 MEDIATION **Tell a friend** ▸ Unit 3, p. 61

a) Read this advert for film and °TV extras and make notes in English under these headings:
- **job title** - **type of show** - **skills needed** - **experience** - **where** - **when** - **pay**

> **Komparsen gesucht**
>
> **Tätigkeit:** Raum Berlin
>
> **Drehtage:** 1. bis 5. Dezember (6 Tage; 2 – 3 Stunden täglich)
>
> **Vergütung:** 40 Euro pro Drehtag
>
> **Für** eine Reality-Sendung. Eine amerikanische Familie zieht von New York City nach Berlin um. Es geht um Freundschaften, aber auch um Mobbing und Auseinandersetzungen. Die Darsteller/innen sprechen Englisch und Deutsch.
>
> **Voraussetzungen:** Du bist zwischen 14 und 19 Jahre alt und wohnst in Berlin oder Umgebung, da weder Fahrt- noch Übernachtungskosten übernommen werden. Du sprichst fließend Deutsch und gutes Englisch. Dreherfahrungen sind von Vorteil.
>
> **Bewerbung:** Per E-Mail, bitte auf Englisch (da amerikanisches Drehteam), an: americanlife@casting100.com
>
> **Einsatzort:** Berlin

! If you can't guess what some important words in the advert are in English, use a dictionary.

▸ Skills file 12, p. 181

b) Now tell your partner about it. Would you like the job? Why (not)?

More help **4** **Your ideal job** ▸ Unit 3, p. 61

You can use this checklist to help you to make notes for your text about an ideal job:

Do you need ...	experience? / special skills? / a driving licence? / qualifications? / ...
Do you have to ...	work with other people? / go to school or college? / do special training? / work indoors or outdoors? / work shifts? / use English? / ...
Can you ...	train on the job? / learn new skills? / ...
What ...	kind of work do you have to do? / hours do you work? / duties do you have? / training do you need? / is the pay like? / holidays do you get? / is the job title?

More challenge 1 **Different countries – different CVs** ▸ Unit 3, p. 62

Compare your CV in German to Paul Schulz's CV in English. Think about these questions:
- What's the same? - What's different? - What do you like especially in an English CV?

Unit 3

More practice 3 A cover letter ▸ Unit 3, p. 63

Apply for this job. Write a cover letter and try to sell yourself.

Schloss Granstein

Are you looking for an exciting and °challenging summer job?
Do you speak some English and good German?
Would you like to live in a castle for the summer?
We are offering a summer job in the souvenir shop in the famous Granstein castle. Come and help us with our many visitors from all over the world. It's a great chance to improve your English.

Apply (in English) to: The Manager, Schloss Granstein

More help 2a The experience of volunteering ▸ Unit 3, p. 65

Some phrases you could use:
(As a volunteer) you could/would probably ...
I can imagine that a volunteer could/would maybe (have to) ...

Possible positive experiences:
- learn to deal with difficult situations
- become more °self-confident
- make new friends
- ...

Possible negative experiences:
- find yourself in difficult situations
- find out that you're not prepared
- discover that you're not able to help
- ...

More practice 4 My volunteer work ▸ Unit 3, p. 65

Imagine you're applying to be an international volunteer. As part of the application, write a text (°max. 200 words) answering these questions:
- In what country would you like to work?
- What would you like to do there?
- What strengths, skills, etc. can you bring to your volunteer work?
- What do you want to get from your volunteer work?

More practice 5 Find someone who ▸ Unit 3, p. 66

Talk to people in your class and find at least one person in the class who ...

1 has been to France.
2 doesn't like tomato soup.
3 is wearing interesting socks.
4 was doing something fun at 8 o'clock yesterday evening.
5 is going to watch a football match this evening.
6 did something exciting last weekend.
7 has never seen any of the Harry Potter films.
8 has an unusual role model.
9 made more than 10 euros pocket money last week.

! Don't forget to ask °follow-up questions to find out more.
Examples: When did you go? (1)
What soup do you like? (2)
Who bought you those socks? (3)
...

More challenge 2 Who saw it? What did you see?

▸ Unit 3, p. 66

Your friend is telling you what he did yesterday, but you can't quite hear what he is saying.
Ask questions about the underlined parts.

1 I saw a great film on TV last night. – Sorry, what ...
2 The story really disturbed me. – Sorry, what ...
3 It described the life of a singer. – Sorry, what ...
4 A new band wrote the music for the film. – Sorry, who ...
5 Lots of people I know watched the film. – Sorry, ...
6 Our TV wasn't working, so I °went round to our friends' house to watch it. – Sorry, ...
7 My mum watched it with me. – Sorry, ...
8 She thought it was brilliant. – Sorry, ... think of it?

! Subject and object questions

You can ask questions
about the **subject** (e.g., ***Who*** *saw it? – **I** did.*)
or about the **object** of a sentence (e.g. ***What*** *did you see? – A **film**.*).

If you ask about the subject, you don't use do, ~~does~~ or did.

▸ Language file 13, p. 189

3a Question tags

▸ Unit 3, p. 67

2.12

Listen again to the interview in task 1 and complete these sentences.

1 - Okay. Emma was born in 1990 in Paris.
- In Paris? But she's British, ...?

2 - And the name of her school is interesting for someone who worked on Harry Potter films.
- It wasn't the Hogwarts School, ...?

3 - I think that she's a great actor, ...?
- Yes, definitely.

4 - But she has also found time to go to university.
- What did she study? She didn't study magic, ...?

More practice 6 Missing!

▸ Unit 3, p. 67

An Irish reporter is gathering information about two local teenagers who got lost in the Australian outback while doing work and travel there. She's interviewing Owen Dunn, who runs the work and travel agency in Dublin. Complete her questions with the *passive*.

! If you're not sure which tense to use, check the answer that comes after the question.

1 Reporter When *were you told* that the two were missing? (you, tell)
Dunn We were told about it three days ago. We got a phone call from the park rangers there.
2 Reporter I understand the boys were doing an organized trek. Who ... by? (the trek, organize)
Dunn It was organized by our travel agency – that's why the park rangers contacted us first.
3 Reporter I see. And the boys' parents? ...? (they, contact)
Dunn Yes, they have. We have been in touch with their parents the whole time.
4 Reporter So what ... about the boys at the moment? (know)
Dunn Well, it's clear that they're safe now.
5 Reporter Oh! ...? (they, find)
Dunn Yes, they've been found in the bush and have been taken to a nearby town.
6 Reporter Well, that's good news. When ...? (find) And who found them?
Dunn That was several hours ago. Two Aboriginal guides spotted them.

▸ Language file 14, p. 190

Unit 3

More challenge 3 What are you laughing at?
► Unit 3, p. 67

Make the follow-up questions.

1 The kids are waving to somebody. – Who *are they waving to?*
2 The teacher is cross with somebody. – Who is she ...
3 I'm looking forward to the weekend. – What ...
4 That girl is smiling at someone. – Who ...
5 My friend Tim is afraid of lots of things. – What exactly ...

Questions with prepositions

In English a preposition (*at*, *to*, etc.) which is closely °linked to a question word usually comes at the end of a question.

This is different to German:

What are you laughing at? – Worüber lachst du?

► Language file 15, p. 190

More challenge 4 A trailer
► Unit 3, p. 71

Imagine you plan to make a film of this story. But first you have to make a two minute trailer to advertise it. Work alone or with a partner.

Step 1: The °voice-over

Write a short voice-over text about the story and make it interesting and exciting. Just tell some details of the story – don't tell the whole story.

Here are some example sentences:

This is a film about Cindy – a sixteen-year-old girl from ...
Cindy wants a summer job at ...
But there's a problem because ...
Cindy's answer to the problem is simple ...
But things get complicated for Cindy when ...
This film is exciting ...

Step 2: A scene from the film

Pick your favourite scene in the story. Write a short dialogue for it. Then get some actors to play the scene and give them their lines.

Practise the scene with your actors. You're the director.

Step 3: Making the trailer

Perform your trailer for the class (remember, you have only two minutes). Read your voice-over. Use a dramatic voice. Use music too, if you like. Your actors should act their scene. Tell the audience why they should watch the film.

More practice 7 A checklist
► Unit 3, p. 72

Make a checklist of the most important things to remember for a job interview. Then share your checklists in class.

More help 3 YOUR TASK Who will get the job? ▸ Unit 3, p. 73

Step 1: Look at the advert

Before you answer the questions, take a closer look at the advert.

Restaurant team member
in busy fast-food restaurant

Improve your service and teamwork skills in our restaurant. We're looking for very hard-working, enthusiastic individuals. Part-time or full-time work. Experience not necessary.

The ideal candidate has to:

- be able to work as part of a team
- speak clearly and listen carefully to guests and staff members
- have a professional, energetic and enthusiastic approach

If you like the sound of the job, please send your CV by email.

Teamwork is mentioned a lot in the advert – so be well prepared for a question on teamwork. Show that you like it.

They expect you to be very hard-working and energetic. So tell them that you have lots of energy.

How you speak and listen to others is important. In the interview you need to show how good your communication skills are.

! Don't forget to think of at least one question about the job.

Step 3: Decide who should get the job

Assessors: use your notes to give feedback to the candidates.

1 How did the candidates present themselves?

You could say things like this:
They all had good handshakes.
Timo didn't have great eye contact.
Nina's body language was very good, very positive.
They all spoke clearly. Timo spoke quietly, and Monique spoke quite fast.
...

2 How good / appropriate were their answers?
Did they say enough?

You could say things like this:
They all gave quite good answers, but Timo was very good because ...
Sometimes the answers were a bit short.
...

3 Did they ask questions?

You could say things like this:
They all asked questions.
Monique asked very good questions.
...

Unit 3 Stop! Check! Go!

//● 1 LANGUAGE Driving in Ireland ▸ *Unit 3, p. 77*

Michael (17), a German student in Dublin, is asking his friend Dylan about how to get a learner licence. Complete his sentences with *question tags*.

1 I don't have to take a driving test, ...?
– No, but you have to take a theory test.
2 OK. But then they'll give me a learner licence, ...?
– Well, no. You need to take an eyesight test too.
3 Oh, right. And then I can practise driving on the motorway, ...?
– No, I'm afraid not. Learner drivers aren't allowed on the motorway.
4 Hm. Learner drivers aren't allowed to drive fast either, ...?
– That's right. They can only go 72 kph.
5 But I won't have to have somebody in the car with me, ...?
– Actually, you will – somebody with a full driving licence.
6 Well, what about you? You've already got your full licence, ...?
– No, I haven't yet. I'm still a learner driver.

More help 6 SPEAKING Who has been important to you? ▸ *Unit 3, p. 79*

You need to think of a person who has been an important influence in your life. It could be someone who:

– is always there when you need help
– gave you advice in a difficult situation (What advice? Give examples.)
– is a good example to you (Why?)
– did something special
– has the same interests or hobbies as you
– spends a lot of time with you

Unit 4

More challenge 1 ***-ing*-form (gerund) or *to*-infinitive after verbs** ▸ *Unit 4, p. 83*

FOCUS

1) ***I enjoy playing games.*** ↔ ***I want to buy a new game.***
After some verbs you **only** use an **-*ing*-form** (a **gerund**), e.g. *dislike, enjoy, finish, imagine, miss, practise.*
After others you **only** use *to* + an **infinitive**, e.g. *would like to ..., want to ..., need to ..., hope to ...*

2) ***I like playing games*** ↔ ***I like to play games*** ⇨ ***same meaning***
After some verbs you can use an **-*ing*-form** (a **gerund**) **or** *to* + an **infinitive** and **the meaning is the same**, e.g. *start, begin, continue, like, love, prefer, hate.*

3) ***I stopped using my phone*** ↔ ***I stopped to use my phone*** ⇨ ***different meaning***
After some verbs you can use an **-*ing*-form** (a **gerund**) **or** *to* + an **infinitive**, but **the meaning is different**.

stop doing something (aufhören, etwas zu tun) ↔ *stop to do something (stoppen / anhalten, um etwas anderes zu tun)*

forget doing something (vergessen, dass man früher etwas getan hat) ↔ *forget to do something (vergessen, später etwas zu tun)*

remember doing something (sich daran erinnern, dass man etwas getan hat) ↔ *remember to do something (daran denken, etwas zu tun)*

▸ *Language file 29, p. 201*

a) Complete the sentences with an **-*ing*-form** (a **gerund**) or *to* + an **infinitive**.

1 I remember ... (switch off) my phone last night. I don't understand why it's still on. ↔ I must remember ... (switch off) my phone tonight. If I don't, Mum will be cross.

2 I've stopped ... (send) my friend texts late at night. I need to go to sleep earlier. ↔ I was doing my homework. But I got a text from my friend and I stopped ... (text) her back.

3 I'll never forget ... (play) Angry Birds for the first time. I thought it was brilliant. ↔ I forgot ... (do) my homework because I was playing a brilliant computer game.

b) Complete the text with **-*ing*-form (gerunds)** or ***to*-infinitives**. Sometimes you can use both.

I think I'm a typical screenager. I really enjoy ... (1 use) social media and I like ... (2 video chat) with my friends. My parents want me ... (3 spend) less time in front of a screen. They get very angry when I don't stop ... (4 read) a text when I'm eating with them. I also love ... (5 play) video games. Sometimes I get into trouble because I don't stop ... (6 play) until really late. I also forget ... (7 do) my homework quite often. I'm trying ... (8 be) less °chaotic. But hey! I'm a teenager. I don't always remember ... (9 do) things. It's normal!

Unit 4

More practice 1 SPEAKING Young people together ▸ Unit 4, p. 83

Partner A: Stay on this page.
Partner B: Go to page 106.

a) Look at the photo and think about these questions:
- What's happening?
- Where are the people?
- What are they doing?
- Do they know each other?
- Are they friends?

b) Describe your photo to your partner. Then listen to her or him. Compare your photos.

c) Talk about these questions.
- How do you communicate with your friends?
- What kind of things do you and your friends do together? ▸ Skills file 10, p. 179

More challenge 2 Digital habits in your peer group ▸ Unit 4, p. 83

Write a paragraph (about 150–180 words) about the digital habits of the teens that you know. These questions can help you:
- Do they prefer to use the internet for news or for school work or just for fun?
- Do they like to surf the net? If so, why?
- Do they like to play games? If so, what kind of games?
- Do they use social media and °messaging a lot? Explain.

More practice 2 What profile pictures say ▸ Unit 4, p. 84

How much do you think profile pictures tell us about a person? Give examples. These words and phrases can help you:

I'm not sure if I think that	profile pictures tell us a lot about a person.

Perhaps a profile picture can tell us that a person	would like to be … is …

artistic • boring • careful • clever • cool • crazy • different • easy-going • energetic • exciting • friendly • fun • independent • interesting • likeable • normal • old-fashioned • popular • romantic • shy • silly • sporty • strange

More practice 3 More on the text ▸ Unit 4, p. 85

a) Which is the most likely title for the written discussion on page 85? Explain your choice.

1 What are selfies? 2 Selfies: Do you love them or hate them?

3 Why have selfies become popular recently?

b) Do you agree with the writer's conclusion about selfies? Why (not)?

You can use one or more of these reasons for your answer:

I think	it's fun to take selfies. it's normal. Everybody takes selfies. a selfie is a nice way to remember a time when you felt good. selfies are boring – who wants to see pictures of other people? people only take selfies because they want to look good or cool.

More help 4 WRITING For and against tattoos ▸ Unit 4, p. 85

Collect ideas: Choose from these arguments for and against tattoos or collect your own ideas.

For

- They're very trendy.
- All my friends have them.
- Lots of celebrities have them.
- They're artistic.

...

Against

- They're very expensive.
- Once you have one, it's hard to get rid of it.
- You can get an °infection.
- Maybe it will be difficult to get a job. °Employers might not like it.

...

Make a plan:

Paragraph 1: introduction – describe the general topic

Today tattoos are becoming more popular.
I don't have any tattoos, but ...
None / Some of my friends have tattoos.
Lots of footballers have tattoos. For example ...
So is this a good idea or not?

Paragraph 2: arguments for (or against)
Are you're against tattoos? Then start with arguments for in this paragraph.
Are you're for tattoos? Then start with arguments against.

Paragraph 3: arguments against (or for)

Firstly / Secondly ...
For example,
On the other hand ...
In other words
Maybe ...
Don't forget that ...
Lots of people say that ....
I'm not so sure about that.

Paragraph 4: conclusion – give your personal opinion

I (definitely) think ...
In my opinion ...
To sum up ...
... tattoos are / aren't a good idea.

Unit 4

More practice 4 Working with the text ▸ Unit 4, p. 87

Finish these sentences with ideas from the text.

1 If teenagers become ad-savvy, ...
2 The advertising industry is interested in teens because ... (two reasons)
3 Ads use special °strategies, for example by showing perfect, beautiful people, or ... (three more examples)
4 The advertising industry is interested in finding out about ...
5 Popular vloggers are interesting for the ad companies because ...

More practice 5 Your own advert ▸ Unit 4, p. 87

If you want to understand how adverts work, you need to make one yourself.
Work in pairs.
°Invent a product (make-up, food, drink, clothes ... anything you like).
Think of a good name for your product.
Think of a slogan for your advert.
Find or make a good jingle.
Then perform the advert for the class.
Ask the class if they can identify your tricks.

More challenge 3 WRITING Your opinion ▸ Unit 4, p. 87

"Teenagers are influenced by all kinds of ads."
Do you agree or disagree with this statement?
Explain your opinion and give examples.

! Write about things like this:
- ads that you and your friends like (and why)
- where you see these ads
- the products that you and your friends buy
- if you are influenced by ads (and how)

More practice 6 A different situation ▸ Unit 4, p. 88

How could things have been different? Match the sentence parts.

1 If Leah had sent emails, only thirty people would have ...
2 If only thirty guests had come, Leah wouldn't have ...
3 If Leah's dad had stayed, he would have ...
4 If Leah's dad had taken his phone, Leah would have ...
5 If Leah had phoned her dad, he would have ...
6 If the police hadn't arrived so quickly, there could have ...

A come home °straight away.
B had any problems.
C phoned him.
D come to the party.
E been more damage.
F stopped the gate-crashers.

//● 3a Oh dear, what a shame!

▸ Unit 4, p. 89

Complete the sentences with the correct form of the verbs in brackets.

1 I was in trouble because I was late. If I … (send) mum a text message to let her know, she … (not be) cross.
2 My test results weren't great. If I … (work) harder, I … (get) better marks.
3 I couldn't do my homework because I forgot my book. If I … (remember) my book, I … (do) my homework.
4 I didn't tell my friend that I was going out. If I … (know) that she wanted to come, I … (phone) her.
5 I don't have enough money for a phone. If I … (work) in the holidays, I … (earn) some.

More practice 7 What would you have done?

▸ Unit 4, p. 89

Read the sentences. Then decide what you would have done.

1 **Ben** Leah didn't invite me to her party, but I went. What would you have done?
You …
2 **Ben** For my birthday my parents said I could have a party or I could go to a theme park. I chose the party.
You …
3 **Ben** My friend and I wanted to go to the cinema. I waited at the cinema but he didn't come, so I went home.
You …
4 **Ben** I was angry because my friend bought the same shirt as me.
You …

More practice 8 An email to Scott

▸ Unit 4, p. 94

Fill in suitable words from the box on the right.

Hi Scott

I was very interested to read … (1) your adventures in 2030. I love stories about the future, but I think that your world is … (2) and I'm very … (3) that I don't live in it. I was very sad when I read that your parents had … (4) of a killer virus. I really liked the … (5), Tammy and Tommy – they're so sweet! But I thought that Shark and his … (6) were horrible. You were … (7) when you helped Tammy and Tommy. And it was nice when the twins gave you some … (8) I thought that it was very exciting when you … (9) over the roofs of the city. I really hope that you … (10) the Virtual Kombat game and find a better life. But I think that your story shows that people can be addicted to … (11), and that's bad.

Best wishes … (12) a big fan

Kirsty

(1) over / about / on / to
(2) scary / fun / comfortable / cold
(3) sad / hopeful / angry / happy
(4) lived / had / died / saw
(5) boys / girls / teens / twins
(6) teens / gang / kids / family
(7) brave / frightened / stupid / quiet
(8) money / drink / meat / bread
(9) drove / rode / escaped / flew
(10) get / win / lose / play
(11) fighting / food / games / fun
(12) to / for / at / from

Unit 4

More challenge 4 WRITING **What happens next** ▸ *Unit 4, p. 94*

Write the next chapter of the story (max 180 words).

More challenge 5 **Writing a book review** ▸ *Unit 4, p. 95*

Choose your favourite book or a book that you have recently read and write a review about it.

> Things you should include in your review:
> - a description of what the book is about (if it's a story, don't °give too much away!)
> - some thoughts about the plot and the characters (e.g. are they strong or weak?)
> - your general opinion of the book

▸ *Skills file 9.8, p. 178*

More practice 9 **Banning social media at night** ▸ *Unit 4, p. 96*

What do Marek, Amy, Tim and Grace think about this idea?
Who agrees? Who disagrees?
Who isn't sure?

More help **3** NOW YOU **Listen and speak** ▸ *Unit 4, p. 97*

Step 1: Prepare your arguments

a) Each group prepares a list of arguments. You will be either for the statement, or against it, or not sure. Choose from this list or use your own ideas:

- If you play video games, your reactions are very fast.
- Playing video games is unhealthy because you sit for so long.
- Video games are often violent. / aren't always violent.
- Playing video games is a good way to get rid of stress.
- When people start playing games, they can't stop.
- Gamers can / can't tell the difference between the game and the real world.
- When you play video games, time °goes by very quickly.

b) Think of examples and reasons to support your arguments like this:

- People often play alone and this is a bad thing because ... (Give a reason.)
- It's true that people sometimes play alone, but on the other hand they also play with other people. (Give an example.)
- Video games are often violent. / aren't always violent. For example ... (List games that you know that are or aren't violent.) In my opinion, ... (Say why you think games are violent or not violent.)

Step 2: Take part in a discussion ▸ Unit 4, p. 97

The observers need a copy of this form. They should make notes.

	very good	OK	needs work
Repeat what the last speaker said.			
Say if you agree or disagree.			
Make your point cleary.			
Give reasons and examples.			
Speak respectfully.			

Unit 4 Stop! Check! Go!

//● 2a LANGUAGE If I had known … ▸ Unit 4, p. 101

Complete the conditional sentences in 1–4 with the right verb forms.

1 I got a PC virus after downloading a game from the internet. If the media buddies … (not help) me to get rid of it, my parents … (take) away my PC.

2 A media buddy told me to change the settings of the app so that only some people can see my posts.
If I … (not do) that, my parents … (see) all my conversations with my friends.

3 I found a website with lots of cool songs. I … (be) in trouble for using an illegal music site if I … (not speak) to a media buddy first.

4 I'm a fool! I bought a new gadget last week because of a cool ad. I … (get) something much better for the same price if I … (speak) to the media buddies.

Wordbank 1: At the doctor's

▸ Unit 1, p. 13

What the doctor says / asks

What's the problem?

Where does it hurt?

What are your symptoms?

How long have you been feeling like this?

What have you eaten today?

Are you on any sort of medication?
Nehmen Sie Medikamente?

Do you have any allergies?
Haben Sie Allergien?

Are you diabetic? / Do you have diabetes?
Sind Sie Diabetiker/in?

Let me take your blood pressure / temperature / pulse.
Lassen Sie mich Ihren Blutdruck / Ihre Temperatur / Ihren Puls messen.

Could you roll up your sleeve?
Könnten Sie den Ärmel hochkrempeln?

Your blood pressure is low / normal / high.
Ihr Blutdruck ist hoch / normal / niedrig.

Open your mouth, please.
Öffnen Sie bitte den Mund.

Show me your tongue, please.
Zeigen Sie mir bitte Ihre Zunge.

Cough, please.
Bitte husten.

You're going to need a few stitches.
Sie müssen genäht werden.

I'll desinfect and dress the wound.
Ich werde die Wunde desinfizieren und verbinden.

I'm going to give you an injection.
Ich werde Ihnen eine Spritze geben.

I'm going to prescribe you some antibiotics.
Ich werde Ihnen ein Antibiotikum verschreiben.

Take two of these pills three times a day.
Nehmen Sie zwei von diesen Tabletten dreimal täglich.

You need an X-ray.
Ich möchte Sie zum Röntgen schicken.

You need to be vaccinated against tetanus.
Sie brauchen eine Tetanusimpfung.

What you say

I've got a cold / cough / temperature.
Ich habe eine Erkältung / Husten / Fieber.

I've got a sore throat.
Ich habe Halsschmerzen.

I've got a headache / stomach ache.
Ich habe Kopfschmerzen / Magenschmerzen.

My arm / back / hand / knee / leg / neck / shoulder hurts. I can't move it.
Ich habe Schmerzen im Arm / Rücken / an der Hand / am Knie / am Fuß / im Nacken / an der Schulter. Ich kann ihn / es / sie nicht bewegen.

I feel sick. Mir ist schlecht.

I feel dizzy. Mir ist schwindlig.

My joints are aching. Ich habe Gliederschmerzen.

I've got diarrhea. Ich habe Durchfall.

I'm constipated. Ich habe Verstopfung.

I've hurt my foot / wrist / arm / ...
Ich habe mich am Fuß / Handgelenk / Arm / ... verletzt.

I've got a swollen foot / arm ...
Mein Fuß / Arm / ... ist geschwollen.

I've sprained my ankle.
Ich habe mir den Knöchel verstaucht.

I'm in a lot of pain.
Ich habe starke Schmerzen.

I think I've pulled a muscle.
Ich glaube, ich habe eine Muskelzerrung.

I can't breathe (properly).
Ich kann nicht (richtig) atmen.

I'm allergic to some antibiotics.
Ich bin allergisch gegen Antibiotika.

▸ INKL p. 103

Wordbank 2: Strengths and weaknesses

▸ Unit 3, p. 59

Strengths

caring	warmherzig, liebevoll	**independent**	unabhängig
confident	selbstbewusst	**motivated**	motiviert
commited	engagiert	**organized**	organisiert, strukturiert
creative	kreativ	**patient**	geduldig
disciplined	diszipliniert	**practical**	geschickt
easy-going	gelassen	**polite**	höflich
energetic	aktiv	**punctual**	pünktlich
flexible	flexibel	**quiet**	ruhig
friendly	freundlich	**reliable**	verlässlich
hard-working	fleißig, tüchtig	**responsible**	verantwortungsbewusst
helpful	hilfsbereit	**sporty**	sportlich
honest	ehrlich, integer	**tidy**	ordentlich

Weaknesses

aggressive	aggressiv	**messy**	unordentlich
dishonest	unehrlich	**selfish**	egoistisch
disorganized	unstrukturiert	**shy**	schüchtern
impolite	unhöflich	**(very) slow**	(sehr) langsam
impatient	ungeduldig	**stubborn**	stur
insecure	unsicher	**undisciplined**	undiszipliniert
lazy	faul	**unfriendly**	unfreundlich

Wordbank 3: Jobs and job titles

► Unit 3, p. 61

Management/Commerce Verwaltung/Handel

administrative assistant Verwaltungsangestellte/r
assistant tax inspector Steuerfachangestelle/r
assistant bank manager Bankkaufmann/-frau
sales representative Industriekaufmann/-frau
insurance sales representative Versicherungskaufmann/-frau
legal assistant Rechtsanwaltsfachangestellte/r
assistant logistics manager Speditionskaufmann/-frau
sales representative in wholesale and foreign trade Kaufmann/-frau im Groß- und Außenhandel
office management assistant Bürokaufmann/-frau
retail assistant manager Kaufmann/-frau im Einzelhandel
sales assistant Verkäufer/in
travel agent Reiseverkehrskaufmann/-frau

Health and care Gesundheit und Pflege

animal keeper Tierpfleger/in
dentist's assistant Zahnarzthelfer/in
doctor's assistant Arzthelfer/in
geriatric assistant/care worker Altenpfleger/in
nursery teacher Erzieher/in
midwife Hebamme/Entbindungspfleger
nutritionist Ernährungsberater/in
optical technician Feinoptiker/in
orthopaedic technician Orthopädietechniker/in
paramedic Sanitäter/in
physiotherapist Physiotherapeut/in, Krankengymnast/in
nurse Krankenpfleger/-schwester

Craft Handwerk

baker Bäcker/in
bricklayer Maurer/in
carpenter Zimmerer, Zimmerin
electrician Elektriker/in
florist Florist/in
joiner Schreiner/in
mechanic Mechaniker/in
metalworker Schlosser/in
painter Maler/in

Service Dienstleistung

beautician Kosmetiker/in
cook Koch, Köchin
assistant hotel manager Hotelkaufmann/-frau
lorry driver LKW-Fahrer/in
postman/-woman Briefträger/in
waiter/waitress Kellner/in

Technology Technik

automotive engineer Fahrzeugtechnik-Ingenieur/in
chemical engineer Chemieingenieur/in
design engineer Konstrukteur/in
electrical engineer Elektroingenieur/in
mechanical engineer Maschinenbauingenieur/in
mechatronics technician Mechatroniker/in
motor vehicle technician Kfz-Mechaniker/in
telecom(munication)s engineer Fernmeldeingenieur/in

IT and Media IT und Medien

digital web analyst Webanalyst/in
IT technician IT-Techniker/in
media designer Mediendesigner/in
media technician Medientechniker/in
programmer Programmierer/in
software engineer Software-Entwickler/in

Wordbank 4: Describing jobs ▸ Unit 3, p. 61

I'd like to work …

- with animals
- in a team
- outside
- abroad
- in a hotel / restaurant
- in an office
- in a hospital / surgery
- in a factory
- in a laboratory
- with food
- with media
- with my hands
- with computers
- with wood / metal / clothes / …
- with people / children

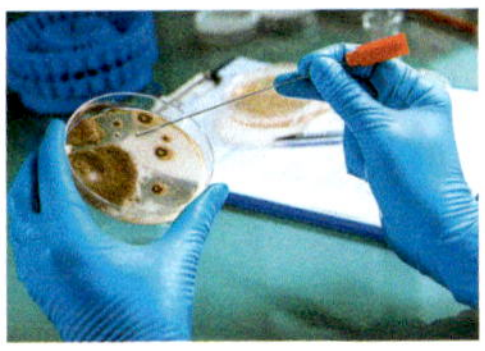

Wordbank 5: In a job interview ▸ Unit 3, p. 73

Why you want the job

I am really interested in this job because I want to gain experience in this area.	Ich bin sehr interessiert an dieser Stelle, weil ich in diesem Bereich Erfahrung sammeln möchte.
I have always wanted to work in this field.	Ich wollte schon immer in diesem Gebiet arbeiten.
I'm interested in …	Ich interessiere mich für …
I would like to develop my … skills.	Ich würde gerne meine …-Fähigkeiten weiterentwickeln.
I really enjoy working in a team.	Ich arbeite sehr gerne im Team.
I think this is a job I could do well, because …	Ich glaube, ich wäre gut in diesem Beruf, weil …

Experience

I have some experience of office work.	Ich habe etwas Erfahrung mit Büroarbeit.
I have already worked at / in …	Ich habe schon in … gearbeitet.
I have helped out in …	Ich habe in … ausgeholfen.
I have done work experience in …	Ich habe ein Praktikum in … gemacht.
I can use standard software.	Ich kann mit Standardsoftware umgehen.

▸ KV 1 ▸ INKL pp. 78–81

TF 1 Oz: Facts for visitors

Australia – an infographic

NICKNAMES

Australia is called 'Oz' or 'Aus', or the land 'down under' because it is 'under' the equator[1].

CURRENCY

Australian dollar (AUD)

THE AUSTRALIAN NATIONAL FLAG

The British flag in the top left-hand corner represents Britain's role in the history of Australia. The Southern Cross, on the right, is a group of stars that Australians can see 'down under', but which can't be seen in Europe.

SIZE

7,700,000 km²
▸ Australia is 21 times bigger than Germany (357,000 km²).

POPULATION

23,600,000
▸ Germany has 3.4 times more people (81,000,000).

GOVERNMENT

Federal parliamentary constitutional monarchy

CLIMATE

The northern third of the country is tropical, with two seasons: a hot wet summer and a warm dry winter. Most of Australia is warm or hot all year, but the coldest winter temperatures are in the south and the warmest winter temperatures are in the north. Most of the country gets only 100 to 500 mm of rain per year and 40 % of Australia is desert.

CAPITAL CITY

Sydney and Melbourne both applied to be the capital, but in the end Canberra was chosen.

LANGUAGE

English

WHERE PEOPLE LIVE

89 % of the population lives in towns or cities. The five largest cities are: Sydney, Melbourne, Brisbane, Perth and Adelaide.
More than 85 % of the population lives near the coast.

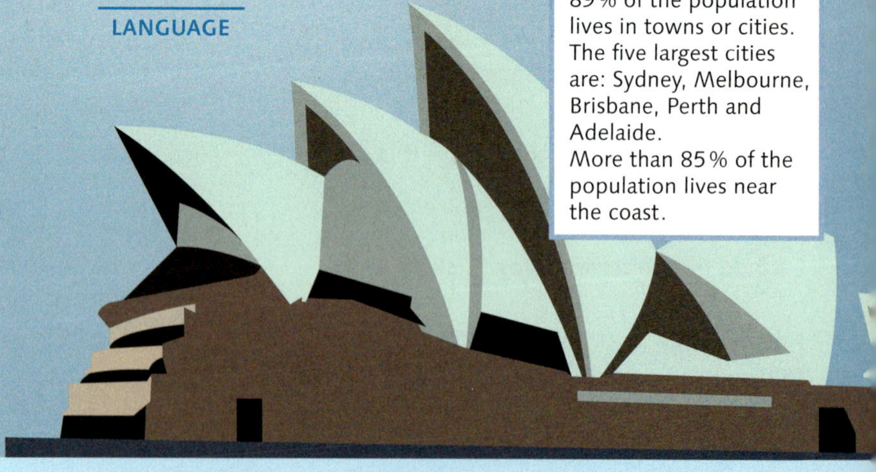

WHEN TO TRAVEL

Most visitors arrive in summer (December to February), when the weather is sunny and warm in places like Sydney, Melbourne and Brisbane. But at that time it's hot and wet in the north, so it's best to visit this area in winter (June to August).

1 Find some more facts about Australia (e.g. online).
Take notes and present them to a partner.
Example: Did you know that … Australia has over 10,000 beaches / you drive on the left in Oz / the seasons in Oz are opposite to those of the northern hemisphere[2] (e.g. Europe) / …?

[1] equator [ɪˈkweɪtə] *Äquator* [2] hemisphere [ˈhemɪsfɪə] *Halbkugel*

▸ KV 4 ▸ INKL pp. 78–81

Oz highlights for visitors

1 **The outback:** The huge deserts in the centre and the west are full of special places, including the big rock Uluru. It's a great place to learn about Aboriginal culture.
2 **Sydney:** Must-sees are Sydney Harbour and Bondi Beach.
3 **Cairns:** From here you can visit the Great Barrier Reef and the tropical rainforests of the north.
4 **Tasmania:** This island is famous for wild landscapes, beautiful waterfalls and clean air.
5 **Australian wildlife:** See animals, birds and plants that aren't found anywhere else in the world, like the platypus[3], the wombat, the koala and the kookaburra[4].

2 Match the pictures A–E to the texts 1–5.

Indigenous Australians and the Stolen Generations

There are two groups of Indigenous Australians: the Torres Strait Islanders from the islands to the north of Queensland, and Aboriginal people from mainland Australia and Tasmania.

No one's land[5]?

When the British arrived at the end of the 18th century, they saw that people were already living there, but they also saw that there were no fences. They said that the land was *terra nullius*, 'no one's land', and they took it for themselves. Indigenous people didn't get their land rights[6] back until 1992, when it was decided that the idea of *terra nullius* was wrong and they were the traditional owners of Australia.

The Founding of Australia, 1788

The Stolen Generations

From 1910 to 1970 at least 100,000 children were forcibly[7] taken from their Aboriginal mothers to be brought up[8] by white foster[9] families or in institutions. They weren't allowed to see their families or speak their own languages. These children are called the Stolen Generations. The film *Rabbit-proof fence* is based on the true story of some girls who were 'stolen' in this way.

Sorry

Finally, in 2008, the Australian government officially said 'sorry' to Indigenous Australians. Many of them were very emotional[10] when Prime Minister Kevin Rudd made his speech because they had waited for so long to hear the word 'sorry'.

Audience at Kevin Rudd's 'Sorry Speech', 13th February 2008

3 Explain the terms 'terra nullius' and 'Stolen Generations' in German.

[3] platypus ['plætɪpəs] *Schnabeltier* [4] kookaburra ['kʊkəbʌrə] *Kookaburra, Lachender Hans (= spezieller australischer Vogel)*
[5] no one's land ['nəʊwʌnz lænd] *Niemandsland* [6] land rights [lænd raɪts] *Bodenrecht* [7] forcibly ['fɔːsəbli] *gewaltsam*
[8] bring up [brɪŋ 'ʌp] *großziehen* [9] foster ['fɒstə] *Pflege-* [10] emotional [ɪ'məʊʃənl] *bewegt, gerührt*

▸ KV 37 ▸ INKL pp. 82–85

TF 2 Waiting for something to happen (from the story *Riot* by David Fermer)

3.06

In the summer of 2011, North London became the scene of street protests and violence after the controversial police shooting of a man in Tottenham. ***Riot*** *is the story of Danny, a teenage boy from Tottenham, who gets caught up in the events.*

Read the beginning of the story and do the task at the end of each part.

Saturday 4 pm

So this is it? This is my life? Hanging out with my mates on a Saturday afternoon with nothing to do but watch people walking up and down Tottenham High Road? They're all out shopping, buying nice things for themselves and their family. All I have in my pocket is £1.50. That's not even enough to buy a Mars bar and a Coke. I can't even afford[1] a kebab. Is this what I came into the world for?

"Hey, lads, see that bird over there?" says Kyle. Kyle is the oldest in our gang. He calls all girls 'birds', like they've got wings and can fly. We're not really a gang. Not like The Smalley Boys or the BWF gang, the guys who do business around here, the ones who deal the drugs. We're just friends who hang out together. We all live on the Broadwater Farm Estate up the road. We've known each other forever.

Kyle points at this Muslim girl who's walking past us. She's done up all nice and pretty, with big long eyelashes[2] and lots of make-up. She's wearing a blue headscarf[3] which sparkles[4] in the afternoon sun.

"I bet she's hot under there," Kyle says with a grin, and we all know he's not talking about her body temperature. "Hey there, beautiful!" he calls out, jumping down from the wall and going over to the girl with a big smile on his face. "How about a little kiss for Uncle Kyle?" The girl takes one look at him and walks off, as if Kyle has got some horrible disease. Kyle just laughs. "What's the problem, love? Aren't I good-looking enough for you?" Kyle can be a real idiot sometimes.

That's what we've been doing all afternoon. Watching people. Talking about people. Laughing at people. That's all. There is nothing else to do. We can't go shopping, we can't go to the cinema, we can't even hang out at McDonald's. No cash, no splash. All we can do is just sit here on this wall, watching people.

"Look at that old man over there. He walks like he just did it in his trousers." Or: "Check out the bird at the cash machine. How much do you think she's taking out? 100? 200? Maybe we should just take her money?"

[1] afford [ə'fɔːd] *sich etwas leisten (können)* [2] eyelash ['aɪlæʃ] *Wimper* [3] headscarf ['hedskɑːf] *Kopftuch* [4] sparkle (v) ['spɑːkl] *funkeln, glitzern*

We don't, of course. We might look like scum[5] to some people, but we're not. We don't steal. We don't do drugs. We don't mess with the law. Drugs are too expensive anyway. No cash, no hash either. Besides, if you get into drugs around here, you're in serious trouble. The best thing that can happen to you is to end up in prison and get clean. It's downhill all the way.

Kyle likes to think he's a real bad guy. Mr Dangerous. Like he's some Mafia boss or something. But he's not. It's just a role he likes to play. I can understand him in a way. It's all he's got. His fantasies, his role play. He hasn't got anything else. He's seventeen and unemployed. At least Todd and Reeko are on a job programme. They're both sixteen, a year older than me. They've finished school. None of them have got any qualifications. Zee too. He's seventeen as well. He works in his dad's shop. His parents are from Pakistan, but that's OK. I'm the only one who's still at school. Everyone calls me 'The Professor'. They say they'll kill me if I don't get a GCSE[6]. Hang me naked from Big Ben if I fail[7]. It's just a joke, of course. I'm not making any promises. You never know what's going to happen around here next.

a) How do Danny and his friends spend their afternoons?

b) Explain why they do what they do.

Saturday 5.30 pm

3.07

Time goes slowly when you don't have anything to do. It's a waiting game. Killing time. Waiting for something to happen. Waiting for the next laugh.

Zee has a cool sense of humour. I get along with him really well, but he's not around much these days. Busy, he says. When he's around, we always have a laugh together.

I get along with Reeko too. Most of the time. Todd's not the sharpest knife in the drawer, if you know what I mean. He and Reeko always do whatever Kyle says. They think Kyle is God. Kyle thinks so too. He's always talking about money. How much things cost, how much people earn, how the banks are corrupt, how one day he's going to make a million. If you heard him talk, you'd think he already owned half of North London. He thinks he's the smartest person in the world.

We're just about to go home when we see this crowd coming down the street. About a hundred people walking towards us really slowly. It looks kind of beautiful, like a funeral procession or some ritual, like the ones you see on TV from India. Some of the people are carrying banners, others are holding cardboard[8] signs.

They're waving their banners and shouting. As they get closer I can read the slogans:

JUSTICE FOR MARK DUGGAN.
WE WANT THE TRUTH.
WHO SHOT MARK DUGGAN?

I didn't know Mark Duggan personally, but I knew of him. He grew up on the Broadwater Farm Estate too. He used to be in the Star Gang, but he quit[9] a while back. So people say. But you can't really quit a gang, can you? Once you're in, you're in for life. You can't just leave. It's not like working at the Post Office. "Sorry, sir, I've found another job. I'd like to hand in my notice if that's OK. Can you give me a reference, please?"

It doesn't work like that.

Anyway, the police killed Mark Duggan on Thursday. They shot him dead. They were following him in connection with a killing at a nightclub. Duggan's best friend got stabbed[10]. The police thought Duggan was going to take revenge. That's why they were following him. To prevent[11] more bloodshed[12]. Or so they say. They stopped Duggan in his car. They said he was carrying a gun and that he shot first. That's why they killed him. No one really knows the truth. Mark's family and friends say Mark would never have been carrying a gun. He wasn't a criminal. Not any more.

---

[5] scum [skʌm] (Schimpfwort) *Abschaum, Dreck* [6] GCSE [dʒiː siː es ˈiː] = General Certificate of Secondary Education *Schulabschluss im britischen Schulsystem* [7] fail [feɪl] *scheitern; hier: durch die Prüfung fallen* [8] cardboard [ˈkɑːdbɔːd] *Karton, Pappe* [9] quit [kwɪt] *verlassen, kündigen* [10] stab [stæb] *niederstechen, erstechen* [11] prevent [prɪˈvent] *verhindern* [12] bloodshed [ˈblʌdʃed] *Blutvergießen*

▸ KV 37 ▸ INKL pp. 82–85

As the protesters pass by, Kyle jumps down from the wall. "Come on, lads. Let's join them," he says.

Todd looks at him like he has no idea what he is talking about.

"What for?" he asks.

"You know ... because ..." At first Kyle can't think of a good reason, then he has a moment of inspiration.

"Because the pigs killed our bro'," he says, gritting his teeth[1]. That's a good enough explanation to get Reeko down from the wall. He punches[2] the air and says, "Yo. We want answers, man."

"That's right," says Kyle, waving a fist. "Or we'll teach them a lesson they won't forget!"

c) What does Danny criticize about Kyle?

d) Describe who Mark Duggan is and what happened to him.

e) Why does Kyle want to join the protesters?

Saturday 5.45 pm

3.08

The crowd stops in front of Tottenham police station. A couple of policemen come out and talk to Mark Duggan's family. The people are waving their banners, chanting, "We want answers! We want answers!" The police listen to what the family has to say. I can see them nodding and holding up their hands, like they're trying to tell the family to be patient, but to me it looks like they're just fobbing them off[3]. They're probably not the right people to be talking to anyway. They're just ordinary coppers[4]. Duggan's family needs to talk to the big boys. The boss.

After a minute or two, the policemen go back into the station while about ten other police officers take up position in front of the main entrance. They stand in a line at the top of the steps, making sure the crowd doesn't try to get into the building.

"What now?" Todd asks.

"Now we wait," Kyle says.

"Wait?" Todd looks confused[5]. "What for?"

Kyle doesn't answer. He doesn't need to. Everyone knows that sooner or later something is going to happen here. It's only a question of time.

That is, everyone knows but Todd.

Zee sees someone he knows in the crowd. Some Asian fellas. He goes over to them. I stay with the others and think about my geography project. I have to hand it in at the end of the summer holidays. I haven't even started yet. I've been putting it off for weeks. If I don't start soon, I'll never finish it in time.

I went to the library yesterday to get some books. I've never been to a library before.

---

[1] grit (one's teeth) [grɪt] *die Zähne zusammenbeißen* [2] punch [pʌntʃ] *mit der Faust schlagen* [3] fob sb. off [fɒb] *abfertigen, abspeisen* [4] copper (*infml*) ['kɒpə] *Bulle, Polyp* [5] confused [kən'fju:zd] *verwirrt*

They let me become a member. For free. The woman there said I could take out eight books at a time. I took out eight books on earthquakes. My bag was so heavy, my shoulder hurt when I got home. I started reading them last night.

I like geography a lot. It's my favourite subject. I like reading about all the layers[6] of the earth, and the heat at the centre of the planet, and the way mountains were formed by tectonic plates pushing the ground together. The changing shapes[7] of rivers over the centuries. The earth is in a permanent state of transformation, even though we can't see it. In a thousand years we probably won't even recognise the world at all.

I'd rather be at home now, reading about earthquakes, but I can't say that. Kyle would just call me a wuss[8]. That's what I don't understand about Kyle. He tells me I should get my qualifications at school, but he doesn't think I need to do anything for it. Like something can come of nothing. But it can't. Nothing comes of nothing, everybody knows that. Maybe that's why Kyle hasn't got anywhere himself.

I try to think of an excuse to go home. It's times like this I wish I had a little sister or a baby brother who I have to look after, but I don't. I'm on my own. I could say I have to look after my mum, but I'm always saying that. Most of the time it's true.

Before I can think of a good excuse to leave, I see a familiar face in the crowd: Riya, a girl from my school. Riya is Asian, like Zee, except her family is from India, not Pakistan. Riya is amazing. She's the most beautiful girl in the world. She has this amazing skin that looks like silk. It really makes you want to touch it. Her eyes are black stones. They're so deep, you could drown in them. When I see those eyes of hers, I just think 'wow'. She's wearing tight jeans and a T-shirt. She has an amazing body. Unlike Zee with his friends, I don't go over to Riya and start talking to her. Riya goes to my school, but we're not friends. We're not even in the same class. She's in Year 10, like me, in a parallel class. She probably doesn't even know who I am. I've never even talked to her. Riya is smart. She's going to go to university one day. A lot of the Asian girls in my school are smart. They work hard. They're ambitious[9]. They want to do something with their lives, become doctors or go to the City and make lots of money on the stock exchange[10]. Riya will make it too. She has success written all over her.

I guess that's why I've never spoken to her before. What would Riya want with a guy like me? She's ten times smarter than I am. She's in completely another league. Plus she's Asian. Not that I have a problem with that. I don't. But her family probably wouldn't want her to go out with a guy like me. Besides, a girl like Riya wouldn't want a boyfriend like me. She doesn't want a loser.

f) Describe what happens when the protesters arrive at the police station.

g) Where would Danny rather be and why?

h) Who is Riya? Why doesn't Danny talk to her?

Saturday 8.20 pm

3.09

I stay at the demo longer than I planned. I just can't leave. Not because of the protest. And not because of Kyle, who's going on about police incompetence and institutional racism. I stay because of Riya. I can't take my eyes off her. I keep looking at her from the side, but she doesn't see me. Every time I look at her, I feel a warm glow[11] in my stomach, a tingling[12] like the bubbles of a fizzy drink. The tingling goes right through my body, to every fingertip and down to my toes. My feet almost lift off the ground. I feel like I'm floating[13].

I've just decided to go home when a group of

[6] layers (of the earth) ['leɪə] *(Erd-)Schichten* [7] shape [ʃeɪp] *Form* [8] wuss (sl) [wʊs] *(Schimpfwort) Waschlappen*
[9] ambitious [æm'bɪʃəs] *ehrgeizig* [10] stock exchange [stɒk ɪks'tʃeɪndʒ] *Börse* [11] glow [gləʊ] *Strahlen, Glühen*
[12] tingling ['tɪŋglɪŋ] *Kribbeln* [13] float [fləʊt] *schweben*

people at the front of the crowd starts shouting. A girl throws a leaflet[1] at one of the policemen at the main entrance. She can't be much older than me. All of a sudden three or four police officers spring into action. They pull out their batons[2] and jump on the girl. They beat her to the ground. The crowd surges[3] forward to protect her. People push and shove me in the back. There's no way out. Even if I wanted to leave, I couldn't. I'm pushed forward as if the ground under my feet is moving. Everyone is shouting and waving their fists and telling the police to leave the girl alone. Then all hell breaks loose. Someone picks up a stone. They hurl[4] it through the air and it hits one of the policemen in the face. Blood explodes from his eyebrow and he goes straight to the ground. The coppers around him look really shocked. They freeze and stare at him like they've never seen blood before. They wake up after a second and help the man to his feet. The girl is still lying on the ground, knees tucked up[5] under her chin like an unborn baby. The police retreat[6] up the steps, carrying their wounded colleague, regrouping. They look scared. They should be.
A couple of people start kicking down an old wall in front of the station. They loosen a couple of bricks[7] and throw them at the police officers. All of a sudden dozens of objects start showering down on the men in uniform. They escape into the building. I look back over my shoulder. About ten or twelve guys are running down the High Road with petrol cans and rags[8] in their hands. Their hoods are up, scarves over their faces. They look like they mean business. I look for Riya, but I can't see her anywhere. The police come out of the building again, more of them this time, armed[9] with riot shields[10] and batons. They look like they mean business too. Some people in the crowd move away from the station. Others start to move forward, ready to fight. Next to me Kyle is throwing stones at the police shouting, "Pigs die! Pigs die!" I look again for Riya, but she's nowhere to be seen.
"Let's get out of here," I say to Kyle, grabbing him by the arm and stopping him from throwing the next stone.
"What for?" Kyle says. He breaks free of my grasp[11] and hurls his stone at the police. "Die, pigs!"
"This is bad, Kyle. Really bad."
"The pigs are bad."
"Yeah, I know, but this is worse." I can feel my heart beating in my throat.
"You wuss," says Kyle.
Typical. Sometimes it's scary how predictable[12] Kyle is. Next to him Todd is going crazy. He's throwing stones like a human howitzer[13].

---

[1] leaflet ['li:flət] *Flugblatt, Broschüre* [2] baton ['bætɒn] *Schlagstock* [3] surge [sɜ:dʒ] *drängen* [4] hurl [hɜ:l] *schleudern, werfen*
[5] tuck [tʌk]: knees tucked up under the chin *(die Knie bis unters Kinn) angezogen* [6] retreat (v) [rɪ'tri:t] *zurückweichen*
[7] brick [brɪk] *Ziegelstein* [8] rag [ræg] *Stofffetzen, Lumpen* [9] armed [ɑ:md] *bewaffnet* [10] riot shield ['raɪət ʃi:ld] *Schutzschild*
[11] grasp (n) [grɑ:sp] *Griff* [12] predictable [prɪ'dɪktəbl] *voraussagbar, berechenbar* [13] howitzer ['haʊɪtsə] *Haubitze*

▸ KV 37 ▸ INKL pp. 82–85

His face is a deep shade of red. The spit is dripping from his mouth. Reeko has run out of ammunition. It's not as if the streets of London are filled with stones. We're not in Gaza here. Reeko looks around, but he can't find any more stones, so he just pulls off one of his shoes and throws it at the police.
"Scum!"
I see Zee pushing his way through the crowd towards us. His T-shirt is torn and soaked in sweat. His eyes are shining.
"You all right, lads?" he asks us.
"Couldn't be better," says Kyle with a smile.
"I'm going to go home and get changed into something more comfortable," Zee explains, pointing at his torn T-shirt. "I don't want to ruin these jeans as well."
Kyle looks puzzled for a moment, then he nods. "Whatever."
"You'll be here when I get back?" Zee asks, talking to me.
I shrug my shoulders. All of a sudden my geography project doesn't feel like the most important thing in the world.
I nod.
"Good. See you in a bit then," says Zee, heading to the back of the crowd. "Be good!"
"Are you gonna stand there all day doing nothing?" Kyle says to me. Next to us someone has kicked over one of the rubbish bins onto the road. People are picking out things from the pile of rubbish. Kyle bends down and picks up an old Coke can.
"Here, take this," he says, pushing me the crushed can of Diet Coke into my hand. "It's better than nothing."
I look at the can in my hand. Only the C and the K are visible. Calvin Klein, I think. Coca-Cola. The big money companies. The ones that make billions from people like us. Maybe Kyle is right. Maybe it is about 'them and us'. The rich and the poor. The bankers and the taxpayers[14]. The corporations and the people who let themselves be brainwashed[15] by advertising. What are the chances of one of us ever becoming one of them? Zero. The lines are drawn just like the lines in front of the police station. And there ain't no one who's gonna cross them.
I pull back my arm, like a catapult preparing to fire, and throw the Coke can into the air. A war cry explodes from my lungs. The sound of my voice surprises me. It's like a giant's voice, deep and booming, as it rings in my ears. It feels good, better than the butterflies in my stomach when I saw Riya. The Coke can crashes against one of the riot shields and drops to the ground, but I'm already looking for my next weapon.

i) Why does Danny stay longer at the demo?

j) Describe what happens after the police beat a protester.

k) Describe how Danny's reaction to the events changes.

More challenge 1 The main characters

Collect adjectives to describe Danny and Kyle. Then write a paragraph about each of them.

More challenge 2 Point of view

Kyle tells a friend about what happened at the demo. Write what he said.

More challenge 3 What happens next?

What happens after the demo? How is Danny affected by his actions? Does he get into trouble? Write the next part of the story.

! You can read the full story about Danny in the Cornelsen reader *Riot*.

[14] taxpayer ['tækspeɪə] *Steuerzahler* [15] brainwash ['breɪnwɒʃ] *einer Gehirnwäsche unterziehen*

TF 3 Job description: Cleaner of the world's oceans

1 A teenager with a vision

a) If you saw rubbish in the ocean or on a beach, how would you react? Tell your partner and give reasons. Then read the text.

Boyan Slat was 16 when he went diving in Greece on a summer holiday. He was shocked. "I saw more plastic than fish," he says. It opened the Dutch teenager's eyes to the problem of plastic pollution in the sea. He began to take interest in the problem. Millions of tonnes of plastic rubbish – bags, bottles, old fishing nets, etc. – are floating around the world's oceans. Seabirds, dolphins and other sea life eat the plastic or get caught in it. Many of them suffer and die. Chemicals in the plastic enter the food chain through the fish we eat, so it's a danger for humans too. Cleaning up plastic pollution is a huge challenge with no easy solutions.

Boyan Slat was interested in how the plastic rubbish is carried by the oceans' currents. These currents move in huge gyres that circle the oceans. The plastic collects in large "patches" inside the gyres.

Key terms

absorb [əb'zɔːb] *aufnehmen, absorbieren*
barrier ['bæriə] *Barriere; Schwelle*
chemical ['kemɪkl] *Chemikalie*
current ['kʌrənt] *Strömung*
float [fləʊt] *treiben, schwimmen*
food chain ['fuːd tʃeɪn] *Nahrungskette*
garbage patch ['gɑːbɪdʒ pætʃ] *Müllstrudel, Müllhalde*
gyre ['dʒaɪə] *Drehung, Strudel*
particle ['pɑːtɪkl] *Stückchen, Teilchen*
pollution [pə'luːʃn] *Umweltverschmutzung*
toxic ['tɒksɪk] *giftig*

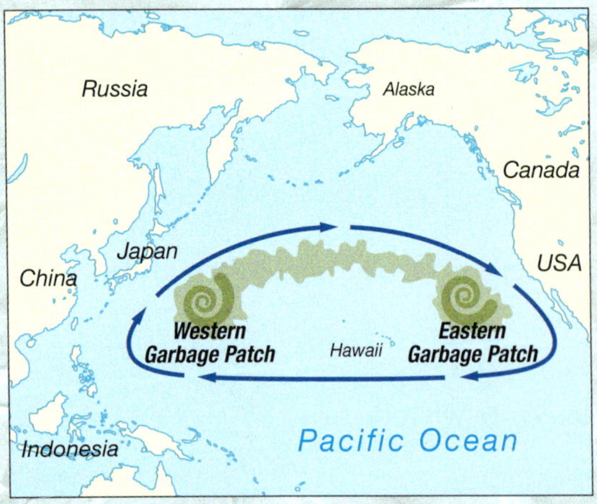

The movement of the plastic gave Slat an idea: a system of swimming barriers that stay in place could catch the plastic. The plastic could then be collected and recycled. Slat worked on his idea in high school and in his first year at Delft University of Technology. Then he decided to go a step further: he left university and started an organization called *The Ocean Cleanup*. Using the internet, he gathered support and money to research and test his idea. Slat and his volunteer team of researchers now plan to have their ocean cleaning system ready by 2020.

b) Answer these questions.

1 Why is the plastic in the oceans a big problem?
2 What role do the ocean currents play?
3 What is Boyan Slat's idea?
4 What has Slat done with his idea so far?

▸ INKL pp. 86–89

2 Slat's ocean cleaning system

a) Look at the photo and the diagrams. Talk about how the system works. You can use the words and phrases in the box.

Activate your English

- The currents move / carry / push / pass …
- The rubbish moves / floats / is carried / collects …
- The barriers stop / catch / collect …
- They are fixed / attached to the ocean floor …
- Sea life can pass under …

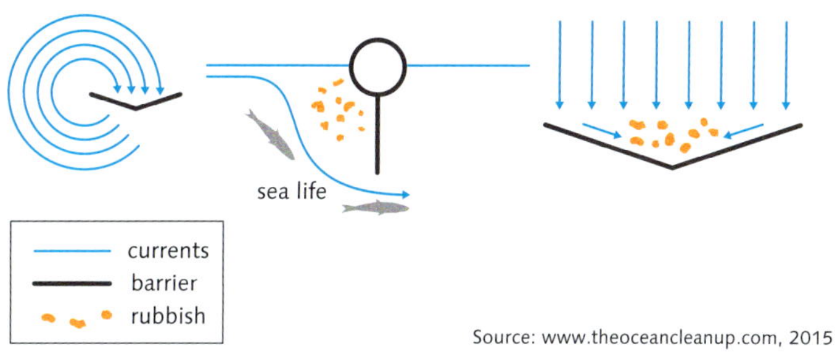

Source: www.theoceancleanup.com, 2015

b) Some experts see problems with Slat's ocean cleaning system. What possible problems could you imagine? Discuss.

3 A complex problem

Boyan Slat's project deals with one part of a much bigger problem. Most of the millions of tonnes of plastic in the sea have been there for a long time (see the infographic). The sun and the movement of the water have broken the plastic down into small particles of less than 5 millimetres. These particles absorb other toxic chemicals, becoming even more dangerous for animals and humans. The plastic particles never break down completely. And they're everywhere, and there is no effective way to get rid of them.

Describe and explain what the graphic shows.

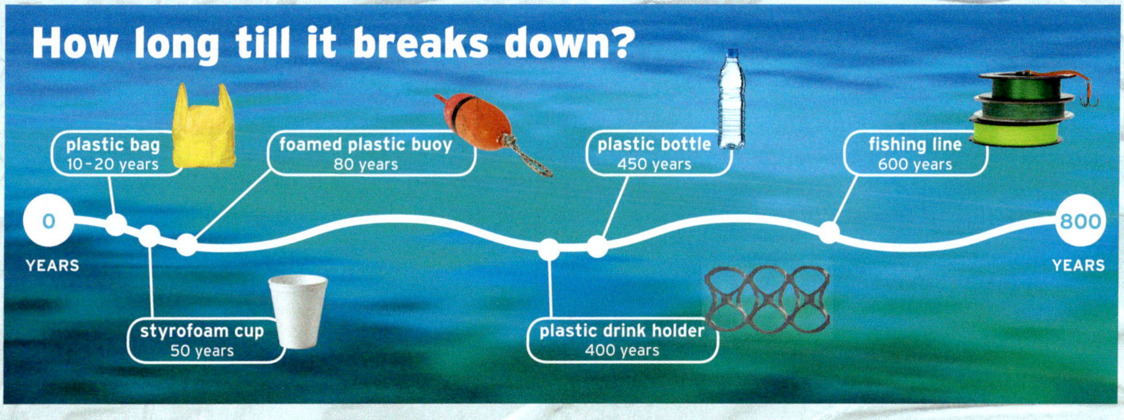

4 Finding solutions

Experts and activists agree on three important areas of action for dealing with plastic pollution:

1 Governments need to reduce or ban the use of throwaway plastic.
2 Businesses need to take responsibility for the life of their plastic products.
3 Consumers need to make the right choices about using and recycling plastic.

a) Choose one of the three areas and talk about why you think it is important. Make notes. Then write a comment for an online forum that discusses possible solutions.

b) Think of concrete ideas how young people can help. Present your ideas to the class.

TF 4 Music in your life

About me
Hi! I'm Bibi. I'm 16 years old. I love technology, photography and fashion. I started this blog ten months ago when my family moved from England to New Zealand. I wanted something to help me to remember this special time in my life. It's also a place for my family and friends back in the UK to read about my adventures on the other side of the world. I really had no idea what I was getting into when I started blogging! I'm pleased and proud to say that people from 45 different countries have liked my blog. A whole new world has opened up for me and I have learned about cultures from all over the world. Welcome everybody!

Posted by Bibi, 17th March
Your favourite song (Yes, you have to choose just one!)
Choosing a favourite is tough, isn't it? But my absolute favourite song of all time is *Wake Me Up* by Avicii. I like Electronic Dance Music because it gives you energy and makes you feel good.

To me this song says wake up, look around you and do something different today. The video is great because it reminds you that you shouldn't waste[1] your time. You should try to enjoy every day. I think the message of the video is: don't be a part of gangs, fighting and hating. Wake up, find out who you really are and just be you. Don't be someone you're not. – So what's your favourite song???

Cara from Wellington, NZ, says:
I find this task too stressful! It's impossible to choose just one song! So here is my favourite song 'this week'. Next week it might change! The song is *What a Wonderful World* by Louis Armstrong. It's a really old song, but I just love it! I am a very positive, happy kind of person. It doesn't matter what is happening around me or how difficult things are, I always think that the world is a wonderful place. That's just how I am, so this song really suits me :-)

[1] waste (v) [weɪst] *verschwenden*

▸ KV 38 ▸ INKL pp. 90–93

Alex from Texas, USA, writes:

Just one song? Just one? It's so hard to choose! I love rock music by bands like Queen, The Beatles and AC/DC. To me this is real music. I think my favourite song is *Black Dog* by Led Zeppelin. I like other music genres – you can find pop, EDM[2] and hip hop on my music player too – but this is a song I could not live without. I first heard it when I was 12. That was when I decided that I wanted to learn to play the guitar. I'm part of a band now and I know how complicated this song is to play. Led Zeppelin are excellent musicians and Robert Plant's voice is amazing. I always sing when I listen to this, but it's not really a song that you can dance to.

Billie in Scotland writes:

All of the stars by Ed Sheeran. I love all of Ed Sheeran's music, but this song reminds me of my grandmother. We were really close and she died five years ago. We used to look at the stars together. She said I was "the brightest[3] star in her sky". Now she is gone, I think she is the brightest star in mine. It reminds me of all the times we sat together watching the stars and talking about the world.

1 Your kind of music – or not?

a) Go online and listen to the songs the blog is about. Which song do you like best? Which song do you like least? Why?

b) Work alone. If you had to choose your own favourite song, what would it be?

c) **Walk around:** Talk to different people about their own favourite song. Ask them to explain their choice.

d) Report the results to the class. What are the most popular songs in your class?

2 Music and me

a) ○ Write a short text about music and you (80–100 words). Think about:
- How important is music to you? Why?
- What kind of music do you listen to?
- How often do you listen to music?
- Where and when do you listen to music?
- Who do you listen to music with?
- What's your favourite song? Why?

OR

b) ● Think of at least one important event in your life (e.g. first day at school, a special family trip, a family event, winning first place in a competition, a concert, ...). Match a song to the event(s). Write a text and explain your choice(s).

[2] EDM = Electronic Dance Music [3] bright [braɪt] *hell, leuchtend*

TF 5 Images in the media: a perfect picture

1 A picture of beauty

a) Choose one of the pictures. Think and make notes about these questions:

- What do you see?
- Where would you expect to find this picture?
- What kind of image of people and/ or life does the picture present?
- How realistic is the image?

Compare your ideas.

b) Find other examples of pictures like these and show them in class. What effect do they have on you?

2 How ads shape our ideas

Did you know that over 90 per cent of the pictures that you see in advertising have been retouched? The media, especially in the digital age, are in the business of presenting false pictures – of lying with images. Everywhere we turn, ads show people with perfect white teeth, a slim or muscular body, clear, wrinkle-free skin, the latest designer clothes. It doesn't matter to advertisers that we never see people like this in real life.
When consumers see images like these again and again, they accept the false ideal that the images present. Then they aren't able to live this way and they feel "less than beautiful". And when consumers don't feel good about themselves, companies profit. It's how clothes, make-up, shampoo, skin cream, weight-loss and fitness programmes and many other products are sold.

Key terms
acne ['ækni] Akne
consumer [kən'sjuːmə] *Verbraucher/in, Käufer/in*
ideal [aɪ'diːəl] *Ideal, Vorbild*
manipulative [mə'nɪpjələtɪv] *manipulativ*
retouch [riː'tʌtʃ] *retuschieren*
shape [ʃeɪp] *formen, gestalten*

a) Complete this sentence: *Ads with idealized images tell consumers …*

b) How does the influence of the media work? Put the lettered boxes in the right order.

A People aren't happy with themselves
B Companies profit
C People accept media's messages
D Media present idealized images
E People look for "help" by buying products

c) Take turns explaining in your own words how the media's influence works.

3 Young people and media influence

a) Read this quote and answer the question: Why are product marketers interested in teens?

"Young people are still forming ideas about who they are, and the people who market products know this. They also know that teens spend a lot of money and are big consumers of media. This makes them big targets for ads on the Web, on TV, in the cinema and in magazines. The average teen sees over 5,260 'attractiveness messages' per year (or at least 14 per day)."

b) Think about these questions, then talk with your partner.

- Where do you usually see ads?
- What kinds of ads get your attention the most?
- Which ads make you want to spend money?

c) Now read the dialogue. Which of these two friends can you identify with more? Why?

Hey Eric, here's that acne cream again. Look at her face – that's before and that's after. Amazing! Maybe I should try it.

Hm. It might be good cream, but come on, Dana, do you really think it made her look like that? Her skin looks perfect.

That's what it says. That photo is dated March and that's her in May. You can see the change. She looks happier too.

Yeah, for the "after" shot they gave her amazing hair, trendy clothes and told her to smile. Be serious! Your skin isn't that bad anyway.

But it could be nicer ...

But there are good creams for half that price, Dana. Why is this stuff so special?

You're so cynical! The ad says "Because you're worth it". I think I'm worth it. Anyway, sometimes you have to spend more to get more.

Go ahead and spend! Then we'll take before and after photos and compare.

d) Talk about the dialogue in class. Which arguments make sense to you and which don't? Explain.

e) Write a letter to the editor of a teen magazine. Describe the effect that ads with "attractiveness messages" have on you. Explain how, in your view, ads can be manipulative or dishonest. Then suggest how they could be improved. The words and phrases in the box may help you.
Read and discuss your letters to the editor in class.

Activate your English

When I see ads that ...
... they make me feel / I often feel excited / hopeful / poor / unsure / less confident / ugly / fat / ...
When ads show people / pictures that ...
If the ads showed / had / didn't show / ...,
then they would / wouldn't ...

EXAM FILE 1

▸ KV 34 A/B ▸ INKL pp. 94–95

> Students who are getting ready for exams at the end of year 9 (level A2/A2+) will find extra practice here. ▸ *Skills file 3, p. 162*

1 READING Signs

a) Where can you see these signs?

1. Ⓐ in a park
   Ⓑ at a pool
   Ⓒ at the beach

2. Ⓐ in a hospital
   Ⓑ by a road
   Ⓒ in a playground

3. Ⓐ at a post office
   Ⓑ on a letter box
   Ⓒ on a computer

b) What information do these signs give? Choose Ⓐ, Ⓑ, Ⓒ or Ⓓ.

1. Ⓐ You can only go to the beach on Sundays between 9.00 and 1.00.
   Ⓑ Dogs are allowed on the beach.
   Ⓒ If you want to surf, you should always do it between the flags.
   Ⓓ There will be lifeguards at the beach on Sunday morning.

2. Ⓐ Let people get on the train before you try to get off.
   Ⓑ Nobody is allowed to get off the train.
   Ⓒ Let people get off the train first.
   Ⓓ People who want to exit the train must use this door.

3. Ⓐ You aren't allowed to bring a mobile into the library.
   Ⓑ You can take calls in the library.
   Ⓒ It's not OK to bring your phone into the library, even if it's off.
   Ⓓ You can have your phone in the library, but put it on silent.

2 LISTENING A strange story

3.10

Listen twice to the story about a boy and a kangaroo. Are the sentences true or false?

1 A boy was visiting an Australian national park with his family.
2 They were worried about the boy because there were salt water crocodiles in the park.
3 The boy was missing all night.
4 The boy said that a kangaroo looked after him.
5 Everybody believed the boy's story about the kangaroo.

3 LANGUAGE Sam, the koala

Complete the text with the correct words in the brackets.

Firefighter gives koala a drink

Sam, a two-year-old koala, became an internet star after a forest fire in Victoria, Australia. Volunteer firefighter David Tree ... (1 found / finds/ find) her and ... (2 gave / give / will give) her some water from a bottle. Another firefighter filmed her with Tree, and the film ... (3 was seen / is seen / saw) by thousands of Australians on the internet. Koalas are often hurt in fires ... (4 but / because / so) they usually spend all ... (5 his / her / their) time up in trees and they move slowly on the ground. The fires spread so quickly that the koalas can't move ... (6 fast / slow / slowly) enough to escape.

Many koalas are hurt every year in forest fires

4 WRITING An email to a host family

You're planning a trip to Australia and looking for a host family. Read this website and write to the family (at least 60 words). Give information about yourself and ask them questions.

We're an average Australian family – mum, dad and three kids. We love meeting new people, and foreign students come and stay with us every year.
We'd like to find out something about you before you come, so tell us:
- your name, age and hobbies,
- why you'd like to come to Australia,
- what you'd like to see while you're here.
Feel free to ask us anything you like about us, our family, our house, our town, etc.

The Hanson family

EXAM FILE 2

► *KV 35 A/B* ► *INKL pp. 96–97*

1 SPEAKING **Tourist talk**

a) Talk to a partner about these questions.

1 What's happening in this picture?
2 What do you think the people are saying?
3 Talk about a holiday that you've had.
4 Describe your dream holiday.

b) ROLE-PLAY At a bus stop in Dublin

PARTNER A

You're at a bus stop and you speak to a tourist.

- help you?
- number 16 to city centre
- tickets on bus
- €2.55 / where from?
- like Dublin?
- how long staying?
- visited Dublin before?
- 'hop-on-hop-off' bus tour
- my bus coming / bye

PARTNER B

You're a tourist in Dublin and you're a little lost.

- bus to city centre?
- where buy bus ticket?
- how much to centre?
- Germany
- Dublin fun / friendly people
- a week / staying in a hostel
- first visit / any good tips?
- good suggestion
- bye / thanks for help ...

2 WRITING **Arriving in London**

a) Anton has just arrived at London Heathrow. He wants to take the Underground train to Covent Garden, so he goes to the ticket office. Complete the dialogue.

1 Clerk Can I help you? Anton ...
2 Clerk That's £4.80, please. Anton ...
3 Clerk It's about 50 minutes. Anton ...
4 Clerk Follow the signs to the Piccadilly Line. Anton ...

b) The train is very full, but Anton sees two seats near the window. Complete the dialogue.

1 Anton ... Man No, I'm sorry, this is for my wife. She's just coming now.
2 Anton ... Man Yes, that one is. I'll move my bag.

▸ KV 35 A/B ▸ INKL pp. 96–97

3 READING 16 – too young to love?

Read the following opinions about teen love.

Mandy It's ridiculous to fall in love when you're 16. You should spend your time with lots of friends – boys and girls! There'll be time for more serious relationships later. I say stay free!

Dwight Of course I believe in teenage love. I have a steady girlfriend – we've known each other for more than a year. We spend all our free time together, sit together in school, have lunch together … we're head over heels in love!

Charlie Some of my friends say that they're in love, but I think that they watch too many soaps on TV. I guess they're just acting because they think you have to have a girlfriend or boyfriend to be cool. I don't think like that. Maybe one day I'll meet the right girl … but I'm not in a hurry!

Anna Some kids really want to fall in love … Sure – it's romantic. When I was a teen, I just wanted romance too. I read the books, saw the films, dreamed the dreams. With my friends, that was all we talked about. I thought I was in love lots of times, but I don't think it really was love. As a teenager I liked the idea of being in love, just like all the other kids.

Said For me falling in love means getting married, having kids, a home, a job … and all that kind of thing. Sure, I want to do that some day, but not now when I'm 16. I have a girlfriend, and she's great! But love … I don't know …

Sofia I totally believe in teen love! I met someone on holidays and we just clicked. It was love at first sight. I never want us to part. We're mad about each other!

Now look at the statements. Are they true, false or not in the text?

1 Mandy feels that 16 is too young for a love relationship.
2 Dwight and his girlfriend fell in love the moment they saw each other.
3 Charlie is happy that his friends are in love. He's hoping that it will happen to him soon.
4 Anna used to dream of being in love, but she never really was.
5 Said is planning to marry his girlfriend and have kids with her.
6 Sofia never expected to fall in love while she was on holiday.

4 WRITING Under pressure

Your friend Ben has sent you this email. Read it and write a reply to him (at least 60 words).

> Hey there!
>
> Cool party last night, wasn't it? Why did you leave so early? And why were you talking to Jordan forever? He's on my "nerd" list. I hope you're not going to go to his party on Saturday. Let's go to the movies!
>
> Ben

▸ KV 36 A/B ▸ INKL pp. 98–99

1 READING **My first real job** (Text adapted from 'Climbing the Golden Arches' by Marissa Nuñez)

a) Read the text.

Two years ago, while my cousin Susie and I were doing our Christmas shopping on Fourteenth Street, we decided to have lunch at a fast food place.
"Look at the job ad," Susie said. "They're hiring. Let's give it a try." I looked at her and said, "Are you serious?" She gave me this look that made it clear that she was.

When Susie and I got home from school one day about a month later, my mother told us that the fast food place had called. They wanted to interview us both. We walked straight over there. They asked us why we wanted to work there and how we felt about tasks like cleaning the bathroom. Then they told us to wait for a while. Finally the manager came out and said we had the job.

Susie worked for only three months, but I stayed on. I liked having a job because I was learning how to be a responsible person. I was meeting all kinds of people. I started making friends with my co-workers and getting to know many customers. And I was in charge of my own money for the first time. I didn't have to go asking Mom for money when I needed something. I could just go and buy it.

Working at a fast food place does have its downsides. The worst thing about the job is that the customers can be real jerks sometimes. They just don't seem to understand the pressure we're under. At times they try to make you look stupid. Or they blame you for a mistake they made. If you don't watch and listen carefully, some of them try to short-change you for some money.

Working here has taught me a lot. The most important thing I've learned is that you have to start at the bottom and work your way up. You need to know how to do all the jobs. I also have more patience and have learned to control my emotions. I've learned how to get along with all different kinds of people. I'd like to have my own business some day, and working at this fast food place has shown me I could do that.

b) Complete the sentences by choosing the correct ending to each sentence.

After applying for the job, Marissa and her cousin
- A waited for months.
- B got an interview after a month.
- C started working straight away.

The job was good because
- A her school friends visited her at work.
- B she didn't have much responsibility.
- C she could earn money.

Sometimes the customers
- A feel under pressure.
- B aren't very understanding.
- C give her too much money.

Marissa has learned that
- A you can't start at the top.
- B you have to do just one job.
- C people are all the same.

2 LANGUAGE A job advert

Read the job advert and complete the text with the correct words in the brackets.

The Sandwich Bar, 14th St, New York

IMMEDIATE OPENINGS

We're looking (1 to/from/for) hard-working, friendly and enthusiastic people who can deliver excellent customer service (2 with/from/at) a smile. Your duties include: preparing and cooking food, serving customers, working (3 in/at/through) the cash desk, and helping to keep the restaurant safe and clean.

You must be able to work quickly (4 so/and/then) be a team player. We (5 need/needed/needs) you to work 11 am to 7 pm and 1 pm to 9 pm. Pay will be discussed (6 by/at/on) the interview.

APPLY HERE

3 LISTENING Looking for work experience

3.11 **a)** You will hear a telephone conversation about work experience twice. Pick A, B or C.

1 Sanjay wants to work at A a cafe. B a school. C a supermarket.
2 The name of the manager is A Robert. B Ms Walker. C Mr Rath.
3 Sanjay can work A for one week. B for two weeks. C for three weeks.
4 Sanjay has to work A seven days a week. B six days a week. C five days a week.
5 In July Sanjay has to send A a CV. B an email. C a letter.

3.12 **b)** You will hear a conversation between Sanjay and Asha twice. Complete the table.

	where they worked	duties (at least 2)	hours	what it was like
Sanjay	…	…	…	…
Asha	…	…	…	…

4 WRITING Jobs and work experience

You want to apply for a job at *The Sandwich Bar*. Write a letter of application (at least 60 words):

– say who you are
– say if you have relevant experience
– say why you'd be good at this job
– say when you could start

Inhalt

STUDY AND LANGUAGE SKILLS — page

SF 1 Dealing with unknown words — 160
SF 2 Using a dictionary — 161
SF 3 Exam skills: How to do better in tests — 163
SF 4 Doing research — 164
SF 5 Working with charts and diagrams — 165

LISTENING AND READING SKILLS

SF 6 Listening — 165
SF 7 READING COURSE
- Skimming — 166
- Scanning — 166
- Finding the main point of a text — 166
- Reading for details — 167
- Reading between the lines — 167
- Marking up and note-taking — 168
- Working with fictional texts — 168

SPEAKING AND WRITING SKILLS — page

SF 8 SPEAKING COURSE
- Giving a presentation — 169
- Successful conversations — 170
- Doing well in job interviews — 170
- Taking part in discussions — 171

SF 9 WRITING COURSE
- The steps of text writing — 171
- Writing a report — 173
- Writing an email / a letter — 173
- Summarizing texts — 174
- Writing a CV — 175
- Writing a cover letter — 176
- A written discussion — 177
- Writing a book or film review — 178

SF 10 Describing photos and pictures — 179
SF 11 VIEWING SKILLS — 180
SF 12 MEDIATION SKILLS — 181

STUDY AND LANGUAGE SKILLS

SF 1 Dealing with unknown words

Du kannst englische Texte verstehen, auch ohne alle Wörter zu kennen. Nicht immer ist Nachschlagen nötig.

- Schau genau auf Titel und (Zwischen-)Überschriften sowie den Zusammenhang (Kontext), in dem das unbekannte Wort steht.
- Achte auf Abbildungen und Bildunterschriften. Was könnte bedeuten "... the Typhoon muscle car that had rocketed past us earlier ..."?
- Viele Wörter sind im Deutschen und in anderen Sprachen dem Englischen ähnlich, z.B. *democracy, humour, loyal, religion, souvenir*.
- Wie ist das Wort aufgebaut? Unbekannte Wörter enthalten oft bekannte Teile.
  - in **Zusammensetzungen** (Komposita, *compounds*), z.B.
    one-way street – *a street where vehicles are allowed to move in one direction only* (Einbahnstraße)
    baby car seat – *a car seat for a baby* (Kindersitz)
  - in **Ableitungen** mit Vor- und Nachsilben (*prefixes and suffixes*), z.B. *antisocial, disappear, multilingual, oversleep, reappear; washable, national, useful, childish, attractive, careless, percentage, performance, foundation, opener, racism, movement, happiness, leadership, pressure*
- Kennst du das Wort evtl. schon in einer anderen Wortart? Z.B. kennst du *campaign* als Nomen. In *We've successfully campaigned against cyberbullying at our school* ist es ein Verb und bedeutet ...?
- Aber: Nicht alle englischen Wörter, die im Deutschen ähnlich sind, haben in beiden Sprachen dieselbe Bedeutung. Achte auf so genannte *false friends*: z.B. heißt *become* „werden" (nicht „bekommen").
- Oft hilft dir der Textzusammenhang (Kontext), also die umstehenden Wörter und Sätze: *In case of a snake bite try to identify the snake, so the doctors can find an anti-venom more quickly.*

two muscle cars

a *Typhoon*

a *Holden Monaro*

! Typical **prefixes** and their meanings:

again / back
re- (*rebuild, remarry*)
after
post- (*post-war, postmodern*)
before
pre- (*premature, preschool*)
do / be more than / too much
out- (*outrun*)
over- (*overeat, overcrowded*)
not / against / opposite
anti- (*anti-war*)
dis- (*disloyal, disorder*)
in- (*incorrect, incredible*)
mis- (*mislead, misuse*)
non- (*non-smoker*)
put in(to)
en- (*endanger, encircle*)

SF 2 Using a dictionary ▸ More challenge 1, p. 28 ▸ Unit 2, p. 38

Wenn du ein Wort nicht erschließen kannst, helfen das *Dictionary* (*English-German* pp. 234–265) oder ein Wörterbuch für das Englische (entweder in Buchform oder im Internet).

usually ['juːʒuəli] meistens, normalerweise I

V

vacation [və'keɪʃn], [veɪ'keɪʃn] *(AE)* Ferien, Urlaub IV
vacuum cleaner ['vækjuəm kliːnə] Staubsauger V 3 (52)
vain [veɪn] eitel V 4 (79)
valley ['væli] Tal IV
value ['væljuː] Wert I **It's good value.** Es ist sein Geld wert. I
vamping ['væmpɪŋ] *spät in der Nacht noch aktiv sein* V 4 (88)

1 Wörterbucheinträge sind immer alphabetisch

- *U* kommt vor *V*
- *value* kommt vor *vegetables*
- *vamping* kommt vor *vampire*

2 Zusammengesetzte Ausdrücke und *idioms*

Der Haupteintrag (z.B. ***ear***) steht farbig oder fett am Anfang. Daneben oder darunter findest du oft zusammengesetzte Wörter oder Redewendungen und Idiome, z.B. ***(be) all ears***.

ear [ɪə] *Substantiv*
1 Ohr **2** Gehör **3** Ähre
IDM **(be) all ears** ganz Ohr sein
(be) up to one's ears in sth. bis zum Hals in etwas stecken
go in one ear and out the other *(umgs)* zum einen Ohr rein- und zum anderen rausgehen

3 Wortarten und Wortbedeutungen

- Oft ist das gleiche Wort ein Nomen (Substantiv), ein Adjektiv oder ein Verb, mit je unterschiedlichen Bedeutungen. Überlege zuerst, zu welcher **Wortart** das gesuchte Wort gehört und suche den passenden Eintrag. Diesen liest du dann genauer.
- Die Ziffern 1, 2 usw. bei einem Eintrag zeigen, dass ein Wort mehrere **Bedeutungen** hat. Lies immer alle Einträge bei der passenden Wortart und entscheide dann, welche Bedeutung in deinem Satz passt. Zusätzlich findest du Verweise auf den Gebrauch im *American* oder *British English* (AE bzw. BE).

  Welche Bedeutungen hat *fall* hier?

  The number of unemployed people has fallen since last fall.
  Is September a summer or a fall month?
  I fell asleep very fast yesterday because I was so tired.

Besonders wenn du ein Wort in einem deutsch-englischen Wörterbuch suchst, achte genau darauf, welche Bedeutung in deinem englischen Satz passt.

fall [fɔːl] *Verb, Substantiv*
***Verb* (fell, fallen)**
1 fallen, stürzen **The book fell off the table.** Das Buch fiel vom Tisch.
2 *(Zahlen)* fallen, sinken, zurückgehen **Their profits have fallen by 30%.** Ihr Gewinn ist um 30% zurückgegangen.
3 in einen Zustand geraten **fall asleep** einschlafen, **fall ill** krank werden, **fall in love (with)** sich verlieben (in)

Substantiv **1** Fall, Sturz
2 falls (Plural, bes. in Namen) (Wasser) fall **the Niagara Falls** die Niagarafälle
3 *(AE)* Herbst
4 *(Zahlen)* Rückgang

4 Weitere Informationen im Wörterbuch

- Die Lautschrift zeigt dir, wie ein Wort ausgesprochen wird.
- Unregelmäßige Verbformen, Pluralformen, Steigerungsformen usw. stehen in Klammern hinter dem Haupteintrag.

go [gəʊ] *Verb* (***went*** [went], ***gone*** [gɒn])

child [tʃaɪld] (***children*** [tʃɪldrən])

5 Online-Wörterbücher

- Wenn du ein Online-Wörterbuch verwenden möchtest, erkundige dich vorher bei deiner Lehrperson, welche zu empfehlen sind.
- Achte auf dieselben Dinge wie bei gedruckten Wörterbüchern.
- Vorteil online: Du kannst dir meist die Aussprache per Audiodatei anhören.

SF 3 Exam skills: How to do better in tests ▸ Exam file, pp. 154–159

VOR DEM TEST

Eine Klassenarbeit oder ein Test in Englisch ist angekündigt? Keine Panik. **Frage** am Tag der Ankündigung deine Lehrperson und **notiere** dir, worum es gehen wird und was du besonders wiederholen solltest.

Nimm dir Zeit zur **Vorbereitung**. Beginne **10 Tage** vor dem Termin. Mach dir einen **Plan**, den du wirklich Tag für Tag abarbeitest. Plane auch einen vorbereitungsfreien Tag ein.

Schätze dich selbst ein

- Bitte deine Lehrperson um einen Selbsteinschätzungsbogen.
- Stell fest, welche Bereiche du noch üben musst. Wenn du unsicher bist, sprich mit deiner Lehrperson.
- Steh am Tag des Tests früh genug auf. Frühstücke etwas Gutes.

WÄHREND DES TESTS

Sei ruhig und optimistisch

- Du bist gut vorbereitet. Konzentriere dich, alles Andere ist jetzt unwichtig.

Lies zuerst alle Arbeitsanweisungen sehr genau.

Vom Einfachen zum Schwereren

- Löse zuerst die einfachen Aufgaben.
- Hake erledigte Aufgaben ab.

Achte auf die Zeit

- Schau beim Arbeiten ab und zu auf die Uhr, damit du weißt, wie viel Zeit dir noch bleibt.
- Nutze die letzten fünf Minuten dazu, alles nochmal durchzulesen und Fehler zu korrigieren.

NACH DEM TEST

Lerne aus deinen Fehlern

- Lies genau durch, was deine Lehrperson korrigiert hat. Gibt es Tipps und Hinweise für dich? Merke sie dir, beachte sie beim nächsten Mal.
- Gibt es ein Kompetenzraster? Lies dir genau durch, wo deine Schwächen und Stärken liegen.
- Berichtige deine Fehler sorgfältig. Frage bei Unsicherheiten deine Lehrperson.
- Führe deine persönliche **Fehlerliste**, in der du Fehler, die du immer wieder machst, sammelst (z.B. in einem kleinen Heft, auf Karteikarten oder als Notizensammlung im Smartphone – Hauptsache, du kannst immer schnell darauf zugreifen).

VOR DEM TEST

Bereite dich wieder sorgfältig vor

- Geh noch einmal deine typischen Fehler der letzten Tests und die Berichtigungen durch.
- Schau dir das Kompetenzraster und eventuelle Tipps der Lehrperson nochmal an.
- Du bist gut vorbereitet. Konzentriere dich ruhig und optimistisch.
- Erstelle und bearbeite wieder deinen Vorbereitungsplan.

SF 4 Doing research ▸ Unit 1, p. 25

1 Nutze unterschiedliche Quellen für deine Recherche

Bei der Informationssuche für ein Referat, eine Präsentation o.Ä. benutze mehrere unterschiedliche Quellen und Medien. Beachte auch die Hinweise zum Skimming und Scanning ▸ Skills file 7.1, 7.2, p. 166.
Gleiche die gefundenen Informationen miteinander ab.

für alle Wissensgebiete
- Lexika (gedruckt und online, ggf. englischsprachig)
- Schulbücher und Begleitmaterialien

für aktuelle Informationen
- Zeitungen, Zeitschriften (gedruckt und online, ggf. englischsprachig)

für geographische und politische Informationen
- Karten und Atlanten (gedruckt und online)

2 Tipps zur Internetrecherche

So wird deine Internetrecherche leichter und bringt bessere Ergebnisse:

Wie suche ich, um weniger und bessere Ergebnisse (*hits*) zu bekommen?
- Überlege dir gute Stichwörter für dein Thema. Bereitest du z.B. eine Präsentation zu *Koalas in Australia* vor, wären *koala bear* und *Australia* ein Anfang. Weitere Ideen: *life of koalas*, *enemies of koalas*, …
- Gib die Stichwörter in eine Suchmaschine ein und setze die Einstellungen auf englischsprachige Websites.

Welche Websites sind zuverlässig?
- Offizielle und zuverlässige Websites im englischsprachigen Internet haben *domain names*, die auf *.gov* oder *.edu* enden.
- Weniger vertrauenswürdig sind Websites von Firmen (*.com*), persönliche Blogs, Fanseiten oder Websites von Interessengruppen. Auch hier kannst du Interessantes finden, solltest aber kritisch bei der Verwendung von Inhalten sein.

Wie verschaffe ich mir einen Überblick?
- Du kannst mit dem Skimming eines Artikels in einem online-Lexikon beginnen, z.B. der englischsprachigen Wikipedia (https://en.wikipedia.org).
- Häufig finden sich im Artikel bzw. am Ende weitere Links zum Thema.
- So findest du auch genauere Stichwörter für deine weitere Recherche.

Wie finde ich Websites wieder?
- Leg dir besonders interessante Websites in die Favoriten deines Webbrowsers. Strukturiere sie in eigenen Ordnern, die du innerhalb der Favoriten anlegen kannst.

Was kommt nach dem Suchen?
- Setz dir ein Zeitlimit für deine Recherche. Danach ordne dein Material. Prüfe, was evtl. fehlt und suche dann gezielt nur danach.

Was tun mit den gefundenen Informationen?
- Mach dir Notizen in weitgehend eigenen Worten ▸ Skills file 7.6, p. 168. *Copy and paste*, also bloßes Zusammenkopieren, ist nicht sinnvoll.
- Zu jeder Notiz vermerke die Quelle (die Webadresse sowie das Zugriffsdatum).

Was tun mit unbekannten Wörtern und Wendungen?
- Unbekannter Wortschatz begegnet dir immer wieder in fremdsprachigen Texten. Für den ersten Überblick musst du nicht jedes Wort genau verstehen – erschließe die Bedeutung ▸ Skills file 1, p. 160.
- Wichtige Wörter schlage im (Online-)Wörterbuch nach, v.a. wenn du sie selbst in deiner Präsentation verwenden willst. Vergiss die Aussprache nicht! Hör dir das neue Wort online an und übe es.

SF 5 Working with charts and diagrams

▸ Text file 3, p. 149

1 Was sind Diagramme und wozu dienen sie?

Diagramme stellen statistische Vergleiche zwischen mindestens zwei Dingen dar. Dabei helfen sie komplexe Informationen zu veranschaulichen und leichter zu verstehen.

2 Welche unterschiedlichen Formen von Diagrammen gibt es?

- Bar charts (Säulendiagramme) beschreiben in der Regel die Anzahl oder Größe von zwei oder mehr Dingen.
- Pie charts (Kreis- / Tortendiagramme) geben einen Überblick über die prozentuale Verteilung.
- Line graphs (Kurvendiagramme) stellen den Zusammenhang zwischen zwei oder mehr Variablen (Parameter) dar.
- Charts (Tabellen) ermöglichen den Vergleich unterschiedlicher Daten anhand von Zahlen.

3 Wie kann ich Diagramme beschreiben?

Um Diagramme zu beschreiben, ist es hilfreich, folgende Struktur zu nutzen.

A: Einleitung
What is the graph / chart about?
The bar / pie chart / line graph is about … / deals with …
The (horizontal) x-axis / (vertical) y-axis shows …
The slices of the pie chart compare …
Du solltest auch sagen, wo du das Diagramm gefunden hast.
It is taken from …

B: Beschreibung der dargestellten Informationen
What does the graph / chart compare? What information does it give?
… has the largest / smallest … is twice / three times … as big as …
There are more than / almost twice as many … as there are …
A majority / minority / … per cent of …
Less than half / more than one third …
The number … grows by … / sinks by … / does not change.

C: Schlussfolgerung
What is the general conclusion?
I was really surprised / shocked by …
So / To sum up / All in all we can say …

4 Worauf muss ich sonst noch achten?

Benutze das **simple present**, wenn das Diagramm sich auf Fakten in der Gegenwart bezieht oder bei allgemeingültigen Aussagen:
More than 55 per cent of the German students under 10 have a smartphone.
Benutze das **simple past** bei Fakten, die in der Vergangenheit liegen:
73 per cent of the 10–12-year-olds had their own TV in 2012.
Benutze das **present perfect**, wenn du dich auf einen Zeitraum beziehst, der von der Vergangenheit bis heute reicht:
The number of young people using social media has nearly doubled since 2011.

What do 10 to 18-years-olds use their mobile for?

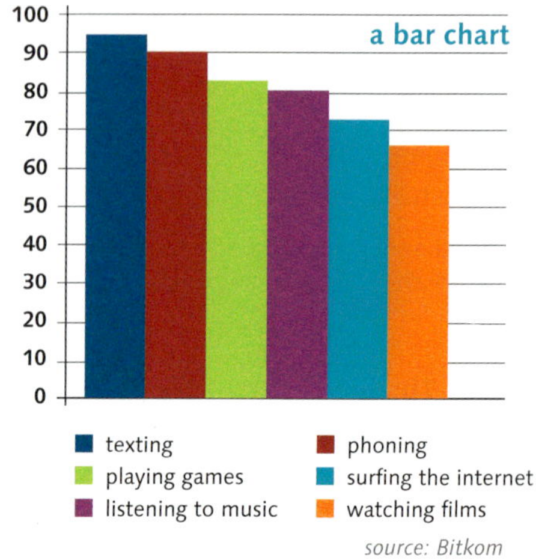

Use of social networks (10–18 yrs)

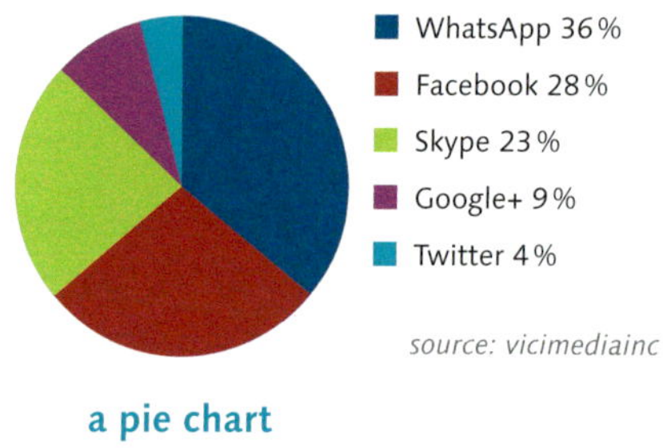

Hours spent on media per day

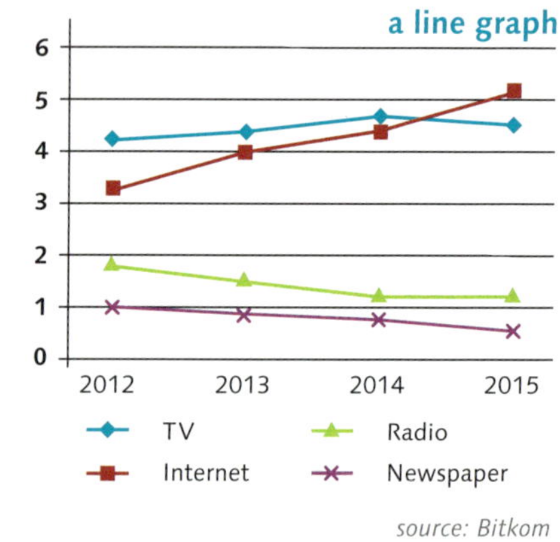

LISTENING AND READING SKILLS

SF 6 Listening

▸ *Unit 1, p. 13* ▸ *Unit 2, p. 36*
▸ *Unit 3, p. 59* ▸ *Unit 4, p. 83*

1 Vor dem Hören: bereite dich vor

- Lies sorgfältig die Aufgabenstellung. Die Aufgaben sagen oft, worum es in dem Text geht oder enthalten Schlüsselwörter.
- Stell dir die Situation oder die Geschichte vor: Worum wird es im Text gehen? Wer wird sprechen? Versuche vorauszuschauen.
- Überlege, was du selbst zum Thema schon weißt und welche englischen Begriffe vorkommen könnten.
- Wenn du dem Hörtext Abbildungen zuordnen sollst, schau sie dir vor dem Hören genau an.
- Konzentriere dich, denn du kannst den Text meist nur bis zu zweimal hören.

> **!** Versuche zu erkennen, **was für eine Art Text** du hören wirst:
> Nachrichten, Werbung, ein Gespräch, ein Interview, eine öffentliche Ansage oder eine *story*?

2 Beim Hören

- Beantworte schon beim ersten Hören möglichst viele Aufgaben (mach dir kurze Notizen, verwende Symbole und Abkürzungen).
- Die Informationen könnten in einer anderen Reihenfolge auftauchen.
- Im Hörtext können andere Wörter benutzt werden als in der Aufgabe, doch die Bedeutung ist ähnlich.
- Gib nicht auf, wenn du etwas nicht verstehst. Bleib ruhig und hör weiter zu. Vielleicht verstehst du beim zweiten Hören mehr.
- Achte auf Signalwörter, die dir das Verstehen erleichtern, z. B.:
  - Reihenfolge (*before, after, then, next, later, first, ...*)
  - Gegensätze (*however, but, ...*)
  - Gründe, Folgen (*because, so, ...*)
  - Vergleiche (*larger/older than ..., more, most, as ... as*)
- Beachte auch, wie etwas gesagt wird: zum Beispiel verärgert oder besorgt, überrascht, freudig? Das kann ein Hinweis auf die Lösung sein.

> **!** Höraufgaben können unterschiedliche **Arten des Zuhörens** von dir verlangen:
> - **detailliertes Hören** Hier musst du genau zuhören, um wichtige Einzelheiten zu erfassen (z. B. bei einer Ansage am Bahnhof die Abfahrtszeit des Zuges).
> - **globales Hören** Hier sollst du verstehen, worum es generell geht, z.B. den Hauptgedanken eines Textes erfassen. Du musst dafür nicht jedes einzelne Wort verstehen.
> - **schlussfolgerndes Hören** Hier werden deine Vorüberlegungen und Vermutungen wichtig. Achte auf die Zusammenhänge. Wird etwas evtl. nur angedeutet, aber nicht vollständig ausgesprochen? Wie klingt die Stimme der Sprecher?

3 Nach dem Hören

- Vervollständige deine Notizen sofort.
- Konzentriere dich beim nächsten Hören auf eventuelle Lücken.
- Manchmal hilft auch Kombinieren (es ist in jedem Fall besser als gar nichts zu schreiben).

> **!** **Tausche** dich mit Mitschülern und -schülerinnen **aus**. Haben sie gute **Tipps und Tricks**, z. B. für kurze Notizen und Symbole?
> Ihr könnt, wenn das erlaubt ist, auch eure Notizen und Lösungen vergleichen.

SF 7 Reading course

1 Skimming ▸ Unit 1, pp. 15, 20 ▸ Unit 3, p. 66

Wofür? Mit dieser Technik verschaffst du dir einen **Überblick**, z.B. über eine Website oder eine Zeitungsseite.

Wie? Du musst nicht jede Einzelheit verstehen, also auch **nicht jedes Wort** lesen und verstehen. Achte vor allem auf Überschriften, Abbildungen und Bildunterschriften, hervorgehobene Wörter und den ersten Satz.

Beispiel: Du möchtest mehr über Australien wissen. Ist dies dafür eine geeignete Website?

Für wen ist sie vor allem gedacht?

☐ Sportler ☐ Touristen ☐ Geschäftsleute

2 Scanning ▸ Unit 1, p. 12 ▸ Unit 3, p. 60, 64 ▸ Unit 4, p. 86

Wofür? Mit dieser Technik kannst du einen Text schnell nach **bestimmten Informationen** durchsuchen.

Wie? Du suchst nur bestimmte Informationen, die du über geeignete **Schlüsselwörter** findest. Lies nur dort genauer, wo sie stehen.

Beispiel: Du möchtest mehr darüber erfahren, was du bei einer Reise nach Australien beachten musst. Welchen Reiter musst du bei der obrigen Website anklicken?

3 Finding the main point of a text

▸ Unit 4, p. 87

Wofür? Um herauszufinden, was die **Hauptaussage** eines Textes ist und wie sie sich aus seinen Hauptgedanken formt.

Wie? Für deinen **Überblick**, worum es in dem Text generell geht, benutzt du das Skimming (siehe 1).

Die **Hauptaussage** eines Textes findest du oft in seinem **ersten Absatz**, und dort oft im **ersten** oder **letzten Satz**.

Jeder **Absatz** eines Textes beinhaltet einen **Hauptgedanken**, der zur Hauptaussage beiträgt. Du findest den Hauptgedanken meist im **ersten** oder **letzten Satz** des Absatzes.

Beispiel: Lies Text **(A)** auf S. 10 noch einmal. Schau dir dann rechts oben die Markierung aus dem ersten Absatz an. Welcher Satz beinhaltet die Hauptaussage des Texts?

Ban on climbing Uluru comes nearer

Together with Sydney Harbour Bridge and the Great Barrier Reef, Uluru is probably the best-known tourist sight in Australia. 200,000 visitors travel there every year, and at the moment they are allowed to climb the rock. But for how long?

But Uluru is more than a tourist sight. For the local Anangu people Uluru is sacred, and they don't climb it. According to their law, only a few people are allowed to go up the rock at special times. That's why they politely ask visitors not to climb the rock.
In the past most visitors went up on the rock. Today more and more people decide not to

4 Reading for details

▸ Unit 2, p. 35

▸ More challenge 1, p. 50

Wofür? Manchmal musst du in einem Text **jedes Detail** im Zusammenhang genau verstehen, z.B. bei Gedichten, Rezepten, Gebrauchsanweisungen und Aufgabenstellungen. In längeren Informationstexten oder Tabellen und Diagrammen ist es oft nur ein bestimmter Bereich, den du detailliert liest, weil du eine Information suchst. Welcher Bereich das ist, findest du mithilfe des Scanning heraus (siehe **2**).

Wie? Lies **jedes Wort** und **jede Zahl** sehr **genau**. Achte auch auf Maßeinheiten. Benutze ein Wörterbuch für unbekannte Wörter.

Beispiel: Wie viele Ziffern musst du hier eingeben, damit der Safe schließt?
Wann sollst du den Safe offen hinterlassen?

OPERATING INSTRUCTIONS
You can operate this safe with your own 4-digit personal code.

TO LOCK: Close the door and enter your own 4-digit code.
Press # (LOCK). The safe will lock automatically and the word CLOSED will be displayed.

TO OPEN: Enter the 4-digit code that was used to lock the safe. It will unlock automatically and the word OPEN will be displayed.

IMPORTANT: Always leave the safe open at checkout.

5 Reading between the lines

▸ Unit 2, pp. 35, 54

▸ More challenge 1, p. 50

Wofür? Wenn du Fragen zu einem Text beantworten sollst, ist es möglich, dass du die Antworten nicht eins zu eins im Text findest. Hier hilft es dir, **Schlussfolgerungen** aus dem Gelesenen zu ziehen. Wichtig ist diese Technik z.B. bei Kommentaren, persönlichen Texten (wie Tagebucheinträgen) und literarischen Texten.

Wie? Einfaches Schlussfolgern bedeutet, dass du Informationen aus **unterschiedlichen Textstellen** zusammenführst.

Beispiel: Sieh dir den Text auf S. 69–70, Parts 3 und 4 an und beantworte Frage 1 rechts.

Manchmal werden im Text **andere Wörter** benutzt als in der Aufgabe, doch die Bedeutung ist ähnlich oder gleich.

Beispiel: Schau im selben Text auf S. 69, in Part 2 die Zeilen 71 – 73 an und beantworte Frage 2 rechts.

Es gibt auch Fragen, auf die du im Text gar keine direkte Antwort findest. Und doch ist sie im Text enthalten, man könnte sagen, sie steht **„zwischen den Zeilen"**. Du musst sie schlussfolgern, also z.B. dein eigenes Wissen, aber auch begründete Vermutungen beim Lesen einbringen.

Beispiel: Lies auf S. 68, in Part 1 die Zeilen 41 – 43 und beantworte Frage 3 rechts.
Die Antwort für Frage 4 findest du auf S. 70, in Part 4, Zeilen 148 – 149 und in Part 5, Zeilen 163 – 175.

(1) How do you know that Cindy has fallen in love with Cal?

(lines 115–120; 148–149)

(2) What does *mature* mean here?
Cynthia sounded much more mature, she thought.
a) showing great understanding and skill ☐
b) fully grown and developed ☐
c) behaving in a responsible way, like an adult ☐
d) no longer young ☐

(3) Does Charlotte believe what her friend says?

(4) What's the difference between Cindy's two names? How are they used in the story?

6 Marking up and note-taking ▸ Unit 4, p. 83

Wofür?

Du hast einen längeren Text mit vielen Fakten vor dir und sollst ihn später zusammenfassen oder inhaltliche Fragen beantworten. Wähle die für diese Aufgabe wichtigen Informationen aus und markiere sie.

Wie?

Du kannst die Stellen mit den für dich wichtigen Informationen z.B.:

- mit Textmarker hervorheben
- umkreisen
- unterstreichen

All das geht nur in elektronischen Texten oder auf Fotokopien bzw. Ausdrucken, aber nicht in geliehenen Büchern.

Being a screenager

Today's teenagers were born into the digital world, a world where screens are everywhere – TV screens, smartphone screens, tablet screens, laptop screens ... The average American teen spends 8.5 hours per day in front of a screen! In Britain it's a little less, about 7 hours per day. These screenagers don't look at only one screen – they usually multitask. They videochat on their smartphone, play a game on their tablet and watch a programme on TV, all at the same time.
Not every teen is like this of course, and many have hobbies and interests away from their screens. But digital technology is part of every teen's world and the attraction of TV, video games and social media is strong. Most teens feel the pressure to do as their friends do.
About 60% of teenagers today watch at least 20 hours of TV per week.
About 94% of teenagers have social media accounts.

Wenn du dir zu den markierten Stellen **Notizen** machst (*note-taking*), kannst du diese später leichter weiterverarbeiten, z.B. für eine Präsentation ▸ *Skills file 8.1, p. 169*, einen Bericht oder eine Zusammenfassung ▸ *Skills file 9.4, p. 174*

> Schreibe nur Schlüsselwörter auf, nutze Ziffern (statt Zahlwörter: **7** statt **sieben**) und Symbole (?, !, ✓, ≠, +, =, ~). Zum Beispiel:
>
> **screenagers:**
> - born into digital world (= world of screens)
> - ~ 8 hrs daily screen time (multitasking)
> - strong attraction + peer pressure
> - ...

7 Working with fictional texts ▸ Unit 2, p. 47 ▸ Unit 3, p. 71 ▸ Unit 4, p. 94

Literarische oder fiktionale Texte, z.B. **Romane *(novels)*** oder **Kurzgeschichten *(short stories)*** handeln von einer erdachten Welt. Der Autor oder die Autorin entwickelt Figuren (*characters*) *und erzählt, was sie tun und fühlen sowie häufig* auch, warum sie sich so verhalten.

Beim Erschließen des Texts achte auf diese Elemente:

- ***characters***: Wer sind die wichtigen Figuren? Wie werden sie beschrieben? In einer Figurencharakterisierung *(characterization)* nenne Namen und Alter. Sage etwas über ihr Verhalten, ihr Aussehen und ihre Persönlichkeit. Wie sprechen sie? Inwiefern verändern sie sich im Lauf der Handlung?
- ***plot***: Der Grundaufbau der Handlung. Fasse knapp zusammen, worum es in der Geschichte geht, was passiert und warum.
- ***setting***: Gib an, zu welcher Zeit und an welchem Ort bzw. welchen Orten sich die Handlung abspielt.
- ***mood***: Welche Stimmung oder Atmosphäre prägt die Geschichte? Ist sie z.B. fröhlich oder spannend, traurig oder gruselig? Verändert sich die Grundstimmung im Verlauf der Handlung? Achte darauf, wie eine Situation beschrieben wird (Adjektive, Vergleiche, Sprachbilder, usw.).

> **USEFUL PHRASES**
> for talking and writing about fictional texts:
>
> The **main character(s)** in this story is / are ...
> - He / She is ... years old and lives in ...
> - He / She is a tall / small / ... person with ...
> - He / She likes / hates ... / typically ...
> - He / She is a strong / weak / brave / reliable / an easy-going ... person.
>
> **Plot:** The text tells the story of ...
> - The story is about ...
> - First ... / Then ... (because of ...) / In the end ...
> - The story is **set** in ... at the beginning of the ... century / just before World War II / ...
>
> The story starts in a very sad **mood**. However, that changes when ...
>
> Reading this story was very exciting. Its mood is scary / threatening / ... because phrases like ... are used.

SPEAKING AND WRITING SKILLS

SF 8 Speaking course

1 Giving a presentation

▸ *Unit 1, pp. 25, 112*
▸ *Unit 4, p. 87*
▸ *More challenge 4, p. 98*

Beachte diese Schritte, damit deine Präsentation erfolgreich wird.

OUTLINE
Topic: The outback

1) Introduction:
   Today I'm going to talk about Australia's most exciting …
2) Main body:
   First: how big
   Second: weather
   Third: animals
   Fourth: people
3) Summary / Conclusion:
   To sum up, I'd love to spend …

a) PLANNING YOUR PRESENTATION

- **Recherchiere** dein Thema ▸ *Skills file 4, p. 164* und fertige dir Notizen an (am besten gleich in Englisch ▸ *Skills file 7.6, p. 168*).
- **Strukturiere** die Informationen, z.B. in einer Mindmap oder einer Gliederung (*outline*). Prüfe nochmal, ob alle Informationen zum Thema passen.
- Wähle die **Form deiner Präsentation** aus: z.B. Vortrag, Folienpräsentation am Computer, Poster.
- Überlege, wie du dein Thema **anschaulich** und **interessant** gestaltest (Beispiele, und Visualisierungen, z.B. Abbildungen, Karten, Diagramme, evtl. Filmausschnitte). Überlege dir einen guten Einstieg.
- Bereite deine **Notizen** für die Präsentation (nur Stichwörter). Notiere kurze Erklärungen zu schwierigeren Begriffen, die deine Zuhörer/innen evtl. nicht verstehen.
- Bereite deine **Materialien** sorgfältig vor (Computerfolien, Fotos usw.): Achte auf Lesbarkeit und Übersichtlichkeit.
- **Übe** deine Präsentation zu Hause und / oder mit Freunden. Achte auf die Zeit. Nummeriere deine Notizzettel bzw. Karteikärtchen. Überprüfe die technischen Hilfsmittel, die du verwenden willst (Laptop, Beamer usw.).

b) GIVING YOUR PRESENTATION

- **Schau** die Zuhörenden **an**. Warte bis es ruhig ist. **Erkläre**, worüber du sprechen wirst und wie deine Präsentation aufgebaut ist.
- **Sprich langsam**, deutlich und möglichst **frei** (d.h. lies nicht nur ab).
- **Schau** die Zuhörenden **an**, **lächle**. Zeige, dass du deinen Vortrag gern hältst.
- Sprich in **kurzen**, **verständlichen Sätzen**. Vermeide zu viele unbekannte oder schwierige Wörter. Erkläre sie bei Bedarf.
- **Verweise** auf deine **Abbildungen** oder Fotos. Erkläre sie bei Bedarf.
- **Beende** deine Präsentation mit einer kurzen **Zusammenfassung** der wichtigsten Punkte, evtl. auch mit einer abschließenden Schlussfolgerung.
- **Bedanke** dich fürs Zuhören und frage, ob jemand **Fragen** hat oder sich äußern möchte.

2 Successful conversations

▸ *Unit 2, p. 49*

Unterhaltungen mit Menschen aus anderen Ländern gelingen gut, wenn du diese Hinweise beachtest. Sei höflich und aufgeschlossen! Verwende häufig *please*, *thank you* und *sorry*.

a) STARTING OFF

- **Eröffne** das Gespräch mit einer freundlichen Anrede oder Frage, möglichst mit etwas **Verbindendem**, z.B. über den Ort, die Situation usw. Mit jemandem, den du zum ersten Mal triffst, sprichst du etwas förmlicher als mit jemandem, den du schon kennst.
- Wenn es angebracht ist, stell dich vor.

USEFUL PHRASES
Excuse me, please.
Do you know ... / Can I sit here?
Hello, how are you?
My name is ... Nice to meet you.
Hi there, are you from Sydney?
Hi, how is it going?
Hi, have you been here before?

b) KEEP THE CONVERSATION GOING

- Zeige dein **Interesse**, indem du Fragen stellst, z.B. auch Nachfragen.
- Antworte nicht nur mit wenigen Worten, das kann unfreundlich wirken.
- Erzähle auch etwas **von dir**, möglichst auf eine **positive** Art (vermeide es, zu jammern oder zu nörgeln).
- Wenn du etwas nicht verstehst, frage höflich nach.
- Wenn du etwas nicht sagen kannst, umschreibe das Wort.

USEFUL PHRASES
Fine, thanks. / Yeah, sure.
Yes, I am. / No, not really.
What about you? Do you like ... / I'm new here in ... / I really like these ...
What do you think ...?
Could you say that again, please?
I don't know the English word. It's something that ... / like ...

c) A GOOD ENDING

- **Beende** das Gespräch so freundlich, wie du es begonnen hast.
- **Bedanke** dich, wenn du um Hilfe gebeten oder z.B. Tipps bekommen hast.
- **Verabschiede** dich höflich.

! Mache dir vor dem Gespräch möglichst klar, mit wem du sprichst. So wirst du z.B. mit Gleichaltrigen informeller umgehen als mit Älteren.
Denke auch an eventuelle kulturelle Unterschiede, z.B. beim Begrüßen und Verabschieden.

3 Doing well in job interviews ▸ *Unit 3, p. 72*

a) PREPARE YOURSELF

- **Bereite dich sorgfältig** auf das Vorstellungsgespräch **vor**. Übe deine **Gesprächsanteile**, z.B. vor einem Spiegel oder mit Freunden. Achte besonders auf eine freundliche, aber angemessen formelle **Körpersprache**.
- Wo liegen deine **Stärken** und **Schwächen**? ▸ *Wordbank 2, p. 137* Was sind deine besonderen **Interessen**?
- **Warum** bewirbst du dich um diese Tätigkeit?
- Welche **Arbeitserfahrungen** hast du? ▸ *Wordbank 5, p. 139*
- **Informiere dich vorab** über das Unternehmen bzw. den Betrieb und bereite auch einige **Fragen** an die Interviewer vor.

USEFUL PHRASES
Good morning, Ms / Mr ...
My name is ... and I'm really interested in this job because I like working with ...
I think this is a job I could do well because I already have some experience with ...
I'm quite good at ... / I'm not very good at ...
I'd like to know if I'll be working in a team or on my own.
Do I have to work at the weekends?

b) IN THE INTERVIEW

- Plane **genügend Zeit** für die Anfahrt und das Finden des genauen Interviewortes ein. Schalte dein **Smartphone stumm**, bevor du dort ankommst.
- **Begrüße** dein Gegenüber freundlich, stell dich nochmal vor.
- Bleib **ruhig**, sei **freundlich** und **positiv**.
- Hör gut zu, sprich **deutlich** und nicht zu schnell. Sieh dein Gegenüber beim Gespräch an.
- Kontrolliere immer mal wieder deine **Köperhaltung**.
- Bleibe **ehrlich**, übertreibe nicht.
- Am Ende des Gesprächs **bedanke** dich und **verabschiede** dich freundlich.

4 Taking part in discussions ▸ Unit 4, p. 97

In einer (Klassen-)Diskussion tauschst du dich über Ideen und Meinungen aus. Dabei sollst du auf die Äußerungen deiner Gesprächspartner/innen eingehen und gleichzeitig deinen eigenen Standpunkt darstellen und begründen.

a) PREPARING A DISCUSSION

- Eine **inhaltliche Vorbereitung** auf das Thema der Diskussion ist sinnvoll, damit du nützliche **Wörter** und **Wendungen** parat hast. Notiere sie dir.
- Mache dich mit **unterschiedlichen Standpunkten** zum Thema vertraut und denke darüber nach, was deine Position ist.
- Notiere dir **Argumente**, die deinen bzw. andere Standpunkte unterstützen. (Beispielsweise in einem Rollenspiel kann deine Aufgabe sein, einen anderen Standpunkt als den eigenen zu vertreten.)
- Bereite deine **erste Äußerung**, mit der du in die Diskussion eintrittst, besonders gut vor.

STATING YOUR OPINION
In my opinion, / view, ...
Well, I'd say ...
(Personally,) I think / feel / believe ...
If you ask me, ...
First of all, ...
To start with, I'd like to point out that ...

b) HAVING THE DISCUSSION

- Wenn du die Diskussion **eröffnest**, beginne mit deinem vorbereiteten **Einstieg**.
- Häufiger wirst du dich auf deine **Vorredner/innen** beziehen. Du kannst ihrem Standpunkt **zustimmen** oder **nicht zustimmen** und dann deine vorbereitete Äußerung und passende **Argumente** vorbringen.
- In jedem Fall **höre** den Argumenten der anderen **genau zu** und beziehe dich in deiner Äußerung darauf.
- Bleibe stets **höflich** und lass andere ausreden.
- Manchmal wirst du **nachfragen** müssen, wenn dir etwas unklar oder unverständlich ist.

ASKING FOR CLARIFICATION
Sorry, I didn't get that. / Are you saying that ... ?
Does your last statement mean that ... ?
Could you please give an example of ... ?

AGREEING
I quite agree. (+)
You're quite right. (+)
I think so too. (+)
You've got a (good) point there. (+)
That's true / right. / That's just it. (++)
I agree completely. (++)
I couldn't agree with you more. (+++)

DISAGREEING
I'm afraid I don't (quite) agree (there). (-)
I'm not so sure, really. (-)
Well, that's one way of looking at it, but ... (-)
It's not as simple as that (I'm afraid). (-)
I don't believe that at all. (--)
I don't agree with you at all. (--)
(Sorry,) I definitely disagree. (--)
(Sorry,) I think you're wrong. (--)

SF 9 Writing course

1 The steps of text writing ▸ Unit 1, pp. 13, 19 ▸ Unit 2, p. 35

a) PLANNING YOUR TEXT

- Über welches Thema willst / sollst du genau schreiben?
- Was für einen Text sollst du schreiben: z.B. eine E-Mail, das Ende einer Geschichte oder einen Sachtext (Beschreibung – *Describe* ...; Erläuterung – *Explain* ...; Erörterung – *Discuss* ...; Zusammenfassung – *Summarize* ...)?
- Sammle Ideen und / oder Argumente – z.B. in einem Mindmap oder in einer Liste.
- Recherchiere die für dein Thema notwendigen Informationen ▸ *Skills file 4, p. 164*.
- Strukturiere dein Material: Schreibe deine geplante Gliederung (*outline*) auf.

Du brauchst
- eine Einleitung (*beginning / introduction*): Hier steht, worum es im Text insgesamt geht.
- einen Hauptteil (*middle / main body*): Dieser Teil ist in mehrere Absätze (*paragraphs*) gegliedert, die Details (Fakten, Beispiele usw.) und Argumente enthalten.
- einen Schluss (*ending / summary / conclusion*): Hier gibst du dem Text ein passendes, einprägsames Ende.

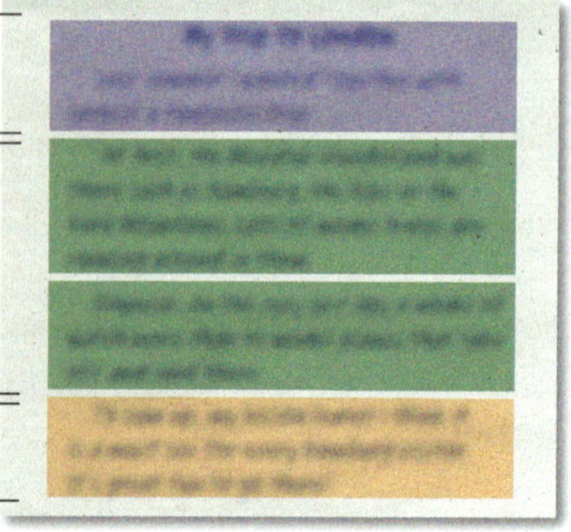

b) WRITING YOUR TEXT

- Nun schreibe den **ersten Textentwurf**. Halte dich an deine Gliederung.
- Beginne für jeden neuen Gedanken einen **neuen Absatz**.
- Jeder Absatz sollte mit einem **Einleitungssatz** (*topic sentence*) beginnen. Er drückt aus, worum es in diesem Absatz gehen wird.
- **Verbinde** deine Sätze mit passenden *linking* und *time phrases*.
- Verwende passende, **ausdrucksstarke** Wörter und Wendungen, z.B.:
  - **Adjektive** (zum näheren Beschreiben von Personen, Dingen, Orten usw.): *a peaceful voice*
  - **Adverbien** zum näheren Beschreiben von Handlungen, Vorgängen und Zuständen: *It was raining terribly.* oder zum Verstärken von Adjektiven: *an extremely sad story*; *He was deeply disappointed.*

USEFUL LINKING PHRASES

Konjunktionen (***conjunctions***): ***but***, ***and***, ***because***, ***so***, ***on the one hand – on the other hand*** (einerseits – andererseits), ***although***, ***however***

Demonstrativpronomen (***demonstrative pronouns***): *This is exactly .... That's the point.*

Relativsätze (***relative clauses***): *The platypus is an animal that I've never seen in real life.*

USEFUL TIME PHRASES

Adverbiale Bestimmungen der Zeit (*time markers*): ***at first***, ***next***, ***finally*** (Reihenfolge) ***for half an hour***, ***just two minutes later*** (Dauer) ***immediately***, ***faster than ...*** (Geschwindigkeit) ***during our holiday***, ***as he arrived***, ***while ...*** (zeitgleiches Geschehen) ***two years ago***, ***last spring*** (Zeitpunkt)

c) CHECKING AND REWRITING YOUR TEXT

- Wenn dein erster Textentwurf geschrieben ist, hast du viel geschafft, bist aber noch nicht fertig. Jetzt solltest du deinen Text **jemand anderem** zu lesen geben und um **Feedback** bitten.
- **Lies** selbst deinen Text **mehrmals** durch, je mit einem anderen Schwerpunkt:
  - Stimmt der **logische Aufbau**, die Struktur (Einleitung – Hauptteil – Schluss)? Sind die Absätze in sich logisch aufgebaut?
  - Sind die Sätze gut verbunden, liest sich der Text **flüssig** (*linking* and *time phrases*)?
  - Prüfe, ob du alle **typischen Fehlerquellen** vermieden hast (wenn du eine persönlich Fehlerliste führst, schau dort nochmal nach).
  - Schau dir ein eventuelles **Feedback** genau an und überlege, was du davon übernehmen willst.
- Schreibe nun deinen Text in der **endgültigen Version**. Lass dir etwas Zeit, dann lies auch diese Version nochmal kritisch durch und verbessere, wo das noch nötig ist.

! Typische Fehlerquellen
- Groß- und Kleinschreibung
- Wörter die ähnlich klingen, aber unterschiedlich geschrieben werden: *your / you're; than – then; quiet – quite*
- unregelmäßige Pluralformen: *woman – women, child – children*
- Wörter mit „stummen" Buchstaben: *know, talk, listen*
- *word order* in Aussagen, Fragen ▸ Language file 11, 12, pp. 190–191
- unregelmäßige Verben und unregelmäßige Schreibungen: *try → tries, tried*
- Präpositionen: *on the internet, in the photo, go by bus, be good at ...*
- Typische Wendungen, z.B.: „Was gibt's zum Abendbrot?" – *What's for dinner?* „Alles Gute!" – *All the best!*

2 Writing a report ▸ Unit 2, p. 37

Auch beim Verfassen eines Berichts beachte *The steps of text writing*. ▸ p. 171
In einem *report* gibst du deinen Lesern kurze und sachliche Informationen.

a) PLANNING YOUR REPORT

Collect ideas
Notiere dir Stichwörter zu den fünf *wh*-Fragen und *how* in einer Mindmap oder Tabelle. Beispiel:

Footballers support refugees

Gelsenkirchen-Schalke, Germany – Yesterday Schalke's former professional footballer Gerald Asamoah and Schalke's fans stood up for human rights and refugees. Ghana born Asamoah started a campaign for refugees earlier this month. His campaign is called *#Stand up for human rights!* and was supported by thousands of fans who stood up holding posters with *#stehtauf* in their hands. Asamoah started the campaign because he wanted to show that everybody could help. He said, "Everybody must show courage and they must hold up a sign that says, "Stand up." The campaign is supported in many social networks by well-known footballers, e.g. Schalke's Benedikt Höwedes or Hamburg's Rene Adler.

Plan the structure of your report
Auch ein Bericht besteht aus *beginning*, *middle* und *end*.
Beginne mit den **wichtigsten Informationen**, um deinen Lesern eine schnelle Orientierung zu ermöglichen. **Weitere Informationen** kannst du ans Ende setzen. Informiere deine Leser kurz und knapp.

b) WRITING YOUR REPORT

Schreibe deinen Bericht auf und bilde Sinnabschnitte. Beachte: Wenn du über Vergangenes berichtest, musst du das *simple past* verwenden.

b) CHECK AND CORRECT YOUR REPORT

Plane auch bei einem *report* mindestens einen Textentwurf und eine gründliche Überarbeitung ein.

3 Writing an email / a letter ▸ Unit 3, p. 63 ▸ Unit 4, pp. 94, 102

- **(E-Mail-)Adresse und Betreff:** Schreibe die korrekte Adresse sowie kurz und deutlich das Thema (*subject*) deiner E-Mail in die entsprechenden Felder. (Das Datum fügt das Programm automatisch ein.)
- **Persönliche Anrede:** E-Mails an **Organisationen** beginnst du mit *Dear Mr … / Dear Mrs … / Dear Ms …* Kennst du den Namen nicht, schreibst du *Dear Sir or Madam*.
  An Zeitungen, Online-Magazine oder Sender kannst du auch *Dear Editor* (Herausgeber/in bzw. Redakteur/in) schreiben.

  An **Freunde** schreibst du z.B. *Dear Lily* oder *Hi Max*.
- **Beginn:** Bedanke dich, wenn das angebracht ist. Sage dann, warum du schreibst und worauf du dich beziehst.

  Thank you for your article …
  I'd like to add my view on …
- **Mittelteil:** Hier teilst du dem Empfänger Wichtiges mit, nimmst Stellung oder kommentierst.

  I (completely) agree with the first part of your …
  However, the second …
- **Schluss:** Schließe mit eventuellen Wünschen und freundlichen Worten:

  An **Organisationen**: *Yours sincerely* (*AE:* nur *Sincerely*) / *Best wishes* / *regards* (+ dein Name), wenn du oben in der Anrede einen Namen geschrieben hast. *Yours faithfully* (+ dein Name), wenn die Anrede keinen Namen enthält.

  An **Freunde**: *Lots of love / All the best / Best wishes* (+ dein Name)

4 Summarizing texts ▸ Unit 1, pp. 11, 12, 23 ▸ Unit 3, p. 71

Wenn du einen Text (mündlich oder schriftlich) zusammenfasst, gibst du die wichtigsten Informationen oder Ereignisse in kurzer Form wieder.

a) PLANNING YOUR SUMMARY

- Lies den Text: Für den ersten Überblick beginne mit dem Skimming und lies danach genauer, aber noch ohne etwas zu markieren oder dir Notizen zu machen.
- Bestimme die **Textsorte**, denn einen erzählenden Text fasst du etwas anders zusammen als einen Sachtext.
- Beim Finden der **wichtigen Informationen** helfen dir die ***5 Wh-questions***. Markiere die wichtigsten Informationen im Text (auf einer Kopie) und fertige dann kurze Notizen an. Mit diesen schreibst du dann deine Zusammenfassung.

ERZÄHLENDE TEXTE (Geschichten, Romane, Romanauszüge usw.):	**SACHTEXTE** (Zeitungs- oder Magazinartikel usw.):
Thema, Ort, Zeit, grobe Handlungszüge	Thema, Fakten, Argumente (und ggf. wichtige Ereignisse)

↓	↓
WHO	**WHAT**
is the text about?	
WHAT happens	**WHAT** are the **main points** or **arguments**
in the text?	
WHERE / WHEN / WHY does it happen?	**WHERE / WHEN / WHY** is it important?

USEFUL PHRASES
- the text / story is about ...
- ... is a story about ...
- the article shows ... / deals with ...

b) WRITING YOUR SUMMARY

- ***beginning / introduction***: Hier nennst du das Thema, Titel und Autor/in des Originaltexts. Bei Zeitungsartikeln solltest du hier auch die Quelle nennen.
- Im **Hauptteil** fasst du die wichtigsten Fakten (eines Sachtexts) bzw. Handlungsschritte (eines erzählenden Textes) zusammen.
  - Fasse dich **kurz** (Der Umfang einer Zusammenfassung ist maximal **20 %** des Originaltexts).
  - Fasse jeden Abschnitt in einem kurzen Satz zusammen.
  - Verwende deine eigenen Worte, schreibe den Text nicht ab.
  - Verwende keine direkte Rede.
  - Verzichte auf Einzelheiten und Beispiele.
  - Schreibe im ***simple present***, auch wenn der Originaltext eine oder mehrere andere Zeitformen verwendet.
  - Verbinde die Sätze und Textteile, so dass sich deine Zusammenfassung gut und flüssig liest. ▸ p. 172

c) CHECK AND CORRECT YOUR SUMMARY

- Auch bei *summaries* plane mindestens einen Textentwurf und eine gründliche Überarbeitung ein.
  - Enthält deine Zusammenfassung das Thema und die wesentlichen Fakten bzw. Handlungsschritte?
  - Hast du unwichtige Einzelheiten weggelassen?
  - Korrigiere Rechtschreib- und Grammatikfehler. ▸ p. 172
  - Ist dein Text logisch aufgebaut und gut zu verstehen?

Falls möglich, überprüft eure Zusammenfassungen im *partner check*.

5 Writing a CV ▸ Unit 3, p. 62

Die Abkürzung CV kommt aus dem Lateinischen (*curriculum vitae*) und bedeutet „Lebenslauf". Es handelt sich dabei um die Zusammenfassung deiner bisherigen Ausbildung, deiner Fähigkeiten und deiner Interessen. Du benötigst einen CV häufig bei Bewerbungen. Im Amerikanischen wird anstelle von CV meist der Begriff *résumé* verwendet.

Adriane Wibbing
Rüterweg 122, 48032 Bielefeld, Germany
Telephone: +49(0)521-549765 Mobile: +4917126282054
Email: ari.wib@mail-bi.de

Personal statement
I am a confident and polite person with good communication and computer skills. I am looking forward to getting more practical work experience in the workplace.

Key Skills
- friendly and well-organized
- strong team member
- good at foreign languages
- good at organizing things

Education
2012 to present: Olof-Palme-Gesamtschule, Bielefeld
2008 – 2012: Regenbogen Grundschule, Herford

Work experience
Travel agency: research on hotels and flights (online and in print catalogues)
Kindergarten: working with small children

Hobbies and interests
My hobbies include travelling, reading books about foreign countries, taking photos and creating photo shows. At school my favourite subjects are foreign languages and geography. I am a member of the school drama club.

References
Mrs Sprengel (class teacher), OPG, Nordhofstraße 75, …
Mrs Diel (manager), Reisebüro Globus-Reisen, Ringstraße 9, …

! In GB und den USA ist **kein Bewerberfoto** in einem CV üblich.

! **Geburtsdatum und -ort** werden in CV in GB und den USA meist **nicht** genannt.

! Beginne mit einem **personal statement**. In einem Absatz beschreibst du dich kurz.

! **Fettgedruckte Überschriften** und eine klare **Gliederung** erleichtern das Lesen.

! Du beginnst die Aufzählung deiner Schulen, Praktika usw. **chronologisch rückwärts**.

! Schreibe zum Schluss einen kurzen **Absatz** zu deinen Hobbys und Interessen.

! Nenne zwei **persönliche Fürsprecher/innen** (Referenzengeber/innen) mit Adresse.

Check and correct your CV:

- Hast du ein weißes Blatt A4-Papier benutzt, das ordentlich und sauber ist?
- Ist dein computergeschriebener CV gut gegliedert und übersichtlich?
- Ist dein CV frei von Rechtschreib- und Grammatikfehlern?
- Denke daran, dass du im CV keine Kurzformen verwendest (~~*I'm*~~ -> *I am* usw.).

! Informiere deine Fürsprecher/innen, dass sich eventuell eine britische oder US-amerikanische Institution bzw. Firma bei ihnen melden wird.

6 Writing a cover letter ▸ Unit 3, p. 63

Ein *cover letter* (auch: *covering letter, letter of application*) ist ein Begleitschreiben zu einer Bewerbung und ist nicht länger als eine Seite. Du musst dabei auf bestimmte Regeln achten.

Lessingstraße 3
46562 Voerde
Germany

Peter Tiger
Peter's Pet shop
Adalbertstraße 10
40545 Düsseldorf

30 May 20...

Dear Mr Tiger

I am writing to you about the advertisement for a pet shop assistant on your website that I saw yesterday. I would like to apply for this job.

I am a student,and I really like pets. Our family has a cat, a dog and two budgies. I take care of them. I am reliable and hard-working and I love working with animals. I am good at English, so I can also take care of your English-speaking customers.

In my last summer holidays I volunteered at the Berlin Zoo. Please find the reference enclosed.

I also enclose my CV and I am looking forward to your answer.

Yours sincerely
Jonathan Held
Jonathan Held

> ! Schreibe **deine Anschrift** und das **Datum** in die rechte obere Ecke.

> ! Die **Anschrift des Adressaten** steht links.

> ! Wenn du den Adressaten **nicht kennst**, beginne mit ***Dear Sir / Madam***. Wenn du den Adressaten **kennst**, beginne mit ***Dear Mr ... / Mrs ... / Ms ...***

> ! Schreibe, **worauf** du dich **beziehst** und um welche **Position** du dich bewirbst.

> ! Nenne **Erfahrungen** und Fähigkeiten, die dich für die Stelle qualifizieren. Erwähne ggf. **Referenzen**.

> ! Ende mit einem **freundlichen Ausblick** oder mit **Dank** vorab.

> ! Wenn du den Adressaten nicht kennst (und oben mit *Dear Sir* or *Madam* beginnst), beende mit ***Yours faithfully***. Wenn du den Adressaten kennst (und oben mit *Dear Mr ... / Mrs ... / Ms ...* beginnst), beende mit ***Yours sincerely***.

Check and correct your cover letter:

- Hast du ein weißes Blatt A4-Papier benutzt, das ordentlich und sauber ist?
- Ist dein computergeschriebener *cover letter* gut gegliedert und übersichtlich?
- Ist dein *cover letter* frei von Rechtschreib- und Grammatikfehlern?
- Denke daran, dass du im *cover letter* keine Kurzformen verwendest (~~*I'm*~~ -> *I am*; ~~*ad*~~ -> *advertisement*; ~~*paper*~~ -> *newspaper* usw.).

> ! Dein Bewerbungsschreiben sollte **kurz** sein, aber das **Wesentliche** enthalten: was genau dich für diese Stelle qualifiziert. Bleib bei der Wahrheit und übertreibe nicht.

7 A written discussion ▸ Unit 4, p. 85

Oft sollst du zu strittigen Fragen schriftlich Stellung nehmen und deine Sichtweise überzeugend darlegen. Zeige dabei, dass du dich gründlich mit dem Thema beschäftigt und die Pro-/ Contra-Argumente abgewogen hast.

a) PREPARING YOUR TEXT

- **Sammle** zuerst alle **Argumente** (z.B. in einem kurzen Brainstorming). Evtl. musst du vorher weiter recherchieren ▸ *Skills file 4, p. 164*
- Ordne deine Argumente gleich beim Sammeln in zwei Listen: ***pro*** und ***contra***.
- Schau dir die Argumentlisten an und bereite so die Gliederung *(outline)* deines Texts vor:
  - Was sind die **besten drei Argumente *contra*** und die **besten drei *pro***? Diese verwendest du, jeweils beginnend mit dem stärksten Argument.
  - **Nummeriere** die Argumente entsprechend dem Schema rechts.
- Notiere deine **Gliederung *(outline)*** gemäß dem Schema rechts.
  - Beginne mit den Argumenten, die **gegen *(contra)*** deine Sichtweise sprechen und stell **danach** die Argumente vor, die deine Meinung **unterstützen *(pro)***. (Auf diese Weise lassen sich die Contra-Argumente wirkungsvoller entkräften. Prinzipiell kannst du aber auch mit den Pro-Argumenten beginnen.)
  - Notiere jeweils **Beispiele** zu den Argumenten.
  - Überlege und notiere, in welche Richtung deine **Schlussfolgerung *(conclusion)*** gehen soll.

OUTLINE FOR A WRITTEN DISCUSSION

Topic: Should computer games be a school subject?

1) Introduction: ...

2) Arguments contra / against
   - 2.1) First argument: ...
   - 2.2) Second argument: ...
   - 2.3) Third argument: ...

3) Arguments pro / for / supporting
   - 2.1) First argument: ...
   - 2.2) Second argument: ...
   - 2.3) Third argument: ...

4) Conclusion: ...

b) WRITING YOUR TEXT

- Nun formuliere mithilfe deiner *outline* die *written discussion* **ausführlich**.
- In der **Einleitung *(introduction)*** stellst du das Thema vor und beschreibst, worum es geht. Geh dabei von einem allgemein bekannten Problem oder einer persönlichen Erfahrung aus.
- Im **Hauptteil *(main body)*** präsentiere die Argumente *contra* und *pro*.
  - Nenne jeweils das Argument.
  - Erläutere es näher und begründe deine Meinung.
  - Unterstütze deine Meinung durch Fakten und Beispiele (aus deiner Recherche bzw. aus eigener Erfahrung).
  - Formuliere logisch und flüssig, verbinde deine Argumente. ▸ *p. 172*
- Am Textende steht deine persönliche **Schlussfolgerung *(conclusion)***. Achtung: Hier keine neuen Argumente und auch keine Argument-Wiederholungen aus dem Hauptteil!

USEFUL PHRASES

... for your introduction:
A lot of people think ...
You often hear people say that ...,
... so the questions is: should ... or not?

... for the main body of your text:
Firstly, ...; Secondly, ...
Another argument for / against ... is ...
For example, ...
People think that because ...
However, a lot of people feel ...
On the one hand, ...
On the other hand, we should not forget ...
So ...; That is why ...; Finally, ...

... for your conclusion:
To sum up, I think / I would say ...
After looking at all the arguments I think / I come to the conclusion that ...

c) CHECK AND CORRECT YOUR TEXT

- Auch bei *written discussions* plane mindestens einen Textentwurf und eine gründliche Überarbeitung ein. ▸ *p. 172*

8 Writing a book or film review ▸ Unit 2, p. 47 ▸ Unit 4, pp. 99, 134

1 Worum geht es?

Nicht nur Fachleute wie Journalisten oder Kritiker schreiben Kritiken zu Filmen oder Büchern, sondern auch viele Nicht-Profis geben zunehmend ihre Meinung zu Büchern und Filmen, die sie gelesen oder gesehen haben, in Internetportalen wieder. Auch Mitschüler sind daran interessiert, wie dir ein Film oder ein Buch gefallen hat.

2 Wie schreibe ich eine Kritik?

Überlege dir vorab, ob du den Film/ das Buch weiterempfehlen oder davon abraten möchtest. Dann baue deine Kritik wie folgt auf.

- **Einleitung** (background information)
  Nenne den Titel und das Genre (z. B. Komödie oder Thriller; Roman oder Sachbuch). Sag etwas über die wichtigsten Schauspieler bzw. Figuren und auch etwas zum Regisseur bzw. Autor. Du kannst wichtige zusätzliche Informationen zum Film oder Buch ergänzen (z.B. gewonnene Preise etc.)

- **Hauptteil** (specific information)
  Gib eine kurze Zusammenfassung: Ort und Zeit der Handlung, Hauptpersonen und die wichtigsten Inhalte. Benutze dafür das **simple present**. Schreibe über den Aufbau, den Handlungs- (*plot*) den Schauplatz (*setting*), die Figuren (*characters*) und die Stimmung (*mood*). ▸ *Skills file 7.7, p. 168*

- **Bewertung und Empfehlung**
  (your opinion and recommendation)
  Schreib, wie dir der Film oder das Buch gefallen hat und sag, woran das lag. Fandest du Handlung spannend und interessant oder langweilig? Warum? Was war ansprechend und ungewöhnlich?

  Falls du einen Film kritisierst: Wie waren die Schauspieler, wie gefiel dir die Filmmusik? Kannst du Buch oder Film empfehlen oder nicht? Wem könnte der Film bzw. das Buch gefallen?

3 Check and correct your review

Plane auch bei einem *review* mindestens einen Textentwurf und eine gründliche Überarbeitung ein.

USEFUL PHRASES
for writing a book or film review

... is a film / book by ...
It's a comedy / thriller / adventure film / documentary ...
The main actors / characters are ...

The film / book is about ...
It's the story of ...
The action takes place in ...
The story begins when ...
Later ... In the end ...

I really enjoyed ...
I think it's one of the best films of the last years because ...
Personally I think the story is exciting / weak / boring ...
The actors are just super / convincing....
The special effects are amazing and the music is wonderful.
If you like action / romantic feelings / to laugh (*film title*) is the movie for you.
I can recommend / wouldn't read this book / watch this film because I'm (not) interested in ...
I think that this film / book will be popular with girls / boys / anybody who likes ...

SF 10 Describing photos and pictures

▸ Unit 1, pp. 30, 104 ▸ Unit 4, pp. 106, 130

Wenn du ein Foto oder ein Bild beschreibst, beachte Folgendes:

1 Beginne allgemein

Sage zunächst, **was** du **allgemein** auf dem Foto oder Bild siehst. Welcher Ort, welche Gegenstände und welche Menschen siehst du? Was tun sie?

In the photo we can see a little girl and a young man.
They're sitting inside a big room, but not together.

2 Beachte eine Reihenfolge

Wen oder **was** siehst du; **wo** befinden sich die Personen oder Gegenstände im Foto?
Du kannst z.B. mit dem beginnen, was im Vordergrund bzw. im Hintergrund des Bildes zu sehen ist.
Benutze **Ortsangaben** wie

in the middle / on the left / on the right
at the top / bottom ...

Ordne die Personen und Dinge einander zu, indem du **Präpositionen** benutzt, z.B.

at / behind / between / in front of / near / next to / on ...

The (little) girl is in the foreground on the left sitting at a table.
The young man is in the background sitting on the floor.
In the background you can see windows and some trees outside.

3 Beschreibe Personen und Handlungen

Wie sehen die Personen aus (z.B. Alter, Kleidung, Gesichtsausdruck)? Um zu beschreiben, was sie gerade tun, benutze das ***present progressive***.

The man is using a laptop.
The girl is smiling.
The girl might be playing with dominoes or she might be building something with them.

4 Formuliere Vermutungen

In welchem **Verhältnis** stehen die Personen wahrscheinlich **zueinander**? Versetze dich in sie hinein und beschreibe, was sie gerade **fühlen** oder **denken** (könnten). Nützliche Wendungen dafür sind z.B.

I think / I'm sure / perhaps / probably / would / could ...

The man might be working or surfing or writing an email. He looks busy. He might be her father.
The girl is probably having fun or is happy that her father is at home.

5 Was denkst du persönlich?

Am Ende der Beschreibung sollst du häufig deine Meinung zur Situation und zum Verhalten der Personen formulieren.

Dabei hilft es, an deine eigenen Erfahrungen in ähnlichen Situationen zu denken. Du könntest auch Fragen stellen, die dir zu dieser Situation einfallen. Nützliche Wendungen sind hier z.B.:

I think / I guess / In my opinion / For me it's absolutely (not) okay / it's alright / it's wrong
If I was (the man / woman ... in the photo), I'd / I wouldn't ... because ...
I remember a similar situation / story ...

Maybe they're going to have a video-call with grandma.

It's also possible that the man is just checking the rules of the domino game online.

SF 11 VIEWING SKILLS

▸ Unit 2, p. 32

1 Vor dem Sehen: bereite dich vor

- Welche Art von Film wirst du sehen: a documentary, a movie, a commercial, a soap, the news, ...? Was weißt du bereits über die Art des Films?
- Lies sorgfältig die Aufgabenstellung. Worum könnte es gehen?
- Worauf musst du besonders achten? Was kann dir beim Verstehen helfen?
- Betrachte die Filmszenen im Buch vor dem Anschauen.

2 Beim Sehen

Häufig sollst du dich zum Schauplatz (*setting*), zu den Figuren (*characters*), zum Handlungsverlauf (*plot*) und zur Stimmung (*mood*) eines Filmausschnitts äußern. Nutze dieses Raster für Notizen:

a classroom in a British school, ... **setting**	four teenagers, a history teacher, ... **characters**
they talk about World War 1, ... **plot**	relaxed, sad, ... **mood**

Versuche beim ersten Sehen die wesentlichen Inhalte des Films zu erfassen. Beim zweiten Sehen kannst du dann auf Einzelheiten achten und deine Notizen ergänzen.

Kameraeinstellungen helfen dir, Inhalte und Gefühle besser zu verstehen.

- close-up
  Ein *close-up* ist eine Nahaufnahme eines Gesichts oder einer Gegenstandes. So kannst du z.B. am Gesichtsausdruck die Gefühle einer Person erkennen.
  What does Patrick look like in this close-up?
- long shot
  Ein *long shot* (auch: *wide shot*), die Totale, gibt dir einen Eindruck der gesamten Szene und des Schauplatzes.
  How many people are there? Where are they? Who are they?

close-up

long shot

Achte auf die Erzählstruktur des Filmes, z. B. monologue. Ein Monolog gibt dir die Möglichkeit, die Motive einer einzelnen Person besser zu verstehen.

Ein *flashback* (Rückblende) verändert die chronologische Reihenfolge. Dadurch kannst du Ereignisse besser verstehen oder erkennen, wieso jemand dieses oder jenes gemacht hat.
Why did the teenagers bully Patrick?
Filmtechniken werden eingesetzt, um z. B. Spannung, Lachen, Angst oder Freude auszulösen.
Weitere wichtige Aspekte beim Anschauen, auf die du achten kannst, um dein Verständnis zu schulen, wie Filme funktionieren: Farbe, Kameraführung, Kontraste, Licht, Perspektive, Schnitt und Ton.

3 Nach dem Sehen

Vervollständige deine Notizen.
Dabei helfen dir die Redewendungen rechts.

USEFUL PHRASES

The film is about .... / It tells the story of ...

The close-ups of .... make it easier to understand ...

The wide shot of the classroom shows ...

The monologues helped me to understand ...

The flashbacks showed ...

There is no music in the film / The music is dramatic / sad / ... because...

I (don't) like the film because ...

SF 12 MEDIATION SKILLS

▸ *Unit 1, pp. 14, 28, 31* ▸ *Unit 3, p. 123* ▸ *Unit 4, pp. 87, 103*

1 Worum geht es?

- Bei der **Mediation** (Sprachmittlung) gibst du englische Informationen auf Deutsch wieder, wie im Beispiel rechts.
- Oder du vermittelst deutsche Informationen **auf Englisch**, z.B. wenn bei dir an der Schule ein Austauschschüler zu Gast ist. Das kann mündlich geschehen (im Gespräch) oder auch schriftlich, wenn du dem Gastschüler z.B. eine Nachricht schreibst.

2 Worauf musst du achten?

- *Mediation* ist keine Übersetzung. Gib also nur **das Wesentliche** sinngemäß in einfachen Sätzen wieder.
- Wenn du **schriftliche Informationen** sprachmitteln sollst:
  - **Scanne** den Text gezielt nach den notwendigen Informationen.
    ▸ *Skills file 7.1, p. 166*
  - Ist der Text länger und du brauchst viele Informationen daraus, **markiere** die wichtigsten Textstellen und mach dir ggf. **Notizen** in deinen eigenen Worten.
    ▸ *Skills file 7.6, p. 168*
- Wenn du **mündliche Informationen** sprachmitteln sollst:
  - **Höre zielgerichtet** auf die notwendigen Informationen.
    ▸ *Skills file 6, p. 165*

Beispiele:

1. Einem englischsprachigen Reisenden in Deutschland sagst du, was eben in der Bahnhofsdurchsage Wichtiges zu hören war.
2. Bei einem Telefonat mit einem englischen Jobanbieter machst du Notizen, die du einem Freund mailst.
3. Du mailst einer künftigen Gastschülerin die wichtigsten Inhalte eurer Schulordnung auf Englisch.

3 Paraphrasieren (Umschreiben)

Wenn es dir schwerfällt, Inhalte auf Englisch wiederzugeben, dann nutze das Umschreiben unbekannter Wörter *(paraphrasing)*. Die folgenden **Strategien** helfen dir.

- Umschreibe mit Wörtern, die eine **ähnliche** oder die **gleiche Bedeutung** haben (Synonyme), mit Vergleichen oder mit **gegensätzlichen** Wörtern (Antonymen):
  It's the same as ... / It's (very) similar to ... / It works like ...
  It's the opposite of ...
  Seine Eltern leben getrennt. – *His parents don't live together.*
- Umschreibe mit dem **Oberbegriff** oder mit **Unterbegriffen**:
  Wir müssen noch ein paar Tulpen und Osterglocken kaufen.
  – *We need (to buy) some flowers.*
  Haben wir ausreichend Geschirr für die Party heute Abend?
  – *Are there enough plates and glasses, etc. for the party?*
- Umschreibe mit einer näheren Erläuterung, z.B. in **Relativsätzen**. ▸ *Language file 25, p. 198*
  It's somebody / a person who is known for ...

Oft hilft das Prinzip ***Keep it simple***. Fällt dir eine einfache Erklärung des gesuchten Begriffs ein? Diese kannst du dann leicht auf Englisch formulieren, z.B. Selbstbedienung – *no waiter / waitress*

4 Kulturelle und regionale Unterschiede

- Manche Alltagsdinge oder Traditionen wird dein Gegenüber eventuell nicht kennen. Du musst dann erklären, was du meinst.
- Natürlich wird es für dich auch Unbekanntes geben, worüber dein Gegenüber selbstverständlich spricht. Dann frage höflich nach.

Schultüte – It's a kind of special bag kids are given on their first day at school. There are sweets in it and little things you need at school, like pens and exercise books.

LANGUAGE FILE

Inhalt

TALKING ABOUT THE PRESENT — page
- LF 1 The simple present — 182
- LF 2 The present progressive — 183

TALKING ABOUT THE PAST
- LF 3 The simple past — 183
- LF 4 The past progressive — 184
- LF 5 The present perfect — 185
- LF 6 *The present perfect progressive — 186
- LF 7 The past perfect — 186

TALKING ABOUT THE FUTURE
- LF 8 The *going to*-future — 187
- LF 9 The *will*-future — 187

- LF 10 Using tenses — 187
- LF 11 Word order in statements — 188
- LF 12 Word order in questions — 189
- LF 13 Subject and object questions — 189
- LF 14 Questions with passives and modals — 190
- LF 15 Questions with prepositions — 190
- LF 16 The comparison of adjectives — 191
- LF 17 Adverbs of manner — 191
- LF 18 Adverbs of frequency — 192
- LF 19 The comparison of adverbs — 192
- LF 20 Indirect speech — 192
- LF 21 Modal verbs and their substitutes — 195
- LF 22 *If* ... (Conditional sentences type 1) — 196
- LF 23 *If* ... (Conditional sentences type 2) — 197
- LF 24 *If* ... (Conditional sentences type 3) — 197
- LF 25 Relative clauses — 198
- LF 26 *Contact clauses — 199
- LF 27 *Participle clauses instead of subordinate clauses — 199
- LF 28 Reflexive pronouns — 200
- LF 29 The *-ing*-form (the gerund) — 200
- LF 30 The passive — 202
- LF 31 Question tags — 203
- LF 32 The definite and the indefinite article — 203
- LF 33 Countable and uncountable nouns — 204
- Grammatical terms — 204

TALKING ABOUT THE PRESENT

LF 1 The simple present (Die einfache Form der Gegenwart)

Mit dem ***simple present*** drückst du aus, was **wiederholt** oder **nie** geschieht. Es steht häufig mit: *always, sometimes, often, never* oder Zeitangaben wie *every day, in the morning, at the weekend, on Monday.*

Bejahte und verneinte Aussagen

I/you/we/they	like	sport.
He/she/it	likes	

I/you/we/they	don't like	sport.
He/she/it	doesn't like	

Bei **bejahten Aussagen** fügst du bei *he/she/it* ein *-s* an das Verb.

! - *he/she/it goes, watches, tries, hurries*

! Das Verb nach doesn't (hier: *like*) steht immer in der Grundform. Das gilt auch für does in Fragen.

***Ja-/Nein*-Fragen und Kurzantworten**

Do you like	sport?	Yes, I do./No, I don't.
Does he like		Yes, he does./No, he doesn't.

Ja-/Nein-Fragen im ***simple present*** beginnst du mit *Do* oder *Does*.

Fragen mit Fragewort

Why do Ben's friends love football?

Wenn die Frage mit einem **Fragewort** anfängt, folgt direkt *do* bzw. *does*.

Fragen mit *Who ▸ *LF 13, p. 189*

Wenn das **Fragewort** *Who* nach dem **Objekt** fragt *(wen? wem?)*, folgt *do* bzw. *does*.
– *Who does Ben like?* **Wen** mag Ben? – *Who/What does Ben dislike?* **Wen/Was** mag Ben nicht?

Fragt *Who* nach dem **Subjekt** *(wer?)*, folgt direkt das Verb – **nie** ~~*do*~~ oder ~~*does*~~.
– *Who likes Ben?* **Wer** mag Ben? – *Who/What makes Ben angry?* **Wer/Was** macht Ben ärgerlich?

LF 2 The present progressive (Die Verlaufsform der Gegenwart)

Mit dem ***present progressive*** sagst du, dass etwas **gerade jetzt** geschieht oder dass jemand **gerade etwas tut**.
Das ***present progressive*** benutzt du auch, um Bilder zu beschreiben.
Häufige Zeitangaben in Sätzen im ***present progressive*** sind: *now, at the moment, just, still, today*.
Eine Verlaufsform gibt es im Deutschen nicht. Man sagt aber z.B.: „Ich bin gerade dabei, etwas zu tun."

Bejahte Aussagen

I'm / You're He's / She's They're	waiting.

Verneinte Aussagen

I'm not / You aren't He / She isn't They aren't	waiting.

Das ***present progressive*** bildest du mit einer Form von ***be*** + ***verb*** + ***-ing***.

! Beachte beim Schreiben:
write → writing *make → making*
plan → planning *stop → stopping*

Ja-/*Nein*-Fragen und Kurzantworten

Am I	waiting?	Yes, I am. / No, I'm not.
Are you Is he / she		Yes, he / she is. / No, ... isn't.
Are they		Yes, they are. / No, they aren't.

Ja-/Nein-Fragen beginnst du mit *Am / Are / Is*:
Is Mia going to football practice?
- Yes, she is. / No, she isn't. She's waiting for Li.

Fragen mit Fragewort

What's Mia doing today? Where is she going first?

Wenn die Frage mit einem **Fragewort** anfängt, steht das Fragewort vor *am / are / is*:
What's Mia doing at the moment?
Where are Mia and her friend going?

Present progressive oder simple present?

Mia is playing football. (***present progressive***)
Mia spielt Fußball. (= gerade, jetzt im Moment)

Mia plays football. (***simple present***)
Mia spielt Fußball. (= regelmäßig, es ist ihr Sport)

Mia often plays football, but she isn't playing today because it's raining.
Mia spielt oft Fußball, aber heute spielt sie nicht, weil es jetzt regnet.

Für den Satz „Mia spielt Fußball." kannst du entweder das ***present progressive*** oder das ***simple present*** benutzen, je nachdem, was du ausdrücken möchtest:

present progressive:	***simple present:***
just, at the moment, now, today	*always, often, sometimes, never, every day / week, on Saturdays*

TALKING ABOUT THE PAST

LF 3 The simple past (Die einfache Form der Vergangenheit)

Mit dem ***simple past*** sagst du, was **zu einer bestimmten Zeit** in der Vergangenheit geschah.
Du verwendest es oft mit Zeitangaben wie *yesterday, last week, in July, two years ago*.

! Freie Wahl: Perfekt oder Präteritum
Mia fuhr gestern zu Li. / Mia ist gestern zu Li gefahren. → ! ***Simple past***
Mia went to Li's yesterday.

a) Regelmäßige Verben (*regular verbs*)

Bejahte Aussagen

I/He/We/...	laughed a lot.

Bei **regelmäßigen** Verben bildest du das ***simple past*** durch Anhängen von ***-ed*** an das Verb:

! Beachte beim Schreiben: *try* → *tried*, *plan* → *planned*, *hurry* → *hurried*

b) Unregelmäßige Verben (*irregular verbs*)

Bejahte Aussagen

I/He/We/...	bought a book.

Lerne die ***simple past***-Formen **unregelmäßiger** Verben.

▸ *Irregular verbs, pp. 266–267*

Verneinte Aussagen

I/He/We/...	didn't know all the people.

Wenn du sagen willst, was **nicht** geschah, setzt du *didn't* vor das Verb in der **Grundform**:
Mia didn't buy a comic yesterday.

Ja-/Nein-Fragen und Kurzantworten

Did you/she /...	like it?	Yes, I did./No, I didn't. Yes, she did./No, she didn't.

! Das Verb *be* (*was/were*) verneinst du **ohne** ~~*did*~~.
The comics weren't new.

Fragen mit *be* (*was/were*) und Kurzantworten

Was I/he/she/it **Were** we/you/they	happy?	Yes he was./No, he wasn't. Yes, we were./No, we weren't.

Ja-/Nein-Fragen im ***simple past*** beginnst du mit *Did*.

! *Ja-/Nein*-Fragen mit *Was/Were* bildest du **ohne** ~~*did*~~, ebenso die Kurzantworten.

Fragen mit Fragewort

What did Mia like best about the comic?

Did folgt direkt auf das **Fragewort**.

! Das Verb nach *did* (hier: *like*) steht immer in der Grundform.

▸ *LF 13, p. 189*

LF 4 The past progressive (Die Verlaufsform der Vergangenheit)

At 5 pm Ben was taking part in a bike race.
Um 17 Uhr **nahm** Ben (gerade) an einem Radrennen **teil**.

His team was racing down a hill when a boy fell.
Sein Team **raste** gerade ..., als ... stürzte.

Mit dem ***past progressive*** drückst du aus, dass eine Handlung in der Vergangenheit **gerade im Gange** war.

Oder du beschreibst, was gerade vor sich ging, als etwas anderes geschah.

Das ***past progressive*** bildest du mit ***was/were*** + *verb* + ***-ing***.

! Beachte beim Schreiben: *verb* + ***-ing***

▸ *LF 2, p. 183*

Bejahte und verneinte Aussagen

I/He/She/It You/We/They	was/wasn't were/weren't	racing.

***Ja-/Nein*-Fragen und Kurzantworten**

Was/Were ... taking ...?	Yes, I/he was./ No, they weren't.

Fragen mit Fragewort

What was Ben doing at 5 pm?

LF 5 The present perfect (Das *present perfect*)

Mia and Li are shopping at the new mall. They've already been to three clothes shops. "We haven't found a shirt for me yet, Mia." "I know, but I'm hungry. I haven't eaten enough today."

! Das ***present perfect*** wird **immer** mit *have/has* gebildet, auch wenn im Deutschen eine Form von „sein" steht.

Das ***present perfect*** drückt aus, dass etwas irgendwann geschehen ist. Der Zeitpunkt ist unwichtig. Es steht häufig mit: *just, already, always, ever, never, not … yet.*

Du bildest das ***present perfect*** mit

have/has **+ 3. Form des Verbs**.

▸ *Irregular verbs, pp. 266–267*

Bejahte Aussagen

I/… 've He/… has	bought …

Verneinte Aussagen

I /… haven't He / … hasn't	bought …

***Ja-/Nein*-Fragen**

Have you/we … Has she/he …	bought …?

Kurzantworten

Yes, I /we … have. / No, I / we … haven't.
Yes, she / … has. / No, she /… hasn't.

Fragen mit Fragewort

Why have Mia and Li gone to the new mall?

Present perfect with *since* and *for*

! Auch wenn im Deutschen das Präsens steht, musst du mit *since* und *for* das ***present perfect*** benutzen:

I've lived next door to Mia **since** my family came to the US. Mia has been my friend **for** six years.

Ich bin Mias Nachbarin seit …

Das ***present perfect*** mit *since* oder *for* drückt aus, **seit wann** oder **wie lange** etwas schon andauert.

Since nennt einen Anfangs**zeitpunkt**: *since 6 am, since 2016, since I was a baby, …*

For umfasst einen **Zeitraum**: *for two months/ years/hours /for a long time.*

*Present perfect or simple past?

! Das ***present perfect*** steht häufig in Sätzen mit Zeitangaben wie *just, already, often, always, never, ever, not … yet, before.*

- um zu sagen, dass etwas **irgendwann** geschehen ist, oft mit **Auswirkungen auf die Gegenwart**.
  Greg has **just** come back from Oz.
- in Fragen mit *ever …?*
  Have you **ever** been to Uluru before, Greg?
- in Sätzen mit *since* und *for*
  His uncle has lived in Oz **since** 2011.

! Das ***simple past*** muss stehen in Sätzen mit Zeitangaben wie *yesterday, last week, in July, two years ago, in 2015.*

- um zu sagen, dass etwas **zu einer bestimmten Zeit** geschehen ist, oft mit genauer Zeitangabe.
  In 2015 Greg's uncle started a bar in Sydney.
- in Berichten und Erzählungen
  Greg asked his mum. Finally she agreed.
- in Fragen mit ***When*** …?
  When did you go on a trip last time?

LF 6 *The present perfect progressive
(Die Verlaufsform des *present perfect*)

Mit dem ***present perfect progressive*** sagst du, dass etwas **in der Vergangenheit** begonnen hat und **bis jetzt andauert** bzw. **gerade vorbei** ist.

Bejahte und verneinte Aussagen

I/…'ve He/…'s	been waiting for two hours.

I … He …	haven't been hasn't been	waiting long.

Häufige Zeitangaben in Sätzen im ***present perfect progressive*** sind:

since 7 am/2010/…/I came here **(Zeitpunkt)**

for two hours/a long time, in recent years **(Zeitraum)**

Du bildest das ***present perfect progressive*** mit ***have/has been*** + *verb* + ***-ing*.**

***Ja-/Nein*-Fragen und Kurzantworten**

Have you/… Has he/…	been waiting long?	Yes, …have/has. No, … haven't/hasn't.

Fragen mit Fragewort

How long have you been waiting?

! Im Deutschen verwendest du meist das Präsens:
How long have you been learning English?
Wie lange lernst du schon Englisch?

LF 7 The past perfect (Das *past perfect*)

When Li arrived at the party, Ben had already gone home. *(Erst ging Ben, dann kam Li.)*

Ben thought that Li had forgotten about the party.

Had he told her about it at all?

! Das ***past perfect*** wird **immer** mit ***had*** gebildet, auch wenn im Deutschen „war" steht.

Mit dem ***past perfect*** (Plusquamperfekt oder **Vor**vergangenheit) drückst du aus, dass etwas noch **vor** etwas anderem in der Vergangenheit stattgefunden hatte.

Du bildest das ***past perfect*** mit
had **+ 3. Form des Verbs (*past participle*).**

▸ *Irregular verbs, pp. 266–267*

Bejahte und verneinte Aussagen

I/… He/…	had/hadn't	forgotten.

***Ja-/Nein*-Fragen und Kurzantworten**

Had I …/he …	forgotten?	Yes, … had. No, … hadn't.

*Simple past or past perfect?

Before Li left home, it had started to rain heavily.

Mit dem ***past perfect*** sagst du, was zeitlich vorangegangen war. Oft stehen dabei Zeitangaben wie *after, when, before, already*.

So Li took an umbrella with her, but she forgot her phone.

! Keine Vorvergangenheit (***past perfect***), wenn etwas zur gleichen Zeit geschieht.

TALKING ABOUT THE FUTURE

LF 8 The *going to*-future (Das Futur mit *going to*)

Mia's going to have a football match next Saturday.
Mia wird nächsten Samstag ... haben.

Her brother Ben isn't going to come to the match.
Ihr Bruder hat nicht vor, es zu sehen.

What are we going to do on Sunday?
Was wollen wir am Sonntag machen?

Is the weather going to be fine?
Wird das Wetter gut?

! *Going to* hat hier nichts mit dem deutschen Wort *gehen* zu tun. Es heißt hier „werden / wollen / vorhaben / beabsichtigen".

Wenn du ausdrücken möchtest, was jemand in der Zukunft **plant** oder **vorhat** sowie für Vorhersagen benutzt du das Futur mit *going to*.

Es wird mit einer Form von *be* (*am / are / is*) gebildet, oft mit den Kurzformen:
'm / 're / 's + going to + verb

Verneinung:
Ben isn't going to be at Mia's match.
But she's not going to be angry with him.

Fragen und Kurzantworten:
Is it going to rain?
- (Look at the sky!) Yes, it is. / No, it isn't.

LF 9 The *will*-future (Das Futur mit *will*)

Bejahte und verneinte Aussagen

I / You / He / She / It We / You / They	will like the concert. won't like all the songs.

Ja-/Nein-Fragen und Kurzantworten

Will	I / you / he / ...	like all the songs?	Yes, ... will. No, ... won't.

Fragen mit Fragewort

Who will win the match tomorrow?
When will we get home?

! Englisch *I will* heißt im Deutschen „ich werde" und nicht „ich will".

Mit dem ***will-future*** kannst du über die Zukunft sprechen, z.B. über **Vermutungen** und **Vorhersagen** oder auch einen spontanen Entschluss äußern.

Eine **Vermutung** beginnt oft mit *I think, I'm sure, Maybe.*
I think I'll enjoy the concert. – I'm sure you will.

Bei **Vorhersagen** geht es oft um Dinge, die man nicht direkt beeinflussen kann:
It'll be winter soon.

Ein **spontaner Entschluss** ist oft ein Hilfsangebot oder ein Versprechen.
I'll get my money and then I'll buy you an ice cream.

Das ***will-future*** wird mit ***will* + Verb** gebildet. Die Kurzform von *will* heißt ***'ll***.
! Die **Verneinung *will not*** wird in der Kurzform zu ***won't***.

NEW LF 10 Using tenses (Die Verwendung der Zeitformen) ▸ Unit 1, p. 19

Du kannst die **wichtigsten Zeitformen des Verbs** im Englischen bilden. Manchmal werden sie anders **gebraucht** als im Deutschen. Das ist wichtig, wenn du **eigene Texte** schreibst.

simple present ▸ LF 1, p. 182

Cycling is Ben's favourite sport. He practises hard. He often wins races. He doesn't like to lose them.

Mit dem ***simple present*** drückst du aus, was wiederholt oder nie geschieht. Du benutzt es, wenn du **Orte, Zustände, Gewohnheiten** und **Vorgänge / Abläufe** beschreibst und bei **Zusammenfassungen**.
▸ Skills file 9.4, p. 174.

present progressive (▸ LF 2, p. 183)

In this photo Ben is cyling down a street. Two boys are following him. A car is just coming from the right.

Mit dem ***present progressive*** drückst du aus, was **gerade geschieht**. Du benutzt es auch bei **Bildbeschreibungen** ▸ Skills file 10, p. 179.

simple past (▸ LF 3, p. 183)

Mia met her friend Li in a cafe yesterday. They didn't eat a lot because it was a very hot day. But they had a big ice cream together.

Mit dem ***simple past*** sagst du, was **zu einer bestimmten Zeit** in der Vergangenheit geschah. Das ***simple past*** verwendest du in **Berichten** und beim **Erzählen**.

***going to*-future** (▸ LF 8, p. 187)

What are Mia, Ben and Li going to do next Sunday?
They're going to go to a concert. (They've already got the tickets.)

Was jemand **in der Zukunft plant** oder **vorhat**, drückst du mit dem ***going to*-future** aus.

***will*-future** (▸ LF 9, p. 187)

Ben: "I'm afraid I won't have time to come to your match, Mia. But I promise I'll be at your next match.

Mit dem ***will*-future** kannst du über die Zukunft sprechen, z.B. über **Vermutungen** und **Vorhersagen**.

LF 11 Word order in statements

(Die Verwendung der Zeitformen) ▸ Unit 3, p. 66

Die Regel zur Wortstellung im englischen Satz ist **subject – verb – object**, kurz **S-V-(O)**.
Subjekt – Prädikat – (Objekt) (Ein Objekt gibt es nicht immer.)

! Anders als im Deutschen wird von **S-V-O** nicht abgewichen, z.B. bei Orts- oder Umstandsangaben *(In englischen Sätzen stellst du nicht um.)* bzw. Zeitangaben *(Gestern wusste ich das noch.)*

subject	verb	object	adverbial *(Adverbialbestimmung)*	
Mia	plays	football.		
She	can't play	an instrument.		
Ben and Mia	have bought	tickets.		
Ben and Mia	are interested in	music.		
They	didn't go		to concerts	last year.

Mia usually plays football. Ben sometimes phones Li.

Die **Adverbien der Häufigkeit** *usually, always, often, sometimes, never* stehen **zwischen Subjekt** und **Verb**.

Mia and Ben have already bought tickets. They are planning how to get to the concert. Have you ever been to a concert?

Die **Adverbien der Zeit**, wie *already, ever, just, never* stehen **vor** dem ***present participle*** (*-ing*-Form) bzw. dem ***past participle*** (dritte Form) **des Verbs**.

Luckily Ben and Mia still got cheap tickets.
Ben und Mia bekamen glücklicherweise noch …

Die **Adverbien**, die sich auf den **gesamten Satz** beziehen, wie *perhaps/maybe, suddenly, finally, of course, at first* stehen meist am **Satzanfang**.

After the date with Li, Ben walked home happily.

Adverbien, die sich auf ein Verb bzw. eine Tätigkeit beziehen, stehen in der Regel **am Satzende**.

Ben had first met Li **at Mia's club two months ago**.

! Gibt es in einem Satz eine **Orts- und** eine **Zeitangabe**, gilt die **Regel „Ort vor Zeit"**.

LF 12 Word order in questions (Die Wortstellung in Fragen)

▸ Unit 3, p. 66

Du erkennst eine Frage daran, dass hier **vor** dem **Subjekt** eine konjugierte (gebeugte) **Verbform** steht.

Fragen mit *do / does* und *did*

Viele Fragen bildest du mit einer Form von *do*, einem Hilfsverb (*auxiliary*). Es „hilft" sozusagen dabei, dass die Wortstellung des zugrundeliegenden Aussagesatzes einfach erhalten bleiben kann. Vergleiche:

Aussagesatz (S-V-O)
Mia and Li play football.

→

Fragesatz (Hilfsverb-S-V-O)
Do Mia and Li play football? (*Ja-/Nein*-Frage)
When do Mia and Li play football? (Frage mit Fragewort)

Weitere Fragesätze:

question word	auxiliary *do(es)/did*	subject	(main) verb	
	Does	Ben	work	on Fridays?
	Did	he and Li	go	to the cinema?
What	does	Ben	watch	on TV?
Where	did	you	buy	that DVD?

Du beginnst die Frage mit (Fragewort +) *do/does/did*, dann folgt das Subjekt und dann das Hauptverb *(main verb)*.

! Keine **Umstellungen** von **Verb** und **Subjekt** wie im Deutschen:
Arbeitet Ben? → *Does Ben work?*

! Das Hauptverb steht **immer** in der **Grundform** (Infinitiv). Gebeugt (konjugiert) wird das Hilfsverb.

Fragen mit Formen von *be* und *have*

Wenn der Fragesatz eine Form von ***be*** oder ***have*** enthält, steht diese **vor** dem **Subjekt**.

question word	verb (forms of *be / have*)	subject	
	Is	Mia	Ben's sister?
	Are	Mia and Li	good friends?
	Have	you	been to school?
Where	were	you	last weekend?
What	are	Mia and Li	planning for Friday?

Ein **Fragesatz** mit *be* oder *have* wird gebildet, indem du die entsprechende Form, z.B. *is, was, were; have, has* **vor** das **Subjekt** stellst.

Fragewörter – *who, what, when, where, why, how, how long* – stehen am **Satzanfang**.

NEW LF 13 Subject and object questions

(Fragen nach dem Subjekt oder dem Objekt) ▸ Unit 3, More challenge 2, p. 125

***Ben** likes Li.*

Who **likes** Li? – **Ben**.
Wer mag Li?

Who **does** **Ben** like? – Li.
Wen mag Ben?

***The noise** disturbed Li.*
What **disturbed** Li? – **The noise.**
Was störte Li? – Der Lärm.
***Li** shut the window.*
What **did** **Li** shut? – **The window.**
Was schloss Li? – Das Fenster.

Mit den Fragewörtern *who/what/which* kannst du nach dem Subjekt oder nach dem Objekt fragen.

Wenn das **Fragewort** nach dem **Subjekt** *(wer?/was?)* fragt, **folgt direkt das Vollverb – nie ~~do~~ oder ~~does~~ als Hilfsverb.**

Wenn das **Fragewort** nach dem **Objekt** fragt *(wen?/wem?/was?)*, **folgt *do* bzw. *does*.**

Nach dem Subjekt der Frage, z.B. *Ben*, steht dann gemäß der **S-V-(O)-Regel** das Hauptverb.

! Das Hauptverb steht in der Grundform (Infinitiv).

NEW LF 14 Questions with passive and modals

(Fragen im Passiv und mit Modalverben) ▸ *More practice 6, p. 125*

Fragen im Passiv

question word	form of *be*	subject	*past participle*	
	Is	Ben	called	*Benny* by his fans?
	Was	he	invited	to a party?
When	were	you	born,	Ben?
Why	isn't	your team	supported	by sponsors?

Da du das Passiv mit ***be + past participle*** bildest, beginnst du *Ja-/Nein*-Fragen mit der Form von ***be***, die hier Hilfsverb ist.

Bei Fragen mit **Fragewort** steht die Form von ***be* zwischen** Fragewort und Subjekt.

Fragen mit Modalverben

question word	*modal verb*	subject	(main) verb	
	Can	Ben	meet	Li on Friday?
	May	she	go	to a party then?
	Should	Li	ask	her parents?
When	will	Ben and Li	meet?	
What else	must	Ben	prepare	for the party?

Ja-/Nein-Fragen mit ***modals*** beginnen mit dem **Modalverb**.

Bei Fragen mit **Fragewort** steht das ***modal* zwischen** Fragewort und Subjekt.

NEW LF 15 Questions with prepositions

(Fragen mit Fragewörtern und Präpositionen) ▸ *More challenge 4, p. 126*

Ben waved goodbye to his team. Then he walked with Li to her house.

Ben and Li spent the afternoon with Li's family. They laughed at her mum's funny stories.

Now they are looking forward to next weekend. They're waiting for a visitor from Germany.

Präpositionen, z.B. *after, at, for, from, in, of, on, to,* stehen **vor Nomen** oder **Pronomen**.

Es gibt auch viele typische **Wendungen** (Verb + Präposition), z.B. *look at, wait for, be afraid of, wave to, ...*

Who did Ben wave goodbye to?
  Wem winkte Ben zum Abschied **zu**?

Who did he walk with?
  Mit wem ging er spazieren?

Who did Ben and Li spend the afternoon with?
  Mit wem verbrachten Ben und Li den Nachmittag?

What did they laugh at?
  Worüber haben sie gelacht/lachten sie?

What are they looking forward to?
  Worauf freuen sie sich?

Who/What are they waiting for?
  Auf wen/Worauf warten sie?

Wenn du **Fragen mit Präpositionen** bildest, stehen die **Fragewörter** *Who/What* **am Anfang**, die **Präpositionen** stehen häufig **am Ende der Frage**.

! Im Deutschen stehen die Präpositionen meist vor dem Fragewort, z.B. *Mit **wem** spielst du gern?* → **Who** do you like to play with?

Häufig gibt es im Deutschen besondere Fragewörter, z.B.
- ***Womit** spielst du gern?* → **What** do you like to play with?

LF 16 The comparison of adjectives (Die Steigerung der Adjektive)

The comparison with *-er* / *-est* and *more* / *most*

Wenn du Personen oder Dinge vergleichst, benutzt du Steigerungsformen.
Mit der 1. Steigerungsform + ***than*** („als") vergleichst du zwei **unterschiedliche** Personen oder Dinge.

Ben thinks English is hard, but maths is harder than English.
But today PE seems to be the hardest of all.

Bei **kurzen** (einsilbigen) Adjektiven und bei Adjektiven mit der Endung *-**y*** hängst du für die Steigerung *-er* und *-est* an das Adjektiv:

cheap	*cheaper*	*(the) cheapest*

! Beachte beim Schreiben:

*nic**e***	*nicer*	*(the) nicest*
*health**y***	*health**ier***	*(the) health**iest***
big	*bigger*	*(the) biggest*

Li prefers a big bowl of ice cream – the biggest she can get.
But she doesn't have enough money for the most expensive one.

Bei **längeren** (zwei- oder dreisilbigen) Adjektiven stellst du ***more*** und ***most*** *vor* das Adjektiv:

expensive	*more expensive*	*(the) most expensive*

Chocolate looks good, it's better than vanilla.
It's the best – and it's cheap too.

! Merke dir die **unregelmäßig** gesteigerten Adjektive, z.B.:

good	*better*	*(the) best*
much / many	*more*	*(the) most*
bad	*worse*	*(the) worst*

The comparison with *as ... as*

Li doesn't think that ice cream is unhealthy.
It's as healthy as all the other things on the menu.

Mit dem Vergleich (***not***) ***as*** ... ***as*** ... kannst du ausdrücken, dass zwei Personen oder Dinge gleich (oder nicht gleich) sind.

LF 17 Adverbs of manner (Adverbien der Art und Weise)

Adjektive beschreiben **Nomen** näher. *Luis was a happy boy after the basketball match.*

Adverbien der Art und Weise beschreiben **Verben** näher. *Luis walked home happily.*

Adverbien der Art und Weise stehen nach dem Verb, oft am Satzende:

Li's morning was going terribly.
*(**Wie** lief der Morgen für Li? – Schrecklich.)*

She couldn't find her ticket and looked for it very carefully, but still couldn't find it.
She left the house angrily.

Then she ran to school fast.
She worked very hard in maths that day.
In the evening her team played well in the basketball match.

So Li walked home happily. She felt good in the end.

Du bildest ein Adverb der Art und Weise meist durch Anhängen von *-ly* an das Adjektiv:

! Merke dir **unregelmäßige** Adverbformen:

Adjektiv	**Adverb**
*Li is a **fast** runner.*	*Li ran **fast**.*
*She had a **hard** day at school.*	*She worked **hard** in class.*
*But she was **good** at sport.*	*She played **well**.*

! Nach den Verben *feel, look, sound, taste, smell* folgt **kein** Adverb, sondern ein Adjektiv.

LF 18 Adverbs of frequency (Adverbien der Häufigkeit)

Diese drücken aus, wie häufig jemand etwas tut oder wie häufig etwas geschieht: *always, usually, often, sometimes, never*. (Zur Wortstellung im Satz ▸ LF 11, p. 188)

Hi guys,
How's it going? I sometimes miss home, but seeing the famous sights of Oz is always exciting! You never get bored. I don't often check my emails because I don't have a lot of time. We usually do lots of things together.
...

Adverbien der Häufigkeit stehen:

- nach ***be***:
  *Uluru **is** always interesting for tourists.*
- vor einem Vollverb:
  *I sometimes **miss** home.*
- bei zusammengesetzten Verbformen nach dem Hilfsverb (*don't, have, ...*):
  *I **don't** often **check** my emails.*

LF 19 Comparison of adverbs (Die Steigerung der Adverbien)

Du kannst auch Adverbien steigern. Du bildest die zwei Steigerungsformen wie bei Adjektiven.

▸ LF 16, p. 191

Ben spoke more slowly to help the new exchange student understand.

Adverbien, die auf ***-ly*** enden, steigerst du mit ***more/most***, z.B.

slowly — *more slowly* — *(the) most slowly*

Of all students, Ben was the most friendly to Moritz.

Everyone was fast, but Li was the fastest.

Einsilbige Adverbien werden mit *-er/-est* gesteigert:

fast — *faster* — *(the) fastest*

The race went well, much better than Li had expected.

! Beachte:

well — *better* — *(the) best*

LF 20 Indirect speech (Indirekte Rede)

Direct speech (Direkte Rede)

Emily says/said, "I like my new friend Kai."
Emily sagt/sagte: „Ich mag meinen neuen Freund Kai."

Mit der **direkten Rede** gibst du ***wörtlich*** wieder, was jemand sagt, schreibt oder denkt (bzw. gesagt/geschrieben/gedacht hat). Direkte Rede steht meist in Anführungszeichen.

Indirect speech (Indirekte Rede)

Emily says _ (that) she likes her new friend Kai.
Emily sagt, dass sie ihren neuen Freund Kai mag.

Mit der **indirekten Rede berichtest** du, was jemand sagt, schreibt oder denkt. Einleitende Verben sind z.B.: *say, tell sb., add, answer, think, explain*.

! Im Englischen steht vor der indirekten Rede **kein** Komma, und *that* („dass") wird oft weggelassen.

! Achte bei der **indirekten Rede** darauf, **wer** spricht bzw. schreibt. Personen und Pronomen sowie Verbformen ändern sich:
"I like my new friend Kai." → *... she likes her new friend Kai.*

NEW Indirect speech: backshift (Indirekte Rede: *backshift*)

▸ Unit 2, p. 40

Emily said_ (that) she liked Kai.
Emily sagte, dass sie Kai mag/gut finden würde.

Steht das einleitende Verb im ***simple past***, z.B. *said, told, added, answered, thought, explained,* verschiebt sich auch die Zeitform des Verbs der ursprünglichen Aussage meist ins ***simple past*** oder ins ***past perfect*** (letzteres häufiger in der Schriftsprache).
Dieses (Rück-)Verschieben in die Vergangenheit heißt auf Englisch ***backshift*** *(of tenses)*.

She told Kai her name was Emily and she hadn't been to this club before.
She was there for the first time.
Sie sagte (zu) Kai, ihr Name sei/wäre Emily und sie wäre noch nie in diesem Club gewesen.
Daher sei/wäre sie zum ersten Mal dort.

Wenn **mehrere Aussagen bzw. Sätze in indirekter Rede** wiedergegeben werden, benötigst du nicht jedes Mal einen neuen Einleitungssatz.

Emily: "I'm 16. I live in Braxton."
➡ Kai to Josh: "Emily told me she's (*was*) 16. And she lives (*lived*) in Braxton."

In der **Umgangssprache** wendet man den ***backshift of tenses*** bei immer noch gültigen (oder allgemeinen) Tatsachen **nicht immer** an.

NEW Indirect speech: questions (Indirekte Rede: Fragen)

▸ Unit 2, p. 41

Kai asked Emily, "Where do you live?"
➡ Kai asked Emily_ where she lived.
Kai fragte Emily, wo sie wohnt/wohne/wohnte.

He also asked, "How did you get here?"
➡ He also wanted to know how she had got there.
Er wollte auch wissen, wie sie hergekommen war.

Bei der Wiedergabe von **Fragen in indirekter Rede** musst du die **gleichen Regeln** wie bei Aussagen beachten:

- **Personen** und **Pronomen ändern** sich je nachdem, wer spricht, denkt oder schreibt.
- Steht das **einleitende Verb** im ***simple past*** (z.B. *asked, wanted to know, wondered, thought),* verschiebt sich auch hier die Zeitform des Verbs, meist ins ***simple past*** oder ***past perfect*** (***backshift*** *of tenses).*

Emily asked, "How often are you at this club?"
➡ Emily asked how often he was at that club.
Emily fragte, wie oft er in diesem Klub sei.

! Wie im Deutschen steht **am Ende** einer indirekten Frage **kein Fragezeichen**, sondern ein **Punkt**.

Fragewörter werden übernommen, jedoch entspricht die Wortstellung im Nebensatz jetzt Aussagesätzen, vgl. ... *how often ~~do/does/did~~ he was* ... -> ***subject*** – ***verb***: **S-V-(O)**

▸ LF 11, p. 188

Kai asked Emily, "Do you like our club?"
➡ Kai asked Emily_ if she liked their club.
Kai fragte Emily, ob sie ihren Klub mochte.

He asked, "Are you a good singer?"
➡ He wanted to know if she was a good singer.
..., ob sie eine gute Sängern sei/wäre/sein würde.

Bei ***Ja-/Nein*-Fragen** wird (wie im Deutschen „ob“) im Englischen ***if*** *(oder whether)* eingefügt. Auch hier gilt die **Wortstellung** von **Aussagesätzen**: **S-V-(O)**.

▸ LF 11, p. 188

He asked, "Can you come to the talent show?"
➡ He asked if she could come to ...
... ob sie kommen könnte.

! Verwechsle ***if*** = **ob** in indirekten Fragen **nicht** mit ***if*** = **falls/wenn**, was du aus *If*-Sätzen kennst.

▸ LF 22–24, pp. 196–198

NEW *Indirect speech: commands, requests, advice*
(Aufforderungen, Bitten, Ratschläge in indirekter Rede) ▸ *Unit 2, p. 41*

Dan told Kai, "Get lost."
➡ Dan told Kai **to** get lost.
Dan forderte Kai auf, zu verschwinden.

And he added, "Don't be a pain!"
➡ And he asked him **not to** be a pain.
Und er fügte hinzu, dass er nicht nerven sollte.

Kai told Emily, "You shouldn't listen to Dan."
➡ Kai told Emily not to listen to Dan.

Emily said to Kai, "Please, walk me home."
➡ Emily asked Kai to walk her home.
Emily bat Kai, sie nach Hause zu begleiten.

Kai asked her, "Can you give me your address, please?"
➡ Kai asked her to give him her address.
Kai bat sie, ihm ihre Adresse zu geben.

Aufforderungen, Befehle und **Ratschläge** werden in **indirekter Rede** meist eingeleitet mit: *tell/told sb.* ***to*** *(do sth.)*

Bei **Verboten** und **Verneinungen** wird vor dem Infinitiv mit *to* das ***not*** eingeschoben:
tell/ told s.b. ***not to*** *(do sth.)*
bzw. *ask/ tasked s.b.* ***not to*** *(do sth.)*

Bitten werden in **indirekter Rede** meist eingeleitet mit: *ask/asked sb.* ***to*** *(do sth.)*.

NEW Indirect speech: More on backshift
(Indirekte Rede: Weiteres zum *backshift*) ▸ *Unit 2, p. 42*

Den ***backshift of tenses*** – das Rückverschieben in eine andere Zeitstufe in der Vergangenheit – hast du in der **indirekten Rede** z.B. bei der Änderung von ***simple present*** in **simple past** kennen gelernt, wenn der **Einleitungssatz im *simple past*** steht, z.B.

Emily says, "I like Kai." ➡ *Later Emily told her best friend (that) she liked Kai.*

Emily said, "Kai is a nice guy."
➡ Emily told her friend Kai was a nice guy.

She told her, "We met at a music club."
➡ She told her they had met at a music club.

She added, "I have never been there before."
➡ She added she had never been there before.

She thought, "Next Saturday I'll meet him again. ...
➡ She thought she would meet him again on Saturday.

"And maybe I can learn more about him."
➡ (And) Maybe she could learn more about him.

!
simple present *(is)* wird ***simple past*** *(was)*

simple past *(met)* wird ***past perfect*** *(had met)*

present perfect *(have been)* wird ebenfalls ***past perfect*** *(had been)*

> ***will (future)*** *(will meet)* wird ***would*** *(would meet)*

> ***can*** *(can learn)* wird ***could*** *(could learn)*

LF 21 Modal verbs and their substitutes
(Modalverben und ihre Ersatzformen)

Modal verbs (modale Hilfsverben) sind z.B. *can, must, should* und ihre Verneinungen. Du benutzt sie, um auszudrücken, was jemand **kann**, **darf**, **muss**, **soll** oder **nicht kann** usw.

Ben's coach said, "You may leave earlier tonight." Ben was happy because he could go to the party and meet Li.

Bens Trainer sagte: „Du darfst heute Abend früher ...". Ben war ..., weil er ... konnte.

Modal verbs haben nur eine Form, z.B. *can*, *must* oder *may* für alle Personen, d.h. kein ***-s*** bei *he/she/it*.

But then his coach added that Ben shouldn't forget the match next week. So Ben asked, "Well, should I stay until the end of practice, after all?"

... ergänzte sein Trainer, dass er ... nicht vergessen sollte. Also fragte Ben „Hm, soll ich doch ...?"

Die **Verneinung** und die **Frage** werden **ohne** ~~do/does/did~~ gebildet.

"Can/May I borrow your black dress for the party, please?" Li asked her mum.
- "Yes, you can/may./No, you can't/may not."

„Darf ich mir bitte dein ... borgen?" ...
- „Ja, du darfst./Nein, du darfst nicht."

Modal verbs dürfen nur in Kurzantworten allein stehen.

Li to Mia: "I'm sorry, I must go now. I have to pick up mum's black dress from the dry-cleaner's. I'm allowed to wear it to the party!"

"I wasn't able to do it yesterday because I had to prepare my presentation on *Native Australians* for tomorrow morning."

Modal verbs haben nur eine ***simple present***-Form. Weitere Zeitformen bildest du **mit anderen Verben** mit ähnlicher Bedeutung:

müssen:	*must*	→ ***have to***
dürfen:	*can/may*	→ ***be allowed to***
können:	*can*	→ ***be able to***

Verneinte Aussagen

You mustn't play in the street.
! Du darfst nicht ...

You don't have to play in a team.
You needn't play in a team.
Du musst/brauchst nicht ...

Verneinte Aussagen

You can't You aren't allowed to Du darfst nicht ...	play in the street. play in a team.

Verneinte Aussagen

The team can't The team isn't able to The team is unable to	win the game today.

Mit diesen Verben kannst du **alle Zeitformen** bilden, auch das *simple present*:

müssen

simple present: *must* oder *have/has to* (muss)
simple past: *had to* (musste)
future: *will have to* (wird ... müssen)

dürfen

simple present: *can/may*
oder *am/are/is allowed to* (darf)
simple past: *was/were allowed to* (durfte)
future: *will be allowed to* (wird ... dürfen)

können (fähig sein)

simple present: *can* oder *am/are/is able to* (kann)
simple past: *could* oder *was/were able to* (konnte)
future: *will be able to* (wird ... können)

Ja-/Nein-Fragen

Can / May Should Must	I / he practise now?

Must I go now?
- No, but you may go.

Do / Did I / you / they Does / Did he / she Muss / Müssen / Musste(n) …	have to practise hard? hart üben / trainieren?

Did he have to go?
- No, he didn't have to go.

Am / Are / Is … Was / Were … Will … be	allowed to …? able to …?

Was he allowed to go?
- Yes, he was.

LF 22 *If* … (Conditional sentences type 1) (Bedingungssätze Typ 1)

Mit ***if***-Sätzen (Bedingungssätzen Typ 1) sagst du, was unter bestimmten Bedingungen geschieht oder geschehen wird: „**Was ist, wenn …**"

Nebensatz
If Mia's team plays well next time,
Hauptsatz
they'll win the summer contest.
Wenn Mias Team nächstes Mal gut spielt, werden sie den Sommer-Wettbewerb gewinnen.

Bedingungssätze bestehen aus zwei Teilsätzen:

Die **Bedingung** wird im ***if***-Satz (Nebensatz) genannt. Das Verb steht im ***simple present***:

If they ***play …,***

Die **Folge für die Zukunft** steht im **Hauptsatz**. Hier steht meist das ***will*-future**:

… they ***will …*** ▸ *LF 9, p. 187*

Their team will only finish in second place _ if they don't fight hard.
Ihr Team wird nur Zweiter sein, wenn sie nicht kämpfen.

= If they don't fight hard, their team will only finish in second place.
Wenn sie nicht kämpfen, wird ihr Team nur Zweiter sein.

Der ***if***-Teil kann am Anfang oder am Ende stehen.

! Anders als im Deutschen setzt man **kein Komma**, wenn der ***if***-Teil am **Ende** steht.

"I'll ask the coach for her advice when I see her."
… wenn ich sie sehe.
(Es steht fest, dass Mia die Trainerin trifft. Dann fragt sie.)

"I'll ask the coach for her advice if I see her."
… falls ich sie sehe. *(Es ist unsicher, ob sie sich treffen.)*

! Nicht verwechseln:
- ***when*** bedeutet „sobald wie", „dann, wenn"
- ***if*** bedeutet „wenn", „falls"

If you need advice, you **can/should** ask the coach.
Wenn ihr Rat braucht, könnt ihr /solltet ihr die Trainerin fragen.

Im **Hauptsatz** können auch stehen:
- *can, must, should* + Infinitiv ▸ *LF 21, p. 195*

Please **phone** me if you want to talk to me.
Bitte ruft mich an, wenn ihr … wollt.

- oder eine Aufforderung bzw. Bitte (ein **Imperativ**).

LF 23 *If* … (Conditional sentences type 2) (Bedingungssätze Typ 2)

Mit Bedingungssätzen Typ 2 sagst du, was unter unwahrscheinlichen oder unsicheren Bedingungen geschehen würde: „**Was wäre, wenn …**“

Nebensatz
If Greg had enough money,
Hauptsatz
he'd travel everywhere.
Wenn Greg genug Geld hätte, würde er …

Hauptsatz
But his friend Tina wouldn't travel
Nebensatz
even if she won a trip around the world.
Aber seine Freundin Tina würde nicht reisen, selbst wenn sie … gewinnen würde.

If you were travelling around the world, you **could** forget about school.
Wenn du auf … wärst, könntest du … vergessen.

Da die **Bedingung** im ***if***-Satz unwahrscheinlich ist (hier: genug Geld), ist unsicher, ob die **Folge** im **Hauptsatz** (hier: das Reisen überall hin) Wirklichkeit wird.
Im Deutschen verwendet man hier oft ***würde/wäre/hätte***.

Auch ***if***-Sätze Typ 2 bestehen wie ***if***-Sätze Typ 1 aus zwei Teilsätzen: ▸ *LF 22, p. 196*

Die (unwahrscheinliche) **Bedingung** steht im ***if***-Satz. Das Verb steht im ***simple past***, z.B. *had, won*.

Die (unsichere) **Folge** steht im **Hauptsatz**. Dort benutzt du *would* (Kurzform ***'d***) bzw. für die Verneinung *wouldn't* + Infinitive.

! Auch bei Typ 2 kein Komma vor dem ***if***-Teil.
Im **Hauptsatz** kann auch *could* + Infinitiv stehen.

Forms of *would*

Bejahte und verneinte Aussagen

I/You/He/… We/…	'd/would/wouldn't	travel to Oz.

Greg would travel everywhere if he could, but Tina wouldn't come with him.

***Ja-/Nein*-Fragen mit Kurzantworten**

Would I/he/we/…	travel to Oz?	Yes, … would. No, … wouldn't.

Would you go on a trip around the world if you had the chance? – Yes, you would.

Fragen mit Fragewort

Where/How/ … would	I/you/he/… …?

Where would you travel first – to the US or to Oz? How would you get there?

NEW LF 24 *If* … (Conditional sentences type 3)
(Bedingungssätze Typ 3) ▸ *Unit 4, p. 89*

Mit Bedingungssätzen Typ 3 **stellst du dir vor**, was **in der Vergangenheit** unter bestimmten Bedingungen hätte geschehen können: „**Was wäre gewesen, wenn …**“

Nebensatz
If it had been warmer,
Hauptsatz
Li would have gone to the beach.
Wenn es wärmer gewesen wäre, wäre Li zum Strand gegangen. *(Es war aber nicht wärmer, und Li war nicht am Strand.)*

Da die **Bedingung** im ***if***-Satz **nicht erfüllt** ist, können über die **Folge** im **Hauptsatz** nur Vermutungen angestellt werden.

Im Deutschen verwendet man oft ***wäre*** *gewesen/gegangen/… oder* ***hätte*** *gehabt/gegeben/…*

Hauptsatz
Li would have phoned Mia
Nebensatz
if she had had her new number.
Li hätte Mia (ja) angerufen, wenn sie deren neue Telefonnummer gehabt hätte. *(Aber sie kannte sie nicht oder hatte sie verlegt.)*

If Li had asked Mia's brother Ben, he could have helped her. … hätte er ihr helfen können.

If she'd asked Ben, he'd have given her Mia's number. … gefragt hätte, hätte er ihr … gegeben.

Die (nicht erfüllte) **Bedingung** steht im ***if*-Satz**. Das Verb steht im ***past perfect*** z.B. *had been, had had, had helped.* ▸ *LF 7, p. 186*

Die (vermutete) **Folge** steht im **Hauptsatz**. Dort benutzt du ***would/wouldn't*** + ***have*** + ***past participle*** (3. Form).

! Auch hier steht kein Komma vor dem ***if***-Teil.

Im **Hauptsatz** kann auch ***could*** + ***have*** + ***past participle*** stehen.

! Die **Kurzform** von ***would*** und von ***had*** ist ***'d***:
he'd (= he would) have given.
she'd (= she had) asked.

LF 25 Relative clauses (Relativsätze)

Mit Relativsätzen sagst du genauer, **wen** oder **was** du meinst.

Is there something wrong with people who don't use social media?

Someone who uses social media often has several profile pictures.

Wenn du **Menschen** genauer beschreibst, benutzt du meistens ***who***:
the man/woman/people/someone ***who*** *…*
der Mann, **der** …/die Frau, **die** …/Leute, **die**…/…

I prefer a profile picture that is creative and different.

But many people use standard pictures that look boring.

Wenn du **Dinge** (oder Tiere) genauer beschreibst, benutzt du meistens ***that***:
a picture/(the) food/animals/the things ***that*** *…*
ein Bild/das Essen, **das** …/Tiere/die Sachen, **die** …

Do you really want people that search your name to see that profile picture?

Vor allem umgangssprachlich kannst du ***that*** auch für Personen benutzen:
the boy/girl/kids/users ***that*** *…*
der Junge, **der** … / das Mädchen, **das** … /Kids, **die** …

Ben chose the photo that/which Li took last summer.

Für Dinge oder Tiere wird auch ***which*** statt *that* verwendet.

! Die Wortstellung im englischen Relativsatz ist anders als im deutschen:
Someone **who uses** social media …
Jemand, **der** soziale Medien **nutzt**, …

Die meisten englischen Relativsätze werden **nicht** durch **Komma** vor *who/that/which* abgetrennt. Es sind so genannte ***defining relative clauses*** (bestimmende Relativsätze). Sie geben Informationen, die zum Verständnis des Satzes unverzichtbar sind.
Ben chose the photo wäre ohne den Relativsatz *that Li took last summer* unverständlich.

LF 26 *Contact clauses (Relativsätze ohne Relativpronomen)

Vergleiche:

Subjekt des Relativsatzes
That's the girl **who** chatted with me yesterday.
Das ist das Mädchen, **das** gestern … hat.

Subjekt des Relativsatzes
These are the pictures **that** were shared the most.
Das sind die Bilder, **die** am häufigsten … wurden.

Objekt **Subjekt** des Relativsatzes
That's the girl ~~who~~ **I** chatted with yesterday.
Das ist das Mädchen, mit **dem** **ich** …

Objekt **Subjekt** des Relativsatzes
These are the pictures ~~that~~ **our friends** shared the most.
Das sind die Bilder, **die** **unsere Freunde** am häufigsten teilten.

Mit oder ohne Relativpronomen (*who/that*)?

Wenn das Relativpronomen (*who/that*) **direkt vor dem Verb** im Relativsatz steht, darfst du es **nicht** weglassen (weil es hier das **Subjekt** des Relativsatzes ist).

Wenn aber **nach** dem Relativpronomen (*who/that*) ein Pronomen oder Nomen folgt und **vor** dem Verb steht, darfst du *who/that* **weglassen**.
(Hier ist das Relativpronomen **Objekt** des Relativsatzes und zum Verständnis nicht unbedingt notwendig.)

Relativsätze **ohne** *who/that* heißen ***contact clauses***.

NEW LF 27 *Participle clauses instead of subordinate clauses

(Partizipialsätze anstelle von Nebensätzen) ▸ *More challenge 2, p. 52*

What are you doing? (*present progressive*)
Reading is fun. (*gerund*)

(1) Walking down the street to the youth club, Ben suddenly noticed a broken shop window.
While he was walking down the street, Ben suddenly noticed a broken shop window.
Während *er … entlang ging, bemerkte Ben plötzlich …*

(2) He looked round, seeing two men near a van.
He looked round **and** saw two men near a van.
Er schaute sich um ***und*** *sah zwei Männer nahe bei …*

(3) Ben shouted loudly, expecting some sort of crime.
Ben shouted loudly **because** he expected some sort of crime.
Ben rief laut, ***weil*** *er irgendeine Art Verbrechen erwartete.*

(4) Having noticed Ben, the men laughed, "It's OK. We're here to put in a new window."
When they noticed Ben, the men laughed, "It's OK …
Als *sie Ben bemerkten, lachten die Männer: „…*

(5) The two men working at the window talked to Ben.
The two men **who were working** … talked to Ben.
Die *zwei Männer, die gerade …, sprachen mit Ben.*

Das ***present participle*** – die **-*ing*-Form** – kennst du schon als Teil des ***present progressive*** (▸ *LF 2, p. 183*) sowie als ***gerund*** (▸ *LF 29, p. 200*).

Partizipalsätze enthalten das ***present participle*** und dienen der **knappen Formulierung** des gesamten Satzes, indem sie einen vollständigen Nebensatz ersetzen. Im Deutschen muss stattdessen ein vollständiger Nebensatz gebildet werden.

Solche **Partizipialsätze** kommen im Englischen vor allem in **geschriebenen** Texten vor.

Partizipialsätze können **ersetzen**:

- **Nebensätze der Zeit**, die mit ***while, when*** beginnen. Damit wird oft Gleichzeitigkeit ausgedrückt (1)
- zwei **Hauptsätze**, die mit ***and*** verbunden wären (2)
- **begründende Nebensätze**, die mit ***because, as*** beginnen (3)
- **Nebensätze**, die etwas als Ergebnis **Folgendes** ausdrücken (4)
- **Relativsätze**, die beschreiben, was gerade vor sich geht (***present progressive***) oder ging (***past progressive***) (5)

LF 28 Reflexive pronouns (Reflexivpronomen)

I ask myself how we can enjoy ourselves this evening.

Ich frage mich, wie wir uns heute Abend amüsieren können.

I think your little sister is old enough to look after herself.

Ich finde, deine …, auf sich selbst aufzupassen.

Reflexivpronomen (***myself***, ***yourself***, ***ourselves***, …) beziehen sich auf das Subjekt: (*I* – ***myself***, *you* – ***yourself***, *people* – ***themselves***):

Subjekt		Reflexivpronomen
I	*asked*	*myself* …
We	*can enjoy*	*ourselves.*
Your sister	*can look after*	*herself.*

Reflexive pronouns

(I)	myself	(ich)	mir / mich
(you)	yourself	(du)	dir / dich
(he)	himself	(er)	sich
(she)	herself	(sie)	sich
(it)	itself	(er / sie / es)	sich

(we)	ourselves	(wir) uns
(you)	yourselves	(ihr) euch
(they)	themselves	(sie) sich

! Den Plural bildest du mit ***-selves***.

! Es gibt Verben, die im Deutschen reflexiv sind, im Englischen jedoch nicht. Das „sich, mich, mir, dir" usw. wird nicht übersetzt, z.B.:

		Beispiele:	
(to) feel	sich fühlen	*He doesn't feel well.*	Er fühlt sich nicht gut.
(to) hide	sich verstecken	*Let's hide!*	Verstecken wir uns!
(to) imagine	sich etwas vorstellen	*I can imagine that.*	Das kann ich mir vorstellen.
(to) look forward to sth.	sich auf etwas freuen	*I'm looking forward to it.*	Ich freue mich darauf.
(to) meet	sich treffen	*Let's meet at six!*	Treffen wir uns um sechs!
(to) remember	sich an etwas erinnern	*I don't remember.*	Ich erinnere mich nicht.
(to) wonder	sich fragen	*I wonder if …*	Ich frage mich, ob …
(to) worry	sich Sorgen machen	*Don't worry.*	Mach dir keine Sorgen.

LF 29 The *-ing*-form (the gerund) (Die *-ing*-Form bzw. das Gerundium)

Du kannst von vielen Verben eine *-ing*-**Form** bilden, etwa für die Verlaufsform (*present progressive*), z.B. *Li is driving to school in her own car today.* ▸ *LF 2, p. 183*

Driving a car is cool.

(Das) **Autofahren** ist cool. / Ein Auto **zu fahren**, ist *cool*.

I love driving a car.

Ich liebe das **Fahren** mit dem Auto. / Ich liebe es, Auto **zu fahren**.

Als ***gerund*** bezeichnet man die *-ing*-Form, wenn sie als **Nomen** verwendet wird, hier z.B. als **Subjekt** oder **Objekt**:

Sport is cool. ◂▸ ***Driving*** *is cool.* **(Subjekt des Satzes)**

I love sport. ◂▸ *I love* ***driving***. **(Objekt des Satzes)**

Im Deutschen wird das ***gerund*** oft durch einen Infinitiv mit „zu" wiedergegeben.

I enjoy **helping** people. So I keep **working** with kids. I'd miss **teaching** them music.

Die ***-ing*-Form** (***gerund***) folgt oft auf bestimmte **Verben** als **Objekt,** z.B. *(dis)like, enjoy, hate, miss, start, finish, …*

I prefer **learning** languages. (or: *I prefer* ***to*** *learn languages.*)
I'll start **learning** German next term.
(or: *I'll start* ***to*** *learn German …*)

! Nach *like/love/hate/imagine/prefer/start/begin* kann auch ***to*** **+ Infinitiv** *folgen:*
love/like to play   *hate to learn*   *begin/start to sing*

! Nach allen übrigen Verben darf **nie der Infinitiv** stehen: *enjoy ~~to help~~*   *miss ~~to learn~~*   *keep ~~to go~~*

I'm good at **playing** basketball. Our team is looking forward to **playing** against Boston City. We've always dreamed of **winning** against them.

Die ***-ing*-Form *(gerund)*** folgt nach **Präpositionen:** *at, about, after, for, in, of, to.*

! Es gibt einige **Wendungen**, denen das ***gerund*** **folgen muss**, z.B.
- *dream of/about …ing*
- *(be) good/bad at …ing*
- *(be) interested in …ing*
- *get used to …ing*
- *look forward to …ing*

NEW *-*ing*-form (gerund) or *to*-infinitive? (Gerundium oder *to*-Infinitiv?)

▸ *Unit 4, More challenge 1, p. 129*

Ben: I enjoy **chatting** with people.

Das ***gerund*** **(*-ing*-form)** folgt meist nach bestimmten Verben als **Objekt**, z.B. *(dis)like, enjoy, hate, start, …*

I want **to tell** them everything.

Nach **bestimmten Verben** darfst du **nur** den ***to*-Infinitiv** verwenden, z.B. *want to, would like to, need to, hope to …*

Li prefers **meeting** people. She prefers **to meet** them in real life.

Nach bestimmten Verben kannst du das ***gerund*** oder den ***to*-Infinitiv** verwenden. Die **Bedeutung** ändert sich **nicht**, z.B. bei *like, love, hate, prefer, start, begin*.

"Stop **chatting** all day long."
Hör auf… zu chatten.
At the door Ben stopped **to check** his emails.
… Ben stehen, **um** seine …

! **Unterschiedliche Bedeutungen** hat die Verwendung von ***gerund*** oder ***to*-Infinitiv** nach diesen Verben:

stop + *gerund* ◂ mit etwas aufhören (… es zu tun)
stop + *to …* ◂ aufhören/anhalten, um etwas anders zu tun
forget + *gerund* ◂ vergessen, was man (früher mal) getan hat
forget + *to …* ◂ vergessen, was später (noch) zu tun ist
remember + *gerund* ◂ sich erinnern, was man mal getan hat
remember + *to …* ◂ daran denken, etwas (noch) zu tun

I'll never forget **skiing** for the first time.
Ich werde nie vergessen, wie ich …

Oh, I won't forget **to send** you the photos.
… darf nicht vergessen, dir die Fotos …

Mum remembers **buying** her first mobile.
… erinnert sich, dass/wie sie …

Will dad remember **to give** me his headphones?
… daran denken, dass er …?

LF 30 The passive (Das Passiv)

Advertising companies make all sorts of ads.
Werbefirmen machen alle Arten von Werbung.

Special ads are made to target teens only.
… Werbung wird gemacht, nur um auf Teens abzuzielen.

"I'm often asked how much money is spent on ads."
Ich werde oft gefragt, … ausgegeben wird.

Of course, ads aren't made for teens only.
Natürlich wird Werbung nicht nur … produziert.

Yesterday a new tablet was presented on TV.
Gestern wurde ein neues Tablet … präsentiert.

Years ago ads for cigarettes were shown everywhere.
Vor Jahren wurde noch Werbung … überall gezeigt.

Slogans are often repeated in ads.
Man wiederholt oft Slogans in der Werbung.

The song in this ad was first sung **by** the *Beatles*.
Das Lied in dieser Werbung wurde zuerst von … gesungen.

New game created by XYZ company

Mit einem **Aktivsatz** sagst du, wer oder was etwas tut. Das Subjekt des Aktivsatzes führt die Handlung aus.

Mit einem **Passivsatz** drückst du aus, mit wem oder was (= womit) **etwas geschieht** ohne zu sagen, wer der/die „Verursachende" ist. (Subjekt ist im Passivsatz der, die bzw. das, womit etwas geschieht.)

Du bildest das Passiv mit einer **Form von *be*** und der **3. Form des Verbs** (***past participle***).

▸ *Irregular verbs, pp. 266–267*

simple present: *am/are/is* **+ *past participle*:**
I'm ***asked*** *…*
how much money is ***spent*** *on …*

simple past: *was/were* **+ *past participle*:**
The street was ***used*** *in …*
… houses that were ***shown*** *…*

! In vielen Passivsätzen wird ***be*** im Deutschen mit ***werden*** ausgedrückt *(werde, wird, wurdest, wurde, …)*.

! Im Deutschen gibt man englische Passivsätze häufig durch einen Aktivsatz mit „man" wieder:

! Will man in einem Passivsatz doch den/die „Verursachende" nennen, verwendet man die Präposition ***by*** (von/durch).

Das Passiv wird oft in Nachrichten verwendet. In Überschriften und Schlagzeilen entfallen zudem meist die Artikel, die Form von *be* sowie Satzzeichen:
~~A~~ new game ~~was~~ created by ~~the~~ XYZ company~~.~~

*The passive: *will*-future and modals
(Das Passiv: *will*-future und Modalverben)

Passivsätze im ***will*-future** *(will/won't)* und mit **Modalverben** bildest du mit ***be* + *past participle***.

The meeting will be held next Friday.
Das Treffen wird … abgehalten/stattfinden.

The pictures can be seen online.
Die Bilder kann man online sehen.

Which problems should be fixed first?
Welche Probleme sollten zuerst gelöst werden?

The email couldn't be sent.
Die E-Mail konnte nicht versendet werden.

will/won't can/can't could/couldn't should/shouldn't may/mustn't must/needn't have to/has to may	**be**	served seen missed booked bought spotted shown taken

LF 31 Question tags (Frageanhängsel)

▸ Unit 3, p. 67

Question tags werden im Englischen **in Gesprächen** oft verwendet. Diese Frageanhängsel an Aussagesätze benutzt man, um **Zustimmung** beim Gesprächspartner zu erreichen.
Sie werden aber auch verwendet als „echte" **Nachfrage**, wenn man unsicher ist.
Im Deutschen kennen wir „…, nicht wahr?" oder „…, nicht?" bzw. auch „ne?/ gell?/woll?/ja?/oder?".

Look, it's a nice day today, isn't it? … nicht wahr?

You and I can go swimming, can't we? …oder?

And Ben has won the game, hasn't he? … ja?

Im Englischen muss das Frageanhängsel aber jeweils unter **Rückbezug** auf das **(Modal-) Verb** und **die Person** des Aussagesatzes neu gebildet werden.

Wenn der **Aussagesatz bejaht** ist, wird das **Frageanhängsel verneint**.
Das Personalpronomen steht wie in einer Frage hinten.

Yeah, that comedy wasn't fine last week, was it?
But we can't expect too much, can we?

Wenn der **Aussagesatz verneint** ist, wird das **Frageanhängsel bejaht**.

The bus to the beach **leaves** at 4 pm, doesn't it?
You **didn't repair** your bike, did you?
And you **don't want** to walk there, do you?

Vollverben werden im Frageanhängsel durch *do/does* im ***simple present*** bzw. *did* im ***simple past*** ersetzt.

LF 32 The definite and the indefinite article
(Der bestimmte und der unbestimmte Artikel)

Der bestimmte Artikel **the** entfällt, wenn ein Nomen ganz allgemein gebraucht wird.
Life here is sometimes hard.

Solche allgemein gebrauchten Nomen sind oft
- **abstrakte Begriffe** wie *life*, *history*, *nature*, *traffic*
- **Stoffbezeichnungen** wie *food*, *oil*, *water*, *air*
- **Nomen im Plural** wie *schools*, *students*, *people*

Wenn diese Nomen aber **näher bestimmt** sind, stehen sie **mit dem bestimmten Artikel *the***.

The film described the life of a singer.
The digital habits of the teens that you know …

! Der bestimmte Artikel steht im Englischen immer bei **Musikinstrumenten**:
play the piano, the guitar, the drums, …

Du benutzt den **unbestimmten Artikel a /an** im Englischen meist genauso wie im Deutschen.

Besonders zu beachten ist der unbestimmte Artikel aber
- **vor Berufsbezeichnungen** wie a teacher, …
  I'm **a student**. Ich bin Schüler/Schülerin.
- **in Wendungen** wie …
  be in a hurry — es eilig haben
  have/take a bath/shower — baden/duschen
  have / take a look — mal sehen/schauen
- **im Sinne von „pro"** wie bei *a month, a kilo*
  Our car does 70 miles ***an hour***. … pro Stunde.
- **vor vielen Krankheiten** wie *a cold*, *a headache*
  I've got ***a temperature***. Ich habe Fieber.

Anders als im Deutschen gibt es **Zeitangaben** sowie viele **Ortsangaben** und viele **Wendungen**, in denen **im Englischen kein bestimmter Artikel** steht. Diese musst du wie Vokabeln lernen.

!

Zeitangaben und Mahlzeiten:	*in May, on Monday, at night, at breakfast, after lunch*	im Mai, am Montag, in der Nacht, zum Frühstück, nach dem Essen
Straßen- und Eigennamen:	*along Main Street, on 14th Street*	entlang der …, in der …
Einrichtungen (allgemein):	*be at school, go to hospital*	in der Schule …, ins Krankenhaus …
Wendungen wie:	*on TV, at work, by bike/car/plane …*	im Fernsehen, bei der Arbeit, mit dem …

LF 33 Countable and uncountable nouns
(Zählbare und nicht zählbare Nomen)

countable nouns

a point	two points
a teenager	many teenagers
a butterfly	these butterflies

uncountable nouns

advice • butter • damage • equipment • health • homework • information • mea • money • music • news • plastic • shopping • traffic • work

! Nicht zählbare Nomen haben **keinen Plural** und stehen **nie** mit ***a/an*** oder Zahlwörtern wie ***one/two/three/...*** .

Die meisten Nomen sind **zählbar**, du benutzt sie auch im **Plural**.

Von **nicht zählbaren** Nomen gibt es **keine Pluralform**, z.B. bei Dingen, die meist als **Masse** gesehen werden, wie *water, sugar, milk, wood, rice, bacon, furniture, ...*
oder **abstrakten** Begriffen, wie *damage, love, peace, ...*

Mit Angaben *wie a piece of, a kilo of* kannst du die Menge oder Anzahl eines nicht zählbaren Nomens bestimmen, z.B.
two pieces of cake, ten kilos of meat, three litres / bottles of milk

Für „viel" verwendest du bei nicht zählbaren Nomen neben *a lot of* auch ***much***, z.B. *much homework, much fun, much money*
Bei zählbaren Nomen heißt es ***many***.

! Anders als im Deutschen sind einige Nomen **nicht zählbar**, d.h. sie haben **keinen Plural**, z.B. *damage, homework, information*.

I need some information about ...	Ich brauche Informationen ...
That's good news!	Das ist eine gute Nachricht! / sind gute Nachrichten!

Grammatical terms (Grammatische Fachbegriffe)

active	['aktɪv]	Aktiv	*Li **went** to the party.*
adjective	['ædʒɪktɪv]	Adjektiv	*good, red, new, boring, ...*
adverb	['advɜːb]	Adverb	*today, there, outside, very, ...*
adverb of frequency	['friːkwənsi]	Häufigkeitsadverb	*always, often, never ...*
adverb of manner	[ædvɜːb əv 'mænə]	Adverb der Art und Weise	*slowly, happily, well, ...*
article	['ɑːtɪkl]	Artikel	*the, a, an*
auxiliary	[ɔːg'zɪliəri]	Hilfsverb (zur Bildung von Fragesätzen, Zeitformen usw.)	***Did** Ben go to the party?*
backshift of tenses	['bakʃɪft]	Rückverschiebung der Zeitformen	*"I'**m** tired." She said (that) she **was** tired.*
comparative	[kəm'pærətɪv]	Komparativ (1. Steigerungsform)	*older; more expensive*
comparison	[kəm'pærɪsn]	Steigerung	*old – older – oldest*
conditional sentence	[kən'dɪʃənl 'sentəns]	Bedingungssatz	*If we win, we'll go to London.*
contact clause	['kɒntækt klɔːz]	Relativsatz ohne Relativpronomen	*She's the girl **I love**.*
defining relative clause	[dɪ'faɪnɪŋ]	bestimmender Relativsatz	*I like teachers **who laugh a lot**.*
direct speech	[ˌdaɪrekt 'spiːtʃ]	direkte Rede	***"**I love my dog.**"***
future	['fjuːtʃə]	Zukunft, Futur	
gerund	['dʒerənd]	Gerundium, *-ing*-Form	*I like **dancing**.*
***going to*-future**	['gəʊɪŋ tʊ fjuːtʃə]	Futur mit *going to*	***I'm going to stay** at home tonight.*
***if*-clause**	['if klɔːz]	*if*-Satz, Nebensatz mit *if*	***If we meet**, we'll talk.*
imperative	[ɪm'perətɪv]	Imperativ (Befehlsform)	***Open** your books. **Don't** talk.*
indirect speech	[ˌɪndərekt 'spiːtʃ]	indirekte Rede	*She said (that) **she loved her dog**.*
infinitive	[ɪn'fɪnətɪv]	Grundform des Verbs, Infinitiv	*go, open, see, read*
***-ing*-form**		Gerundium, *-ing*-Form	*I like **dancing**.*
irregular verb	[ɪ'regjələ 'vɜːb]	unregelmäßiges Verb	*go – went – gone*
main clause	[ˌmeɪn 'klɔːz]	Hauptsatz	*If we meet, **we'll talk**.*
main verb	[meɪn vɜːb]	Hauptverb (trägt die Hauptbedeutung im Satz)	*Did Ben **go** to the party?*

modal verb	[ˌməʊdl ˈvɜːb]	Modalverb, modales Hilfsverb	*can, must, should, may, …*
negative statement	[ˈnegətɪv]	verneinter Aussagesatz	*I don't like oranges.*
noun	[naʊn]	Nomen, Substantiv	*Ben, girl, man, time, name, …*
object	[ˈɒbdʒɪkt]	Objekt	*Ben has* ***an idea****.*
object question		Objektfrage, Frage nach dem Objekt	***Who did*** *Mrs Miller invite to tea?*
participle clause	[ˌpɑːtɪsɪpl ˈklɔːz]	Partizipialsatz	*Li shook her head,* ***laughing out loud****. The man* ***waiting at the bus stop*** *wis my uncle.*
passive	[ˈpæsɪv]	Passiv	*Lots of films* ***are made*** *in LA.*
past participle	[pɑːst ˈpɑːtɪsɪpl]	Partizip Perfekt, 3. Form des Verbs	*happened, eaten, gone, …*
past perfect	[ˌpɑːst ˈpɜːfɪkt]	*past perfect* (Vorvergangenheit, Plusquamperfekt)	*I* ***had*** *already* ***gone*** *to bed when they arrived.*
past progressive	[pɑːst prəˈgresɪv]	Verlaufsform der Vergangenheit	*He* ***was playing*** *a drum.*
persononal pronoun	[pɜːsənl ˈprəʊnaʊn]	Personalpronomen	*I, you, he, she, it, we, they, …*
plural	[ˈplʊərəl]	Plural, Mehrzahl	*sweets, carrots, sheep, …*
positive statement	[ˈpɒzətɪv]	bejahter Aussagesatz	*I like oranges.*
possessive determiner	[pəˌzesɪv dɪˈtɜːmɪnə]	Possessivbegleiter	*my, your, his, her, its, our, their*
possessive pronoun	[pəˌzesɪv ˈprəʊnaʊn]	Possessivpronomen	*mine, yours, his, hers, ours, theirs*
preposition	[prepəˈzɪʃn]	Präposition	*after, at, in, next to, under, with, …*
present participle	[ˌpreznt ˈpɑːtɪsɪpl]	Partizip Präsens	*checking, phoning, trying, planning, going, …*
present perfect	[preznt ˈpɜːfɪkt]	*present perfect*	*He* ***has drunk*** *your water.*
present progressive	[preznt prəˈgresɪv]	Verlaufsform der Gegenwart	*They****'re having*** *lunch.*
pronoun	[ˈprəʊnaʊn]	Pronomen, Fürwort	
question	[ˈkwestʃən]	Frage(satz)	*What did you do yesterday?*
question tag	[ˈkwestʃn tag]	Frageanhängsel	*isn't he?, are you?, can't we?, …*
question word	[ˈkwestʃən wɜːd]	Fragewort	*what?, when?, where?, how?, …*
reflexive pronoun	[rɪˌfleksɪv ˈprəʊnaʊn]	Reflexivpronomen	*myself, yourself, himself, …*
regular verb	[ˈregjələ ˈvɜːb]	regelmäßiges Verb	*help – helped – helped*
relative clause	[ˌrelətɪv klɔːz]	Relativsatz	*This is the dog* ***that bit me****.*
relative pronoun	[ˌrelətɪv ˈprəʊnaʊn]	Relativpronomen	*who, that, which*
short answer	[ʃɔːt ˈɑːnsə]	Kurzantwort	*Yes, I am./No, I don't./…*
simple past	[sɪmpl ˈpɑːst]	einfache Form der Vergangenheit	*I* ***loved*** *the holidays.*
simple present	[sɪmpl ˈpreznt]	einfache Form der Gegenwart	*I always* ***go*** *to school by bike.*
singular	[ˈsɪŋgjələ]	Singular, Einzahl	
statement	[ˈsteɪtmənt]	Aussage(satz)	
subject	[ˈsʌbdʒɪkt]	Subjekt	***My dad*** *is working.*
subordinate clause (*also*: sub-clause)	[səˈbɔːdɪnət klɔːz] [ˈsʌbklɔːz]	Nebensatz	*I like cycling* ***because I like the sport****.*
superlative	[suˈpɜːlətɪv]	Superlativ	*cheapest, most expensive, …*
tense	[tens]	Zeitform des Verbs	
time word / time phrase	[ˈtaɪm wɜːd] [ˈtaɪm freɪz]	Zeitangabe	*yesterday, this morning, after school, …*
verb	[vɜːb]	1. Verb 2. Prädikat	*go, help, look, see, …* *Reading* ***can be*** *fun.* ***Did*** *Ben* ***go*** *to the party?*
***will*-future**	[ˈwɪl fjuːtʃə]	Futur mit *will*	*I think our trip* ***will be*** *fun.*
***yes*/*no*-question**	[ˈjes ˈnəʊ kwestʃən]	Entscheidungsfrage / Frage ohne Fragewort / Ja- / Nein-Frage	*Are you 15? Do you like films?*
word order		Wortstellung (im Satz)	

Im **Vocabulary** werden folgende **Abkürzungen** verwendet:

sb. = somebody	sth. = something	jn. = jemanden	jm. = jemandem
pl = plural (Mehrzahl)	*BE = British English*	*AE = American English*	*infml = informal* (umgangssprachlich)

Unit 1: Life down under

p. 8	**kangaroo** [kæŋgə'ruː]	Känguru	a **kangaroo** 
	Aboriginal [æbə'rɪdʒənl]	Aborigine- *(die Ureinwohner/innen Australiens betreffend)*	! **Aboriginal** Australian = australische/r Ureinwohner/in
	the outback ['aʊtbæk]	*das Hinterland Australiens*	
	landscape ['lændskeɪp]	Landschaft	
	nickname ['nɪkneɪm]	Spitzname	His name is "Hundt". "Bello" is his **nickname**.
	climate ['klaɪmət]	Klima	! Aussprache: **climate** ['klaɪmət]
p. 9	**reef** [riːf]	Riff	rocks or a sandbank under the water in the sea
	road trip ['rəʊd trɪp]	Autoreise	

Theme 1

p. 10	**ban (on)** [bæn]	Verbot (von)	There's a ~ **on** smoking here. *(= Rauchverbot)* noun: **ban** – verb: **ban** *(verbieten)*
	best-known [best 'nəʊn]	der/die/das bekannteste; am bekanntesten	**well-known – better-known – best-known**
	flat [flæt]	flach, eben	! **flat** = **1.** Wohnung; **2.** flach, eben
	according to ... [ə'kɔːdɪŋ]	laut ...; ... zufolge	**According to** my mum, I was the cutest baby in the world.
	one in five	eine/r/s von fünf(en)	**One in three** children in the UK have never climbed a tree. ! Auf **One in xxx children/teens/cars/...** kann ein Verb im Plural oder im Singular folgen: **One in three** kids **have** never climbed ... *oder* **One in three** kids **has** never climbed ...
	original [ə'rɪdʒənl]	original, ursprünglich, Original(-)	They're showing the short version on TV. The ~ film is 30 minutes longer. ! Betonung auf der 2. Silbe: o<u>ri</u>ginal [ə'rɪdʒənl]
	citizen ['sɪtɪzn]	Bürger/in	
	diverse [daɪ'vɜːs]	unterschiedlich, vielfältig	London has a very rich and ~ culture.
p. 11	**exam** [ɪg'zæm]	Prüfung	! **take/do an exam** = eine Prüfung machen **final (school) exam** = (Schul-) Abschlussprüfung
	shark [ʃɑːk]	Hai	a **shark** 
	spider ['spaɪdə]	Spinne	 **spiders**

likely ['laɪkli]	wahrscheinlich	Take a raincoat – it**'s likely to** rain, they said. ! **be likely to do sth.** = wahrscheinlich etwas tun (werden)
jellyfish ['dʒelifɪʃ], *pl* **jellyfish**	Qualle	 some **jellyfish** in the sea
which	der, die, das; die *(Relativpronomen)*	songs **which** I know / the cat **which** is in our garden ! Das Relativpronomen **which** benutzt du nur für Dinge und Tiere.
allergic (to) [ə'lɜːdʒɪk]	allergisch (gegen)	I can't eat that. I'm **allergic to** nuts.
sting [stɪŋ]	(Insekten-)Stich	
sting [stɪŋ], **stung, stung** [stʌŋ]	stechen *(Insekt)*; brennen	Be careful – bees can **~**. Your eyes **~** if there's a lot of smoke.
human ['hjuːmən]	Mensch; menschlich	animals and **humans / human beings** *(Menschen)* **human** life *(menschlich)* It's only **human**. *(nur menschlich)*
honey ['hʌni]	Honig	Bees make **~**. It's sweet.

Theme 2

p. 12 **litre** ['liːtə]	Liter	! *English:* 10 **litres** per person *German:* 10 **Liter** pro Person
break down	eine Panne haben, kaputtgehen *(Auto)*	 Their car **broke down** on their way to the coast.
vehicle ['viːəkl]	Fahrzeug	Cars and buses, for example, are **~s**.
heat [hiːt]	Hitze, Wärme	**heat ◄► cold** **heat stress** = Hitzestress, Wärmebelastung des Körpers
shade [ʃeɪd]	Schatten	
shadow ['ʃædəʊ]	Schatten	
light [laɪt], **lit, lit** [lɪt]	anzünden	**light a fire** = (ein) Feuer machen
torch [tɔːtʃ]	Taschenlampe; Fackel	

	suffer (from) ['sʌfə]	leiden (an), erleiden	I often **suffer from** headaches. *(leiden an)* He **suffered** a heart attack. *(Er erlitt einen Herzinfarkt.)*
	cool down [ku:l 'daʊn]	sich abkühlen; sich beruhigen	
	bite [baɪt]	Biss, (Insekten-)Stich	verb: **bite, bit, bitten** – noun: **bite**
	identify [aɪ'dentɪfaɪ]	erkennen, identifizieren	be able to say who or what sb. or sth. is
	as soon as	sobald; so bald wie	I'll call you **as ~ as** I'm home. ! **as soon as possible** = so bald wie möglich
p. 13	**care** [keə]	Sorgfalt, Vorsicht	Choose your words **with care**. *(sorgfältig, mit Bedacht)*
	bleed [bli:d], **bled, bled** [bled]	bluten	verb: **bleed, bled, bled** – noun: **blood**
	redness ['rednəs]	Rötung, Röte	

-ness

Die Endung **-ness** wird verwendet, um Nomen aus Adjektiven zu bilden. Beispiele:

cleverness	Schlauheit	**friendliness**	Freundlichkeit	**redness**	Rötung, Röte
darkness	Dunkelheit	**happiness**	Glück	**sadness**	Traurigkeit
fitness	Fitness	**illness**	Krankheit	**weakness**	Schwäche

	take sb.'s **temperature**	(bei jm.) Fieber messen	You feel very hot. I think we should **take your ~**.
	lifeguard ['laɪfgɑ:d]	Rettungsschwimmer/in; Bademeister/in	

Theme 3

p. 14	**crew** [kru:]	Mannschaft, Team; Clique	
	body ['bɒdi]	Körper	
	paint [peɪnt]	lackieren, (be)malen, *(mit Farbe)* streichen	verb: **paint** – noun: **painting** = Gemälde, Bild; Malerei **body painting** = Körperbemalung
	wide [waɪd]	breit, weit	The river is too **~**. We can't get across. **wide ◄► narrow** (schmal)
p. 15	**indigenous (to)** [ɪn'dɪdʒənəs]	einheimisch (in)	• **indigenous people** = Einheimische, Ureinwohner/innen • **indigenous Australian** = australische/r Ureinwohner/in
	inland [ɪn'lænd]	landeinwärts, im Landesinneren/ins Landesinnere	
	gather ['gæðə]	sammeln; (sich) versammeln	Many people had **~ed** to watch the parade.
	disease [dɪ'zi:z]	Krankheit	! • **disease** wird für ansteckende oder sehr ernsthafte Erkrankungen verwendet: She has a blood **disease**. Thousands of trees died from **disease**. • Das allgemeinere Wort für „Krankheit" ist **illness**: After a week of **illness**, she went back to school.

	lifestyle ['laɪfstaɪl]	Lebensstil	
	forever [fər'evə], **for ever**	für immer, ewig (lange)	I hope they arrive soon. We can't wait **~**.
	way of life	Lebensweise	
	say sorry	sich entschuldigen	I gave you lots of extra work. I really want to **say ~**.
	generation [dʒenə'reɪʃn]	Generation	
	face sth. [feɪs]	vor etwas stehen *(Problem)*; einer Sache ins Auge sehen, sich einer Sache stellen; einer Sache entgegentreten	Jamie, **~** the facts. You'll never be a professional football player. As a single parent, I have to **~** problems other parents don't have to deal with.
	health [helθ]	Gesundheit	noun: **health** – adjective: **healthy** Apples are **good for your ~**. = Äpfel sind **gesund**.
	dot [dɒt]	Punkt, Pünktchen	**dot painting** = Punktmalerei; Punktgemälde
	plant [plɑːnt]	Pflanze	noun: **plant** – verb: **plant** (pflanzen)
	dig [dɪg], **dug, dug** [dʌg]	graben	He's **digging** a hole.
	fantastic [fæn'tæstɪk]	fantastisch, wunderschön	

Background theme

p. 16	**Sydney rocks.** *(infml)* [rɒks]	Sydney bringt's. / In Sydney geht die Post ab.	
p. 17	**architecture** ['ɑːkɪtektʃə]	Architektur	! Betonung auf der 1. Silbe: <u>ar</u>chitecture ['ɑːkɪtektʃə]
	tourism ['tʊərɪzəm]	Tourismus	! Betonung auf der 1. Silbe: <u>tou</u>rism ['tʊərɪzəm]
	trade [treɪd]	Handel	buying and selling things
	list [lɪst]	auflisten, aufzählen	verb: **list** – noun: **list** (Liste)
	liveable ['lɪvəbl]	lebenswert	We should try to make this a better, **~** world for everybody!
	colony ['kɒləni]	Kolonie	! Betonung auf der 1. Silbe: <u>co</u>lony ['kɒləni]
	compete (with) [kəm'piːt]	konkurrieren (mit); *(in Wettbewerben)* antreten (gegen)	verb: **compete (with)** – noun: **competition**
	media *(pl)* ['miːdiə]	Medien	The story of the pop star who died at the age of 27 was in all the **~**. It's so much faster to use **~** like the phone or email than to write letters.
	neither ['naɪðə]	keine/r/s *(von beiden)*	Should I buy the green dress or the red dress? – I would buy **neither**. **Neither of them** looks good on you.

Focus on language

p. 18	**enter** ['entə]	sich anmelden, teilnehmen *(Wettbewerb)*	Jay has **~ed** a marathon. He has only two more months to train!
	remote [rɪ'məʊt]	entlegen, abgelegen	far away from places where other people live

	the nearest …	der/die/das nächstgelegene …	! • **nearest** = nächstgelegen *(räumlich)*: The **nearest** shop is just round the corner. • **next** = nächstfolgend *(Reihenfolge)*: We have to get off at the **next** stop.
	upside down [ʌpsaɪd 'daʊn]	verkehrt herum, auf dem/den Kopf	Can you read when the book is ~ **down**?
	tyre ['taɪə]	Reifen	
	waterproof ['wɔːtəpruːf]	wasserdicht, wasserfest, wasserundurchlässig	You need ~ clothes and a ~ watch if you want to go sailing.
	race [reɪs]	rasen, schnell fahren	verb: **race** – noun: **race** (Wett-)Rennen **racer** = Rennfahrer/in
	stick with sth.	bei etwas bleiben	
p. 19	**regular** ['regjələ]	regelmäßig, normal	adjective: **regular** – our **regular** customers; a **regular** verb adverb: **regularly** – We meet **regularly** every Friday afternoon.
	simple ['sɪmpl]	einfach, simpel	
	panic ['pænɪk]	in Panik geraten	Everything's OK. Don't ~. (Keine Panik. / Immer mit der Ruhe.)

Text

p. 20	**swerve** [swɜːv]	*(das Auto/Steuer)* herumreißen, *(mit dem Auto)* ausweichen	Suddenly, an animal ran out into the road. I **swerved** and nearly hit a tree.
	adapted from [ə'dæptɪd frɒm]	basierend auf, (frei) nach	
	ponytail ['pəʊniteɪl]	Pferdeschwanz *(Frisur)*	
	waistcoat ['weɪskəʊt]	Weste	! Aussprache – das „t" in der Mitte wird nicht gesprochen: **waistcoat** ['weɪskəʊt]
	turn up	auftauchen, erscheinen	= arrive
	be familiar (to sb.**/with** sth.**)** [fə'mɪliə]	(jm.) vertraut sein / (mit etwas) vertraut sein	Who's that guy over there? He looks ~, but I can't think of how I might know him.
	chin [tʃɪn]	Kinn	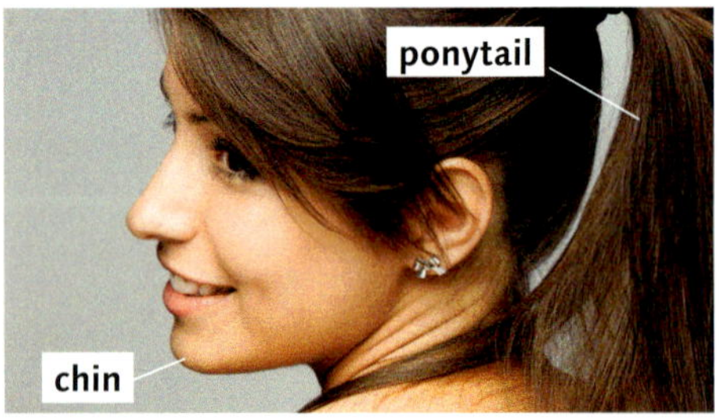
	threaten ['θretn]	(be)drohen	They **~ed** him with a knife and he ran away.
p. 21	**stripe** [straɪp]	Streifen	
	whose [huːz]	wessen	

his [hɪz]	seiner, seine, seins *(zu „he")*	Is this your bike? – No, it's **his**. (Ist dies dein Rad? – Nein, das ist seins.)

Possessivpronomen (possessive pronouns)

I	**my** dog	**mine**	*meiner, meine, meins*	we	**our** dog	**ours**	*unserer, unsere, unseres*
you	**your** dog	**yours**	*deiner, deine, deins*	you	**your** dog	**yours**	*eurer, eure, eures*
he	**his** dog	**his**	*seiner, seine, seins*	they	**their** dog	**theirs**	*ihrer, ihre, ihrs*
she	**her** dog	**hers**	*ihrer, ihre, ihrs*				

be up for sth. *(infml)*	bei etwas dabei sein, mitmachen	We're going to the disco tonight. **Are you ~ for it?** (Bist du dabei? / Machst du mit?)
risk [rɪsk]	riskieren, wagen	Don't ride your bike without a helmet! You're **~ing** your life! verb: **risk** – noun: **risk** (Risiko)
clearing ['klɪərɪŋ]	Lichtung	
boot [buːt]	Kofferraum *(Auto)*	**!** **boot** = **1.** Stiefel; **2.** Kofferraum *(Auto)*
appear (to be/do) [ə'pɪə]	auftauchen, erscheinen; (zu sein/tun) scheinen	**appear ◄► disappear** A car **appeared** behind us. *(auftauchen)* He **appeared** ten minutes late. *(erscheinen)* There **appears** to be a problem. *(scheinen)*
overtake [əʊvə'teɪk], **overtook** [əʊvə'tʊk], **overtaken** [əʊvə'teɪkən]	überholen	pass another vehicle because you are going faster
pull over	anhalten, an den Straßenrand fahren	= pull in
bully ['bʊli]	tyrannisieren, mobben	verb: **bully** – noun: **bully** (Mobber/in, Tyrann/in)
goat [gəʊt]	Ziege	
hitchhiker ['hɪtʃhaɪkə]	Anhalter/in, Tramper/in	
hood [hʊd]	Kapuze	
p. 22 **engine** ['endʒɪn]	Motor	

sink [sɪŋk], **sank** [sæŋk], **sunk** [sʌŋk]	sinken	**sink down** in your seat = auf dem Sitz zusammensinken, nach unten rutschen
fuel ['fjuːəl]	Treibstoff, Kraftstoff	
kind of glamorous ['glæmərəs]	irgendwie glamourös	**!** **1.** a **kind of** puzzle (eine Art Rätsel); **2. kind of** cool (irgendwie cool)
counter ['kaʊntə]	(Verkaufs-)Schalter, Ladentheke	
fingernail ['fɪŋgəneɪl]	Fingernagel	
nail polish ['neɪl pɒlɪʃ]	Nagellack	**polish** = Lack; Politur
stud [stʌd]	(Ohr-/Nasen-)Stecker	
campground *(AE)* ['kæmpgraʊnd]	Campingplatz	= *BE* **campsite** ['kæmpsaɪt]
press [pres]	drücken	"If you have general questions, please ~ 1."
redial [riː'daɪəl]	die Wahlwiederholung betätigen	

Speaking course

p. 24	**attention** [ə'tenʃn]	Aufmerksamkeit	This advert is a real **attention-getter**! *(Blickfang; etwas, was Aufmerksamkeit erregt)* Please **pay attention**! *(aufpassen)*
	structure ['strʌktʃə]	Struktur	noun: **structure** – verb: **structure** (strukturieren, gliedern)
	materials *(pl)* [mə'tɪəriəlz]	Materialien, Hilfsmittel	
	make sure that …	darauf achten, dass …; dafür sorgen, dass …	**Make ~** that you turn off the lights when you leave the room.
	visuals *(pl)* ['vɪʒuəlz] (*kurz für*: **visual materials**)	visuelle Materialien/Hilfsmittel	
	audience ['ɔːdiəns]	Publikum; Zuschauer/innen, Zuhörer/innen	! Auf **audience** kann ein Verb im Plural oder im Singular folgen: The **audience was/were** very noisy.
	presenter [prɪ'zentə]	Referent/in	someone who gives a presentation
p. 25	**screen** [skriːn]	Leinwand; Bildschirm	

Unit 2: Respect

p. 32	**delete** [dɪ'liːt]	löschen	I **deleted** the message **from** my phone. (… die Nachricht <u>auf</u> meinem Telefon …)
	chronological [krɒnə'lɒdʒɪkl]	chronologisch	In this book you have a ~ and an alphabetical word list.
	monologue ['mɒnəlɒg]	Monolog, Selbstgespräch	**monologue ◄► dialogue**
	flashback ['flæʃbæk]	Rückblende	
p. 33	**cyberbullying** [saɪbə'bʊliɪŋ]	Cybermobbing	
	victim ['vɪktɪm]	Opfer	No one should be a ~ of cyberbullying.
	bystander ['baɪstændə]	Zuschauer/in, *(unbeteiligte/r)* Beobachter/in	Lots of **~s** saw the man fall, but nobody helped him.
	horrible ['hɒrəbl]	schrecklich	It's ~ to tell those untrue stories about Kim.

Theme 1

p. 34	**deal with** sth. [diːl], **dealt, dealt** [delt]	umgehen mit etwas, mit etwas fertigwerden, klarkommen	We have to **~ with** these questions before we can continue. I find it hard to **~ with** stress.
	peer pressure [pɪə 'preʃə]	Gruppendruck, Gruppenzwang	
	pressure ['preʃə]	Druck	
	peer [pɪə]	Gleichaltrige/r, Ebenbürtige/r, jemand aus derselben sozialen Gruppe	
	classmate ['klɑːsmeɪt]	Mitschüler/in	
	influence ['ɪnfluəns]	beeinflussen	Even today, the Beatles still ~ musicians all over the world. verb: **influence** – noun: **influence** (Einfluss)
	(just) for fun	(nur) zum Spaß	What do you learn Turkish for? – Oh, **just for ~**!
	tease sb. [tiːz]	jn. hänseln, sich über jn. lustig machen	

novel ['nɒvl]	Roman	
go after sb./sth.	hinter etwas/jm. her sein	I'm **going** ~ a job in a hotel.
act [ækt]	handeln, sich verhalten; so tun, als ob	

act

- I'm going to **act** in a play. — **Theater spielen; schauspielern**
- We have to **act** fast! — **handeln**
- He **acted** like a little kid. — **sich verhalten**
- I **acted** stupid. (= I acted as if I was stupid.) — **so tun, als ob**

lose weight [weɪt]	abnehmen *(Gewicht)*, dünner werden	You want to ~ **weight**? Why? You're not too fat! **weight** = Gewicht
attractive [ə'træktɪv]	attraktiv	= good-looking
weigh [weɪ]	wiegen	verb: **weigh** – noun: **weight**
... like ... *(infml)*	... irgendwie ... / ..., keine Ahnung, ...	
along *(infml)*	mit-	Come **along** to the party! *(mitkommen)* I'll drag you **along**. *(mitschleifen)* Sing **along**! *(mitsingen)* Bring your friends **along**. *(mitbringen)*
p. 36 **solution (to a problem)** [sə'lu:ʃn]	Lösung (eines Problems)	! *English:* **the solution to** this problem *German:* **die Lösung für** dieses Problem / **die Lösung** dieses Problems
lately ['leɪtli]	in letzter Zeit	Have you seen any good films ~? ! **late** = spät; zu spät – **lately** = in letzter Zeit
further ['fɜ:ðə]	weiter; weitere	Stop there. Don't walk any ~. Do you have any ~ questions?
(just) the two of us/you	(nur) wir/ihr beide	We met at the station, and then **the two of** ~ walked home together.
be/feel comfortable (with) ['kʌmftəbl]	sich wohlfühlen (bei/mit)	! **comfortable** = **1. a ~ bed/chair/car** (bequem) **2.** I don't **feel ~ with** big groups of people. (sich wohlfühlen bei/mit)
suggestion [sə'dʒestʃən]	Vorschlag	verb: **suggest sth.** – noun: **suggestion**

Theme 2

p. 37 **frustrating** [frʌ'streɪtɪŋ]	frustrierend	
frustrate [frʌ'streɪt]	frustrieren	
illustrate ['ɪləstreɪt]	veranschaulichen; illustrieren, bebildern	Can you give examples to ~ what you mean?
discrimination (against sb.) [dɪskrɪmɪ'neɪʃn]	Diskriminierung *(eines Menschen)*	! **discrimination against** women/black people = Diskriminierung **von** Frauen/Schwarzen
prejudice ['predʒudɪs]	Vorurteil, Voreingenommenheit	Some people still have a ~ against girls and think that girls aren't good at maths.
teammate ['ti:mmeɪt]	Mannschaftskamerad/in	someone who is in the same team as you

	racist ['reɪsɪst]	Rassist/in; rassistisch	! Betonung auf der 1. Silbe: **ra**cist ['reɪsɪst]
	call [kɔːl]	Ruf, Schrei	! **call** = **1.** rufen; anrufen; **2.** (Telefon-)Anruf; **3.** Ruf, Schrei
	a shame [ʃeɪm]	eine Schande; schade	**It's a ~ (that)** you can't come over! **What a ~** you can't come over! (**Wie schade**, dass …)
	support [sə'pɔːt]	Unterstützung	verb: **support** – My parents always **~** my dreams and plans. noun: **support** (Unterstützung) – My parents are a great **~**.
	action ['ækʃn]	Aktion, Handlung	! **take action** = Maßnahmen ergreifen, etwas unternehmen
p. 38	**kick** [kɪk]	treten; *(Sport)* schießen	! **kick** = **1.** treten, schießen; *(infml) (Gewohnheit/ Idee)* aufgeben, sich davon befreien; **2.** Tritt, Stoß, Kick
p. 39	**campaign** [kæm'peɪn]	Kampagne	

Focus on language

p. 40	**Don't be a pain.**	Nerv nicht. / Geh mir/uns nicht auf die Nerven.	
	walk sb. **home**	jn. zu Fuß nach Hause begleiten	It's late – I'll **walk you to the station**!
	direct [də'rekt]	direkt, unmittelbar	**direct ◄► indirect**
p. 41	**actor** ['æktə]	Schauspieler/in	
	order ['ɔːdə]	Reihenfolge	! **order** = **1.** bestellen; **2.** Bestellung; **3.** Reihenfolge
	command [kə'mɑːnd]	Befehl	
	request [rɪ'kwest]	Wunsch, Bitte; Anfrage	
p. 42	**interest** ['ɪntrəst]	Interesse	! Betonung auf der 1. Silbe: **in**terest ['ɪntrəst]
	skating ['skeɪtɪŋ]	*(= ice skating)* Schlittschuhlaufen; *(= roller skating)* Rollschuhlaufen	
	instead [ɪn'sted]	stattdessen	No fish and chips for me, thank you. I'll have a salad **~**, please.
	copy ['kɒpi]	kopieren, abschreiben	verb: **copy** – noun: **copy** (Kopie, Exemplar)

Text

p. 43	**extract** ['ekstrækt]	Auszug *(aus einem Buch, Film)*	! Betonung auf der 1. Silbe: **ex**tract ['ekstrækt]
	spooky ['spuːki]	unheimlich, gruselig	! „**Spook**" *(infml)* is another word for a ghost.
	board sth. **up** [bɔːd 'ʌp]	etwas mit Brettern vernageln/ zunageln	The old house was **boarded up**.
	weed [wiːd]	(Un-)Kraut	**Weeds were** growing in our garden. *(Unkraut wuchs …)*
	front garden [frʌnt 'gɑːdn]	Vorgarten	

	curtain ['kɜːtn]	Vorhang, Gardine	 **curtains**
	freeze, froze, frozen	erstarren	Rivers and lakes sometimes ~ in winter. Suddenly the lights went out, and I **froze**.
	warn sb. (about/against/ of sth.) [wɔːn]	jn. warnen (vor etwas / davor, etwas zu tun)	The teacher **~ed** Josie that she had to work harder. ! They **warned me not to go** there. Sie **warnten mich davor, dort hinzugehen.**
	See for yourself.	Sieh selbst! / Sehen Sie selbst!	
	squatter ['skwɒtə]	Hausbesetzer/in	**squat** = (ein Haus/Grundstück) besetzen
	of one's own	eigene(r, s)	Do you have a room **of your ~**? I don't have a car **of my ~** – I share one with my sister.
p. 44	**candle** ['kændl]	Kerze	
	respectable [rɪ'spektəbl]	anständig, angesehen, ehrbar	
	hammer ['hæmə]	hämmern	verb: **hammer** – noun: **hammer** (Hammer)
	have every right to do sth.	guten Grund / das Recht haben, etwas zu tun	I **have every ~ to** be here. (Es ist mein gutes Recht, hier zu sein.)
	busybody ['bɪzibɒdi]	Wichtigtuer/in	
	tramp [træmp]	Obdachlose/r, Stadtstreicher/in	
	bedtime ['bedtaɪm]	Schlafenszeit	= time to go to bed
	Off you go!	Dann mal los! / Ab mit dir!	
p. 45	**this** bad, **that** bad	so schlecht/schlimm	= so bad; as bad as this/that
	college ['kɒlɪdʒ]	höhere Schule, Fach(hoch-) schule	
	backpack ['bækpæk]	als Rucksacktourist/in unterwegs sein	verb: **backpack** – noun: **backpack** (Rucksack)
	keep an eye on sb./sth.	jn./etwas im Auge behalten, ein (wachsames) Auge haben auf jn./etwas	**Keep an ~** on your little brother, please. I have to make a phone call.
	builder ['bɪldə]	Bauunternehmer/in	
p. 46	**back and forth** [fɔːθ]	hin und her	Do you travel **back and ~** all the time between where you live and where you work?
	blow [bləʊ], **blew** [bluː], **blown** [bləʊn]	blasen (in); wehen *(Wind)*	! **1.** The wind is **blowing** = der Wind weht **2. blow** your whistle = in die Pfeife blasen, pfeifen
p. 47	**setting** ['setɪŋ]	Schauplatz *(z.B. Film/ Geschichte)*	The ~ of the film is a small village in Cornwall.

	plot [plɒt]	Handlung(sverlauf) *(z.B. Film/ Geschichte)*	the story that a play, book, film tells us

Speaking course

p. 48	**conversation** [kɒnvə'seɪʃn]	Gespräch, Unterhaltung	a talk among people; a chat
	dos and don'ts *(pl)* [du:z ən 'dəʊnts]	was man tun und lassen sollte	What are the **dos and ~** in the computer room?
p. 49	**step by step**	Schritt für Schritt	
	by the way	übrigens	"Hi Dad. Yes, Dad, I took out the rubbish. And I did my homework. ... Oh, **by the ~**, Dad, I got a part in the school play today."
	pleased [pli:zd]	froh, erfreut, zufrieden	**Pleased to meet you.** = Freut mich, Sie kennenzulernen.
	See you around.	Bis dann.	
	sometime ['sʌmtaɪm]	irgendwann	! • **sometime** = irgendwann: We must meet again **sometime**. • **sometimes** = manchmal: We **sometimes** go to the park after school.
	paraphrase ['pærəfreɪz]	umschreiben, mit anderen Worten sagen	Mr Parker, I don't know what Joanna meant. Could you ~ what she said?

Unit 3: Looking forward

p. 56	**training** ['treɪnɪŋ]	Ausbildung	! **training** = **1.** Ausbildung; **2.** Training
	sauce [sɔ:s]	Sauce	! Aussprache: **sauce** [sɔ:s]
	ingredient [ɪn'gri:diənt]	Zutat, Bestandteil	What **~s** do you need to make scones?
	takeaway ['teɪkəweɪ]	Essen zum Mitnehmen	If we don't feel like cooking, we often get a Chinese **~**.
	pick sth. **up**	etwas kaufen, etwas *(aus einem Geschäft)* mitbringen	→ **pick** • **pick sth. up** = etwas hochheben, aufheben • **pick sth. up** = etwas kaufen, mitbringen *(aus Geschäft)* • **pick sb. up** = jn. abholen
	washing machine ['wɒʃɪŋ məʃi:n]	Waschmaschine	
	vacuum cleaner ['vækjuəm kli:nə]	Staubsauger	
	iron ['aɪən]	bügeln	verb: **iron** – noun: **iron** (Bügeleisen) **do the ironing** = bügeln ! Aussprache – das „r" wird nicht gesprochen: **iron** ['aɪən]

vacuum cleaner

washing machine

iron

	earn [ɜːn]	verdienen *(Geld)*	! *German* **„Geld verdienen"** = **1.** *(Gehalt bekommen)* **earn money** **2.** *(Profit machen)* **make money**
	manage ['mænɪdʒ]	verwalten, regeln	My brother is too young to ~ his own money.
	budget ['bʌdʒɪt]	haushalten *(sparsam sein)*	verb: **budget** – noun: **budget** (Budget, Haushalt) ! Betonung auf der 1. Silbe: **bud**get ['bʌdʒɪt]
	I often **run out of** money.	Mir geht oft das Geld aus. / Bei mir wird oft das Geld knapp.	→ **run out** (knapp werden, zu Ende gehen) • **Time is running out.** (Die Zeit wird knapp.) • **I'm running out of time.** (Ich habe keine Zeit mehr.) • **It was so hot that the shops ran out of cold drinks.** (…, dass den Geschäften die kalten Getränke ausgingen.)
	overspend (on sth.**)** [əʊvə'spend]**, overspent, overspent** [əʊvə'spent]	zu viel Geld ausgeben (für etwas)	= spend too much money
p. 57	**skill** [skɪl]	Fähigkeit, Fertigkeit	Her computer **~s** are amazing.

Theme 1

p. 58	**strength** [streŋθ]	Stärke, Kraft	One of my **~s** is that I speak three languages. **strength** ◄► **weakness** **strong** ◄► **weak**
	work experience ['wɜːk ɪkspɪəriəns]	Praktikum/Praktika; Arbeitserfahrung(en)	
	criticism ['krɪtɪsɪzəm]	Kritik	**react to criticism well** = mit Kritik gut umgehen (können), Kritik vertragen ! *German* Kritik = **1.** *(an etwas/jm.)* **criticism**; **2.** *(Rezension eines Buchs/Films)* **review**
	confident ['kɒnfɪdənt]	(selbst)sicher; zuversichtlich	He's very shy. He'd like to become more ~. The interview went very well. I'm ~ I'll get the job.
	energetic [enə'dʒetɪk]	energisch, energiereich	We need an ~ person for this job.
	enthusiastic [ɪnθjuːzi'æstɪk]	begeistert	Look at those flowers! You can see how ~ Joan is about gardening.
	punctual ['pʌŋktʃuəl]	pünktlich	= on time
	reliable [rɪ'laɪəbl]	zuverlässig, verlässlich	She's a very ~ person. If she says she will do something, then she will really do it.
p. 59	**study** ['stʌdi]	studieren; lernen	She wants to ~ history when she's finished school. I'll stay at home this afternoon and ~ for tomorrow's test.
	university [juːnɪ'vɜːsəti]	Universität	
	identity [aɪ'dentəti]	Identität	My native language is part of my ~. (Meine Muttersprache ist Teil meiner Identität.)

Theme 2

p. 60	**advertisement** [əd'vɜːtɪsmənt] *(infml auch:* **ad** [æd], **advert***)*	Anzeige, Inserat, Annonce	You find job **~s** in newspapers and on the internet. noun: **advertisement** – verb: **advertise sth.** (Werbung machen für etwas)
	assistant [ə'sɪstənt]	Helfer/in, Assistent/in	**early years teaching assistant** = Hilfskraft im Kindergarten, Sozialassistent/in ! Betonung auf der 2. Silbe: as**sis**tant [ə'sɪstənt]
	communication [kəmjuːnɪ'keɪʃn]	Kommunikation, Verständigung	
	(working) hours *(pl)*	Arbeitszeit(en)	Cooks have long **working ~** – up to 14 hours a day. **opening hours** *(pl)* = Öffnungszeiten
	salary ['sæləri]	Lohn, Gehalt	the money that employees get for doing their job
	apply (for) [ə'plaɪ]	sich bewerben (um)	Did your brother **~ for** the job? – Yes, but he didn't get it.
	stylist ['staɪlɪst]	Friseur/in; (Mode-)Stylist/in	
	lead [liːd], **led, led** [led]	führen, leiten	This road **~s** to York. Who will **~** the discussion?
	career [kə'rɪə]	Karriere; (schulischer/beruflicher) Werdegang	
	up to ['ʌp tə]	bis (zu)	This tree can get **~ to** 35 metres high.

German „bis“

• **zeitlich** meist:	**until**	I had to work **until** ten o'clock last night. We lived in Austria **until** I was eight years old.
• **„bis jetzt“**:	**up to now/so far**	**Up to now/So far** everything has been OK.
• **„von ... bis ...“**:	**from ... to ...**	We're open **from** Monday **to** Friday **from** 9 **to** 5.
• **„bis zu“** + Menge/Zahl:	**up to**	There'll be **up to** 200 guests. You can earn **up to** £60,000 here.
• **räumlich** meist:	**as far as/up to**	Walk **as far as/up to** the school, then turn left.

	CV (= curriculum vitae) *(BE)* [siː 'vi, kərɪkjələm 'viːtaɪ]	Lebenslauf	
	trainee [treɪ'niː]	Auszubildende/r, Trainee	
	qualification [kwɒlɪfɪ'keɪʃn]	(Schul-)Abschluss, Qualifikation	What **~s** do you need for this job?
	instructor [ɪn'strʌktə]	Lehrer/in	
	qualify ['kwɒlɪfaɪ]	(sich) qualifizieren	Pete's Pasta Place is looking for a **qualified** cook. verb: **qualify** – noun: **qualification**
p. 61	**apprentice** [ə'prentɪs]	Lehrling, Auszubildende/r	an **~ stylist** *(Frisörlehrling)*, an **office ~** *(Bürolehrling)*
	organization [ɔːgənaɪ'zeɪʃn]	Organisation	

department [dɪ'pɑːtmənt]	Abteilung	
take care of sb./sth. [keə]	sich um jn./etwas kümmern	**care** = Versorgung, Betreuung child**care** = Kinderbetreuung health **care** = Gesundheitsversorgung
knowledge (of/about) ['nɒlɪdʒ]	Wissen (von/über), Kenntnis(se) (von/in)	**knowledge** of art (Wissen auf dem Gebiet der Kunst), **knowledge** of geography (Kenntnisse der Geographie, geografische Kenntnisse), **knowledge** about nature (Wissen über die Natur)
flexible ['fleksəbl]	flexibel	! Betonung auf der 1. Silbe: **<u>flex</u>**ible ['fleksəbl]
shift [ʃɪft]	Schicht *(bei der Arbeit)*	! *English:* I **work shifts** at a restaurant. *German:* Ich **arbeite im Schichtdienst** …
at all times	jederzeit, ständig	= all the time, always
duty ['djuːti]	Pflicht, Aufgabe; Dienst	! *English:* **on duty** – *German:* **im Dienst**
suitable ['suːtəbl]	geeignet, passend	Jeans aren't ~ clothes for a job interview.

Theme 3

p. 62 **social** ['səʊʃl]	gesellschaftlich, sozial; gesellig	**social skills** *(pl)* = Sozialkompetenz **social media** *(pl)* = soziale Medien/Dienste ! Betonung auf der 1. Silbe: <u>**so**</u>cial ['səʊʃl]
organizational [ɔːgənaɪ'zeɪʃənl]	organisatorisch	noun: **organization** – adjective: **organizational**
basic ['beɪsɪk]	einfach, elementar	• adjective: **basic** We stayed at a cheap, **basic** hotel. • adverb: **basically** (im Prinzip, grundsätzlich) **Basically** I like your idea. But I'd like to discuss some of the details.
resort [rɪ'zɔːt]	Urlaubsort	a **ski ~**, a **seaside ~**
education [edʒu'keɪʃn]	(Schul-)Bildung	You need a good ~ if you want to get a good job.
key skills *(pl)* ['kiː skɪlz]	Schlüsselqualifikationen, -kompetenzen	
key [kiː]	Schlüssel; Schlüssel-	I can't drive home – I've lost my car **~s**! The coach plays a ~ role for any sports team.
achievement [ə'tʃiːvmənt]	Errungenschaft, Leistung	Learning to play the guitar is quite an ~.
reference ['refrəns]	Referenz, Empfehlung; jd., der eine Referenz erteilt	I listed my coach and my maths teacher as **~s**.
p. 63 **cover letter** ['kʌvə letə]	Anschreiben, Begleitschreiben, Motivationsschreiben	
director [də'rektə]	Geschäftsführer/in, Chef/in	somebody who runs a company
Dear Sir/Madam [sɜː, 'mædəm]	Sehr geehrte Damen und Herren	
enclose [ɪn'kləʊz]	beifügen, beilegen *(einem Brief)*	Please ~ a copy of your driving licence.

Yours faithfully *(BE)* ['feɪθfəli]	Mit freundlichen Grüßen *(Briefschluss)*	

Beginning and ending formal letters

	You start with:	You end with:
• If you know the person's name:	**Dear Ms Jones** **Dear Mr Brown**	*(BE:)* **Yours sincerely** *(AE:)* **Sincerely**
• If you don't know the person's name:	**Dear Sir/Madam**	*(BE:)* **Yours faithfully** *(AE:)* **Sincerely** *or* **Sincerely yours** *or* **Yours truly**

responsibility [rɪspɒnsə'bɪləti]	Aufgabe, Zuständigkeit	adjective: **responsible (for)** – noun: **responsibility**
requirement [rɪ'kwaɪəmənt]	Voraussetzung, Anforderung	something that is needed
attitude (to/towards) ['ætɪtju:d]	Einstellung, (Geistes-)Haltung (zu/gegenüber)	What's your ~ **to(wards)** cheap clothes?

Background theme

p. 64	**target** ['tɑ:gɪt]	Ziel	I am the ~ of a lot of fashion adverts. If you want to sell something, you have to know your ~ **group** *(Zielgruppe)*.
	below [bɪ'ləʊ]	unten; unter, unterhalb (von)	Look at the pictures ~. Write your name ~ all the other names on the list, please.
	ability [ə'bɪləti]	Fähigkeit, Können	have the **ability** to do something = be **able** to do something
	certificate [sə'tɪfɪkət]	Urkunde, Bescheinigung	Do you get a ~ at the end of the course?
	valid ['vælɪd]	aktuell, gültig	You need a ~ passport to travel to the USA.
	people with special needs [ni:d]	Menschen mit besonderen Bedürfnissen / Förderbedarf	= people who need help, people with a disability
	assist (with) [ə'sɪst]	assistieren, helfen (bei)	Could you ~ me **with** my English cover letter, please?
	reserve [rɪ'zɜ:v]	Schutzgebiet	a protected area for animals and plants
	organic [ɔ:'gænɪk]	biologisch, Bio-	I always buy ~ meat because the animals are treated better.
	tropical ['trɒpɪkl]	tropisch, Tropen-	
	rainforest ['reɪnfɒrɪst]	Regenwald	
	system ['sɪstəm]	System	! Betonung auf der 1. Silbe: **sys**tem ['sɪstəm]
p. 65	**(landscape) gardener** ['gɑ:dnə]	(Landschafts-)Gärtner/in	I love making plans for attractive gardens, so I became a **landscape ~**.
	camel ['kæml]	Kamel	! Betonung auf der 1. Silbe: **ca**mel ['kæml]
	explore [ɪk'splɔ:]	erforschen, erkunden	travel around a place and learn more about it

Focus on language

p. 66	**be (good) friends with** sb.	mit jm. (gut) befreundet sein	**I'm friends** with Joe and Jack. = Joe and Jack are my friends.
	... though. [ðəʊ]	... aber ..., ... trotzdem ...	She was born in France. She isn't French **~**. (= ... She isn't French, however.) ! Das Adverb **though** steht am Satzende, anders als die deutschen Entsprechungen.
	admire [əd'maɪə]	bewundern	We stopped at the lake to ~ the view.
	equal ['i:kwəl]	gleich(berechtigt)	Everyone gets an ~ number of biscuits! Husband and wife should be ~ partners.
	for sure	ganz sicher, ganz bestimmt	! *English:* ..., **that's for sure.** *German:* ..., **das ist (ganz) sicher.** *English:* **One thing is for sure:** ... *German:* **Eins ist sicher:** ...
p. 67	**She's ..., isn't she?**	Sie ist ..., nicht wahr?	You **weren't** at Dave's party last Saturday, **were you**?
	interviewer ['ɪntəvju:ə]	Interviewer/in	

Text

p. 68	**blurb** [blɜ:b]	Klappentext *(eines Buches)*	the text on the back cover of a book that tells the reader what the book is about
	pretend (to be sth.) [prɪ'tend]	so tun, als ob (man etwas wäre)	They **~ed to be** ill so that they could miss school.
	in order to ['ɔ:də]	um ... zu	We should go there early **in ~ to** get good seats.
	realize sth. ['ri:əlaɪz]	etwas erkennen, sich einer Sache bewusst werden	When I got home, I **~d** that I had left my bag on the train.
	complicated ['kɒmplɪkeɪtɪd]	kompliziert	! Betonung auf der 1. Silbe: **com**plicated ['kɒmplɪkeɪtɪd]
	lie (to sb.) [laɪ]	(jn. an)lügen	What he said wasn't true. He **lied to** me. Schreibung: **lie, lied** – He **lied** to me. aber: **lying** – Stop **lying** to me.
	lie	Lüge	**lügen** = **lie** *oder* **tell a lie/tell lies**
	clerk [klɑ:k]	Angestellte/r	**(front) desk clerk** = Empfangsmitarbeiter/in
	immediately [ɪ'mi:diətli]	sofort, umgehend, unmittelbar	When I call my dog, she comes **~**. ! **immediate** = sofortige/r/s
	hand sb. sth. [hænd]	jm. etwas (an)reichen, aushändigen	Can you ~ (= give) me the sugar, please?
	application form [æplɪ'keɪʃn fɔ:m]	Bewerbungsformular, Antragsformular	**application** = Bewerbung, Antrag **form** = Formular
	on one's own	alleine, selbstständig *(ohne Unterstützung)*	I repaired this **on my ~** – nobody helped me.
	boardwalk ['bɔ:dwɔ:k]	Steg, Uferpromenade *(aus Holz)*	 a boardwalk

	a friend of Cindy's / of hers / of mine	ein/e Freund/in von Cindy / von ihr / von mir	→ **a friend of Cindy's / of hers / of mine** • Charlotte is **a friend of Cindy's**. (= eine von Cindys Freundinnen) • Josie is **Charlotte's friend**. (= Charlottes (beste) Freundin) ! a friend of **mine/his/hers/ours** (*nicht:* … of ~~me/him/her/us~~)
	program *(AE)* ['prəʊgræm]	Programm	! **programme** *(BE)* / **program** *(AE)* = **1.** Programm; **2.** (Fernseh-/Radio-)Sendung
p. 69	**storey** *(BE)* / **story** *(AE)* ['stɔːri]	Stock, Stockwerk, Etage	→ **German „Stock(werk)"** • When you want to say where someone lives or works: **floor** Our offices are on the sixth **floor**. • When you want to say how high a building is: **storey** *(BE)* / **story** *(AE)* The building is 14 **storeys** high.
	unattractive [ʌnə'træktɪv]	unattraktiv	**attractive** ◄► **unattractive**
	mature [mə'tʃʊə]	reif, vernünftig	
	lipstick ['lɪpstɪk]	Lippenstift	 **lips** **a lipstick**
	cheerful ['tʃɪəfl]	fröhlich, gut gelaunt	
	curly ['kɜːli]	lockig	 **curly hair** ◄► **straight hair** They have **curly** hair.
	graveyard ['greɪvjɑːd]	Friedhof	**graveyard shift** *(infml)* = Nachtschicht
	lady ['leɪdi]	Dame	
	machine [mə'ʃiːn]	Maschine, Gerät	**drinks machine** = Getränkeautomat
	neon ['niːɒn]	Neon; neonfarbig	
	can [kæn]	Dose	 **a can of juice** **a can of cola** **a can of tomatoes**
	accept [ək'sept]	akzeptieren, annehmen	I've asked 20 people to my party and 13 have already **~ed** the invitation.
	credit card ['kredɪt kɑːd]	Kreditkarte	
	slam [slæm]	(zu-, hin)knallen	**slam down the phone** = den Hörer aufknallen

	fire sb. ['faɪə]	jn. feuern, entlassen	You'll get me **fired**. (Du schaffst es noch, dass ich gefeuert werde.)
p. 70	**pull back**	sich zurückziehen, zurückweichen	! *English:* **pull back one's hair** *German:* **sich die Haare zusammenbinden**
	I get it. *(infml)*	Ich verstehe. / Ich kapiere.	
	sandals *(pl)* ['sændlz]	Sandalen	 **sandals**
	foolish ['fuːlɪʃ]	töricht, dumm	noun: **fool** – adjective: **foolish**
p. 71	**appearance** [ə'pɪərəns]	Erscheinung(sbild), Aussehen	You should have an appropriate ~ at a job interview. verb: **appear** – noun: **appearance**

Speaking course

p. 72	**job interview**	Vorstellungsgespräch	
	chest [tʃest]	Brust(korb)	the top part of the front of the body, between the shoulders and the stomach
p. 73	**individual** [ɪndɪ'vɪdʒuəl]	Einzelne/r, Individuum; Person	
	necessary ['nesəsəri]	notwendig, nötig, erforderlich	Some changes will be ~. (= Some changes will have to be made.)
	candidate ['kændɪdət]	Bewerber/in, Kandidat/in	! Betonung auf der 1. Silbe: <u>**can**</u>didate ['kændɪdət]
	approach [ə'prəʊtʃ]	Ansatz, Herangehensweise	This isn't working. Let's try a different ~.
	greet [griːt]	begrüßen	
	contact sb. ['kɒntækt]	Kontakt aufnehmen zu, sich melden bei	verb: **contact** – noun: **contact** (Kontakt)

Unit 4: Generation *like*

p. 81	**argument** ['ɑːgjumənt]	Argument; Streit	→ **argument** • Prepare your **arguments** before you start the discussion. (= **Argument**) • Mum and dad had an **argument** last night. They shouted a lot. (= **Streit**) ! Betonung auf der 1. Silbe: <u>ar</u>gument ['ɑːgjumənt]

Theme 1

p. 82	**digital** ['dɪdʒɪtl]	digital	! Betonung auf der 1. Silbe: <u>di</u>gital ['dɪdʒɪtl]
	average ['ævərɪdʒ]	durchschnittlich, Durchschnitt	The ~ age of students in our year is 16.5 years. I practise the piano two hours a day **on ~**. (= im Durchschnitt, durchschnittlich)
	multitask [mʌlti'tɑːsk]	mehrere Tätigkeiten gleichzeitig ausführen	
	video-chat ['vɪdiəʊ tʃæt]	*sich per Videokonferenz unterhalten*	
	at the same time	zur selben Zeit, gleichzeitig	He chats, reads a magazine and watches TV, all **at the same ~**.

	attraction [ə'trækʃn]	Attraktion; Anziehungskraft	The British Museum is one of London's biggest tourist **~s**.
	the pros and cons *(pl)* [prəʊz ənd 'kɒnz]	das Pro und Kontra; das Für und Wider	What are **the pros and ~** (= the reasons for and against) buying a new car now?
p. 83	**habit** ['hæbɪt]	(An-)Gewohnheit	something you do regularly Smoking is a bad **~**.
	be a drifter ['drɪftə]	sich treiben lassen *(ziellos vor sich hinleben)*	I spend a lot of time on the internet. I think **I'm a** digital **~**.
	butterfly ['bʌtəflaɪ]	Schmetterling	**butterflies** 
	convince [kən'vɪns]	überzeugen	His idea might have been good, but his arguments weren't very **convincing**.

Theme 2

p. 84	**profile** ['prəʊfaɪl]	Profil; Beschreibung, Portrait	! Betonung auf der 1. Silbe: **pro**file ['prəʊfaɪl]
	standard ['stændəd]	normal, üblich, Standard-	adjective: **standard** – noun: **standard** (Norm, Standard)
	imaginative [ɪ'mædʒɪnətɪv]	einfallsreich, kreativ	He's a great cook and so ~! He can make anything taste great!
	arty *(infml)* ['ɑːti]	(gewollt) künstlerisch	being, or wanting to be, very artistic and interested in art
	creative [kri'eɪtɪv]	kreativ	! Betonung auf der 2. Silbe: cre**a**tive [kri'eɪtɪv]
	pair [peə]	Paar	! a **pair** of shoes a **pair** of trousers *(eine Hose)* a **pair** of jeans *(eine Jeans)* a **pair** of glasses *(eine Brille)*
	put sth. **up (on social media)** [pʊt 'ʌp]	etwas (in soziale Medien) (ein)stellen	
p. 85	**vain** [veɪn]	eitel	He's so **~**. He spends all of his time looking in the mirror and checking his hair.
	critic ['krɪtɪk]	Kritiker/in	! *English:* **critic** – *German:* **Kritiker/in** *English:* **criticism** – *German:* **Kritik**
	depressing [dɪ'presɪŋ]	deprimierend	
	astronaut ['æstrənɔːt]	Astronaut/in	an **astronaut** ! Betonung auf der 1. Silbe: **as**tronaut ['æstrənɔːt] 
	self-portrait ['pɔːtreɪt]	Selbstporträt	
	in other words	mit anderen Worten	
	modern-day [mɒdn 'deɪ]	modern, von heute	Remember those old-fashioned telephones? Well, **~-day** phones are mobiles!
	although [ɔːl'ðəʊ] *(kurz auch:* **though** [ðəʊ])	obwohl	We stayed up and watched the late film, **although** we were really tired. *(oder:* …, **though** we were really tired.)

Theme 3

p. 86	**target** sb. ['tɑːɡɪt]	auf jn. zielen *(jn. als Zielgruppe haben/wählen)*, jn. ins Visier nehmen	Fashion companies often ~ young adults. verb: **target** – noun: **target** (Ziel)
	savvy *(infml)* ['sævi]	versiert, gewieft, erfahren	→ **savvy** wird oft an andere Wörter angehängt: **ad-savvy** versiert/gewieft/erfahren im Umgang mit Werbung **media-savvy** versiert/gewieft/erfahren im Umgang mit Medien **net-savvy** interneterfahren **tech-savvy** technikversiert
	fit in [fɪt 'ɪn]	dazugehören; hineinpassen	There are some students in my sister's class who just don't ~ **in**.
	billboard *(AE)* ['bɪlbɔːd]	Plakatwand, Werbeplakat	
	reduce (by) [rɪ'djuːs]	reduzieren, verringern (um)	Oh look, they have **~d** the price.
	advertiser ['ædvətaɪzə]	Werber/in, Werbetreibende/r	
	design [dɪ'zaɪn]	entwerfen, gestalten, entwickeln	A landscape gardener plans and **~s** gardens.
	unnatural [ʌn'nætʃrəl]	unnatürlich	Adverb: **unnaturally** beautiful/white/perfect (unnatürlich schön/weiß/perfekt)
	repeat [rɪ'piːt]	wiederholen	Could you ~ that, please? (= Could you say/do that again, please?)
	sample ['sɑːmpl]	Muster, Probe(exemplar)	We were given free **~s** of fair-trade chocolate. It tasted great!
	advertising ['ædvətaɪzɪŋ]	Werbung, Reklame	

adverts and advertising

- **advertise (sth.)** ['ædvətaɪz] – Werbung machen (für etwas)
- **advertising** ['ædvətaɪzɪŋ] – Werbung, Reklame
- **advertisement,** *infml auch:* **ad, advert** – Anzeige, Inserat, Annonce
- **advertiser** ['ædvətaɪzə] – Werber/in, Werbetreibende(r)

p. 87	**irritate** ['ɪrɪteɪt]	(ver)ärgern, irritieren	Pop-up ads ~ me so much!

Focus on language

p. 88	**gatecrash (a party)** ['ɡeɪtkræʃ]	(bei einer Party) ungebeten erscheinen	**gatecrasher** = nicht eingeladene Person (die eine Party sprengt)
	control [kən'trəʊl]	kontrollieren, regulieren	Should parents ~ how much TV their kids watch?
	reach (sb./a place) [riːtʃ]	(jn./einen Ort) erreichen	If we leave now, we'll ~ London before dinner.

	damage (to) *(no pl)* ['dæmɪdʒ]	Schaden, Schäden (an)	The fire destroyed part of the kitchen, but there was no **~ to** the house. (…, aber es gab keine Schäden am Haus / aber das Haus wurde nicht beschädigt.)
	clean-up ['kliːn ʌp]	Reinemachen, Hausputz	
	fault [fɔːlt]	Fehler, Schuld	Don't blame me! It wasn't my ~!
	learn a/your lesson	eine/deine Lektion lernen	**teach sb. a lesson** = jm. eine Lektion erteilen
p.89	**type (of)** [taɪp]	Art, Sorte, Typ (von)	What ~ of person is she? Quiet? Noisy? Funny? Shy?
	message ['mesɪdʒ]	Nachrichten schicken/ austauschen	My best friend and I ~ all the time. verb: **message** – noun: **message** (Nachricht, Mitteilung)
	crash (into) [kræʃ]	einen Unfall haben, zusammenstoßen (mit)	If you don't drive more carefully, we'll ~! He drove too fast and **~ed** into a tree.

Text

p.90	**heavyweight** ['heviweɪt]	Schwergewicht; Schwergewichts-	(in boxing:) weighing over 79.5 kilos = of the heaviest class
	virtual ['vɜːtʃʊəl]	virtuell	❗ Betonung auf der 1. Silbe: **<u>vir</u>**tual ['vɜːtʃʊəl]
	combat ['kɒmbæt]	Kampf	noun: **combat** – verb: **combat** (kämpfen (gegen))
	turn away	sich abwenden, sich wegdrehen	
	unwanted [ʌn'wɒntɪd]	unerwünscht	
	killer ['kɪlə]	Mörder/in	
	virus ['vaɪrəs], *pl* **viruses** ['vaɪrəsɪz]	Virus	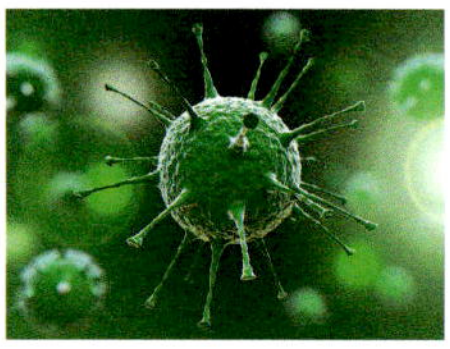 
	spread (sth.) [spred], **spread, spread**	etwas verbreiten *(Virus, Krankheit)*; sich ausbreiten	The disease is **~ing**. *(breitet sich aus)* Some wild animals can ~ diseases. *(verbreiten)*
	go crazy	verrückt werden	the vegetables **went** bad, tyres can **go** flat, apples can **go** brown ❗ **Go** *(werden)* wird nur in bestimmten Zusammenhängen verwendet, z.B. für Farben oder bei Verschlechterungen.
	take over	die Macht übernehmen	
	catch sth.	sich mit etwas anstecken; sich etwas einfangen *(Krankheit)*	Wear a warm jacket so that you don't ~ a cold!
	realistic [riːə'lɪstɪk]	realistisch	I want to see all the sights in London. – Come on, be ~. We only have two days.
	the most realistic game **ever**	das realistischste Spiel, das es je gegeben hat	
	energy ['enədʒi]	Energie	❗ Betonung auf der 1. Silbe: **<u>en</u>**ergy ['enədʒi]

	(chocolate/energy) bar [bɑː]	(Schoko-/Energie-)Riegel	**chocolate bars** 
	torture ['tɔːtʃə]	Folter	**torture** = **1.** Folter; **2.** foltern
	return [rɪ'tɜːn]	zurückkehren, zurückkommen	come back or go back
	I haven't eaten **in days.**	Ich habe tagelang nichts gegessen.	
	be on	laufen, gezeigt werden *(Kino, Theater)*	What**'s ~** at the theatre this evening?
p. 91	**backstreet** ['bækstriːt]	*(kleinere)* Seitenstraße *(weitab von den Hauptstraßen)*	
	rich [rɪtʃ]	reich	**rich ◄► poor**
	lad *(infml)* [læd]	Junge, junger Kerl	a boy or a young man
	hug [hʌg]	umklammern; umarmen	They're **hugging** each other. 
	leave sb. **alone**	jn. in Ruhe lassen	Go away and **~** me **alone**! ! *English:* Leave me **alone**. *German:* Lass mich **in Ruhe**.
	sis *(infml)* [sɪs]	Schwester *(kurz für:* sister*)*	
	step	treten *(einen Schritt tun)*	Please **~** closer and have a look! verb: **step** – noun: **step** (Schritt; Stufe)
	finder ['faɪndə]	Finder/in	! **Finders keepers, losers weepers.** *etwa:* Was man findet, darf man behalten. (Wer's findet, darf's behalten, wer's verloren hat, muss weinen.)
	creep up (on sb.) [kriːp], **crept, crept** [krept]	sich heranschleichen (an jn.)	Two men **crept ~ on** me from behind and stole my bag. ! **creep** = schleichen, kriechen
	pick on sb.	auf jm. herumhacken, jn. drangsalieren	Stop **~ing on** Luke just because he has red hair!
	back away (from) [bæk]	zurückweichen (von)	! **back** = **1.** zurück; **2.** Rücken, Rückseite; **3. back away** = zurückweichen
	weapon ['wepən]	Waffe	
	till [tɪl]	bis	= until
	... is bad news.	... ist gefährlich. / ... ist (gar) nicht gut.	You can't trust him. He**'s bad ~**.
p. 92	**close** [kləʊs]	dicht, eng	hold each other **close**, a **close** friend *(eng)* stand **close** to each other *(dicht)*
	fear (of) [fɪə]	Angst (vor)	I have a **fear of** spiders. (= I'm afraid of /scared of spiders.)
	addicted (to) [ə'dɪktɪd]	süchtig (nach), abhängig (von)	He smokes a lot. He's **~ to** cigarettes.

	frightened ['fraɪtnd]	verängstigt	→ **frighten, frightened, frightening** • **it frightens me** = es macht mir Angst • **be frightened of** sth. = vor etwas Angst haben • **it's frightening** = es ist beängstigend
	leather ['leðə]	Leder	made of **leather** 
	grin (at sb.) [grɪn]	(jn. an)grinsen	Look at him! He's **grinning at** us. 
	no need for … / no need to do sth. [ni:d]	kein Grund für … / kein Grund, etwas zu tun	There's **no ~ for** tears. There's **no ~ to** cry. Everything will be fine.
	know sth. **like the back of one's hand**	etwas wie seine Westentasche kennen; etwas in- und auswendig kennen	the **back of your hand** 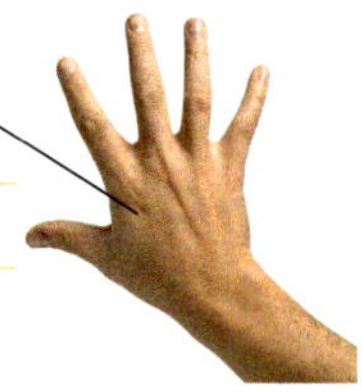
	short cut [ʃɔ:t 'kʌt]	Abkürzung	
	close on sb.	jm. näher kommen, zu jm. aufholen	They were coming closer. = They **~d on** me.
	fire escape ['faɪər ɪskeɪp]	Feuertreppe, Notausgang	
	ladder ['lædə]	*(die)* Leiter	
p.93	**edge** [edʒ]	Rand, Kante	
	flash [flæʃ]	*(das)* (Auf-)Blitzen	
	point a knife/gun at sb.	ein Messer/eine Waffe auf jn. richten	
	mobile ['məʊbaɪl]	mobil	adjective: **mobile** – noun: **mobile (phone)**
p.95	**fictional** ['fɪkʃənl]	erfunden, fiktiv	Is this story real or is it **~**?
	unlike [ʌn'laɪk]	anders als, im Gegensatz zu	**Unlike** some other systems, this one is very reliable.
	come true	wahr werden	**a dream come true** = ein wahr gewordener Traum

German „werden"

Man verwendet am häufigsten **get** oder **become** für das deutsche „werden". Das Verb **get** ist etwas umgangssprachlicher als **become**.	**get/become** **angry, nervous, old, cold, windy, dark interesting, funny**
! Vor Nomen wird nur **become** verwendet.	She **became** a **doctor**/a **singer**/a successful **boxer**. *Sie wurde Ärztin/Sängerin/eine erfolgreiche Boxerin.*
Wenn es um Farben oder Verschlechterungen geht, kannst du **go** verwenden.	food can **go** bad, apples **go** brown, bread **goes** hard, I thought I'd **go** crazy
Und es gibt einige feststehende Ausdrücke mit **come**.	**come** true, **come** alive

orphan ['ɔ:fn]	Waise	a child whose parents have died

	characterization [kærəktəraɪˈzeɪʃn]	Charakterisierung	noun: **characterization** – verb: **characterize**
	characterize [ˈkærəktəraɪz]	charakteristisch sein für; beschreiben, darstellen	Modern architecture **characterizes** this part of the city. *(charakteristisch sein für)* How would you **characterize** Scott in this story? *(beschreiben)*

Speaking course

p. 96	**shocking** [ˈʃɒkɪŋ]	schockierend	→ **shock, shocked, shocking** • **it shocked us** = es hat uns schockiert • **be/look shocked** = schockiert sein/ aussehen • **shocking news** = schockierende Nachrichten
	vamping [ˈvæmpɪŋ]	spät in der Nacht noch aktiv sein	! Das Wort **vamping** kommt von **vampire** [ˈvæmpaɪə] („Vampir") – Vampire sind auch nachtaktiv.
	point	Argument	→ **point** • **Make your point.** = Sag, wie du darüber denkst. • **That's a good point.** = Das ist ein (gutes) Argument.
	express [ɪkˈspres]	ausdrücken, zum Ausdruck bringen	"In my opinion" and "I think" are useful phrases to ~ your opinion.
	gallery [ˈgæləri]	Galerie	! Betonung auf der 1. Silbe: **gall**ery [ˈgæləri]
	invention [ɪnˈvenʃn]	Erfindung	I don't think it's true that every ~ makes life easier.
	waste [weɪst]	Verschwendung	That guy's an idiot, and talking to him is a complete ~ of time.
p. 97	**above** [əˈbʌv]	oben; über, oberhalb (von)	**above** ◄► **below**
	arrange [əˈreɪndʒ]	arrangieren; (an)ordnen	Let's ~ a date when we can meet. Do you want to ~ these books alphabetically **by** author? *(... alphabetisch nach Autoren ...)*
	observer [əbˈzɜːvə]	Beobachter/in	somebody who watches something
	sheet [ʃiːt]	Blatt *(Papier)*	= a piece of paper
	moderator [ˈmɒdəreɪtə]	Moderator/in *(z.B. bei Debatten)*	
	speaker [ˈspiːkə]	Sprecher/in; Redner/in	! **speaker** = **1.** Lautsprecher; **2.** Sprecher/in; Redner/in
	respectful (to) [rɪˈspektfl]	respektvoll (gegenüber)	• adjective: **respectful** If you are **respectful to** your teachers, most of them will be **respectful to** you. • adverb: **respectfully** Speak **respectfully** when you are having a discussion. You will be more successful.
	persuade [pəˈsweɪd]	überreden, überzeugen	She's so good! We must ~ her to enter the competition.

MORE CHALLENGE 1

p.26	°**spare room** [speə 'ruːm]	Gästezimmer	
	°**surroundings** *(pl)* [sə'raʊndɪŋz]	Umgebung	
	°**shower** ['ʃaʊə]	(sich) duschen	! *English:* **shower** *or* **have a shower** *or* **take a shower** *German:* **(sich) duschen** *English:* **have a bath** *or* **take a bath** *German:* **baden** *(in der Wanne)*
	°**bath** [bɑːθ]	Badewanne	
	°**bathtub** ['bɑːθtʌb]	Badewanne	 **bathtubs**
	°**cupboard** ['kʌbəd]	Schrank	! Aussprache: **cupboard** ['kʌbəd]
	°**what ... anyway?** ['eniweɪ]	was/welche/r/s ... überhaupt?	But you know I don't like fish! **What kind of fish is it, ~?** (Was für eine Art Fisch ist es denn überhaupt?)
	°**put** sb. **at ease** [iːz]	jn. beruhigen, jm. die Befangenheit nehmen	My new boss introduced me to everyone and that helped to **~ me at ~**.
	°**idiom** ['ɪdiəm]	Redewendung	
p.27	°**run (a program)**	(ein Programm) anbieten, abhalten	
	°**at once** [wʌns]	auf einmal, gleichzeitig	One after the other, please. Don't talk all **at ~**.
	°**guide** (sb. somewhere) [gaɪd]	(jn. an einen Ort) führen, begleiten	! **guide** = **1.** *(Person)* Reiseleiter/in, Fremdenführer/in; **2.** *(Buch)* Reiseführer; Ratgeber; **3.** führen, begleiten
	°**I suppose** [sə'pəʊz]	ich denke, ich glaube, ich nehme an	Getting tickets for that show will be hard, I **suppose**. **suppose** = glauben, denken, annehmen
	°**go along**	vorangehen, Fortschritte machen	**as I went along** = nach und nach
	°**limit** sb./sth. **to** ['lɪmɪt]	jn./etwas begrenzen, beschränken auf	I'm trying to ~ myself **to** two hours TV a day.
	°**vocabulary** [və'kæbjələri]	Wortschatz, Vokabular	you have a wide ~ = you know many words you have a limited ~ = you don't know many words
	°**construct** [kən'strʌkt]	(auf)bauen, konstruieren	
	°**gap** [gæp]	Lücke; Kluft	Please write the missing words into the **~s**. Do you think there's a ~ between what you learn at school and what you need in life?

°**few**	wenige	I talked to **a few** people at the party. *(einige, ein paar)* Only **few** people came to the party. *(nur wenige)* **!** German „weniger": I have **less** money than Jack. *(money = unzählbar)* So I can buy **fewer** things. *(things = zählbar)*
°**normally** ['nɔːməli]	normalerweise	It's unusual that Dave is late. **Normally** he's on time.
p. 28 °**risky** ['rɪski]	riskant	noun: **risk** *(Risiko)* – verb: **risk** *(riskieren)* – adjective: **risky**
°**chief** [tʃiːf]	Haupt-; leitende/r	I'm the ~ dogwalker at home. (= It's mostly me who walks the dog.)
°**poison** ['pɔɪzn]	Gift	**poison** 
°**be/feel uncomfortable** [ʌn'kʌmftəbl]	sich unbehaglich fühlen	Everyone was looking at me. I felt so ~.
°**moon** [muːn]	Mond	the **moon** 

MORE CHALLENGE 2

p. 50 °**keep up** (**with** sb.)	(mit jm.) Schritt halten	
°**elementary school** *(AE)* [elɪ'mentri skuːl]	Grundschule	= *BE* **primary school**
°**middle school** *(AE)* ['mɪdl skuːl]	Mittelschule *(für 11- bis 14-Jährige)*	
°**abroad** [ə'brɔːd]	im/ins Ausland	My friend Emily has never been ~.
°**call** sb. **names**	jn. beschimpfen	He was really angry. Mike had **called him** ~ in front of the whole class.
°**beyond** [bɪ'jɒnd]	über … hinaus, weiter als	Spending some time abroad helped me to see ~ my own culture.
°**hardship** ['hɑːdʃɪp]	Not, Mühsal, harte Umstände	My grandparents experienced lots of ~ when they arrived in New York as teenagers.
°**able-bodied** [eɪbl 'bɒdid]	(körperlich) gesund	Some **~-bodied** people never think about people with disabilities.
°**rare** [reə]	selten	Wow! That's a ~ kind of bike. Where did you get it?
°**condition** [kən'dɪʃn]	Leiden, Erkrankung	Alan has a rare ~ which makes him sleep 15 hours a day.
°**properly** ['prɒpəli]	richtig, ordentlich, korrekt	My mum always says I don't set the table ~.
°**display** [dɪ'spleɪ]	zeigen, zur Schau stellen	There are always lots of mobile phones **~ed** in the shop window.
°**rather than** ['rɑːðə]	anstelle von, (an)statt	Olivia prefers to wear trousers ~ **than** dresses.

	°**taunt** [tɔːnt]	Spott, höhnische Bemerkung	
	°**admit** [əd'mɪt]	zugeben, (ein)gestehen	My brother sometimes cries, but he would never ~ it!
p. 51	°**doorway** ['dɔːweɪ]	Eingang *(Tür)*	You have to go five steps up to the ~, …
	°**barrier** ['bæriə]	Barriere	… another ~ for wheelchair users.
p. 52	°**replace (with)** [rɪ'pleɪs]	ersetzen, austauschen	I should get rid of my old phone and ~ it **with** a new one.
	°**dock** [dɒk]	Dock, Hafen, Mole	
	°**encourage** [ɪn'kʌrɪdʒ]	ermutigen, unterstützen	My friends **encouraged** me to apply for the job, and I got it!
	°**rather** ['rɑːðə]	ziemlich	He felt ~ sad. (= quite sad) ! **rather** = ziemlich **rather than** = anstelle von, (an)statt

MORE CHALLENGE 3

p. 74	°**overseas** [əʊvə'siːz]	Übersee-, Auslands-	
	°**congratulations (on** sth.) [kəngrætʃʊ'leɪʃnz]	herzlichen Glückwunsch (zu etwas)	**Congratulations on** your fantastic exam results!
	°**set** sth. **up**	etwas einrichten, aufbauen	I'd like to ~ **up** my own business.
	°**palm (tree)** [pɑːm]	Palme	a **palm tree** on a **sandy** beach 
	°**sandy** ['sændi]	sandig, Sand-	
p. 75	°**imagination** [ɪmædʒɪ'neɪʃn]	Fantasie, Vorstellungskraft	
	°**minor character** [maɪnə 'kærəktə]	Nebenfigur *(in Roman, Film usw.)*	
	°**flatmate** ['flætmeɪt]	Mitbewohner/in	One of our ~**s** moved away, so we're looking for someone to share our flat with us.
	°**interview** ['ɪntəvjuː]	befragen, interviewen	verb: **interview** – noun: **interview** (Interview; Vorstellungsgespräch)
p. 76	°**work long hours**	lange arbeiten, Überstunden machen	If you **work ~ hours** on one day, you should be allowed to take time off on another day.

MORE CHALLENGE 4

p. 98	°**analysis** [ə'næləsɪs], *pl* **analyses** [ə'næləsiːz]	Analyse	
	°**location** [ləʊ'keɪʃn]	Ort *(Standort; Einsatzort)*	
	°**reaction (to)** [ri'ækʃn]	Reaktion (auf)	verb: **react (to)** – noun: **reaction (to)**
p. 99	°**gift** [gɪft]	Geschenk	= present
	°**lively** ['laɪvli]	lebendig, lebhaft	My grandma is still very ~ at 85. She goes dancing twice a week.
	°**get lucky**	Glück haben	I wrote many applications, but then I **got ~** and found a job.
	°**sell, sold, sold**	sich verkaufen (lassen)	Beatles songs still ~ quite well, even after all these years.
	°**Incredibly** [ɪn'kredəbli], **…**	Unglaublicherweise … / Es ist kaum zu glauben, aber …	**Incredibly,** my ring was still on my desk five hours after I had forgotten it there.

°**even though**	auch wenn, obwohl *(betont)*	*English:* He's world-famous, **even though** he isn't really an artist. *German:* ... weltberühmt, **und das, obwohl** er gar kein wirklicher Künstler ist.
°**sum** [sʌm]	Summe, Betrag	
°**hint** [hɪnt]	Hinweis	
°**in fact** [ɪn 'fækt]	eigentlich, um genau zu sein	My homework wasn't hard. **In ~** it only took me 10 minutes.
°**make** sth. **up**	etwas erfinden, sich etwas ausdenken	a **made-up** character, story etc. (eine erfundene Figur, Geschichte usw.)
°**entertaining** [entə'teɪnɪŋ]	unterhaltsam	The concert wasn't very **~**. I wanted to leave after 20 minutes.
°**aspect** ['æspekt]	Aspekt	There are many **~s** to think about before you go on a student exchange.
°**recommend** sth. **(to** sb.**)** [rekə'mend]	(jm.) etwas empfehlen	I can ~ the music store on 3rd Street. They have great stuff!
p. 100 °**poetry** ['pəʊətri]	Dichtung, Lyrik, Poesie	= poems
°**rose** [rəʊz]	Rose	
°**violet** ['vaɪələt]	Veilchen *(Blume)*	a **violet** 
°**brick** [brɪk]	Ziegel(-)	
°**but**	nur *(formell, gehoben)*	It is **but** a dream. = It is **only** a dream.
°**within** [wɪ'ðɪn]	innerhalb (von), in	
°**intelligent** [ɪn'telɪdʒənt]	intelligent	! Betonung auf der 2. Silbe: in**tel**ligent [ɪn'telɪdʒənt]
°**cultured** ['kʌltʃəd]	kultiviert, gebildet	
°**regret** [rɪ'gret]	bedauern, bereuen	I'm so sorry! I really ~ what I did to you.

Im **Dictionary** werden folgende **Abkürzungen und Symbole** verwendet:

sb. = somebody sth. = something jn. = jemanden jm. = jemandem
pl = *plural* (Mehrzahl) *BE* = British English *AE* = American English *infml* = *informal* (umgangssprachlich)

°Mit diesem Kringel sind Wörter markiert, die nicht zum Lernwortschatz gehören, sowie Tabuwörter *(taboo)*, die anstößig oder verletzend sein können.

Tipps zur Arbeit mit einem Wörterbuch findest du im Skills file auf Seite 161.

A

a [ə] ein, eine I **£10 a week** 10 Pfund pro Woche II
°**A levels** ['eɪ levlz] *(pl, BE)* Abitur
ability [ə'bɪləti] Fähigkeit, Können V 3 (64)
able ['eɪbl]: **be able to do sth.** etwas tun können, in der Lage sein etwas zu tun III
°**able-bodied** [eɪbl 'bɒdid] (körperlich) gesund
aboard [ə'bɔːd] an Bord I
Aboriginal [æbə'rɪdʒənl] Aborigine- *(die Ureinwohner/innen Australiens betreffend)* V 1 (8) **Aboriginal Australian** australische/r Ureinwohner/in V 1 (8)
about [ə'baʊt]:
1. ungefähr I
2. über I **about me** über mich I **good about my house** gut an meinem Haus I **What about you?** Und du? / Was ist mit dir? I
above [ə'bʌv] oben; über, oberhalb (von) V 4 (97)
°**abroad** [ə'brɔːd] im/ins Ausland
absolute ['æbsəluːt] absolut IV
accent ['æksent] Akzent III
accept [ək'sept] akzeptieren, annehmen V 3 (69)
accident ['æksɪdənt] Unfall II
accommodation [əkɒmə'deɪʃn] Unterkunft III
according to ... [ə'kɔːdɪŋ] laut ...; ... zufolge V 1 (10)
account [ə'kaʊnt] Account, Konto V 4 (82)
ache [eɪk] Schmerz(en) II
achievement [ə'tʃiːvmənt] Errungenschaft, Leistung V 3 (62)
°**acre** ['eɪkə] *Flächenmaß; ca. 4 000 m²*
across [ə'krɒs] (quer) über das II
act [ækt]:
1. Theater spielen, schauspielern II
2. handeln, sich verhalten; so tun, als ob V 2 (34)
°3. aufführen, spielen
°**act out** vorspielen, aufführen
acting school ['æktɪŋ skuːl] Schauspielschule V 3 (67)
action ['ækʃn]:
1. Action *(spannende Filmhandlung)* IV
2. Aktion, Handlung V 2 (37)
take action Maßnahmen ergreifen, etwas unternehmen V 2 (37) °**go into action** einen Einsatz haben

active ['æktɪv] aktiv II
activity [æk'tɪvəti] Aktivität, Tätigkeit II
actor ['æktə] Schauspieler/in V 2 (41)
actually ['æktʃuəli] eigentlich; tatsächlich III
ad [æd] *(infml)* Anzeige, Inserat, Annonce V 3 (60)
adapted from [ə'dæptɪd frɒm] basierend auf, (frei) nach V 1 (20)
adapter [ə'dæptə] Adapter III
add (to) [æd] hinzufügen (zu) III
addicted (to) [ə'dɪktɪd] süchtig (nach), abhängig (von) V 4 (92)
°**addition** [ə'dɪʃn]: **in addition (to) ...** zusätzlich (zu) ...
address [ə'dres] Adresse I
admire [əd'maɪə] bewundern V 3 (66)
admission [əd'mɪʃn] Eintritt(spreis) IV
°**admit** [əd'mɪt] zugeben, (ein)gestehen
adopt [ə'dɒpt] adoptieren; *(Tier)* bei sich aufnehmen II
adult ['ædʌlt] Erwachsene/r II
advantage [əd'vɑːntɪdʒ] Vorteil IV
adventure [əd'ventʃə] Abenteuer I
advert ['ædvɜːt] Anzeige, Werbung I
advertise (sth.) ['ædvətaɪz] Werbung machen (für etwas) V 3 (60)
advertisement [əd'vɜːtɪsmənt] Anzeige, Inserat, Annonce V 3 (60)
advertiser ['ædvətaɪzə] Werber/in, Werbetreibende/r V 4 (86)
advertising ['ædvətaɪzɪŋ] Werbung, Reklame V 4 (86)
advice [əd'vaɪs] Rat(schlag), Ratschläge II **a piece of advice** ein Rat(schlag) IV
°**advise** [əd'vaɪz] (be)raten
afraid [ə'freɪd]: **be afraid (of)** Angst haben (vor) IV **I'm afraid** leider, ich fürchte III
African American [æfrɪkən ə'merɪkən] afroamerikanisch; Afroamerikaner/in IV
after ['ɑːftə]:
1. nachdem III
2. nach *(zeitlich)* I
after that danach IV
after-class activities *(pl)* [ɑːftə klɑːs æk'tɪvətiz] AGs *(freiwillige Veranstaltungen nach Unterrichtsschluss)* IV
afternoon [ɑːftə'nuːn] Nachmittag I
in the afternoon am Nachmittag I
again [ə'gen] wieder, noch einmal I
against [ə'genst] gegen II
age [eɪdʒ] Alter I
aggressive [ə'gresɪv] aggressiv IV

ago [ə'gəʊ]: **a long time ago** vor langer Zeit II
agree [ə'griː]: **agree with sb./sth.** jm. zustimmen; mit etwas einverstanden sein II °**agree (about sth.)** übereinstimmen, sich einig sein (in etwas) °**agree (on) sth.** vereinbaren, sich einigen auf
agriculture ['ægrɪkʌltʃə] Landwirtschaft IV
air [eə] Luft II
airport ['eəpɔːt] Flughafen III
alarm clock [ə'lɑːm klɒk] Wecker I
alcohol ['ælkəhɒl] Alkohol III
alive [ə'laɪv] lebendig, am Leben II
come alive lebendig werden, (wieder) aufleben II
all [ɔːl] alle(s) I **all over the country** überall im Land, im ganzen Land II
all summer den ganzen Sommer I
in all insgesamt III
all right [ɔːl 'raɪt] gut; in Ordnung; OK IV
allergic (to) [ə'lɜːdʒɪk] allergisch (gegen) V 1 (11)
alligator ['ælɪgeɪtə] Alligator IV
allowed [ə'laʊd]: **be allowed to do sth.** etwas tun dürfen III °**be allowed** erlaubt sein
almond ['ɑːmənd] Mandel III
almost ['ɔːlməʊst] fast, nahezu, beinahe IV
alone [ə'ləʊn] allein II **leave sb. alone** jn. in Ruhe lassen V 4 (91)
along [ə'lɒŋ]:
1. **along the road** die Straße entlang II
2. **(come/sing/...) along** *(infml)* mit-(kommen/singen/...) V 2 (34)
drag sb. along *(infml)* jn. mitschleifen V 2 (34) °**as I went along** nach und nach °**go along** vorangehen, Fortschritte machen
alphabet ['ælfəbet] Alphabet I
already [ɔːl'redi] schon II
also ['ɔːlsəʊ] auch II
although [ɔːl'ðəʊ] obwohl V 4 (85)
altogether [ɔːltə'geðə] insgesamt IV
always ['ɔːlweɪz] immer I
am [eɪ'em]: **9 am/9 a.m.** 9 Uhr morgens/vormittags I
amazing [ə'meɪzɪŋ] erstaunlich II
ambulance ['æmbjələns] Krankenwagen II
among [ə'mʌŋ] unter, zwischen *(mehreren Personen oder Dingen)* IV

°**amputate** ['æmpjuteɪt] amputieren
an [ən] ein, eine I
°**analysis,** *pl* **analyses** [ə'næləsɪs], [ə'næləsi:z] Analyse
ancient ['eɪnʃənt] uralt, antik IV
and [ænd], [ənd] und I
angry ['æŋgri] wütend II
animal ['ænɪml] Tier I
announcement [ə'naʊnsmənt] Durchsage, Ansage; Bekanntgabe, Ankündigung IV
another [ə'nʌðə] ein/e andere/r/s; noch ein/e I
answer ['ɑ:nsə]:
1. Antwort II
2. antworten (auf), beantworten II
°**anti-** ['ænti] Anti-, Gegen- **anti-venom** Gegengift
any ['eni] jegliche/r/s, jede/r beliebige IV **Any ideas?** Irgendwelche Ideen? I **(at) any time** zu jeder Zeit, jederzeit IV **It wasn't just any car.** Es war kein beliebiges / nicht einfach irgendein Auto. V 1 (21) **not (...) any more** nicht mehr II **we don't have any** wir haben kein/e II
anybody ['enibɒdi] (irgend)jemand; jede/r (beliebige) IV **not ... anybody** niemand IV
anyone ['eniwʌn] (irgend)jemand; jede/r (beliebige) IV **not ... anyone** niemand IV
anything ['eniθɪŋ]:
1. *(in Fragen)* (irgend)etwas III **Would you like anything else?** Möchten Sie sonst noch etwas? I
2. **not (...) anything** nichts II
anytime ['enitaɪm] jederzeit IV
anyway ['eniweɪ]: **Anyway, ...** Also, ... / So, ... / Gut, ... III °**what ... anyway?** was/welche/r/s ... überhaupt?
anywhere ['eniweə]: **not ... anywhere** nirgendwo(hin) III
apartment *(AE)* [ə'pɑ:tmənt] Wohnung IV
app [æp] App V 4 (85)
appear (to be/do) [ə'pɪə] auftauchen, erscheinen; (zu sein/tun) scheinen V 1 (21)
appearance [ə'pɪərəns] Erscheinung(sbild), Aussehen V 3 (71)
appetite ['æpɪtaɪt] Appetit III
apple ['æpl] Apfel I
application [æplɪ'keɪʃn] Bewerbung, Antrag V 3 (68)
application form [æplɪ'keɪʃn fɔ:m] Bewerbungsformular, Antragsformular V 3 (68)
apply (for) [ə'plaɪ] sich bewerben (um) V 3 (60)
appointment [ə'pɔɪntmənt] Termin; Verabredung II
apprentice [ə'prentɪs] Lehrling, Auszubildende/r V 3 (61)
approach [ə'prəʊtʃ] Ansatz, Herangehensweise V 3 (73)
appropriate [ə'prəʊpriət] angemessen, passend, geeignet IV
April ['eɪprəl] April I
aquarium [ə'kweəriəm] Aquarium I
arch [ɑ:tʃ] Bogen *(z.B. Torbogen)* III
archery ['ɑ:tʃəri] Bogenschießen II
architecture ['ɑ:kɪtektʃə] Architektur V 1 (17)
are [ɑ:] bist, sind, seid I **The posters are £ 1.** Die Poster kosten £ 1. I
area ['eəriə] Gebiet, Gegend III
arena [ə'ri:nə] Arena V 4 (90)
argue ['ɑ:gju:] argumentieren; streiten IV
argument ['ɑ:gjumənt] Argument; Streit V 4 (81)
arm [ɑ:m] Arm II
army ['ɑ:mi] Armee IV **join the army** zur Armee gehen IV
around [ə'raʊnd]:
1. in ... umher III
2. um ... herum III
3. umher(-) II
around here hier in der Nähe II **get around** sich fortbewegen *(mobil sein)* IV **walk around** umhergehen II
arrange [ə'reɪndʒ] arrangieren; (an)ordnen V 4 (97)
arrest sb. [ə'rest] jn. festnehmen, verhaften IV
arrival [ə'raɪvl] Ankunft III
arrive [ə'raɪv] ankommen II
°**arsehole** ['ɑ:shəʊl] *(taboo)* Arschloch
art [ɑ:t] Kunst I
article ['ɑ:tɪkl] Artikel III
artist ['ɑ:tɪst] Künstler/in III
artistic [ɑ:'tɪstɪk] künstlerisch; künstlerisch begabt IV
arty ['ɑ:ti] *(infml)* (gewollt) künstlerisch V 4 (84)
as [æz], [əz]:
1. als, während II
2. da, weil IV
3. **as a footballer** als Fußballer/in III
4. **as fast as he could** so schnell (wie) er konnte II
5. **as much as ...** bis zu ...; nicht weniger als ... IV
ask [ɑ:sk]:
1. fragen I
ask questions Fragen stellen I **ask sb. about sth.** sich bei jm. nach etwas erkundigen II
2. **ask sb. to do sth.** jn. bitten, etwas zu tun II
asleep [ə'sli:p]: **be asleep** schlafen IV **fall asleep** einschlafen IV
°**aspect** ['æspekt] Aspekt
assembly [ə'sembli] Schulversammlung I
°**assess** [ə'ses] beurteilen, bewerten
°**assessor** [ə'sesə] Prüfer/in, Gutachter/in
assist (with) [ə'sɪst] assistieren, helfen (bei) V 3 (64)
assistant [ə'sɪstənt] Helfer/in, Assistent/in V 3 (60) **early years teaching assistant** Hilfskraft im Kindergarten, Sozialassistent/in V 3 (60)
astronaut ['æstrənɔ:t] Astronaut/in V 4 (85)
at [æt], [ət]: **at 1 o'clock** um 1 Uhr / um 13 Uhr I **at a restaurant** in einem Restaurant I **at home** zu Hause, daheim I **at least** wenigstens, zumindest II **at MARTINS** bei MARTINS I **at night** nachts, in der Nacht I **at school** in der Schule I **at the bottom** unten, am unteren Ende I **at the cinema** im Kino I **at the moment** im Moment, gerade I **at the same time** zur selben Zeit, gleichzeitig V 4 (82) **at the top** oben, am oberen Ende; an der Spitze I **at the weekend** am Wochenende I **at this school** auf/an dieser Schule I **at work** bei der Arbeit, am Arbeitsplatz I **be good at sth.** etwas gut können; gut in etwas sein III
ate [eɪt], [et] *siehe* **eat**
attack [ə'tæk] angreifen II
attention [ə'tenʃn] Aufmerksamkeit V 1 (24) **pay attention (to)** achten (auf), aufpassen (auf) V 1 (24)
attention-getter [ə'tenʃn getə] Blickfang; etwas, was Aufmerksamkeit erregt V 1 (24)
attic ['ætɪk] Dachboden IV **in the attic** auf dem Dachboden IV
attitude (to/towards) ['ætɪtju:d] Einstellung, (Geistes-)Haltung (zu/gegenüber) V 3 (63)
attract [ə'trækt] anziehen, anlocken IV
attraction [ə'trækʃn] Attraktion; Anziehungskraft V 4 (82)
attractive [ə'træktɪv] attraktiv V 2 (34)
audience ['ɔ:diəns] Publikum; Zuschauer/innen, Zuhörer/innen V 1 (24)
°**audio** ['ɔ:diəʊ] Audio-, Ton-
August ['ɔ:gəst] August I
aunt [ɑ:nt] Tante I
°**Aussie** ['ɒzi] *(infml)* Australier/in
author ['ɔ:θə] Autor/in IV
autumn ['ɔ:təm] Herbst II
available [ə'veɪləbl] erhältlich, verfügbar, *(Stelle)* frei IV **be available** zur Verfügung stehen, Zeit haben V 3 (63)
avatar ['ævətɑ:] Avatar *(virtuelle Figur)* V 4 (84)
average ['ævərɪdʒ] durchschnittlich, Durchschnitt V 4 (82) **on average** im Durchschnitt, durchschnittlich V 4 (82)
avoid [ə'vɔɪd] (ver)meiden IV
°**aware** [ə'weə]: **be aware of sth.** etwas wissen, sich einer Sache bewusst sein

away [ə'weɪ] weg, fort I
awesome ['ɔːsəm] *(AE, infml)* klasse, stark, großartig IV

B

baby ['beɪbi] Baby I
babysitter ['beɪbisɪtə] Babysitter I
babysitting ['beɪbisɪtɪŋ] Babysitten I
back [bæk]:
1. zurück I
back and forth hin und her V 2 (46)
2. Rücken; Rückseite II
at the back hinten, im hinteren Teil IV **know sth. like the back of one's hand** etwas wie seine Westentasche kennen; etwas in- und auswendig kennen V 4 (92) **the back of the hand** der Handrücken V 4 (92)
back away (from) [bæk] zurückweichen (von) V 4 (91)
background ['bækgraʊnd] Hintergrund III
backpack ['bækpæk]:
1. Rucksack V 2 (45)
2. als Rucksacktourist/in unterwegs sein V 2 (45)
backstreet ['bækstriːt] *(kleinere)* Seitenstraße *(weitab von den Hauptstraßen)* V 4 (91)
backyard [bæk'jɑːd] *(AE)* (Hinter-)Hof, Garten hinter dem Haus IV
bacon ['beɪkən] Speck IV
bad [bæd] schlecht; schlimm I **... is bad news.** ... ist gefährlich. / ... ist (gar) nicht gut. V 4 (91)
badge [bædʒ]:
1. Anstecknadel, Button III
2. Abzeichen, Dienstmarke IV
badger ['bædʒə] Dachs II
badminton ['bædmɪntən] Badminton, Federball IV
bag [bæg] Tasche I
bagel ['beɪgl] Bagel *(ringförmiges Brötchen)* IV
baggage ['bægɪdʒ] Gepäck III
baggage reclaim [rɪ'kleɪm] Gepäckausgabe III
baggy ['bægi] weit (geschnitten), sackig *(Kleidung)* IV
bagpipes *(pl)* ['bægpaɪps] Dudelsack III
bake [beɪk] backen II
baked potato [beɪkt pə'teɪtəʊ] Ofenkartoffel *(in der Schale gebacken)* II
baker ['beɪkə] Bäcker/in IV
bakery ['beɪkəri] Bäckerei III
balcony ['bælkəni] Balkon I
ball [bɔːl] Ball I
balloon [bə'luːn] Ballon III
ballroom dancing [bɔːlruːm 'dɑːnsɪŋ] Standardtanz II
ban [bæn]:
1. verbieten IV
be banned verboten sein/werden IV
2. **ban (on)** Verbot (von) V 1 (10)
banana [bə'nɑːnə] Banane III
band [bænd] Band, Musikgruppe I
bank [bæŋk]:
1. Bank *(Geldinstitut)* II
2. Ufer III
Baptist ['bæptɪst] Baptist/in; Baptisten- IV
bar [bɑː]:
1. Bar II
2. **(chocolate/energy) bar** (Schoko-/Energie-)Riegel V 4 (90)
barbecue ['bɑːbɪkjuː] Grillfest, Grillparty II
barbecued ['bɑːbɪkjuːd] gegrillt IV
bark (at sb.) [bɑːk] (jn. an)bellen II
barn [bɑːn] Scheune, Stall I
°**barrier** ['bæriə] Barriere
baseball ['beɪsbɔːl] Baseball II
°**based on** [beɪst] basierend auf
basic ['beɪsɪk] einfach, elementar V 3 (62)
basically ['beɪsɪkli] im Prinzip, grundsätzlich V 3 (62)
basketball ['bɑːskɪtbɔːl] Basketball I
bat [bæt]:
1. Fledermaus III
2. Schläger *(Sport)* IV
°**bath** [bɑːθ] Badewanne **have/take a bath** baden *(in der Wanne)*
bathroom ['bɑːθruːm]:
1. Bad(ezimmer) I
2. *(AE)* Toilette *(in Privathäusern)* IV
°**bathtub** ['bɑːθtʌb] Badewanne
battle ['bætl]:
1. Wettstreit, Battle *(im Rap)* I
2. Schlacht; Kampf IV
be [biː], **was/were, been** sein I **I want to be a baker.** Ich möchte Bäcker/in werden. IV
beach [biːtʃ] Strand I **on the beach** am Strand I
bean [biːn] Bohne III
bear [beə] Bär I
beat [biːt]:
1. *(Musik)* Beat, Rhythmus I
2. **beat, beat, beaten** schlagen, besiegen III
beaten ['biːtn] *siehe* **beat**
became [bɪ'keɪm] *siehe* **become**
because [bɪ'kɒz] weil I
because of [bɪ'kɒz əv] wegen IV
become [bɪ'kʌm], **became, become** werden II
bed [bed] Bett I
bed and breakfast (B&B) [bed ən 'brekfəst] Frühstückspension; Zimmer mit Frühstück III
bedroom ['bedruːm] Schlafzimmer I
bedtime ['bedtaɪm] Schlafenszeit V 2 (44)
bee [biː] Biene III
been [biːn] *siehe* **be**
before [bɪ'fɔː]:
1. bevor; vor *(zeitlich)* I
2. vorher; zuvor II
began [bɪ'gæn] *siehe* **begin**
begin [bɪ'gɪn], **began, begun** anfangen, beginnen II
beginning [bɪ'gɪnɪŋ] Anfang III
begun [bɪ'gʌn] *siehe* **begin**
behave [bɪ'heɪv] sich benehmen; sich verhalten IV
behind [bɪ'haɪnd] hinter I
beige [beɪʒ] beige V 3 (69)
believe (in) [bɪ'liːv] glauben (an) II
bell [bel] Glocke; Klingel III
°**bellhop** ['belhɒp] *(AE)* Hotelpage
belly button ['beli bʌtn] *(infml)* Bauchnabel IV
belong to sb./sth. [bɪ'lɒŋ] jm. gehören, zu etwas gehören IV
belongings *(pl)* [bɪ'lɒŋɪŋz] Sachen, Besitz IV
below [bɪ'ləʊ] unten; unter, unterhalb (von) V 3 (64)
belt [belt] (Gepäck-)Band III
bend [bend] Kurve III
beside [bɪ'saɪd] neben III
best [best] beste(r, s); am besten I
Best wishes Viele Grüße ... *(Briefschluss)* I **like sth. best** etwas am liebsten mögen II **the best of both worlds** das Beste von beidem I
best-known [best 'nəʊn] der/die/das bekannteste; am bekanntesten V 1 (10)
bet [bet], **bet, bet** wetten III
better ['betə] besser I **do better** besser abschneiden II **like sth. better** etwas lieber mögen II
better-known [betə 'nəʊn] bekannter V 1 (10)
between [bɪ'twiːn] zwischen I
°**beyond** [bɪ'jɒnd] über ... hinaus, weiter als
big [bɪg]:
1. groß I
2. dick, schwer *(Person)* V 1 (22)
bike [baɪk] Fahrrad I
biking ['baɪkɪŋ] *(das)* Radfahren IV
billboard ['bɪlbɔːd] *(AE)* Plakatwand, Werbeplakat V 4 (86)
bin [bɪn] (Müll-)Eimer II
°**biography** [baɪ'ɒgrəfi] Biografie
bird [bɜːd] Vogel I
birthday ['bɜːθdeɪ] Geburtstag I
Happy birthday! Herzlichen Glückwunsch zum Geburtstag! I **It's her birthday.** Sie hat Geburtstag. I
biscuit ['bɪskɪt] Keks, Plätzchen I
bit [bɪt] *siehe* **bite**
bit [bɪt]: **a bit** ein bisschen I
bite [baɪt]:
1. Biss, (Insekten-)Stich V 1 (12)
2. **bite, bit, bitten** beißen II
bitten ['bɪtn] *siehe* **bite**
black [blæk] schwarz I
blame sb. (for) [bleɪm] jm. die Schuld geben (an), jm. Vorwürfe machen (wegen) III
blanket ['blæŋkɪt] Decke *(zum Zudecken u. Ä.)* I

blazer ['bleɪzə] Blazer *(Jackett, oft Teil der Schuluniform)* I
bled [bled] *siehe* **bleed**
bleed [bli:d], **bled, bled** bluten V 1 (13)
blew [blu:] *siehe* **blow**
blind [blaɪnd] blind II
block [blɒk] (Häuser-)Block IV
block of flats [blɒk əv 'flæts] Mehrfamilienhaus, Wohnblock I
blog [blɒg] Blog *(Internet-Tagebuch)* II
blogger ['blɒgə] Blogger/in IV
blond [blɒnd] blond V 4 (91)
blood [blʌd] Blut IV
blouse [blaʊz] Bluse II
blow [bləʊ], **blew, blown** blasen (in); wehen *(Wind)* V 2 (46)
blown [bləʊn] *siehe* **blow**
blue [blu:] blau I
blues [blu:z] Blues *(Musikrichtung)* IV
blurb [blɜ:b] Klappentext *(eines Buches)* V 3 (68)
blush [blʌʃ] erröten, rot werden III
BMX [bi: em 'eks] BMX-Rad I
board [bɔ:d] Tafel I
board [bɔ:d]:
1. einsteigen, an Bord gehen IV
2. **board sth. up** etwas mit Brettern vernageln/zunageln V 2 (43)
boardwalk ['bɔ:dwɔ:k] Steg, Uferpromenade *(aus Holz)* V 3 (68)
boat [bəʊt] Boot; Schiff II
body ['bɒdi] Körper V 1 (14)
body painting ['bɒdi peɪntɪŋ] Körperbemalung V 1 (14)
bodybuilder ['bɒdibɪldə] Bodybuilder/in V 1 (22)
boil [bɔɪl] zum Kochen bringen, kochen *(sieden)* III
bold [bəʊld] fett (gedruckt) III
bonfire ['bɒnfaɪə] *(großes Freuden-)* Feuer II
book [bʊk]:
1. Buch I
2. buchen, reservieren III
booking ['bʊkɪŋ] Buchung, Reservierung; Bestellung III
bookshop ['bʊkʃɒp] Buchladen II
°**boomerang** ['bu:məræŋ] Bumerang
boot [bu:t]:
1. Stiefel II
2. Kofferraum *(Auto)* V 1 (21)
booth [bu:ð] Nische, (Sitz-)Ecke *(im Restaurant)* IV
bored [bɔ:d] gelangweilt II **feel bored** Langeweile haben II
boredom ['bɔ:dəm] Langeweile IV
boring ['bɔ:rɪŋ] langweilig I
born [bɔ:n]: **be born** geboren sein/werden IV
borough ['bʌrə] *(AE)* (Stadt-)Bezirk IV
borrow ['bɒrəʊ] (aus)leihen, sich borgen I
boss [bɒs] Boss, Chef/in III
bossy ['bɒsi] herrisch, rechthaberisch I
both [bəʊθ] beide I **the best of both worlds** das Beste von beidem I
bottle ['bɒtl] Flasche I
bottom ['bɒtəm]:
1. unteres Ende I
at the bottom unten, am unteren Ende I
2. Gesäß, Po III
bought [bɔ:t] *siehe* **buy**
bowling ['bəʊlɪŋ] Bowling, Kegeln II
box [bɒks] Kasten, Kiste, Kästchen I
box [bɒks] boxen III
boxer ['bɒksə] Boxer/in III
boy [bɔɪ] Junge I
boycott ['bɔɪkɒt]:
1. Boykott IV
2. boykottieren IV
boyfriend ['bɔɪfrend] (fester) Freund I
°**bracket** ['brækɪt] Klammer
brave [breɪv] mutig III
bread [bred] Brot I
break [breɪk]:
1. Kurzurlaub, (kurze) Schulferien IV
2. Pause I
at break in der Pause *(zwischen Schulstunden)* II
break [breɪk], **broke, broken** (zer)brechen; kaputtgehen; kaputtmachen III **break a contract** einen Vertrag verletzen, brechen IV **break down** eine Panne haben, kaputtgehen *(Auto)* V 1 (12)
breakfast ['brekfəst] Frühstück I
have breakfast frühstücken I
°**brick** [brɪk] Ziegel(-)
bridge [brɪdʒ] Brücke II
brief [bri:f] kurz (gefasst), knapp IV
be brief sich kurzfassen IV
brilliant ['brɪliənt] genial, toll III
bring [brɪŋ], **brought, brought** bringen, mitbringen I
Britain ['brɪtn] Großbritannien II
British ['brɪtɪʃ] britisch I
brochure ['brəʊʃə] Broschüre, Prospekt I
broke [brəʊk] *siehe* **break**
broken ['brəʊkən]:
1. *siehe* **break**
2. zerbrochen, kaputt III
brother ['brʌðə] Bruder I
brought [brɔ:t] *siehe* **bring**
brown [braʊn] braun I
°**buddy** ['bʌdi] Freund/in, Kumpel
budget ['bʌdʒɪt]:
1. Budget, Haushalt V 3 (56)
2. haushalten *(sparsam sein)* V 3 (56)
budgie ['bʌdʒi] Wellensittich II
buffalo, *pl* **buffalo** *or* **buffaloes** ['bʌfələʊ] Büffel; Bison IV
°**buffet** ['bʊfeɪ] Büfett
build [bɪld], **built, built** bauen II
builder ['bɪldə] Bauunternehmer/in V 2 (45)
building ['bɪldɪŋ] Gebäude III
built [bɪlt] *siehe* **build**
bull [bʊl] Stier, Bulle I
bully ['bʊli]:
1. Mobber/in, Tyrann/in V 1 (21)
2. tyrannisieren, mobben V 1 (21)
bump into [bʌmp 'ɪntə] zusammenstoßen mit; zufällig treffen IV
burger ['bɜ:gə] Hamburger *(Frikadelle)* II
burn [bɜ:n] brennen; verbrennen IV
burst [bɜ:st], **burst, burst** brechen, bersten, platzen IV **burst with excitement** vor Aufregung ganz außer sich sein IV
bus [bʌs] Bus I **go by bus** mit dem Bus fahren I **on the bus** im Bus I
bus station ['bʌs steɪʃn] Busbahnhof I
bus stop ['bʌs stɒp] Bushaltestelle II
bush [bʊʃ] Busch III
business ['bɪznəs] Geschäft, Betrieb III **start a business** ein Geschäft aufmachen, einen Betrieb gründen/eröffnen III
business people ['bɪznəs pi:pl] Geschäftsleute III
business person ['bɪznəs pɜ:sn] Geschäftsperson III
business studies *(pl)* ['bɪznəs stʌdi:z] Wirtschaft(slehre) *(Unterrichtsfach)* III
busker ['bʌskə] Straßenmusiker/in III
busy ['bɪzi]: **be busy** beschäftigt sein; viel zu tun haben I **The kitchen is too busy.** In der Küche ist zu viel los. I
busybody ['bɪzibɒdi] Wichtigtuer/in V 2 (44)
but [bʌt], [bət]:
1. aber I
°2. nur *(formell, gehoben)*
butter ['bʌtə] Butter II
butterfly ['bʌtəflaɪ] Schmetterling V 4 (83)
buy [baɪ] **bought, bought** kaufen I
by [baɪ]:
1. **go by bus** mit dem Bus fahren I
2. **written by …** geschrieben von … III
3. **by the trail** am Weg, neben dem Weg IV **side by side** Seite an Seite IV
4. **come by** *(AE)* vorbeikommen, vorbeischauen *(besuchen)* IV °**go by** *(Zeit)* vergehen
Bye. [baɪ] Tschüs. I
bystander ['baɪstændə] Zuschauer/in, (unbeteiligte/r) Beobachter/in V 2 (33)

C

cable ['keɪbl] Kabel; Seil *(aus Draht/Stahl)* IV
cafe ['kæfeɪ] Café I
cafeteria [kæfə'tɪəriə] *(AE)* Kantine; Cafeteria IV
cage [keɪdʒ] Käfig I
cake [keɪk] Kuchen, Torte I
calculator ['kælkjuleɪtə] Taschenrechner I
calendar ['kælɪndə] Kalender IV

calf, *pl* **calves** [kɑːf], [kɑːvz] Kalb IV
call:
1. (Telefon-)Anruf II
2. Ruf, Schrei V 2 (37)
3. rufen; anrufen; nennen II
be called heißen *(genannt werden)* III °**call sb. names** jn. beschimpfen
calm [kɑːm] ruhig, still; besonnen III
came [keɪm] *siehe* **come**
camel ['kæml] Kamel V 3 (65)
camera ['kæmərə] Fotoapparat; Kamera I
camp [kæmp]:
1. zelten, campen IV
2. (Zelt-)Lager II
make camp sein Lager/Zelt aufschlagen V 1 (19)
campaign [kæm'peɪn] Kampagne V 2 (39)
camper ['kæmpə] Camper/in IV
campground ['kæmpgraʊnd] Campingplatz V 1 (22)
camping ['kæmpɪŋ] Camping I
campsite ['kæmpsaɪt] Campingplatz V 1 (22)
can [kæn], [kən] können I **I can't (= cannot) do my homework.** Ich kann meine Hausaufgaben nicht machen. I
can [kæn] Dose V 3 (69)
°**cancer** ['kænsə] Krebs *(Erkrankung)*
candidate ['kændɪdət] Bewerber/in, Kandidat/in V 3 (73)
candle ['kændl] Kerze V 2 (44)
candy ['kændi] *(AE)* Süßigkeiten II
canoe [kə'nuː] Kanu, Paddelboot I
canteen [kæn'tiːn] Kantine, (Schul-)Mensa I
cap [kæp] Kappe, (Schirm-)Mütze II
capital ['kæpɪtl]:
1. Hauptstadt III
2. **capital (letter)** Großbuchstabe II
captain ['kæptɪn] Kapitän/in II °**fire captain** Brandmeister/in
caption ['kæpʃn] Bildunterschrift III
car [kɑː] Auto I
car park ['kɑː pɑːk] Parkplatz II
card [kɑːd] Karte I
care [keə]:
1. Sorgfalt, Vorsicht V 1 (13)
with care sorgfältig, mit Bedacht V 1 (13)
2. Versorgung, Betreuung V 3 (61)
take care of sb./sth. sich um jn./etwas kümmern V 3 (61)
care [keə]: **I care about you.** Du bist mir nicht egal. / Du liegst mir am Herzen. IV **People don't care.** Es ist den Leuten egal. / Den Leuten ist alles egal. IV **Who cares?** Wen interessiert das? / Was soll's? / Na und? IV
career [kə'rɪə] Karriere; (schulischer/beruflicher) Werdegang V 3 (60)
careful ['keəfl] vorsichtig; sorgfältig II **drive carefully** vorsichtig fahren II
carnival ['kɑːnɪvl] Karneval III
carpenter ['kɑːpəntə] Schreiner/in IV
°**carpet** ['kɑːpɪt] Teppich **red carpet event** Promi-Veranstaltung mit rotem Teppich
carriage ['kærɪdʒ] Kutsche II
carrot ['kærət] Möhre, Karotte II
carry ['kæri] tragen; befördern, transportieren IV
cart [kɑːt] Wagen *(Einkaufswagen, Golfwagen etc.)* IV
cartoon [kɑː'tuːn] Zeichentrickfilm; Comic II
°**case** [keɪs] Fall **in (the) case of** im Falle von
casino [kə'siːnəʊ] (Spiel-)Kasino IV
castle ['kɑːsl] Burg II
cat [kæt] Katze I **Has the cat got his tongue?** Hat's ihm die Sprache verschlagen? IV
catch [kætʃ], **caught, caught** (ein)fangen, erwischen III **catch sth.** sich mit etwas anstecken; sich etwas einfangen *(Krankheit)* V 4 (90)
category ['kætəgəri] Kategorie IV
cathedral [kə'θiːdrəl] Kathedrale, Dom III
Catholic ['kæθlɪk] Katholik/in; katholisch II
cattle *(pl)* ['kætl] Vieh, Rinder IV
caught [kɔːt] *siehe* **catch**
cave [keɪv] Höhle II
CCTV camera [siː siː tiː 'viː] Überwachungskamera III
CD [siː 'diː] CD I
CD player [siː'diː pleɪə] CD-Player II
celebrate ['selɪbreɪt] feiern II
celebrity [sə'lebrəti] Prominente/r, Promi V 3 (60)
cell phone ['sel fəʊn] *(AE)* Handy IV
Celsius (C) ['selsiəs] Celsius IV
cent [sent] Cent III
central ['sentrəl] zentral III
centre ['sentə] Zentrum, (Stadt-)Mitte I
cereals *(pl)* ['sɪəriəlz] Getreide-, Frühstücksflocken II
certificate [sə'tɪfɪkət] Urkunde, Bescheinigung V 3 (64)
chain [tʃeɪn] Kette I
chainsaw ['tʃeɪn sɔː] Kettensäge IV
chair [tʃeə] Stuhl I
challenge ['tʃælɪndʒ] Herausforderung III
°**challenging** ['tʃælɪndʒɪŋ] anspruchsvoll, (heraus)fordernd
chance [tʃɑːns] Chance, Gelegenheit II
change [tʃeɪndʒ]:
1. Veränderung, Wechsel III
2. (ver)ändern; wechseln IV
change (clothes) sich umziehen, sich andere Sachen anziehen II **change (trains)** umsteigen *(Zug)* III
channel ['tʃænl] Kanal II
chant [tʃɑːnt] Sprechgesang I
°**chaotic** [keɪ'ɒtɪk] chaotisch
°**chapter** ['tʃæptə] Kapitel
character ['kærəktə] Figur, Person *(in Roman, Film usw.)* III
characterization [kærəktəraɪ'zeɪʃn] Charakterisierung V 4 (95)
characterize ['kærəktəraɪz] charakteristisch sein für; beschreiben, darstellen V 4 (95)
charge [tʃɑːdʒ] (auf)laden *(Batterie, Handy)* III
charity ['tʃærəti] wohltätige Organisation II **charity shop** *Geschäft, das gespendete Waren für wohltätige Zwecke verkauft* II
chart [tʃɑːt] Diagramm, Tabelle IV
chase [tʃeɪs] verfolgen, jagen III
chat [tʃæt]:
1. **chat (with)** plaudern, „chatten", sich unterhalten (mit) II
2. Unterhaltung; Chat II
have a chat eine Unterhaltung führen, sich unterhalten II
cheap [tʃiːp] billig, preiswert II
check [tʃek]:
1. (Über-)Prüfung, Kontrolle IV
2. (über)prüfen, kontrollieren II
check a website auf einer Website nachschauen II **check sb./sth. out** *(infml)* sich etwas anschauen, anhören; etwas ausprobieren IV
check in [tʃek 'ɪn] einchecken III
check-in ['tʃek ɪn] Check-in, Einchecken III
checklist ['tʃeklɪst] Checkliste V 1 (24)
cheek [tʃiːk] Wange IV
cheer [tʃɪə] jubeln, *(Sportler/innen)* anfeuern IV
cheerful ['tʃɪəfl] fröhlich, gut gelaunt V 3 (69)
cheerleader ['tʃɪəliːdə] Cheerleader *(Stimmungsanheizer/in bei Sportereignissen)* IV
cheese [tʃiːz] Käse IV
chest [ʧest] Brust(korb) V 3 (72)
chicken ['tʃɪkɪn] Huhn; (Brat-)Hähnchen I
°**chief** [tʃiːf] Haupt-; leitende/r
child, *pl* **children** [tʃaɪld], ['tʃɪldrən] Kind I
childcare ['tʃaɪldkeə] Kinderbetreuung V 3 (61)
chili ['tʃɪli] Chili *(scharfes Gewürz)* IV
chill [tʃɪl] *(infml)* relaxen, sich ausruhen II
chin [tʃɪn] Kinn V 1 (20)
chip [tʃɪp] Stück(chen), Splitter IV
chipmunk ['tʃɪpmʌŋk] Streifenhörnchen I
chips *(pl)* [tʃɪps] Pommes frites I **(potato) chips** *(AE)* Kartoffelchips IV
chocolate ['tʃɒklət] Schokolade I
choice [tʃɔɪs] (Aus-)Wahl IV
choose [tʃuːz], **chose, chosen** (aus)wählen II

chore [tʃɔː] (Haus-)Arbeit, *(lästige)* Pflicht II **do chores** (Haus-)Arbeiten erledigen II
chose [tʃəuz] *siehe* **choose**
chosen ['tʃəuzn] *siehe* **choose**
Christmas ['krɪsməs] Weihnachten II
chronological [krɒnə'lɒdʒɪkl] chronologisch V 2 (32)
church [tʃɜːtʃ] Kirche I
cinema ['sɪnəmə] Kino I
circle ['sɜːkl] Kreis II
circus ['sɜːkəs] runder Platz *(in einer Stadt)* III
citizen ['sɪtɪzn] Bürger/in V 1 (10)
city ['sɪti] (Groß-)Stadt I
city slicker ['slɪkə] *(infml)* Großstadtsnob III
civil rights *(pl)* [sɪvl 'raɪts] Bürgerrechte IV
class [klɑːs]:
1. Klasse I
2. Unterricht; Kurs II
class teacher ['klɑːs tiːtʃə] Klassenlehrer/in I
classmate ['klɑːsmeɪt] Mitschüler/in V 2 (34)
classroom ['klɑːsruːm] Klassenraum I
clean [kliːn]:
1. sauber machen, putzen I
2. sauber IV
cleaner ['kliːnə] Reinigungskraft V 3 (60)
cleaning ['kliːnɪŋ]: **do the cleaning** sauber machen, putzen V 3 (69)
clean-up ['kliːn ʌp] Reinemachen, Hausputz V 4 (88)
clear [klɪə]:
1. klar, deutlich II
2. (auf-/ab-/weg)räumen; *(Augen z.B. von Tränen)* frei machen IV
clearing ['klɪərɪŋ] Lichtung V 1 (21)
clerk [klɑːk] Angestellte/r V 3 (68)
clever ['klevə] schlau, klug II
cleverness ['klevənəs] Klugheit V 1 (13)
click (on) [klɪk] klicken (auf) III
climate ['klaɪmət] Klima V 1 (8)
climb [klaɪm] klettern (auf) II
cloak [kləuk] Umhang IV
clock [klɒk] (Wand-, Stand-, Turm-) Uhr I
close [kləuz] schließen, zumachen I **close on sb.** jm. näher kommen, zu jm. aufholen V 4 (92) **close sth. down** etwas schließen, stilllegen *(Fabrik, Geschäft)* III **closed** gesperrt *(Straße)* V 1 (18)
close [kləus]:
1. dicht, eng V 4 (92)
2. **close (to)** nahe (bei, an) IV **step closer** näher treten, näher (heran)kommen IV
3. genau *(eingehend)* IV **look closely** genau/näher hinschauen IV

clothes *(pl)* [kləuðz] Kleidung(sstücke) II
cloud [klaud] Wolke II
cloudy ['klaudi] wolkig, bewölkt II
club [klʌb] Klub I **Join the club.** Da bist du nicht der/die Einzige. II
clue [kluː] Hinweis III
coach [kəutʃ] Trainer/in II
coast [kəust] Küste II **on the coast** an der Küste II
coat [kəut] Mantel; Jacke III
cocoa ['kəukəu] Kakao II
coconut ['kəukənʌt] Kokosnuss III
cod, *pl* **cod** [kɒd] Kabeljau, Dorsch III
coffee ['kɒfi] Kaffee I
cold [kəuld]:
1. kalt II
2. Erkältung II
collar ['kɒlə] Halsband II
collect [kə'lekt] sammeln II
college ['kɒlɪdʒ] höhere Schule, Fach(hoch)schule V 2 (45)
colony ['kɒləni] Kolonie V 1 (17)
colour ['kʌlə] Farbe I
°**column** ['kɒləm] Spalte
comb [kəum]:
1. Kamm IV
2. **comb (your hair)** (sich die Haare) kämmen IV
combat ['kɒmbæt]:
1. Kampf V 4 (90)
2. kämpfen (gegen) V 4 (90)
°**combine** [kəm'baɪn] verbinden, kombinieren
come [kʌm]: **came, come:**
1. (mit)kommen I
come by *(AE)* vorbeikommen, vorbeischauen (besuchen) IV **Come on!** Na los! / Komm(t) (schon)! I **come up** aufgehen (Sonne) I **the sea's coming in** die Flut kommt; das Wasser steigt I **when it comes to ...** wenn es um ... geht IV
2. werden II
come alive lebendig werden, (wieder) aufleben II **come true** wahr werden V 4 (95) **a dream come true** ein wahr gewordener Traum V 4 (95)
comedy ['kɒmədi] Comedyshow; Komödie II
comfortable ['kʌmftəbl] bequem, gemütlich II **be/feel comfortable (with)** sich wohlfühlen (bei/mit) V 2 (36) **make yourself comfortable** es sich gemütlich machen III
comic ['kɒmɪk] Comic II
command [kə'mɑːnd] Befehl V 2 (41)
comment ['kɒment]:
1. Kommentar III
°2. **comment on sth.** etwas kommentieren
commercial [kə'mɜːʃl] kommerziell *(auf Gewinn ausgerichtet)* IV

common ['kɒmən] häufig, weit verbreitet, gewöhnlich IV °**have sth. in common** etwas gemeinsam haben
°**communicate (with sb.)** [kə'mjuːnɪkeɪt] (mit jm.) kommunizieren; sich (mit jm.) verständigen
communication [kəmjuːnɪ'keɪʃn] Kommunikation, Verständigung V 3 (60)
community [kə'mjuːnəti] Gemeinschaft, Gemeinde IV **community service** gemeinnützige Arbeit, Sozialdienst IV
community college [kə'mjuːnəti kɒlɪdʒ] weiterführende Schule *(BE)* I
company ['kʌmpəni] Firma, Gesellschaft IV
compare [kəm'peə] vergleichen IV °**compare (with/to)** vergleichbar sein (mit), sich vergleichen lassen (mit)
compass ['kʌmpəs] Kompass II
compete (with) [kəm'piːt] konkurrieren (mit); *(in Wettbewerben)* antreten (gegen) V 1 (17)
competition [kɒmpə'tɪʃn] Wettbewerb III
complain (about/of) [kəm'pleɪn] sich beschweren (über); jammern III
complete [kəm'pliːt]:
1. vollständig, komplett IV
°2. vervollständigen
complicated ['kɒmplɪkeɪtɪd] kompliziert V 3 (68)
computer [kəm'pjuːtə] Computer I
concert ['kɒnsət] Konzert I
conclusion [kən'kluːʒn] Schluss(folgerung) IV **draw conclusions** Rückschlüsse ziehen IV
°**condition** [kən'dɪʃn] Leiden, Erkrankung
confectionery [kɒn'fekʃənəri] Süßwaren III
confident ['kɒnfɪdənt] (selbst)sicher; zuversichtlich V 3 (58)
confirm [kən'fɜːm] bestätigen III
confiscate ['kɒnfɪskeɪt] konfiszieren, beschlagnahmen III
°**congratulations (on sth.)** [kəngrætʃu'leɪʃnz] herzlichen Glückwunsch (zu etwas)
connect (with/to) [kə'nekt] verbinden (mit) IV
connection [kə'nekʃn]: Verbindung, Anschluss III
cons [kɒnz]: **the pros and cons** *(pl)* das Pro und Kontra; das Für und Wider V 4 (82)
°**construct** [kən'strʌkt] (auf)bauen, konstruieren
contact ['kɒntækt]:
1. Kontakt III
2. **contact sb.** Kontakt aufnehmen zu, sich melden bei V 3 (73)
continent ['kɒntɪnənt] Kontinent; europäisches Festland IV

continue [kən'tɪnjuː] weitergehen, weitermachen, (sich) fortsetzen IV **continue to ...** weitergehen, weiterfahren, weiterreisen nach ... IV
contract ['kɒntrækt] Vertrag IV **break a contract** einen Vertrag verletzen, brechen IV
control [kən'trəʊl]:
1. kontrollieren, regulieren V 4 (88)
2. Kontrolle I
lose control die Kontrolle verlieren I
conversation [kɒnvə'seɪʃn] Gespräch, Unterhaltung V 2 (48)
convince [kən'vɪns] überzeugen V 4 (83)
convincing [kən'vɪnsɪŋ] überzeugend V 4 (83)
cook [kʊk]:
1. kochen, *(Essen)* zubereiten I
2. Koch, Köchin I
cooker ['kʊkə] Herd III
cookie ['kʊki] Keks, Plätzchen III
cool [kuːl]:
1. kühl II
2. cool I
play it cool *(infml)* sich cool geben IV
cool down [kuːl 'daʊn] sich abkühlen; sich beruhigen V 1 (12)
°**coolhunter** ['kuːlhʌntə] Trendscout *(Person, die Trends aufspürt)*
°**cope (with)** [kəʊp] zurechtkommen, fertig werden (mit)
copy ['kɒpi] kopieren, abschreiben V 2 (42)
corn [kɔːn] *(BE)* Korn, Getreide; *(AE)* Mais IV
cornbread ['kɔːnbred] Maisbrot IV
corner ['kɔːnə] Ecke I **corner of your eye** Augenwinkel IV **pets corner** Streichelzoo I
correct [kə'rekt]:
1. korrigieren, berichtigen II
2. korrekt IV
cost [kɒst], **cost, cost** kosten *(Geld)* III
costs *(pl)* [kɒsts] Kosten V 3 (60) **travel costs** Reisekosten V 3 (60)
costume ['kɒstjuːm] Kostüm, Verkleidung II
cottage ['kɒtɪdʒ] Häuschen, Hütte II
cotton ['kɒtn] Baumwolle IV
°**couch potato** ['kaʊtʃ pəteɪtəʊ] Stubenhocker/in; Faulpelz, der ständig vor dem Bildschirm/Fernseher hängt
cougar ['kuːgə] *(bes. AE)* Puma IV
could [kʊd]:
1. **he could** er konnte II
2. **I could** ich könnte II
°**counsellor** ['kaʊnsələ] Berater/in
count [kaʊnt] zählen III
counter ['kaʊntə] (Verkaufs-)Schalter, Ladentheke V 1 (22)
country ['kʌntri] Land I **in the country** auf dem Land I
country (music) ['kʌntri] Countrymusic *(Musikrichtung)* IV
country bumpkin ['bʌmpkɪn] *(infml)* Landei, Bauerntrampel III
countryside ['kʌntrisaɪd] Land(schaft); Natur III
couple ['kʌpl] Paar III **a couple (of)** ein paar; ein Paar III
course [kɔːs] Kurs(us) III
court [kɔːt] Platz, Court *(Tennis, Basketball)* IV
cousin ['kʌzn] Cousin/e I
°**cover** ['kʌvə]:
1. Einband, Umschlag *(Buch)*
2. bedecken
cover letter ['kʌvə letə] Anschreiben, Begleitschreiben, Motivationsschreiben V 3 (63)
cow [kaʊ] Kuh I
°**cowardly** ['kaʊədli] feige
crab [kræb] Krebs *(Tier)* I
cracker ['krækə] Cracker *(Gebäck)* IV
crash (into) [kræʃ] einen Unfall haben, zusammenstoßen (mit) V 4 (89)
crazy ['kreɪzi] verrückt I **go crazy** verrückt werden V 4 (90)
cream [kriːm]:
1. Sahne I
2. Creme II
creative [kri'eɪtɪv] kreativ V 4 (84)
credit card ['kredɪt kɑːd] Kreditkarte V 3 (69)
creep [kriːp], **crept, crept** schleichen, kriechen V 4 (91) **creep up (on sb.)** sich heranschleichen (an jn.) V 4 (91)
crept [krept] *siehe* **creep**
crew [kruː] Mannschaft, Team; Clique V 1 (14)
crime [kraɪm] Kriminalität; Verbrechen IV
crime series, *pl* **crime series** ['kraɪm sɪəriːz] Krimiserie II
°**cripple** ['krɪpl] Krüppel *(beleidigend)*
crisps *(pl)* [krɪsps] (Kartoffel-)Chips I
critic ['krɪtɪk] Kritiker/in V 4 (85)
criticism ['krɪtɪsɪzəm] Kritik V 3 (58) **react to criticism well** mit Kritik gut umgehen können, Kritik vertragen V 3 (58)
crocodile ['krɒkədaɪl] Krokodil I
cross [krɒs]:
1. Kreuz II
2. überqueren II
3. **cross (with)** böse, sauer (auf) III
crossroads, *pl* **crossroads** ['krɒsrəʊdz] (Straßen-)Kreuzung III
crowded ['kraʊdɪd] überfüllt, vollgestopft III
crown [kraʊn] Krone IV
cruise [kruːz]:
1. Kreuzfahrt, Schiffsreise IV
2. herumfahren (in) *(ohne Ziel)* IV
cry [kraɪ] weinen II
cucumber ['kjuːkʌmbə] (Salat-)Gurke III
culture ['kʌltʃə] Kultur III
°**cultured** ['kʌltʃəd] kultiviert, gebildet
cup [kʌp] Tasse I
°**cupboard** ['kʌbəd] Schrank
cupcake ['kʌpkeɪk] Cupcake *(kleiner runder Kuchen)* III
curious about ['kjʊəriəs] neugierig auf II
curly ['kɜːli] lockig V 3 (69)
curry ['kʌri] Curry(gericht), Curry- III
curtain ['kɜːtn] Vorhang, Gardine V 2 (43)
cushion ['kʊʃn] Kissen I
customer ['kʌstəmə] Kunde, Kundin I
cut [kʌt], **cut, cut** schneiden; *(Rasen)* mähen II **cut down trees** Bäume abholzen IV
cute [kjuːt] niedlich, süß I
CV (= curriculum vitae) [siː 'viː], [kərɪkjələm 'viːtaɪ] *(BE)* Lebenslauf V 3 (60)
cyberbullying ['saɪbə'bʊliɪŋ] Cybermobbing V 2 (33)
cycle ['saɪkl] Rad fahren III
cycle tour ['saɪkl tʊə] Radtour III

D

dad [dæd] Papa, Vati I
daily ['deɪli] täglich II
damage (to) ['dæmɪdʒ] *(no pl)* Schaden, Schäden (an) V 4 (88)
dance [dɑːns]:
1. tanzen I
2. Tanz(veranstaltung) III
dancer ['dɑːnsə] Tänzer/in III
danger ['deɪndʒə] Gefahr II
dangerous ['deɪndʒərəs] gefährlich I
dare [deə]:
1. Mutprobe IV
2. **dare sb. to do sth.** jn. herausfordern, etwas zu tun IV
dark [dɑːk] dunkel II
darkness ['dɑːknəs] Dunkelheit IV
dart [dɑːt] (Wurf-)Pfeil II
dartboard ['dɑːtbɔːd] Dartscheibe II
date [deɪt]:
1. Datum I
2. Verabredung, Date *(auch die Person, mit der man ausgeht)* IV
daughter ['dɔːtə] Tochter I
day [deɪ] Tag I **day-to-day** tagtäglich V 3 (61) **I haven't eaten in days.** Ich habe tagelang nichts gegessen. V 4 (90) **in the old days** früher II **one day** eines Tages IV **the next day** am anderen/nächsten Tag III **the other day** neulich III **three-day trip** dreitägiger Ausflug II
day out, *pl* **days out** [deɪ 'aʊt] (Tages-)Ausflug II
dead [ded] tot III °**The phone went dead.** Die Leitung war tot.
deadly ['dedli] tödlich IV
deal [diːl] Geschäft; Vereinbarung II **a big deal** eine große Sache, viel Aufhebens III **It's a deal!** Abgemacht! II

deal with sth. [diːl], **dealt, dealt**:
1. umgehen mit etwas, mit etwas fertigwerden, klarkommen V 2 (34)
°2. *(Problem)* behandeln, sich befassen mit
dealt [delt] *siehe* **deal**
dear [dɪə]: **Dear ...** Liebe/r ... I **Dear Sir/Madam** Sehr geehrte Damen und Herren V 3 (63) **Oh dear.** Oje! I
debate [dɪ'beɪt] debattieren, diskutieren IV
December [dɪ'sembə] Dezember I
decide (to do sth.) [dɪ'saɪd] beschließen, (sich) entscheiden (etwas zu tun) IV
decision [dɪ'sɪʒn] Entscheidung III **make a decision** eine Entscheidung fällen III
deck [dek] Deck IV **on deck** an Deck IV
deep [diːp] tief III
definite ['defɪnət] klar, deutlich, sicher III
definitely ['defɪnətli] auf jeden Fall; ganz bestimmt III
degree [dɪ'griː] Grad II
delete [dɪ'liːt] löschen V 2 (32)
den [den] Versteck; Hobbyraum II
department [dɪ'pɑːtmənt] Abteilung V 3 (61)
department store [dɪ'pɑːtmənt stɔː] Kaufhaus IV
departure [dɪ'pɑːtʃə] Abfahrt; Abflug III
depressing [dɪ'presɪŋ] deprimierend V 4 (85)
deputy ['depjuti] Stellvertreter/in; stellvertretende/r IV **deputy prime minister** Vizepremierminister/in IV **deputy sheriff** Hilfssheriff IV
descended [dɪ'sendɪd]: **be descended from** abstammen von IV
describe [dɪ'skraɪb] beschreiben I
°**description** [dɪ'skrɪpʃn] Beschreibung
desert ['dezət] Wüste IV
°**desert island** [dezət 'aɪlənd] einsame Insel
design [dɪ'zaɪn] entwerfen, gestalten, entwickeln V 4 (86)
designer [dɪ'zaɪnə] Designer/in IV
desk [desk] Schreibtisch I **front desk** Rezeption, Empfang *(z.B. Hotel)* V 3 (68)
desk clerk ['desk klɑːk] Empfangsmitarbeiter/in V 3 (68)
dessert [dɪ'zɜːt] Nachspeise, Dessert II
destroy [dɪ'strɔɪ] zerstören, vernichten II
detail ['diːteɪl] Detail, Einzelheit III
°**detailed** ['diːteɪld] ausführlich, detailliert
detective [dɪ'tektɪv] Detektiv/in III
diagram ['daɪəgræm] Diagramm III
dialogue ['daɪəlɒg] Dialog I
diary ['daɪəri] Tagebuch; Kalender I
dictionary ['dɪkʃənri] Wörterbuch, *(alphabetisches)* Wörterverzeichnis I
dictionary entry ['dɪkʃənri entri] Wörterbucheintrag II
did [dɪd] *siehe* **do** **I didn't want to ... (= did not)** ich wollte nicht ... II **Which club did you join?** In welchen Klub bist du eingetreten? II
°**didgeridoo** [dɪdʒəri'duː] Didgeridoo
die [daɪ] sterben II
difference ['dɪfrəns] Unterschied I **make a difference** etwas bewirken, etwas ausmachen I
different ['dɪfrənt] verschieden; anders I
difficult ['dɪfɪkəlt] schwierig I
dig [dɪg], **dug, dug** graben V 1 (15)
digital ['dɪdʒɪtl] digital V 4 (82)
diner ['daɪnə] *(AE)* (kleines, preiswertes) Restaurant IV
dining room ['daɪnɪŋ ruːm] Esszimmer III
dinner ['dɪnə] Abendessen I
dinosaur ['daɪnəsɔː] Dinosaurier III
direct [də'rekt] direkt, unmittelbar V 2 (40)
direction [də'rekʃn] Richtung IV **directions** *(pl)* Wegbeschreibung(en) II
director [də'rektə] Geschäftsführer/in, Chef/in V 3 (63)
dirty ['dɜːti] schmutzig III
disability [dɪsə'bɪləti] Behinderung IV
disabled [dɪs'eɪbld] (körper)behindert I
disadvantage [dɪsəd'vɑːntɪdʒ] Nachteil IV **at a disadvantage** im Nachteil IV
disagree [dɪsə'griː] nicht zustimmen, widersprechen III °**disagree (about sth.)** nicht übereinstimmen, sich nicht einig sein (in etwas)
disappear [dɪsə'pɪə] verschwinden IV
disappoint sb. [dɪsə'pɔɪnt] jn. enttäuschen IV **disappointed (with)** enttäuscht (von) II **disappointing** enttäuschend IV
disaster [dɪ'zɑːstə] Katastrophe, Unglück III
disco ['dɪskəʊ] Disco III
discover [dɪ'skʌvə] entdecken II
discrimination (against sb.) [dɪskrɪmɪ'neɪʃn] Diskriminierung (eines Menschen) V 2 (37)
discuss [dɪ'skʌs] diskutieren III
discussion [dɪ'skʌʃn] Diskussion I
disease [dɪ'ziːz] Krankheit V 1 (15)
disgusting [dɪs'gʌstɪŋ] ekelhaft, widerlich IV
dish [dɪʃ] Gericht *(Mahlzeit)*; Schüssel III
°**dishonest** [dɪs'ɒnɪst] unehrlich
dishwasher ['dɪʃwɒʃə] Geschirrspülmaschine II
dislike ['dɪslaɪk] nicht mögen IV
dislikes ['dɪslaɪks]: **likes and dislikes** *(pl)* Vorlieben und Abneigungen III
°**display** [dɪ'spleɪ] zeigen, zur Schau stellen
disturb [dɪ'stɜːb] stören III
dive [daɪv]:
1. einen Kopfsprung machen I
2. (ein)tauchen II
diver ['daɪvə] Taucher/in III
diverse [daɪ'vɜːs] unterschiedlich, vielfältig V 1 (10)
divorce [dɪ'vɔːs] (Ehe-)Scheidung IV **get a divorce** sich scheiden lassen IV
DJ ['diː dʒeɪ] DJ *(Discjockey)* IV
do [duː], **did, done** machen, tun I **do a paper round** Zeitungen austragen II **do better** besser abschneiden II **do sport** Sport treiben I **dos and don'ts** *(pl)* was man tun und lassen sollte V 2 (48) **she doesn't like ...** sie mag ... nicht I **you do have ...** du hast (ja/wohl) doch ... IV
°**dock** [dɒk] Dock, Hafen, Mole
doctor ['dɒktə] Arzt, Ärztin II
documentary [dɒkju'mentri] Dokumentarfilm II
dog [dɒg] Hund I **dogs' home** Hundeheim II
doll [dɒl] Puppe IV **doll's house** Puppenhaus IV
dollar ($) ['dɒlə] Dollar IV
done [dʌn] *siehe* **do** **Well done.** Gut gemacht! I
donkey ['dɒŋki] Esel I
door [dɔː] Tür I
°**doorway** ['dɔːweɪ] Eingang *(Tür)*
dormitory ['dɔːmətri] Schlafsaal III
°**dossier** ['dɒsieɪ] Mappe, Dossier
dot [dɒt] Punkt, Pünktchen V 1 (15)
dot painting ['dɒt peɪntɪŋ] Punktmalerei; Punktgemälde V 1 (15)
down [daʊn] hinunter, herunter II **down the hill** den Hügel hinunter I **look down your nose at sb.** herabblicken auf jn. IV
downside ['daʊnsaɪd] Nachteil III
downstairs [daʊn'steəz] (nach) unten *(die Treppe hinunter)* I
downtown [daʊn'taʊn] *(AE)* (im/ins) Stadtzentrum IV
drag [dræg] ziehen, schleifen IV **drag sb. along** *(infml)* jn. mitschleifen V 2 (34)
°**dragon** ['drægən] Drachen
drama ['drɑːmə]:
1. Schauspiel, darstellende Kunst I
2. Drama IV
dramatic [drə'mætɪk] dramatisch IV
drank [dræŋk] *siehe* **drink**
draw [drɔː], **drew, drawn** zeichnen; ziehen IV
drawing ['drɔːɪŋ] Zeichnung IV
drawn [drɔːn] *siehe* **draw**

dream [driːm]:
1. Traum I
a dream come true ein wahr gewordener Traum V 4 (95)
2. **dream (of/about sth.)** träumen (von etwas) IV
°**dreamy** ['driːmi] traumhaft, verträumt
dress [dres]:
1. sich kleiden, sich anziehen IV
get dressed up sich schick anziehen III
2. Kleid II
3. Kleidung IV
formal dress formelle Kleidung, Gesellschaftskleidung IV **formal evening dress** Abendkleid, festliche Abendgarderobe IV
drew [druː] *siehe* **draw**
drifter ['drɪftə]: **be a drifter** sich treiben lassen *(ziellos vor sich hinleben)* V 4 (83)
drink [drɪŋk]:
1. Getränk I
2. **drink, drank, drunk** trinken I
°**drive** [draɪv] (Auto-)Fahrt
drive [draɪv], **drove, driven**:
1. *(mit dem Auto)* fahren II
2. (an)treiben *(Tiere)* III
driven ['drɪvn] *siehe* **drive**
driver ['draɪvə] Fahrer/in III
driver's license ['draɪvəz laɪsns] *(AE)* Führerschein IV
driving licence ['draɪvɪŋ laɪsns] Führerschein III
driving test ['draɪvɪŋ test] Fahrprüfung, Führerscheinprüfung IV
drop [drɒp] Drop *(Bonbon)* III
drove [drəʊv] *siehe* **drive**
drown [draʊn] ertrinken III
drug [drʌg] Droge, Rauschgift; Arzneimittel IV
drum [drʌm] Trommel I **drums** *(pl)* Schlagzeug I
drummer ['drʌmə] Trommler/in II
drunk [drʌŋk] *siehe* **drink** **be drunk** betrunken sein IV **get drunk** sich betrinken IV
dry [draɪ]:
1. trocknen III
2. trocken IV
duck [dʌk] Ente I
°**due to** ['djuː tə] aufgrund, wegen
dug [dʌg] *siehe* **dig**
dull [dʌl] langweilig, trist, öde IV
dumb [dʌm] dumm III
dump [dʌmp]:
1. (Müll-)Abladeplatz, Deponie III
2. abladen *(Müll)* III
dumper ['dʌmpə] Umweltsünder/in *(jemand, der illegal Müll entsorgt)* III
dung [dʌŋ] Dung, Mist IV
during ['djʊərɪŋ] während III
duty ['djuːti] Pflicht, Aufgabe; Dienst V 3 (61) **on duty** im Dienst V 3 (61)
DVD [diːviː'diː] DVD III

E

each [iːtʃ] jede(r, s) (einzelne) II
each other einander, sich (gegenseitig) IV
eagle ['iːgl] Adler IV
ear [ɪə] Ohr II
early ['ɜːli] früh I
earn [ɜːn] verdienen *(Geld)* V 3 (56)
earth [ɜːθ] Erde II
earthquake ['ɜːθkweɪk] Erdbeben IV
°**ease** [iːz]: **put sb. at ease** jn. beruhigen, jm. die Befangenheit nehmen
east [iːst] Osten; nach Osten II
eastbound ['iːstbaʊnd] in Richtung Osten III
Easter ['iːstə] Ostern IV
eastern ['iːstən] östlich, Ost- IV
easy ['iːzi] einfach, leicht I **Take it easy.** *(infml)* Reg dich nicht auf. / Bleib mal locker. III
easy-going [iːzi 'gəʊɪŋ] gelassen, locker II
eat [iːt], **ate, eaten** essen; fressen I
eaten ['iːtn] *siehe* **eat**
edge [edʒ] Rand, Kante V 4 (93)
editor ['edɪtə] Herausgeber/in, Redakteur/in IV **letter to the editor** Leserbrief IV
education [edʒu'keɪʃn] (Schul-)Bildung V 3 (62)
°**effect** [ɪ'fekt] (Aus-)Wirkung, Einfluss, Effekt
e-friend ['iːfrend] E-Mail-Freund/in II
e.g. [iː 'dʒiː] z.B. (zum Beispiel) II
egg [eg] Ei III
eight [eɪt] acht I
either ['eɪðə]: **not … either** auch nicht II
electronics [ɪlek'trɒnɪks] Elektronik II
°**elementary school** [elɪ'mentri skuːl] *(AE)* Grundschule
elephant ['elɪfənt] Elefant I
elevator ['elɪveɪtə] *(AE)* Lift, Fahrstuhl IV
eleven [ɪ'levən] elf I
else [els]: **Would you like anything else?** Möchten Sie sonst noch etwas? I
email ['iːmeɪl]:
1. E-Mail I
2. **email sb./sth.** jn. anmailen/etwas mailen IV
embankment [ɪm'bæŋkmənt] (Straßen-, Bahn-, Fluss-)Damm III
embarrassed [ɪm'bærəst] verlegen II
embarrassing [ɪm'bærəsɪŋ] peinlich IV
emergency [i'mɜːdʒənsi] Notfall II
emergency services Rettungsdienste II
employee [ɪm'plɔɪiː] Arbeitnehmer/in III
°**employer** [ɪm'plɔɪə] Arbeitgeber/in
empty ['empti]:
1. leer II
2. leeren II
°**emu** ['iːmju] Emu

enclose [ɪn'kləʊz] beifügen, beilegen *(einem Brief)* V 3 (63)
°**encourage** [ɪn'kʌrɪdʒ] ermutigen, unterstützen
end [end]:
1. (be)enden IV
2. Ende, Schluss I
in the end schließlich, zum Schluss II
ending ['endɪŋ] Endung; Ende *(Text, Geschichte)* II
enemy ['enəmi] Feind/in III
energetic [enə'dʒetɪk] energisch, energiereich V 3 (58)
energy ['enədʒi] Energie V 4 (90)
engine ['endʒɪn] Motor V 1 (22)
engineer [endʒɪ'nɪə] Ingenieur/in; Techniker/in III
England ['ɪŋglənd] England I
English ['ɪŋglɪʃ] Englisch; englisch I
°**English-speaking** ['ɪŋglɪʃ spiːkɪŋ] englischsprachig
enjoy [ɪn'dʒɔɪ] genießen II **Enjoy your meal.** Guten Appetit! III
enough [ɪ'nʌf] genug II
enter ['entə] sich anmelden, teilnehmen *(Wettbewerb)* V 1 (18)
°**entertaining** [entə'teɪnɪŋ] unterhaltsam
enthusiastic [ɪnθjuːzi'æstɪk] begeistert V 3 (58)
entrance ['entrəns] Eingang; Zutritt II
entry ['entri]:
1. Eintritt, Zutritt III
2. Eintrag *(Wörterbuch)* II
episode ['epɪsəʊd] Episode; Folge *(z.B. einer TV-Serie)* III
equal ['iːkwəl] gleich(berechtigt) V 3 (66)
equipment [ɪ'kwɪpmənt] Ausrüstung, Ausstattung III
eraser [ɪ'reɪzə] *(AE)* Radiergummi IV
e-reader ['iː riːdə] E-Book-Reader II
escalator ['eskəleɪtə] Rolltreppe III
escape (from) [ɪ'skeɪp] entkommen (aus), fliehen (vor/aus) IV
especially [ɪ'speʃəli] insbesondere II
etc. [et'setərə] usw. (und so weiter) II
EU (= European Union) [iː 'juː] EU (Europäische Union) III
euro (€) ['jʊərəʊ] Euro III
Europe ['jʊərəp] Europa III
European [jʊərə'piːən] Europäer/in; europäisch IV
European Union [jʊərəpiːən 'juːniən] Europäische Union III
even ['iːvn]:
1. ausgeglichen; gleich(mäßig); gerade *(Zahl)* IV
2. sogar, selbst III
not even (noch) nicht einmal IV
evening ['iːvnɪŋ] Abend I **in the evening** abends, am Abend I
event [ɪ'vent] Ereignis II
ever ['evə] jemals, schon einmal III
Have you ever …? Hast du (schon) jemals …? III **the most realistic**

game ever das realistischste Spiel, das es je gegeben hat V 4 (90)
every ['evri] jede(r, s) I
everybody ['evribɒdi] jeder; alle I
everyone ['evriwʌn] jeder; alle II
everything ['evriθɪŋ] alles II
everywhere ['evriweə] überall(hin) II
exact [ɪg'zækt] genau, exakt IV
exam [ɪg'zæm] Prüfung V 1 (11) **final (school) exam** (Schul-)Abschlussprüfung V 1 (11) **take/do an exam** eine Prüfung machen V 1 (11)
example [ɪg'zɑːmpl] Beispiel II **for example** zum Beispiel II
excellent ['eksələnt] ausgezeichnet, hervorragend IV
except (for) [ɪk'sept] außer, bis auf IV
exchange [ɪks'tʃeɪndʒ] (Schüler-)Austausch III
excited [ɪk'saɪtɪd] aufgeregt, gespannt I
excitement [ɪk'saɪtmənt] Aufregung, Spannung, Begeisterung IV **burst with excitement** vor Aufregung ganz außer sich sein IV
exciting [ɪk'saɪtɪŋ] aufregend I
Excuse me, ... [ɪks'kjuːz miː] Entschuldigung, ... / Entschuldigen Sie, ... I
exercise ['eksəsaɪz] Übung, Aufgabe I
exercise book ['eksəsaɪz bʊk] (Schul-)Heft I
exit ['eksɪt] Ausgang III
expect [ɪk'spekt] erwarten III
expensive [ɪk'spensɪv] teuer I
experience [ɪk'spɪəriəns]:
1. Erfahrung; Erlebnis III
in my experience nach meiner Erfahrung V 2 (35)
2. **experience sth.** etwas erfahren, erleben II
experiment [ɪk'sperɪmənt] Experiment II
expert ['ekspɜːt] Experte, Expertin II
explain sth. to sb. [ɪk'spleɪn] jm. etwas erklären II
explore [ɪk'splɔː] erforschen, erkunden V 3 (65)
express [ɪk'spres] ausdrücken, zum Ausdruck bringen V 4 (96)
extra ['ekstrə] Extra-, zusätzliche(r, s) II **°(TV) extra** Statist/in, Komparse/-in *(Fernsehen)*
extract ['ekstrækt] Auszug *(aus einem Buch, Film)* V 2 (43)
extreme [ɪk'striːm] extrem IV
extremely [ɪk'striːmli] extrem, äußerst IV
eye [aɪ] Auge II **corner of your eye** Augenwinkel IV **keep an eye on sb./sth.** jn./etwas im Auge behalten, ein (wachsames) Auge haben auf jn./etwas V 2 (45)
°**eyesight** ['aɪsaɪt] Sehkraft

F

face [feɪs]:
1. Gesicht I
2. **face sth.** vor etwas stehen *(Problem)*; einer Sache ins Auge sehen, sich einer Sache stellen; einer Sache entgegentreten V 1 (15)
fact [fækt] Tatsache, Fakt IV **°in fact** eigentlich, um genau zu sein
fair [feə] fair IV
faithfully ['feɪθfəli]: **Yours faithfully** Mit freundlichen Grüßen *(Briefschluss)* V 3 (63)
fall [fɔːl] *(AE)* Herbst IV
fall [fɔːl], **fell, fallen** fallen; hinfallen I
fallen ['fɔːlən] *siehe* **fall**
false [fɔːls] falsch I
familiar [fə'mɪliə]: **be familiar (to sb./with sth.)** (jm.) vertraut sein / (mit etwas) vertraut sein V 1 (20)
family ['fæməli] Familie I **family name** Familienname, Nachname IV **family tree** Familienstammbaum I **family-friendly** familienfreundlich III
famous ['feɪməs] berühmt II
fan [fæn] Fan III
fancy ['fænsi] ausgefallen, extravagant, schick IV
fantastic [fæn'tæstɪk] fantastisch, wunderschön V 1 (15)
fantasy ['fæntəsi] Fantasie; Fantasy *(Literatur-, Filmgattung)* II
FAQ (= frequently asked questions) [ef eɪ 'kju], [friːkwəntli ɑːskt 'kwestʃənz] häufig gestellte Fragen III
far [fɑː] weit (entfernt) II **far away** weit weg II **so far** bis jetzt, bis hierher II
farm [fɑːm]:
1. Bauernhof, Farm I
2. Landwirtschaft betreiben V 1 (15)
farm animal ['fɑːm ænɪml] Nutztier; *im Plural:* Vieh III
farmer ['fɑːmə] Bauer, Bäuerin; Landwirt/in III
farmhouse ['fɑːmhaʊs] Bauernhaus III
farmyard ['fɑːmjɑːd] Hof *(eines Bauernhauses)* III
°**fascinate** ['fæsɪneɪt] faszinieren
°**fascinating** ['fæsɪneɪtɪŋ] faszinierend
fashion ['fæʃn] Mode III
fast [fɑːst] schnell I
fast-food restaurant [fɑːst fuːd 'restrɒnt] Schnellimbiss V 3 (73)
fat [fæt] dick, fett II
father ['fɑːðə] Vater I
fault [fɔːlt] Fehler, Schuld V 4 (88)
favourite ['feɪvərɪt]:
1. Lieblings- I
favourite colour Lieblingsfarbe I
°2. Liebling, Favorit/in
fear (of) [fɪə] Angst (vor) V 4 (92)
feather ['feðə] Feder *(eines Vogels)* IV
February ['februəri] Februar I
fed [fed] *siehe* **feed** **feel fed up** genervt sein, sauer sein; die Nase voll haben I
feed [fiːd], **fed, fed** füttern I
feedback ['fiːdbæk] *(no pl)* Feedback *(Rückmeldung)* III
feel [fiːl], **felt, felt** sich fühlen; fühlen I
feeling ['fiːlɪŋ] Gefühl I
feet [fiːt] *Plural von* **foot** III
fell [fel] *siehe* **fall**
°**fellow student** ['feləʊ] Mitschüler/in
felt [felt] *siehe* **feel**
female ['fiːmeɪl] weiblich III
fence [fens] Zaun III
ferry ['feri] Fähre I
festival ['festɪvl] Fest II
few [fjuː]:
1. **a few** ein paar, einige II
°2. wenige
fictional ['fɪkʃənl] erfunden, fiktiv V 4 (95)
field [fiːld] Feld; Weide I **in the field** auf der Weide I
fight [faɪt] Kampf; Schlägerei IV
fight [faɪt], **fought, fought**:
1. kämpfen II
2. bekämpfen V 1 (11)
fight your way through sich durchkämpfen durch V 2 (45)
fighter ['faɪtə] Kämpfer/in V 4 (90)
figure ['fɪgə] Person *(Gestalt)*; Figur IV
°**file** [faɪl] Datei; Ordner, Liste
fill [fɪl] füllen II **fill out** ausfüllen V 3 (69) **°fill in** einsetzen: ausfüllen
film [fɪlm]:
1. Film I
2. filmen III
film star ['fɪlm stɑː] Filmstar III
final ['faɪnl] Finale III
finally ['faɪnəli] schließlich, endlich II
find [faɪnd], **found, found** finden I
find out herausfinden II **find out about sth.** sich über etwas informieren II
finder ['faɪndə] Finder/in V 4 (91)
Finders keepers, losers weepers. Was man findet, darf man behalten. *(Redensart)* V 4 (91)
fine [faɪn] gut, in Ordnung; schön I
I'm fine. Mir geht es gut. I
fine [faɪn]:
1. Geldstrafe IV
2. zu einer Geldstrafe verurteilen IV
finger ['fɪŋgə] Finger III
fingernail ['fɪŋgəneɪl] Fingernagel V 1 (22)
finish ['fɪnɪʃ]:
1. Ziel *(beim Sport)* II
2. beenden, zu Ende machen II
finish the milk die Milch alle machen, aufbrauchen IV **finish your drink** austrinken IV **finish your meal** aufessen IV
fire ['faɪə] Feuer II
fire escape ['faɪər ɪskeɪp] Feuertreppe, Notausgang V 4 (92) **fire escape ladder** Feuerleiter V 4 (92)
fire sb. ['faɪə] jn. feuern, entlassen V 3 (69) **you'll get me fired** du

schaffst es noch, dass ich entlassen werde V 3 (69)
fire station ['faɪə steɪʃn] Feuerwache I
firefighter ['faɪəfaɪtə] Feuerwehrmann, Feuerwehrfrau I
firework ['faɪəwɜ:k] Feuerwerkskörper II **fireworks** *(pl)* Feuerwerk II
first [fɜ:st]:
1. erste(r, s) I
2. zuerst, als Erstes I
at first zuerst, am Anfang II **the first morning** der erste Morgen I
first aid [fɜ:st 'eɪd] Erste Hilfe II
first-aid kit Erste-Hilfe-Set, Verbandkasten II
Firstly, … ['fɜ:stli] Erstens … III
fish [fɪʃ]:
1. Fisch(e) I
2. fischen, angeln III
fist [fɪst] Faust II
fit [fɪt] fit II
°**fit** [fɪt] passen (zu)
fit in [fɪt 'ɪn] dazugehören; hineinpassen V 4 (86)
fitness ['fɪtnəs] Fitness V 1 (13)
five [faɪv] fünf I **Give me five!** Gib mir fünf! *(Aufforderung zum „Abklatschen", Geste der Freude/Begrüßung)* II
fix sth. [fɪks] *(infml)* etwas in Ordnung bringen; reparieren IV
flag [flæg] Fahne, Flagge II
flash [flæʃ]:
1. *(das)* (Auf-)Blitzen V 4 (93)
2. flash a torch mit einer Taschenlampe leuchten/blinken V 4 (93)
flashback ['flæʃbæk] Rückblende V 2 (32)
flashlight ['flæʃlaɪt] *(AE)* Taschenlampe IV
flat [flæt] Wohnung I **block of flats** *(pl)* Mehrfamilienhaus, Wohnblock I
flat [flæt] flach, eben V 1 (10)
°**flatmate** ['flætmeɪt] Mitbewohner/in
flew [flu:] *siehe* **fly**
flexible ['fleksəbl] flexibel V 3 (61)
flight [flaɪt] Flug III
flight connection ['flaɪt kənekʃn] Anschlussflug III
flood [flʌd] überfluten, überschwemmen IV
°**flooding** ['flʌdɪŋ] Flut, Überschwemmung, Hochwasser
floor [flɔ:]:
1. Fußboden III
2. Etage, Stock(werk) IV
flour ['flaʊə] Mehl III
flower ['flaʊə] Blume; Blüte II
flown [fləʊn] *siehe* **fly**
flute [flu:t] (Quer-)Flöte IV
fly [flaɪ], **flew, flown**:
1. fliegen I
2. rasen *(z.B. Auto)* V 1 (21)
flyer ['flaɪə] Flyer *(Handzettel)* II
focus ['fəʊkəs]:
1. focus on sth. sich auf etwas konzentrieren IV
°**2.** Schwerpunkt
fog [fɒg] Nebel II
foggy ['fɒgi] nebelig II
folks *(pl)* [fəʊks] Leute IV
follow ['fɒləʊ] folgen; verfolgen I
follower ['fɒləʊə] Anhänger/in, Fan V 4 (86)
°**follow-up** ['fɒləʊ ʌp] Anschluss-, Folge-
food [fu:d] Essen, Lebensmittel; Futter I
fool [fu:l] Dummkopf III
foolish ['fu:lɪʃ] töricht, dumm V 3 (70)
foot, *pl* **feet** [fʊt], [fi:t] Fuß III **on foot** zu Fuß III °**put your foot down** Gas geben *(Auto)*
football ['fʊtbɔ:l] Fußball I
footballer ['fʊtbɔ:lə] Fußballspieler/in III
for [fɔ:], [fə] für I **for a few minutes** ein paar Minuten (lang) II **for example** zum Beispiel II **for lots of reasons** aus vielen Gründen III **for two months** seit zwei Monaten III **great for making friends** großartig, um Freunde zu finden II **What's for homework?** Was haben wir als Hausaufgabe(n) auf? I
force sb. to do sth. [fɔ:s] jn. zwingen, etwas zu tun IV **they were forced from their land** sie wurden von ihrem Land vertrieben IV
forecast ['fɔ:kɑ:st] Vorhersage II
foreground ['fɔ:graʊnd] Vordergrund III
°**foreign** ['fɒrən] ausländisch, fremd **foreign language** Fremdsprache
forest ['fɒrɪst] Wald III
forever, for ever [fər'evə] für immer, ewig (lange) V 1 (15)
forget [fə'get], **forgot, forgotten** vergessen I **forget about sth.** (etwas) vergessen, nicht mehr an etwas denken II
forgot [fə'gɒt] *siehe* **forget**
forgotten [fə'gɒtn] *siehe* **forget**
form [fɔ:m] Formular V 3 (68)
°**form** [fɔ:m]:
1. Form
2. (sich) formen, bilden
formal ['fɔ:ml] formell IV **formal dress** formelle Kleidung, Gesellschaftskleidung IV **formal evening dress** Abendkleid, festliche Abendgarderobe IV
forth [fɔ:θ]: **back and forth** hin und her V 2 (46)
fortune ['fɔ:tʃu:n] Vermögen IV **cost a fortune** ein Vermögen kosten IV
forward ['fɔ:wəd] vorwärts, nach vorne II **look forward to** sich freuen auf II **look forward to doing sth.** sich darauf freuen, etwas zu tun IV
fought [fɔ:t] *siehe* **fight**
found [faʊnd] *siehe* **find**
four [fɔ:] vier I
fox [fɒks] Fuchs II
freak [fri:k] Freak, Fan II
°**freak out** [fri:k 'aʊt] *(infml)* ausflippen
freak sb. out [fri:k 'aʊt] *(infml)* jn. ausflippen lassen, ein Horror sein für jn. IV
free [fri:] frei; kostenlos I **free-time activities** Freizeitaktivitäten II **run freely** frei herumlaufen III
freedom ['fri:dəm] Freiheit IV
freeze [fri:z], **froze, frozen**:
1. gefrieren II
2. erstarren V 2 (43)
freezing ['fri:zɪŋ] eisig, eiskalt II
French fries [frentʃ 'fraɪz] *(pl, AE)* Pommes frites IV
frequent ['fri:kwənt] häufig III
fresh [freʃ] frisch I
Friday ['fraɪdeɪ], ['fraɪdi] Freitag I
fridge [frɪdʒ] Kühlschrank III
fried egg [fraɪd 'eg] Spiegelei IV
friend [frend] Freund/in I **a friend of Cindy's / of hers / of mine** ein/e Freund/in von Cindy /von ihr / von mir V 3 (68) **be (good) friends with sb.** mit jm. (gut) befreundet sein V 3 (66)
friendliness ['frendlinəs] Freundlichkeit V 1 (13)
friendly ['frendli] freundlich I **get friendly with sb.** sich mit jm. anfreunden IV
friendship ['frendʃɪp] Freundschaft IV
frighten sb. jm. Angst machen V 4 (92)
frightened ['fraɪtnd] verängstigt V 4 (92) **be frightened of sth.** Angst haben vor etwas V 4 (92)
frightening beängstigend V 4 (92)
frisbee ['frɪzbi] Frisbee I
from [frɒm] von, aus I **from Monday to Friday** von Montag bis Freitag I **Where are you from?** Wo kommst du her? I
front [frʌnt]: **at the front** vorn, im vorderen Teil IV **in front of** vor I
front desk [frʌnt 'desk] Rezeption, Empfang *(z.B. Hotel)* V 3 (68)
front desk clerk [frʌnt 'desk klɑ:k] Empfangsmitarbeiter/in V 3 (68)
front garden [frʌnt 'gɑ:dn] Vorgarten V 2 (43)
froze [frəʊz] *siehe* **freeze**
frozen ['frəʊzn] *siehe* **freeze**
fruit [fru:t] Obst I
frustrate [frʌ'streɪt] frustrieren V 2 (37)
frustrated [frʌ'streɪtɪd] frustriert II
frustrating [frʌ'streɪtɪŋ] frustrierend V 2 (37)
fry [fraɪ] braten IV
frying pan ['fraɪɪŋ pæn] Bratpfanne IV
fuel ['fju:əl] Treibstoff, Kraftstoff V 1 (22)
full (of) [fʊl] voll (mit, von) I
full-time job [fʊl 'taɪm] Ganztagsjob, Vollzeitjob IV

fun [fʌn] Spaß I **(just) for fun** (nur) zum Spaß V 2 (34) **it's fun** es macht Spaß I **she's fun** es macht Spaß, mit ihr zusammenzusein I
fund-raising ['fʌnd reɪzɪŋ] Spendenaktion; Spenden- IV **fund-raising event** Ereignis zur Beschaffung von Geld/Spenden IV
funny ['fʌni] witzig, komisch II
furniture ['fɜːnɪtʃə] Möbel(stücke) IV
furry ['fɜːri] flauschig; pelzig I
further ['fɜːðə] weiter; weitere V 2 (36)
future ['fjuːtʃə] Zukunft II

G

°**gadget** ['gædʒɪt] Gerät, technischer Krimskrams
gallery ['gæləri] Galerie V 4 (96)
game [geɪm] Spiel I
gamer ['geɪmə] Gamer/in *(Computerspieler/in)* V 4 (90)
gaming ['geɪmɪŋ] *(das)* Spielen am Computer V 4 (94)
gang [gæŋ] Gang *(Bande)* V 4 (92)
°**gap** [gæp] Lücke; Kluft
garage ['gærɑːʒ]:
1. (Auto-)Werkstatt II
2. Garage I
garage sale Garagenflohmarkt I
garbage ['gɑːbɪdʒ] *(AE)* Abfall, Müll IV
garbage can ['gɑːbɪdʒ kæn] *(AE)* Abfalleimer, Mülleimer IV
garden ['gɑːdn] Garten I
gardener ['gɑːdnə] Gärtner/in V 3 (65)
gas [gæs]:
1. Gas IV
2. *(AE)* Benzin IV
gate [geɪt] Tor; Flugsteig III
gatecrash (a party) ['geɪtkræʃ] (bei einer Party) ungebeten erscheinen V 4 (88)
gatecrasher ['geɪtkræʃə] nicht eingeladene Person (die eine Party sprengt) V 4 (88)
gateway (to) ['geɪtweɪ] Tor (zu) IV
gather ['gæðə] sammeln; (sich) versammeln V 1 (15)
gave [geɪv] *siehe* **give**
gear [gɪə] Ausrüstung II
geek [giːk] *jemand, der sich sehr stark für etwas begeistert (und manchmal deswegen belächelt wird)* III
gel [dʒel] Gel *(Haarstyling)* IV
general ['dʒenrəl] allgemein III
generally ['dʒenrəl] im Allgemeinen IV
generation [dʒenə'reɪʃn] Generation V 1 (15)
geography [dʒi'ɒgrəfi] Geografie, Erdkunde I
German ['dʒɜːmən]:
1. deutsch; Deutsch I
2. Deutsche, Deutscher II
Germany ['dʒɜːməni] Deutschland I
get [get], **got, got**:
1. bekommen I
2. werden II
3. **get sth.** (sich) etwas holen, (sich) etwas besorgen II
4. **get (to)** gelangen, (hin)kommen (nach) II
get around sich fortbewegen *(mobil sein)* IV **get into (a car)** (in ein Auto) einsteigen IV **get lost** sich verirren, sich verlaufen II **Get lost!** Verschwinde(t)! II **get off (a bus)** aussteigen (aus einem Bus) III **get off (your bike)** absteigen (vom Fahrrad) III **get on a plane/bus/train** in ein Flugzeug / einen Bus / einen Zug einsteigen III **get out (of a car)** (aus einem Auto) aussteigen IV **get out of** herauskommen aus, herausfinden aus II **get started** anfangen, loslegen III **get to do sth.** etwas tun können/dürfen; die Möglichkeit haben/bekommen, etwas zu tun IV **get up** aufstehen I **I get it.** *(infml)* Ich verstehe. / Ich kapiere. V 3 (70) **You got it.** *(infml)* Genau! / Du hast es! V 1 (20)
ghost [gəʊst] Gespenst, Geist III
giant ['dʒaɪənt] riesig; Riese/Riesin IV
°**gift** [gɪft] Geschenk
giggle ['gɪgl] kichern III
gingerbread ['dʒɪndʒəbred] Lebkuchen, Honigkuchen III
girl [gɜːl] Mädchen I
girlfriend ['gɜːlfrend] (feste) Freundin I
gist [dʒɪst]: **the gist** das Wesentliche; die Kernaussage(n) IV
give [gɪv], **gave, given** geben I **give a talk** einen Vortrag halten II **Give me five!** Gib mir fünf! *(Aufforderung zum „Abklatschen", Geste der Freude/Begrüßung)* II **give up** aufgeben, aufhören (mit) IV °**give sth. away** etwas verraten
given ['gɪvn] *siehe* **give**
glad [glæd]: **I'm glad** ich bin froh II
glamorous ['glæmərəs] glamourös V 1 (22)
glasses *(pl)* ['glɑːsɪz] *(eine)* Brille I
°**glee club** ['gliː klʌb] Schulchor *(an amerikan. High Schools, führt eine Mischung aus Gesang und Tanz auf)*
°**global** ['gləʊbl] weltweit, global
go global auf globaler Ebene tätig werden
glove [glʌv] Handschuh II
go [gəʊ], **went, gone** gehen; fahren I
go after sb./sth. hinter etwas/jm. her sein V 2 (34) **go crazy** verrückt werden V 4 (90) **Go for it!** Nichts wie ran! II **go off** klingeln *(Wecker)*; losgehen *(Alarmanlage, Waffe)* IV
go off (to a place) (los)gehen, (los) fahren (nach/zu) IV **Go to sleep!** Schlaf jetzt! I **go with** passen zu, gehören zu I **Here we go!** *(infml)* Jetzt geht's los! II **How's it going?** Wie geht's? / Wie läuft's? I **I must go.** *(am Telefon)* Ich muss Schluss machen. I **I'm going to bring ...** ich werde ... mitbringen I °**go (a) round to ...** zu ... gehen °**go along** vorangehen, Fortschritte machen
°**as I went along** nach und nach
goat [gəʊt] Ziege V 1 (21)
God [gɒd] Gott III
gold [gəʊld] Gold III
gold mining ['gəʊld maɪnɪŋ] Goldabbau IV
golden ['gəʊldn] golden, aus Gold IV
gone [gɒn] *siehe* **go** **be gone** weg sein, nicht (mehr) da sein IV
good [gʊd] gut I **Good boy. / Good dog.** Braver Junge. / Braver Hund. II
Good morning. Guten Morgen. I
be good at sth. etwas gut können; gut in etwas sein III **be good with sth.** gut mit etwas umgehen können III **I'm good.** *(AE)* Mir geht es gut. IV **It's good value.** Es ist sein Geld wert. / Es ist preiswert. I
Goodbye. [gʊd'baɪ] Auf Wiedersehen! I
good-looking [gʊd 'lʊkɪŋ] gut aussehend IV
goody ['gʊdi] gute Sache; leckere Sache III
gospel (music) ['gɒspl] Gospel(musik) IV
got [gɒt] *siehe* **get**
government ['gʌvənmənt] Regierung; Regierungs- IV
gown [gaʊn] Robe; (Fest-)Kleid IV
GPS [dʒiː piː 'es] GPS III
grab [græb] packen, greifen (nach), ergreifen IV
grade [greɪd] *(AE)* Klasse, Jahrgang; (Schul-)Note IV
°**grader** ['greɪdə]: **tenth grader** Zehntklässler/in
graduation [grædʒu'eɪʃn] (Schul-/Studien-)Abschluss; Abschlussfeier IV
graffiti [grə'fiːti] Graffiti IV
grand [grænd] groß(artig) III
grandad ['grændæd] Opa III
granddaughter ['grændɔːtə] Enkelin IV
grandfather ['grænfɑːðə] Großvater I
grandma ['grænmɑː] Oma I
grandmother ['grænmʌðə] Großmutter I
grandpa ['grænpɑː] Opa I
grandparents *(pl)* ['grænpeərənts] Großeltern I
grandson ['grænsʌn] Enkel IV
granny ['græni] Oma I
grass [grɑːs] Gras; Rasen II
grave [greɪv] Grab IV
graveyard ['greɪvjɑːd] Friedhof V 3 (69)
graveyard shift Nachtschicht V 3 (69)
great [greɪt] toll, großartig I
Great Britain [greɪt 'brɪtn] Großbritannien II
green [griːn] grün I
greet [griːt] begrüßen V 3 (73)

grew [gruː] *siehe* **grow**
grey [greɪ] grau I
grill party ['grɪl] Grillparty IV
grin (at) [grɪn] (an)grinsen V 4 (92)
groceries *(pl)* ['grəʊsəriz] Lebensmittel IV
grocery store ['grəʊsəri stɔː] *(AE)* Lebensmittelgeschäft IV
ground [graʊnd] (Erd-)Boden II
group [gruːp] Gruppe I
grow [grəʊ], **grew, grown**:
1. wachsen II
2. anbauen, anpflanzen IV
grow up aufwachsen; erwachsen werden IV **Money doesn't grow on trees.** Das Geld liegt nicht auf der Straße. *(Redewendung)* II
growl (at) [graʊl] (an)knurren IV
grown [grəʊn] *siehe* **grow**
guard [gɑːd] Wärter/in; Wache III
guess [ges] (er)raten I **I guess** ich nehme an, ich glaube IV
guest [gest] Gast III
guide [gaɪd]:
1. Ratgeber, Einführung III
2. Reiseführer *(Buch, Website)* IV
3. Reiseleiter/in, Fremdenführer/in III
°4. **guide (sb. somewhere)** (jn. an einen Ort) führen, begleiten
guitar [gɪ'tɑː] Gitarre I
gun [gʌn] Schusswaffe IV
guy [gaɪ] Typ, Kerl I **guys** *(pl)* Leute *(Anrede)* I
gym [dʒɪm] Turnhalle, Sporthalle; Fitnessstudio III
gymnastics [dʒɪm'næstɪks] Turnen, Gymnastik II

H

habit ['hæbɪt] (An-)Gewohnheit V 4 (83)
had [hæd] *siehe* **have**
hair [heə] Haar, Haare II
hairdresser ['heədresə] Frisör/in II
hairdryer ['heədraɪə] Föhn, Haartrockner II
hairy ['heəri] behaart, haarig II
half [hɑːf] halbe(r, s) I **half an hour** eine halbe Stunde II **half past 6** halb 7 I **sixteen and a half** sechzehneinhalb V 3 (69)
half-brother ['hɑːf brʌðə] Halbbruder I
half-sister ['hɑːf sɪstə] Halbschwester I
halfway [hɑːf'weɪ] auf halbem Wege, halb(wegs) IV
hall [hɔːl]:
1. Flur, Diele I
2. Gang, Korridor II
hallway ['hɔːlweɪ] *(AE)* Korridor, Gang IV
ham [hæm] Schinken III **Black Forest ham** Schwarzwälder Schinken III
hammer ['hæmə]:
1. Hammer V 2 (44)
2. hämmern V 2 (44)
hamster ['hæmstə] Hamster I
hand [hænd]:
1. Hand II
know sth. like the back of one's hand etwas wie seine Westentasche kennen; etwas in- und auswendig kennen V 4 (92) **on the one hand** einerseits III **on the other hand** andererseits III **put up your hand** sich melden III **the back of the hand** der Handrücken V 4 (92)
2. **hand sb. sth.** jm. etwas (an)reichen, aushändigen V 3 (68)
handball ['hændbɔːl] Handball IV
handshake ['hændʃeɪk] Händedruck, Handschlag IV
hang (from) [hæŋ], **hung, hung** hängen (an) IV **hang out** rumhängen, abhängen II
happen ['hæpən] geschehen, passieren I
°**happily** ['hæpɪli] mit Vergnügen, gern(e)
happiness ['hæpinəs] Glück V 1 (13)
happy ['hæpi] glücklich, froh I
Happy birthday! Herzlichen Glückwunsch zum Geburtstag! I **happy ending** Happy End *(glückliches Ende)* II **be happy with sth.** mit etwas zufrieden sein III °**be happy to do sth.** gerne etwas tun
harbour ['hɑːbə] Hafen I
hard [hɑːd] schwer, schwierig; hart I
Hard luck! Pech (gehabt)! III **rain hard** stark regnen V 1 (19) **try hard** sich (sehr) bemühen, sich anstrengen IV
°**hardship** ['hɑːdʃɪp] Not, Mühsal, harte Umstände
hard-working [hɑːd 'wɜːkɪŋ] fleißig III
harmonica [hɑː'mɒnɪkə] Mundharmonika IV
has [hæz], [həz]: **it has** es (er, sie) hat I
hat [hæt] Hut, Mütze I
hate [heɪt] hassen I
haunted ['hɔːntɪd]: **a haunted castle** ein Schloss, in dem es spukt III
have [hæv], **had, had** haben I **Have a good day.** Ich wünsche dir einen schönen Tag. / Schönen Tag (noch). I **have breakfast** frühstücken I **have lunch** (zu) Mittag essen I **have to do sth.** etwas tun müssen II **I'll have ...** ich nehme ... *(beim Essen, im Restaurant)* II **I've lived here all my life.** Ich wohne hier schon mein ganzes Leben (lang). III
he [hiː] er I
head [hed]:
1. Kopf II
2. **head for sth.** auf etwas zugehen/zusteuern IV
head south Richtung Süden gehen/fahren IV
headache ['hedeɪk] Kopfschmerzen II
heading ['hedɪŋ] Überschrift III
headline ['hedlaɪn] Schlagzeile IV
headset ['hedset] Headset V 4 (93)
health [helθ] Gesundheit V 1 (15)
Apples are good for your health. Äpfel sind gesund. V 1 (15)
health care ['helθ keə] Gesundheitsversorgung V 3 (61)
healthy ['helθi] gesund II
hear [hɪə], **heard, heard** hören I
heard [hɜːd] *siehe* **hear**
heart [hɑːt] Herz III
heat [hiːt] Hitze, Wärme V 1 (12)
heat stress Hitzestress, Wärmebelastung des Körpers V 1 (12)
heavy ['hevi] schwer III
heavyweight ['heviweɪt] Schwergewicht; Schwergewichts- V 4 (90)
heel [hiːl] Absatz *(Schuh)* III **(high) heels** *(pl)* hochhackige Schuhe III
held [held] *siehe* **hold**
helicopter ['helɪkɒptə] Hubschrauber IV
Hello. [hə'ləʊ] Hallo. I
helmet ['helmɪt] Helm I
help [help]:
1. Hilfe I
2. helfen I
Help yourselves. Bedient euch! / Greift zu! III
helpful ['helpfl] hilfsbereit; hilfreich, nützlich III
helpless ['helpləs] hilflos II
her [hɜː], [hə] sie; ihr I
her father [hɜː] ihr Vater I
here [hɪə] hier; hierher I **Here you are.** Bitte schön. / Hier, bitte. I
heritage ['herɪtɪdʒ] Erbe IV
hero, *pl* **heroes** ['hɪərəʊ] Held/in III
hers [hɜːz] ihre/r, ihrs *(zu „she")* V 1 (21)
herself [hɜː'self] sie/sich selbst *(zu „she")* III
Hi. [haɪ] Hallo. I **Say hi to everybody.** Grüß alle. I
hid [hɪd] *siehe* **hide**
hidden ['hɪdn] *siehe* **hide**
hide [haɪd], **hid, hidden** verstecken; sich verstecken I
high [haɪ] hoch II **high heels** *(pl)* hochhackige Schuhe III °**high five** *Handschlag mit erhobener Hand, Geste der Freude z.B. über einen Sieg*
high school ['haɪ skuːl] *(BE etwa:)* Gesamtschule I
high street ['haɪ striːt] Hauptstraße *(mit vielen Geschäften)* III
Highlands ['haɪləndz]: **the Highlands** *(pl)* das schottische Hochland III
highlight ['haɪlaɪt] Höhepunkt, Schlaglicht, Highlight IV
highway ['haɪweɪ] *(AE)* Fernstraße IV
hike [haɪk] wandern IV
hill [hɪl] Hügel I
him [hɪm] ihm, ihn I
himself [hɪm'self] er/sich selbst III
°**hint** [hɪnt] Hinweis
hip hop ['hɪp hɒp] Hip-Hop II
hire ['haɪə] mieten, leihen III

his [hɪz]:
1. sein/e *(zu „he")* I
2. seiner, seine, seins *(zu „he")* V 1 (21)

historic [hɪ'stɒrɪk] historisch *(berühmt, denkwürdig)* II
history ['hɪstri] Geschichte I
hit [hɪt]:
1. Hit III
2. **hit, hit, hit** schlagen; prallen, stoßen gegen/auf IV
3. **hit sb./sth.** jn./etwas treffen IV

hitchhiker ['hɪtʃhaɪkə] Anhalter/in, Tramper/in V 1 (21)
hobby ['hɒbi] Hobby I
hockey ['hɒki] Hockey III
hold [həʊld], **held, held** halten II
hole [həʊl] Loch III
hole punch ['həʊl pʌntʃ] Locher I
holiday ['hɒlədeɪ] Urlaub I **holidays** Ferien I
home [həʊm] Heim, Zuhause I **at home** zu Hause, daheim I **dogs' home** Hundeheim II **go home** nach Hause gehen I
homecoming ['həʊmkʌmɪŋ] *(AE)* Ehemaligentreffen *(Schule)* IV
homeless ['həʊmləs] obdachlos IV
homesick ['həʊmsɪk]: **be/feel homesick** Heimweh haben II
homework ['həʊmwɜːk] Hausaufgabe(n) I **do your homework** Hausaufgaben machen I **I forgot my homework.** Ich habe meine Hausaufgaben vergessen. I **What's for homework?** Was haben wir als Hausaufgabe(n) auf? I
honest ['ɒnɪst] ehrlich IV
honey ['hʌni] Honig V 1 (11)
hood [hʊd] Kapuze V 1 (21)
hooded ['hʊdɪd]: **a hooded figure** eine Person/Gestalt mit Kapuze V 1 (21)
hoodie ['hʊdi] Kapuzenpullover I
hoot [huːt] hupen III
hoover ['huːvə] staubsaugen II
hope [həʊp]:
1. hoffen I
2. Hoffnung IV

hopeful ['həʊpfl] zuversichtlich, hoffnungsvoll III
horrible ['hɒrəbl] schrecklich V 2 (33)
horror ['hɒrə] Horror IV
horse [hɔːs] Pferd II
hospital ['hɒspɪtl] Krankenhaus I
host [həʊst] Gastgeber/in III
host family ['həʊst fæməli] Gastfamilie III
hostel ['hɒstl] Hostel *(günstige Unterkunft für Reisende)* IV
hot [hɒt] heiß I
hot dog ['hɒt dɒg] Hot Dog *(heißes Würstchen in einem Brötchen)* IV
hot spot ['hɒt spɒt] Anziehungspunkt V 1 (11) **tourist hot spot** touristischer Anziehungspunkt V 1 (11)
hotel [həʊ'tel] Hotel III
hound [haʊnd] (Jagd-)Hund II
hour ['aʊə] Stunde II **opening hours** *(pl)* Öffnungszeiten V 3 (60) **working hours** *(pl)* Arbeitszeit(en) V 3 (60) **°work long hours** lange arbeiten, Überstunden machen
house [haʊs] Haus I
housework ['haʊswɜːk] Hausarbeit *(Arbeit im Haus/Haushalt)* IV
how [haʊ] wie I **How are you doing?** *(AE)* Wie geht's? / Wie geht es dir/euch/Ihnen? IV **How are you?** Wie geht's? / Wie geht es dir/euch/Ihnen? I **How much are …?** Was (Wie viel) kosten? I **How much is …?** Was (Wie viel) kostet? I **how to do sth.** wie man etwas tut / tun kann / tun soll III **How's it going?** Wie geht's? / Wie läuft's? I
however [haʊ'evə] allerdings, jedoch IV
hug [hʌg] umklammern; umarmen V 4 (91)
huge [hjuːdʒ] riesig, Riesen- III
human ['hjuːmən] Mensch; menschlich V 1 (11)
human being [hjuːmən 'biːɪŋ] Mensch V 1 (11)
hundred ['hʌndrəd]: **a hundred, one hundred** (ein)hundert I
hung [hʌŋ] *siehe* **hang**
hunt [hʌnt] jagen IV
hurricane ['hʌrɪkən] Hurrikan, Orkan IV
hurry ['hʌri] sich beeilen; eilen I **Hurry up.** Beeil dich! / Beeilt euch! IV **be in a hurry** es eilig haben IV
hurt [hɜːt], **hurt, hurt** verletzen; wehtun II **be hurt** verletzt sein II **get hurt** sich verletzen II
husband ['hʌzbənd] (Ehe-)Mann IV

I

I [aɪ] ich I **I'm (= I am)** ich bin I
ice [aɪs] Eis *(gefrorenes Wasser)* III
ice cream [aɪs 'kriːm] (Speise-)Eis I
ice hockey ['aɪs hɒki] Eishockey II
ice rink ['aɪs rɪŋk] Schlittschuhbahn II
ice skates *(pl)* ['aɪs skeɪts] Schlittschuhe II
ice skating ['aɪs skeɪtɪŋ] Schlittschuhlaufen II
iced tea [aɪst 'tiː] Eistee IV
ICT (Information and Communication technology) [aɪ siː 'tiː], [ɪnfə'meɪʃn ənd kəmjuːnɪ'keɪʃn teknɒlədʒi] Informations- und Kommunikationstechnologie I
idea [aɪ'dɪə] Idee I
ideal [aɪ'dɪəl] ideal III
identify [aɪ'dentɪfaɪ] erkennen, identifizieren V 1 (12)
identity [aɪ'dentəti] Identität V 3 (59)
°idiom ['ɪdiəm] Redewendung
idiot ['ɪdiət] Idiot/in I
if [ɪf]:
1. wenn, falls II
2. ob II

°ignorance ['ɪgnərəns] Ignoranz, Unwissenheit
ignore [ɪg'nɔː] nicht beachten, ignorieren IV
ill [ɪl] krank II
illegal [ɪ'liːgl] illegal; verboten III
illness ['ɪlnəs] Krankheit IV
illustrate ['ɪləstreɪt] veranschaulichen; illustrieren, bebildern V 2 (37)
illustration [ɪlə'streɪʃn] Abbildung, Illustration II
image ['ɪmɪdʒ] Image; Bild IV
°imagination [ɪmædʒɪ'neɪʃn] Fantasie, Vorstellungskraft
imaginative [ɪ'mædʒɪnətɪv] einfallsreich, kreativ V 4 (84)
imagine sth. [ɪ'mædʒɪn] sich etwas vorstellen III
immediate [ɪ'miːdiət] sofortige/r/s V 3 (68)
immediately [ɪ'miːdiətli] sofort, umgehend, unmittelbar V 3 (68)
immigrant ['ɪmɪgrənt] Einwanderer, Einwanderin IV
immigration [ɪmɪ'greɪʃn] Einwanderung IV
impaired [ɪm'peəd] beeinträchtigt, behindert IV **visually impaired** sehbehindert IV
impatient [ɪm'peɪʃnt] ungeduldig III
important [ɪm'pɔːtnt] wichtig I
impress [ɪm'pres] beeindrucken IV **impressed** beeindruckt IV
improve [ɪm'pruːv] (sich) verbessern III
in [ɪn] in I **in English** auf Englisch I **in the afternoon** am Nachmittag I **in the country** auf dem Land I **in the end** schließlich, zum Schluss II **in the evening** abends, am Abend I **in the field** auf der Weide I **in the middle** in der Mitte I **in the morning** morgens, am Morgen I **in the photo** auf dem Foto I **in the picture** auf dem Bild I **in town** in der Stadt I **I haven't eaten in days.** Ich habe tagelang nichts gegessen. V 4 (90) **one in five** eine/r/s von fünf(en) V 1 (10) **°in fact** eigentlich, um genau zu sein
inch [ɪntʃ] Zoll *(Längenmaß; 1 inch = 2,54 cm)* IV
°include [ɪn'kluːd] einschließen
included [ɪn'kluːdɪd] inbegriffen III
including [ɪn'kluːdɪŋ] einschließlich; darunter (auch) III
incredible [ɪn'kredəbl] unglaublich IV
°Incredibly, … [ɪn'kredəbli] Unglaublicherweise … / Es ist kaum zu glauben, aber …
independence (from) [ɪndɪ'pendəns] Unabhängigkeit (von) IV
independent (of/from) [ɪndɪ'pendənt] unabhängig (von) III
Indian ['ɪndiən]: **(American) Indian** Indianer/in; indianisch IV

indigenous (to) [ɪn'dɪdʒənəs] einheimisch (in) V 1 (15) **indigenous Australian** australische/r Ureinwohner/in V 1 (15) **indigenous people** Einheimische, Ureinwohner/innen V 1 (15)
indirect [ɪndə'rekt] indirekt V 2 (40)
individual [ɪndɪ'vɪdʒuəl] Einzelne/r, Individuum; Person V 3 (73)
°**indoors** [ɪn'dɔːz] innen, drinnen
industry ['ɪndəstri] Industrie IV
infected [ɪn'fektɪd] entzündet IV
°**infection** [ɪn'fekʃn] Infektion
influence ['ɪnfluəns]:
1. beeinflussen V 2 (34)
2. Einfluss V 2 (34)
°**inform sb.** [ɪn'fɔːm] jn. informieren
information [ɪnfə'meɪʃn] Information(en) I
information desk [ɪnfə'meɪʃn desk] Informationsstand I
ingredient [ɪn'griːdiənt] Zutat, Bestandteil V 3 (56)
inland [ɪn'lænd] landeinwärts, im Landesinneren/ins Landesinnere V 1 (15)
inline skates *(pl)* [ɪnlaɪn 'skeɪts] Inlineskates I
inside [ɪn'saɪd]:
1. drinnen; nach drinnen I
2. **inside a T-shirt** in einem T-Shirt II
3. **the inside** das Innere, die Innenseite IV
install [ɪn'stɔːl] installieren, einbauen III
instead [ɪn'sted] stattdessen V 2 (42)
°**instruction** [ɪn'strʌkʃn] Anweisung
instructor [ɪn'strʌktə] Lehrer/in V 3 (60)
instrument ['ɪnstrəmənt] Instrument I
°**insurance** [ɪn'ʃʊərəns] Versicherung **take out insurance** Versicherungen/eine Versicherung abschließen
integrate ['ɪntɪgreɪt] integrieren IV
°**intelligent** [ɪn'telɪdʒənt] intelligent
interest ['ɪntrəst]:
1. Interesse V 2 (42)
°2. **interest sb.** jn. interessieren
interested (in) ['ɪntrəstɪd] interessiert (an) II
interesting ['ɪntrəstɪŋ] interessant I
international [ɪntə'næʃnəl] international III
internet ['ɪntənet] Internet II
interview ['ɪntəvjuː]:
1. Interview I
°2. befragen, interviewen
interviewer ['ɪntəvjuːə] Interviewer/in V 3 (67)
intimidate [ɪn'tɪmɪdeɪt] einschüchtern IV
intimidating [ɪn'tɪmɪdeɪtɪŋ] einschüchternd, bedrohlich IV
into ['ɪntu], ['ɪntə] in (... hinein) I °**be into sth.** *infml* interessiert sein an etwas, etwas gerne tun
°**intonation** [ɪntə'neɪʃn] Intonation
introduce sb. to sb./sth. [ɪntrə'djuːs] jm. jn./etwas vorstellen, jn. mit jm./etwas bekanntmachen III
introduction (to) [ɪntrə'dʌkʃn] Einleitung, Einführung (in) IV
°**invent** [ɪn'vent] erfinden
invention [ɪn'venʃn] Erfindung V 4 (96)
°**investor** [ɪn'vestə] Investor/in
invisible [ɪn'vɪzəbl] unsichtbar IV
invitation (to) [ɪnvɪ'teɪʃn] Einladung (zu, nach) I
invite (to) [ɪn'vaɪt] einladen (zu, nach) I
°**involved** [ɪn'vɒlvd]: **get involved in** sich engagieren (in/bei), mitmachen (bei)
Irish ['aɪrɪʃ] irisch, aus Irland III
iron ['aɪən]:
1. Bügeleisen V 3 (56)
2. bügeln V 3 (56)
ironing ['aɪənɪŋ]: **do the ironing** bügeln V 3 (56)
irritate ['ɪrɪteɪt] (ver)ärgern, irritieren V 4 (87)
is [ɪz] *(er/sie/es)* ist I **The calculator is £ 1.** Der Taschenrechner kostet 1 Pfund. I
island ['aɪlənd] Insel II
it [ɪt] er, sie, es I
its [ɪts] sein/e, ihr/e II
itself [ɪt'self] es/sich selbst III

J

jacket ['dʒækɪt] Jacke, Jackett II
jam [dʒæm] Marmelade I
January ['dʒænjuəri] Januar I
jazz [dʒæz] Jazz IV
jealous ['dʒeləs] eifersüchtig, neidisch II
jeans *(pl)* [dʒiːnz] Jeans II
jelly ['dʒeli] *(AE)* Marmelade IV
jellyfish, *pl* **jellyfish** ['dʒelifɪʃ] Qualle V 1 (11)
Jewish ['dʒuːɪʃ] jüdisch IV
°**jigsaw** ['dʒɪgsɔː] Puzzle
jingle ['dʒɪŋgl] Jingle *(Werbemelodie, -song)* V 4 (86)
job [dʒɒb] Job, (Arbeits-)stelle I **do a great/good/bad job** großartige/gute/schlechte Arbeit leisten III **Good job!** *(AE)* Gut gemacht! IV **on the job** am Arbeitsplatz IV
job interview Vorstellungsgespräch V 3 (72)
jogging ['dʒɒgɪŋ] Jogging III
join [dʒɔɪn]: **join a club** sich einem Klub anschließen; in einen Klub eintreten I **join the army** zur Armee gehen IV **Join the club.** Da bist du nicht der/die Einzige. II
joke [dʒəʊk]:
1. Witz, Scherz II
She can take a joke. Sie versteht Spaß. III
2. Witze machen, scherzen II
You're joking! Du machst wohl Witze! II
journal ['dʒɜːnl] Tagebuch, Journal IV
journalist ['dʒɜːnəlɪst] Journalist/in IV
journey ['dʒɜːni]:
1. Reise II
2. reisen IV
judo ['dʒuːdəʊ] Judo II
juice [dʒuːs] Saft I
July [dʒu'laɪ] Juli I
jump [dʒʌmp]:
1. **jump (up)** (hoch)springen II
2. *(vor Schreck)* zusammenzucken III
June [dʒuːn] Juni I
junk food ['dʒʌŋk fuːd] Junkfood *(ungesundes Essen)* II
just [dʒʌst]:
1. gerade (eben) II
2. nur, bloß; einfach III
3. **just like Berry** genau wie Berry II

K

°**K** [keɪ]: **£20K** zwanzigtausend Pfund (= £ 20.000)
kangaroo [kæŋgə'ruː] Känguru V 1 (8)
keep [kiːp], **kept, kept** aufbewahren; (be)halten III **keep away from** sich fernhalten von IV **Keep it up!** Weiter so! II **Keep me posted!** Halt mich auf dem Laufenden! III °**keep up (with sb.)** (mit jm.) Schritt halten
keeper ['kiːpə]: **Finders keepers, losers weepers.** Was man findet, darf man behalten. *(Redensart)* V 4 (91)
kept [kept] *siehe* **keep**
ketchup ['ketʃəp] Ketschup III
kettle ['ketl] Wasserkocher *(elektrisch)* III
key [kiː] Schlüssel; Schlüssel- V 3 (62)
key skills *(pl)* ['kiː skɪlz] Schlüsselqualifikationen, -kompetenzen V 3 (62)
kick [kɪk]:
1. Tritt, Stoß, Kick V 2 (38)
2. treten; *(Sport)* schießen V 2 (38)
3. *(infml) (Gewohnheit/Idee)* aufgeben, sich davon befreien V 2 (38)
kickboxer ['kɪkbɒksə] Kickboxer/in V 4 (90)
kid [kɪd]:
1. Kind, Jugendliche/r I
2. **Are you kidding?** *(infml)* Machst du Witze? / Willst du mich auf den Arm nehmen? IV
kill [kɪl] töten, umbringen IV
killer ['kɪlə] Mörder/in V 4 (90)
kilogram, kilo ['kɪləgræm], ['kiːləʊ] Kilo(gramm) IV
kilometre (km) ['kɪləmiːtə] Kilometer II **kilometres per hour (kph)** Kilometer pro Stunde (km/h) III
kilt [kɪlt] Kilt, Schottenrock III
kind [kaɪnd] nett, freundlich II
kind (of) [kaɪnd] Art, Sorte II **kind of glamorous** irgendwie glamourös V 1 (22)
king [kɪŋ] König II

Kingdom ['kɪŋdəm]: **the United Kingdom (the UK)** das Vereinigte Königreich III
kiss [kɪs]:
1. Kuss I
2. (sich) küssen III
kitchen ['kɪtʃɪn] Küche I
kitten ['kɪtn] Kätzchen, junge Katze II
knee [niː] Knie II
knew [njuː] *siehe* **know**
knife, *pl* **knives** [naɪf], [naɪvz] Messer III
knock (on sth.) [nɒk] (an)klopfen (an etwas) III
know [nəʊ], **knew, known** wissen; kennen I **get to know** kennenlernen III
knowledge (of/about) ['nɒlɪdʒ] Wissen (von/über), Kenntnis(se) (von/in) V 3 (61)
known [nəʊn] *siehe* **know**
kph (kilometres per hour) [keɪ piː 'eɪtʃ] Kilometer pro Stunde (km/h) III

L

lab [læb] Labor I
label ['leɪbl] Etikett, Schild(chen) III
lad [læd] *(infml)* Junge, junger Kerl V 4 (91)
ladder ['lædə] *(die)* Leiter V 4 (92)
lady ['leɪdi] Dame V 3 (69)
ladylike ['leɪdilaɪk] damenhaft IV
°**laid** [leɪd] *siehe* **lay**
lain [leɪn] *siehe* **lie**
lake [leɪk] (Binnen-)See II
lamp [læmp] Lampe I
land [lænd]:
1. landen III
2. Land *(Grund und Boden)* IV
by land auf dem Landweg IV
landscape ['lændskeɪp] Landschaft V 1 (8)
landscape gardener [lændskeɪp 'gɑːdnə] Landschaftsgärtner/in V 3 (65)
lane [leɪn] Gasse, Weg, Sträßchen II
language ['læŋgwɪdʒ] Sprache I
lantern ['læntən] Laterne II
°**lapse** [læps]: **time lapse** Zeitraffer *(Film)*
laptop ['læptɒp] Laptop II
large [lɑːdʒ] groß IV
lasagne [lə'zænjə] Lasagne II
last [lɑːst] letzte(r, s) I **at last** schließlich, endlich III
late [leɪt] spät I °**have a late night** lange aufbleiben, spät ins Bett gehen
lately ['leɪtli] in letzter Zeit V 2 (36)
later ['leɪtə] später I **See you later.** Bis später. I
laugh [lɑːf]:
1. lachen I
laugh at lachen über, sich lustig machen über III
2. *(ein)* Lachen I
with a laugh mit einem Lachen I
°**launch** [lɔːntʃ] *(Produkt)* auf den Markt bringen, einführen
law [lɔː] Gesetz IV
lay [leɪ] *siehe* **lie**
°**lay** [leɪ], **laid, laid** legen
lazy ['leɪzi] faul I
lead [liːd]:
1. (Hunde-)Leine III
2. lead, led, led führen, leiten V 3 (60)
leader ['liːdə] Leiter/in, (An-)Führer/in II
league [liːg] Liga *(Sport)* II
lean [liːn] lehnen IV
learn [lɜːn] lernen I **learn a/your lesson** eine/deine Lektion lernen V 4 (88)
°**learner** ['lɜːnə] Lernende/r
°**learner licence** ['lɜːnə laɪsns] *Führerschein für Begleitetes Fahren*
least [liːst] *(der/die/das)* wenigste, am wenigsten IV **at least** wenigstens, zumindest II
leather ['leðə] Leder V 4 (92)
leave [liːv], **left, left**:
1. abfahren, losfahren II
2. *(jemanden)* verlassen; weggehen I
3. zurücklassen II
leave sb. alone jn. in Ruhe lassen V 4 (91)
led [led] *siehe* **lead**
left [left]:
1. *siehe* **leave**
2. links; nach links I
on the left links, auf der linken Seite I
leg [leg] Bein I **I have a sore leg.** Mein Bein tut weh. I
legal ['liːgl] legal IV
legend ['ledʒənd] Legende, Sage II
lemon ['lemən] Zitrone IV
lend sb. sth. [lend], **lent, lent** jm. etwas leihen III
lent [lent] *siehe* **lend**
less [les] weniger II
lesson ['lesn] (Unterrichts-)Stunde I
learn a/your lesson eine/deine Lektion lernen V 4 (88) **teach sb. a lesson** jm. eine Lektion erteilen V 1 (22)
let [let], **let, let** lassen IV **Let's …** Lass(t) uns … I
letter ['letə]:
1. Brief I
letter to the editor Leserbrief IV
2. Buchstabe II
letter box ['letə bɒks] Briefkasten II
°**level** ['levl] Niveau, Grad, Stufe
library ['laɪbrəri] Bücherei, Bibliothek IV
°**licence** ['laɪsns] Lizenz, Erlaubnis
license ['laɪsns] *(AE)*: **driver's license** Führerschein IV
lie [laɪ]:
1. Lüge V 3 (68)
tell a lie/lies lügen V 3 (68)
2. lie (to sb.) (jn. an)lügen V 3 (68)
lie [laɪ], **lay, lain** liegen III
life, *pl* **lives** [laɪf], [laɪvz] (das) Leben I
way of life Lebensweise V 1 (15)
lifeguard ['laɪfgɑːd] Rettungsschwimmer/in; Bademeister/in V 1 (13)
°**life-saving** ['laɪf seɪvɪŋ] lebensrettend, Rettungs-
lifestyle ['laɪfstaɪl] Lebensstil V 1 (15)
lift [lɪft] Lift, Fahrstuhl IV
light [laɪt]:
1. Licht, Lampe II
2. leicht; hell IV
3. light, lit, lit anzünden V 1 (12)
light a fire (ein) Feuer machen V 1 (12)
lighthouse ['laɪthaʊs] Leuchtturm II
like [laɪk] mögen I **I don't like …** ich mag … nicht I **I'd (= I would) like …** Ich hätte gern … / Ich möchte … I
like [laɪk]:
1. als ob, als wenn IV
2. wie I
like that so *(auf diese Art)* IV **like this** so, auf diese Art III **… like …** *(infml)* … irgendwie … / …, keine Ahnung, … V 2 (34) **just like Berry** genau wie Berry II **something like this / like that** so etwas II **What's it like?** Wie ist es? / Wie sieht es aus? I
likeable ['laɪkəbl] sympathisch IV
likely ['laɪkli] wahrscheinlich V 1 (11)
be likely to do sth. wahrscheinlich etwas tun (werden) V 1 (11)
likes and dislikes *(pl)* ['dɪslaɪks] Vorlieben und Abneigungen III
°**limit sb./sth. to** ['lɪmɪt] jn./etwas begrenzen, beschränken auf
line [laɪn]:
1. U-Bahn-Linie III
2. Reihe; Zeile III
link [lɪŋk]:
1. Verbindung; Link IV
°**2. link (to)** verbinden (mit)
lion ['laɪən] Löwe IV
lip [lɪp] Lippe V 3 (69)
lipstick ['lɪpstɪk] Lippenstift V 3 (69)
list [lɪst]:
1. Liste II
2. auflisten, aufzählen V 1 (17)
listen (to) ['lɪsn] (sich etwas) anhören; zuhören I
listener ['lɪsənə] Zuhörer/in III
lit [lɪt] *siehe* **light**
litre ['liːtə] Liter V 1 (12)
litter ['lɪtə] Abfall II
litter bin ['lɪtə bɪn] Mülleimer, Abfalleimer II
little ['lɪtl]:
1. klein I
2. wenig IV
a little ein wenig, ein bisschen III
live [lɪv] leben, wohnen I
liveable ['lɪvəbl] lebenswert V 1 (17)
°**lively** ['laɪvli] lebendig, lebhaft
lives [laɪvz] *Plural von* **life** I

living history [lɪvɪŋ 'hɪstri] *etwa:* Geschichte zum Anfassen II
living room ['lɪvɪŋ ru:m] Wohnzimmer I
lobby ['lɒbi] Eingangshalle IV
local ['ləʊkl] örtlich, Orts-, Lokal- III
°**location** [ləʊ'keɪʃn] Ort *(Standort; Einsatzort)*
locker ['lɒkə] Spind, Schließfach IV
°**logical** ['lɒdʒɪkl] logisch
logo ['ləʊgəʊ] Logo V 4 (90)
Londoner ['lʌndənə] Londoner/in III
lonely ['ləʊnli] einsam I
long [lɒŋ] lang II **no longer** nicht mehr IV
look [lʊk]:
1. sehen, schauen I
2. aussehen I
3. **Let's have a look.** Lass(t) uns mal nachschauen. II
Look, Adam. Sieh mal/Schau mal, Adam. I **look after** sich kümmern um; aufpassen auf I **look at sth.** sich etwas anschauen I **look down your nose at sb.** herabblicken auf jn. IV **look for** suchen; Ausschau halten nach I **look forward to** sich freuen auf II **look forward to doing sth.** sich darauf freuen, etwas zu tun IV **look into sth.** etwas prüfen III **look up a word** ein Wort nachschlagen *(im Wörterbuch)* IV
loot [lu:t] plündern IV
looter ['lu:tə] Plünderer/Plünderin IV
lose [lu:z], **lost, lost** verlieren I **lose control** die Kontrolle verlieren I
loser ['lu:zə] Verlierer/in III **Finders keepers, losers weepers.** Was man findet, darf man behalten. *(Redensart)* V 4 (91)
lost [lɒst] *siehe* **lose** **Get lost!** Verschwinde(t)! II **I'm not lost.** Ich habe mich nicht verlaufen/verirrt. I
lot [lɒts]: **lots of** viel/e I **a lot (of)** viel/e; sehr II
loud [laʊd] laut III
love [lʌv]:
1. lieben, sehr mögen I
I'd love to come. (= I would love to come.) Ich komme sehr gern. / Ich würde sehr gern kommen. I
2. *freundliche Anrede, auch bei Unbekannten* III
3. Liebe I
Give her my love. Grüß sie von mir. III **in love (with)** verliebt (in) I
Lots of love Alles Liebe / Liebe Grüße III
lovely ['lʌvli] schön; nett, lieb II
low [ləʊ] niedrig, tief II
luck [lʌk]: **bad luck** Pech IV **Good luck.** Viel Glück! IV **Hard luck!** Pech (gehabt)! III
luckily ['lʌkɪli] glücklicherweise, zum Glück III
lucky ['lʌki]: **you're lucky** du hast Glück I °**get lucky** Glück haben
lunch [lʌntʃ] Mittagessen I **have lunch** (zu) Mittag essen I
lunch box ['lʌntʃ bɒks] Brotdose II
lunchtime ['lʌntʃtaɪm] Mittagszeit II

M

machine [mə'ʃi:n] Maschine, Gerät V 3 (69) **drinks machine** Getränkeautomat V 3 (69)
madam ['mædəm] meine Dame, gnädige Frau V 3 (63) **Dear Sir / Madam** Sehr geehrte Damen und Herren V 3 (63)
made [meɪd] *siehe* **make**
madhouse ['mædhaʊs] Irrenhaus I
magazine [mægə'zi:n] Zeitschrift II
magic ['mædʒɪk] Zauberei, Magie II
magical ['mædʒɪkl] magisch; zauberhaft II
magician [mə'dʒɪʃn] Zauberer/Zauberin II
mailman/-woman ['meɪlmən, -wʊmən] *(AE)* Briefträger/in IV
main [meɪn] hauptsächlich, Haupt- IV
make [meɪk], **made, made** machen, herstellen I **make a difference** etwas bewirken, etwas ausmachen I **make friends** Freunde finden II **make money** Geld verdienen III **make sb. do sth.** jn. dazu bringen, etwas zu tun II **make sb./sth. sth.** jn./etwas zu etwas machen IV **make sure that ...** darauf achten, dass ...; dafür sorgen, dass ... V 1 (24) **be made of** aus etwas (gemacht) sein IV °**make sth. up** etwas erfinden, sich etwas ausdenken
make-up ['meɪkʌp] Make-up II
mall [mɔ:l] Einkaufszentrum III
mam [mæm] *(in Irland)* Mama, Mutti III
man, *pl* **men** [mæn], [men] Mann I
manage ['mænɪdʒ] verwalten, regeln V 3 (56)
management ['mænɪdʒmənt] Leitung, (Geschäfts-)Führung III
manager ['mænɪdʒə] Geschäftsführer/in, Manager/in III
manga ['mæŋgə] Manga II
manners *(pl)* ['mænəz] Manieren, Umgangsformen IV
many ['mæni] viele II **how many?** wie viele? II
map [mæp]:
1. Landkarte, Stadtplan I
2. kartografieren, *(Entwicklung)* verfolgen IV
March [mɑ:tʃ] März I
°**marine** [mə'ri:n] Meeres-
mark [mɑ:k] kennzeichnen, markieren III
market ['mɑ:kɪt] Markt I
married (to) ['mærid] verheiratet (mit) II **get married (to sb.)** (jn.) heiraten IV
mask [mɑ:sk] Maske II
match [mætʃ] Spiel, Wettkampf II
°**match** [mætʃ] passen zu **match (with)** zuordnen
°**mate** [meɪt] Freund/in, Kumpel
materials *(pl)* [mə'tɪəriəlz] Materialien, Hilfsmittel V 1 (24)
math [mæθ] *(AE)* Mathe(matik) IV
maths [mæθs] Mathe(matik) I
matter ['mætə]:
1. von Bedeutung sein, wichtig sein II
It doesn't matter. Es/Das ist egal. II
2. **What's the matter?** Was ist denn? / Was ist los? II
mature [mə'tʃʊə] reif, vernünftig V 3 (69)
°**maximum (= max)** ['mæksɪməm] Höchst-, maximal; Maximum
May [meɪ] Mai I
°**may** [meɪ]: **it may be ...** es ist vielleicht ...
maybe ['meɪbi] vielleicht I
mayonnaise [meɪə'neɪz] Majonäse III
maze [meɪz] Irrgarten, Labyrinth II
me [mi:] mich; mir I **It's me.** Ich bin's. I
meadow ['medəʊ] Wiese IV
meal [mi:l] Mahlzeit, Essen III **Enjoy your meal.** Guten Appetit! III
mean [mi:n]:
1. geizig II
2. gemein, fies I
mean [mi:n], **meant, meant**:
1. bedeuten I
2. meinen *(sagen wollen)* I
meaning ['mi:nɪŋ] Bedeutung IV
meant [ment] *siehe* **mean**
meat [mi:t] Fleisch II
mechanic [mɪ'kænɪk] Mechaniker/in III
medal ['medl] Medaille III
media *(pl)* ['mi:diə] Medien V 1 (17) **social media** soziale Medien/Dienste V 3 (62)
°**mediation** [mi:di'eɪʃn] Vermittlung, Sprachmittlung
meet [mi:t], **met, met** kennenlernen; treffen I **Nice to meet you.** Freut mich, dich/euch/Sie kennenzulernen. I
member ['membə] Mitglied IV
memorial (to sb./sth.) [mə'mɔ:riəl] Denkmal (für jn./etwas), Gedenkstätte IV
men [men] *Plural von* **man** I
mention ['menʃn] erwähnen III
menu ['menju:] Speisekarte III
mess [mes]:
1. Durcheinander, Chaos II
What a mess! Was für ein Durcheinander/Chaos! II
2. **mess with sb./sth.** herumspielen, Spielchen treiben mit jm./etwas IV
message ['mesɪdʒ]:
1. Botschaft, Aussage III
2. Nachricht, Mitteilung I
message in a bottle Flaschenpost I
leave a message eine Nachricht hin-

terlassen III **take a message** *(jm.)* etwas ausrichten III
3. Nachrichten schicken/austauschen V 4 (89)

°**messaging** ['mesɪdʒɪŋ] (Nachrichten-, Bild-)Übermittlung; das Versenden von SMS
messy ['mesi] unordentlich I
met [met] *siehe* **meet**
metal ['metl] Metall IV
metre ['mi:tə] Meter II
mice [maɪs] *Plural von* **mouse** III
middle ['mɪdl] Mitte I **in the middle** in der Mitte I **in the middle of nowhere** am Ende der Welt III
°**middle school** ['mɪdl sku:l] *(AE)* Mittelschule *(für 11- bis 14-Jährige)*
midnight ['mɪdnaɪt] Mitternacht III
might [maɪt]: **you might miss home** es könnte sein, dass du dein Zuhause vermisst III
migrant ['maɪgrənt] Zuwanderer/Zuwanderin III
mile [maɪl] Meile *(ca. 1,6 km)* II
milk [mɪlk]:
1. Milch II
2. melken IV
milkshake ['mɪlkʃeɪk] Milchshake II
million ['mɪljən] Million III
°**millionaire** [mɪljə'neə] Millionär/in
mind [maɪnd] aufpassen auf, achten auf IV **I don't mind.** Es macht mir nichts aus. III
mind map ['maɪnd mæp] Gedankenkarte, Wörternetz I
mine [maɪn] meine, meiner, meins II
mining ['maɪnɪŋ] Bergbau IV **gold mining** Goldabbau IV
°**minor character** [maɪnə 'kærəktə] Nebenfigur *(in Roman, Film usw.)*
minus ['maɪnəs] minus II
minute ['mɪnɪt] Minute I
mirror ['mɪrə] Spiegel I
Miss [mɪs]:
1. Miss Borowski Frau Borowski *(Anrede für unverheiratete Frauen)* I
2. Fräulein *(BE: Anrede für Lehrerin)* II
miss [mɪs]:
1. vermissen I
2. verpassen II
3. übersehen, überhören *(nicht mitbekommen)* II
°**missing** ['mɪsɪŋ]: **be missing** fehlen
mistake [mɪ'steɪk] Fehler II **by mistake** aus Versehen II
mix [mɪks] Mix, Mischung III
mobile ['məʊbaɪl]:
1. mobil V 4 (93)
2. *(kurz für:* **mobile phone***)* Handy I
moccasin ['mɒkəsɪn] Mokassin IV
model ['mɒdl] Fotomodell, Model V 3 (66)
moderator ['mɒdəreɪtə] Moderator/in *(z.B. bei Debatten)* V 4 (97)
modern ['mɒdn] modern I
modern-day [mɒdn 'deɪ] modern, von heute V 4 (85)
modest ['mɒdɪst] bescheiden; anständig, sittsam IV
mom [mɒm], [mɑ:m] *(AE)* Mutti, Mama IV
moment ['məʊmənt] Moment I **at the moment** im Moment, gerade I
Monday ['mʌndeɪ], ['mʌndi] Montag I
money ['mʌni] Geld I **Money doesn't grow on trees.** Das Geld liegt nicht auf der Straße. *(Redewendung)* II **it's a money-saver** es spart Kosten III **make money** Geld verdienen III **pocket money** Taschengeld II
monitor ['mɒnɪtə] Monitor, Bildschirm III
monkey ['mʌŋki] Affe I
monologue ['mɒnəlɒg] Monolog, Selbstgespräch V 2 (32)
monster ['mɒnstə] Monster III
month [mʌnθ] Monat I
mood [mu:d] Stimmung, Laune IV
°**moon** [mu:n] Mond
more [mɔ:] mehr, weitere I **more and more** immer mehr III **more popular** beliebter II
morning ['mɔ:nɪŋ] Morgen I **Good morning.** Guten Morgen. I **in the morning** morgens, am Morgen I
most [məʊst]: **most popular** am beliebtesten II **(the) most sports** die meisten Sportarten II
mostly ['məʊstli] meistens; hauptsächlich II
motel [məʊ'tel] Motel IV
mother ['mʌðə] Mutter I
°**motivate** ['məʊtɪveɪt] motivieren
°**motorway** ['məʊtəweɪ] Autobahn
motto ['mɒtəʊ] Motto III
mountain ['maʊntən] Berg II
mouse, *pl* **mice** [maʊs], [maɪs] Maus III
mouth [maʊθ] Mund I
move [mu:v]:
1. (sich) bewegen III
2. move (to) (um)ziehen (nach) II **move house** umziehen *(an einen neuen Wohnort)* III
movement ['mu:vmənt] Bewegung IV
movie ['mu:vi] *(bes. AE)* Film IV
movie theater ['mu:vi θɪətə] *(AE)* Kino IV
MP3 player [empi:'θri: pleɪə] MP3-Player I
Mr Brown ['mɪstə] Herr Brown I
Mrs Ford ['mɪsɪz] Frau Ford *(Anrede für verheiratete Frauen)* I
Ms Lee [mɪz], [məz] Frau Lee *(allgemeine Anrede für Frauen)* I
much [mʌtʃ] viel II **as much as ...** bis zu ...; nicht weniger als ... IV **How much is/are ...?** Was (Wie viel) kostet/kosten ...? I **How much?** Wie viel? II **miss/love sb. so much** jn. so sehr vermissen/lieben II **Thanks very much.** Vielen Dank. II
mud [mʌd] Schlamm, Matsch II
muddy ['mʌdi] matschig III
muffin ['mʌfɪn] Muffin II
multitask [mʌlti'tɑ:sk] mehrere Tätigkeiten gleichzeitig ausführen V 4 (82)
mum [mʌm] Mama, Mutti I
mummy ['mʌmi] Mumie II
°**muscle car** ['mʌsl kɑ:] Muscle-Car *(Serienmodell, nachgerüstet mit besonders starkem Motor)*
°**muscular dystrophy** [mʌskjələ 'dɪstrəfi] Muskeldystrophie
museum [mju'zi:əm] Museum I
music ['mju:zɪk] Musik I
musical ['mju:zɪkl] Musical I
musician [mju'zɪʃn] Musiker/in I
must [mʌst] müssen I **mustn't do** nicht tun dürfen I **a must** *(infml)* ein Muss, eine Notwendigkeit IV **I must go.** *(am Telefon)* Ich muss Schluss machen. I
mutter ['mʌtə] murmeln, brummeln IV
my [maɪ] mein/e I
myself [maɪ'self] mich, mir (selbst) I
mysterious [mɪ'stɪəriəs] geheimnisvoll II
mystery ['mɪstri] Geheimnis II

N

nail [neɪl] Nagel III
nail polish ['neɪl pɒlɪʃ] Nagellack V 1 (22)
name [neɪm]:
1. (be)nennen III
2. Name I
What's your name? Wie heißt du? I
°**call sb. names** jn. beschimpfen
narrow ['nærəʊ] eng, schmal III
nation ['neɪʃn] Nation, Volk IV
national ['næʃnəl] national, National- II
national anthem [næʃnəl 'ænθəm] Nationalhymne III
national park [næʃnəl 'pɑ:k] Nationalpark II
native ['neɪtɪv] einheimisch, Heimat-; Einheimische/r IV
Native American [neɪtɪv ə'merɪkən] amerikanische/r Ureinwohner/in IV
natural ['nætʃrəl] natürlich, Natur- III
natural history Naturkunde III
nature ['neɪtʃə] (die) Natur IV
near [nɪə] nahe (bei), in der Nähe von I **near to the city** nah am Stadtzentrum II
nearby [nɪə'baɪ] nahe gelegen, in der Nähe IV
nearest ['nɪərɪst]: **the nearest ...** der/die/das nächstgelegene ... V 1 (18)
nearly ['nɪəli] fast II
necessary ['nesəsəri] notwendig, nötig, erforderlich V 3 (73)
necklace ['nekləs] (Hals-)Kette IV
need [ni:d]:
1. brauchen, benötigen I
need to do sth. etwas tun müssen III

2. Bedürfnis V 3 (64)
people with special needs Menschen mit besonderen Bedürfnissen / Förderbedarf V 3 (64)
3. no need for … / no need to do sth. kein Grund für … / kein Grund, etwas zu tun V 4 (92)
negative ['negətɪv] negativ I
°**negativity** [negə'tɪvəti] negative Einstellung
neighbour ['neɪbə] Nachbar/in II
neighbourhood ['neɪbəhʊd] Nachbarschaft, Gegend, Viertel II
neighbouring ['neɪbərɪŋ] benachbart IV
neither ['naɪðə] keine/r/s *(von beiden)* V 1 (17)
neon ['ni:ɒn] Neon; neonfarbig V 3 (69)
nerd [nɜ:d] *hochintelligente, aber kontaktarme Person* IV
nervous ['nɜ:vəs] nervös, aufgeregt I
net [net] *kurz für* Internet V 4 (82)
network ['netwɜ:k] Netz; Wortnetz I
°**networking website** [netwɜ:kɪŋ 'websaɪt] Online-Kommunikationsplattform
never ['nevə] nie, niemals I **I've never had …** ich habe (noch) nie … gehabt II
new [nju:] neu I
New Yorker [nju: 'jɔ:kə] New Yorker/in IV
newcomer ['nju:kʌmə] Neuling IV
news [nju:z] Nachrichten I **… is bad news.** … ist gefährlich. / … ist (gar) nicht gut. V 4 (91)
newsagent ['nju:zeɪdʒənt] Zeitungshändler/in II
newsletter ['nju:zletə] Mitteilungsblatt, Informationsblatt II
newspaper ['nju:zpeɪpə] (Tages-)Zeitung II
next [nekst] nächste(r, s) I **Next, please.** Der/Die Nächste, bitte. I **Next …** Als Nächstes … II **the next day** am anderen/nächsten Tag III
next to ['nekst tə] neben I
nice [naɪs] nett, schön I
nickname ['nɪkneɪm] Spitzname V 1 (8)
night [naɪt] Nacht I **at night** nachts, in der Nacht I
nine [naɪn] neun I
nineties ['naɪnti:z]: **the 90s** die Neunzigerjahre II
no [nəʊ]:
1. nein I
2. kein, keine I
No./no. *pl* **Nos./nos.** ['nʌmbə] Nr. III
nobody ['nəʊbədi] niemand II
nod (to sb.) [nɒd] (jm. zu)nicken IV
noise [nɔɪz] Geräusch; Lärm I
noisy ['nɔɪzi] laut, voller Lärm I
°**nomadic** [nəʊ'mædɪk] nomadisch, Nomaden-
non- [nɒn] Nicht- III
none [nʌn] keine(r, s) II
°**non-profit** [nɒn'prɒfɪt] gemeinnützig
normal ['nɔ:ml] normal I
°**normally** ['nɔ:məli] normalerweise
north [nɔ:θ] Norden; nach Norden II **north-east** Nordosten; nach Nordosten II **north-west** Nordwesten; nach Nordwesten II
northbound ['nɔ:θbaʊnd] in Richtung Norden III
northern ['nɔ:ðən] nördlich, Nord- IV
nose [nəʊz] Nase IV **look down your nose at sb.** herabblicken auf jn. IV
nosey ['nəʊzi] neugierig IV
nosy ['nəʊzi] neugierig IV
not [nɒt] nicht I **I'm not a boy.** Ich bin kein Junge. I **I'm not ten.** Ich bin nicht zehn. I **She's …, isn't she?** Sie ist …, nicht wahr? V 3 (67)
note [nəʊt]:
1. Notiz II
take notes (sich) Notizen machen *(beim Lesen oder Zuhören)* II
°**2. note down** aufschreiben, notieren
nothing ['nʌθɪŋ] nichts I
notice ['nəʊtɪs]:
1. (be)merken IV
2. Notiz, Aushang, Anzeige III
noticeboard ['nəʊtɪs bɔ:d] Schwarzes Brett *(Blog, Klassenraum)* IV
novel ['nɒvl] Roman V 2 (34)
November [nəʊ'vembə] November I
now [naʊ] nun, jetzt I **right now** gerade jetzt, genau jetzt III
nowhere ['nəʊweə] nirgendwo(hin) III **in the middle of nowhere** am Ende der Welt III
number ['nʌmbə] Zahl, Ziffer, Nummer I
nut [nʌt] Nuss I

O

oatmeal ['əʊtmi:l] Hafermehl, Haferbrei IV
observer [əb'zɜ:və] Beobachter/in V 4 (97)
ocean ['əʊʃn] Ozean IV
o'clock [ə'klɒk]: **at 1 o'clock** um 1 Uhr / um 13 Uhr I
October [ɒk'təʊbə] Oktober I
of [ɒv], [əv] von I **(just) the two of us** (nur) wir beide V 2 (36) **the last day of the holidays** der letzte Tag der Ferien/der letzte Ferientag I
of course [əv 'kɔ:s] natürlich, selbstverständlich II
off [ɒf]:
1. weg von; hinunter von III
Off you go! Dann mal los! / Ab mit dir! V 2 (44) **get off (a bus)** aussteigen (aus einem Bus) III **get off (your bike)** absteigen (vom Fahrrad) III **go off (to a place)** (los)gehen, (los)fahren (nach/zu) IV °**off they went** dann zogen sie los
2. get/have a day off einen Tag frei bekommen/haben IV
3. go off klingeln *(Wecker)*; losgehen *(Alarmanlage, Waffe)* IV
offer ['ɒfə]:
1. (an)bieten III
2. Angebot III
office ['ɒfɪs] Büro III
official [ə'fɪʃl] offiziell, amtlich IV
often ['ɒfn], ['ɒftən] oft I
OK [əʊ'keɪ] okay, gut, in Ordnung I
old [əʊld] alt I **in the old days** früher II
old-fashioned [əʊld 'fæʃənd] altmodisch IV
Olympic [ə'lɪmpɪk] olympisch III **the Olympics** *(pl)* die olympischen Spiele III
omelette ['ɒmlət] Omelett I
on [ɒn] auf I **on 1st March** am 1. März I **on Loch Ness** am Loch Ness III **on Monday** am Montag I **on the beach** am Strand I **on the bus** im Bus I **on the job** am Arbeitsplatz IV **on the phone** am Telefon I **on the way to …** auf dem Weg zu/nach … I **be on** laufen, gezeigt werden *(Kino, Theater)* V 4 (90) **drive/run/go on** weiterfahren/-laufen/-gehen IV **Go on.** Ach, komm! / Na los, mach schon! II
once [wʌns] einmal, einst III
°**at once** auf einmal, gleichzeitig
one [wʌn] eins I **the only one** der/die Einzige IV
online [ɒn'laɪn] online, Online- II
only ['əʊnli]:
1. erst II
2. nur, bloß I
3. the only student der/die einzige Schüler/in I
onto the road ['ɒntu], ['ɒntə] auf die Straße III
open ['əʊpən]:
1. öffnen; aufschlagen *(Buch)* I
2. offen, geöffnet II
opening hours *(pl)* ['əʊpənɪŋ aʊəz] Öffnungszeiten V 3 (60)
opinion [ə'pɪnjən] Meinung III **in my opinion** meiner Meinung nach III
opposite ['ɒpəzɪt] Gegenteil II
optimistic [ɒptɪ'mɪstɪk] optimistisch IV
or [ɔ:] oder; sonst I
orange ['ɒrɪndʒ]:
1. orange(farben) I
2. Orange, Apfelsine I
°**orchestra** ['ɔ:kɪstrə] Orchester
order ['ɔ:də]:
1. bestellen III
2. Bestellung IV
3. Reihenfolge V 2 (41)
4. in order to um … zu V 3 (68)
organic [ɔ:'gænɪk] biologisch, Bio- V 3 (64)
organization [ɔ:gənaɪ'zeɪʃn] Organisation V 3 (61)

organizational [ɔ:gənaɪ'zeɪʃənl] organisatorisch V 3 (62)
organize ['ɔ:gənaɪz] organisieren IV
original [ə'rɪdʒənl] original, ursprünglich, Original(-) V 1 (10)
orphan ['ɔ:fn] Waise V 4 (95)
other ['ʌðə] andere(r, s) I **in other words** mit anderen Worten V 4 (85) **the other day** neulich III
our ['aʊə] unser/e I
ours [ɑ:z], ['aʊəz] unsere/r, unseres V 1 (21)
ourselves [aʊə'selvz] wir/uns selbst III
out [aʊt]:
1. **go out** rausgehen, weggehen; ausgehen II
school is out die Schule ist aus/vorbei I
2. **out of ...** aus ... (heraus/hinaus) I
outback ['aʊtbæk]: **the outback** *das Hinterland Australiens* V 1 (8)
outdoor ['aʊtdɔ:]: **outdoor (sport)** (Sport) für draußen / im Freien II
outdoor shop Geschäft für Outdoor-Bekleidung und -Ausrüstung III
outdoors [aʊt'dɔ:z] im Freien, draußen I **the outdoors** die freie Natur V 3 (62)
outfit ['aʊtfɪt] Outfit III
outlaw ['aʊtlɔ:] Bandit/in, Geächtete/r IV
out-of-town (shopping centre) [aʊt əv 'taʊn] (Einkaufszentrum) außerhalb der Stadt III
outside [aʊt'saɪd]:
1. außerhalb (von) III
2. draußen; nach draußen I
3. **the outside** das Äußere, die Außenseite IV
over ['əʊvə] über III **over 300** über / mehr als 300 III **over there** da drüben, dort drüben I **all over the country** überall im Land, im ganzen Land II **be over** vorbei sein, zu Ende sein I **walk over (to)** hinübergehen (zu) IV
°**overseas** [əʊvə'si:z] Übersee-, Auslands-
overspend (on sth.) [əʊvə'spend], **overspent, overspent** zu viel Geld ausgeben (für etwas) V 3 (56)
overspent [əʊvə'spent] *siehe* **overspend**
overtake [əʊvə'teɪk], **overtook, overtaken** überholen V 1 (21)
overtaken [əʊvə'teɪkən] *siehe* **overtake**
overtook [əʊvə'tʊk] *siehe* **overtake**
owl [aʊl] Eule II
own [əʊn]:
1. **own sth.** etwas besitzen IV
2. **your own lanterns** deine/eure eigenen Laternen, eigene Laternen II
3. **make sth. your own** etwas in deinen Besitz bringen II
of one's own eigene(r, s) V 2 (43)
on one's own alleine, selbstständig *(ohne Unterstützung)* V 3 (68)
owner ['əʊnə] Besitzer/in II
ox, *pl* oxen [ɒks], ['ɒksn] Ochse IV

P

p [pi:]: **50p** fünfzig Pence I
pack [pæk] packen, einpacken II
packet (of) ['pækɪt] Packung, Päckchen, Tüte II
page (= p.) [peɪdʒ] (Buch-, Heft-)Seite I **What page is it?** Auf welcher Seite sind wir? / Auf welcher Seite steht das? I
paid [peɪd] *siehe* **pay**
pain [peɪn] Schmerz; Plage III **Don't be a pain.** Nerv nicht. / Geh mir/uns nicht auf die Nerven. V 2 (40) **What a pain!** So ein Mist! / Es nervt. III
paint [peɪnt] lackieren, (be)malen, *(mit Farbe)* streichen V 1 (14)
painter ['peɪntə] Maler/in V 1 (14)
painting ['peɪntɪŋ] Gemälde, *(gemaltes)* Bild; Malerei V 1 (14) **body painting** Körperbemalung V 1 (14) **dot painting** Punktmalerei; Punktgemälde V 1 (15)
pair [peə] Paar V 4 (84)
palace ['pæləs] Palast III
°**palm (tree)** [pɑ:m] Palme
pan [pæn] Pfanne IV
panic ['pænɪk] in Panik geraten V 1 (19) **Don't panic.** Keine Panik. / Immer mit der Ruhe. V 1 (19)
pants [pænts] *(pl, AE)* (eine) Hose IV
paper ['peɪpə]:
1. Papier I
2. Zeitung II
do a paper round Zeitungen austragen II
parade [pə'reɪd] Parade, Umzug IV
paradise ['pærədaɪs] Paradies IV
paragraph ['pærəgrɑ:f] Absatz *(im Text)* III
paraphrase ['pærəfreɪz] umschreiben, mit anderen Worten sagen V 2 (49)
parents *(pl)* ['peərənts] Eltern I
park [pɑ:k]:
1. Park I
2. **park (a car)** parken III
parliament ['pɑ:ləmənt] Parlament III
part [pɑ:t] Teil II **take part (in)** teilnehmen (an), mitmachen (bei) III
partly ['pɑ:tli] teilweise III
partner ['pɑ:tnə] Partner/in I
part-time job [pɑ:t 'taɪm] Teilzeitjob, Halbtagsjob IV
party ['pɑ:ti] Party I **have a party** eine Party feiern I
party-goer ['pɑ:ti gəʊə] Partygast V 4 (88)
pass [pɑ:s]: **visitor pass** Besucherausweis IV
pass sb./sth. [pɑ:s]:
1. an jm./etwas vorbeigehen, vorbeifahren IV
2. **Pass the ball!** Spiel ab! III
passenger ['pæsɪndʒə] Passagier/in, Fahrgast II
passport ['pɑ:spɔ:t] (Reise-)Pass III
past [pɑ:st]:
1. **past the shop** am Geschäft vorbei II
2. **half past 6** halb 7 I
quarter past 6 viertel nach 6 I
past [pɑ:st] Vergangenheit II
pasta ['pæstə] Pasta, Nudeln III
pasty ['pæsti] Pastete *(mit Fleisch- oder Gemüsefüllung)* II
path [pɑ:θ] Weg, Pfad III
patient ['peɪʃnt] geduldig III
pattern ['pætn] *(wiederkehrendes)* Muster, Schema IV
pavement ['peɪvmənt] Gehweg, Bürgersteig IV
pay [peɪ]:
1. Bezahlung, Lohn IV
2. **pay (for sth.), paid, paid** (etwas be)zahlen III
it doesn't pay very well es wird nicht besonders gut bezahlt IV
PC (= police constable) [pi: 'si:], [pəli:s 'kʌnstəbl] Polizeimeister/in III
PC (= personal computer) [pi: 'si:], [pɜ:sənl kəm'pju:tə] PC IV
PE (physical education) [pi: 'i:], [fɪzɪkl edʒu'keɪʃn] (Schul-)Sport I
peaceful ['pi:sfl] friedlich, friedfertig IV
peanut ['pi:nʌt] Erdnuss II **peanut butter** Erdnussbutter II
peck sb. [pek] jm. ein Küsschen geben IV
pedestrian [pə'destriən] Fußgänger/in, Fußgänger- III
peer [pɪə] Gleichaltrige/r, Ebenbürtige/r, jemand aus derselben sozialen Gruppe V 2 (34)
peer pressure [pɪə 'preʃə] Gruppendruck, Gruppenzwang V 2 (34)
pelican ['pelɪkən] Pelikan IV
pen [pen] Kugelschreiber, Stift; Füller I
pence [pens] Pence *(Plural von Penny)* III
pencil ['pensl] Bleistift I
pencil case ['pensl keɪs] Federmäppchen I
pencil sharpener ['pensl ʃɑ:pnə] Bleistiftanspitzer I
penfriend ['penfrend] Brieffreund/in II
penny ['peni] Penny II
people ['pi:pl] Leute, Menschen I
per cent, percent [pə 'sent] Prozent IV
per hour/person [pɜ:], [pə] pro Stunde/Person III
perfect ['pɜ:fɪkt] perfekt II
°**perform** [pə'fɔ:m] aufführen **perform well/badly** eine gute/schlechte Leistung zeigen

°**performance** [pəˈfɔːməns] Vorstellung, Aufführung
perhaps [pəˈhæps] vielleicht III
period [ˈpɪəriəd] (Unterrichts-)Stunde IV
person [ˈpɜːsn] Person I
personal [ˈpɜːsənl] persönlich IV
personal computer [pɜːsənl kəmˈpjuːtə] PC IV
personal statement [pɜːsənl ˈsteɪtmənt] persönliche Beschreibung, Selbstbeschreibung V 3 (62)
personality [pɜːsəˈnæləti] Persönlichkeit; Charakter II
perspective [pəˈspektɪv] Perspektive IV **put sth. in perspective** etwas in Beziehung setzen, relativieren IV
persuade [pəˈsweɪd] überreden, überzeugen V 4 (97)
pet [pet] (Haus-)Tier I
petrol [ˈpetrəl] Benzin IV
°**pharmacist** [ˈfɑːməsɪst] Apotheker/in
°**pharmacy** [ˈfɑːməsi] Apotheke
phone [fəʊn]:
1. Telefon I
on the phone am Telefon I
2. anrufen I
°**phone for an ambulance** einen Krankenwagen rufen
phone call [ˈfəʊn kɔːl] (Telefon-)Anruf II
phone number [ˈfəʊn nʌmbə] Telefonnummer I
photo [ˈfəʊtəʊ] Foto I **take photos** Fotos machen II
photographer [fəˈtɒgrəfə] Fotograf/in IV
phrase [freɪz] Ausdruck, (Rede-)Wendung I
piano [piˈænəʊ] Klavier I
pick [pɪk] (aus)wählen, aussuchen II **pick on sb.** auf jm. herumhacken, jn. drangsalieren V 4 (91) **pick sth. up** etwas aufheben *(vom Boden)*, etwas hochheben II **pick sth. up** etwas kaufen, etwas *(aus einem Geschäft)* mitbringen V 3 (56) °**pick out** heraussuchen, auswählen °**pick sb. up** jn. abholen
picnic [ˈpɪknɪk] Picknick I
picture [ˈpɪktʃə]:
1. Bild I
2. **picture sth.** etwas abbilden; sich etwas vorstellen IV
pie [paɪ] (gedeckter) Obstkuchen; Pastete IV
piece [piːs] Stück IV **a piece of advice** ein Rat(schlag) IV
piercing [ˈpɪəsɪŋ] Piercing II
pig [pɪg] Schwein I
pilgrim [ˈpɪlgrɪm] Pilger/in II
°**pilot** [ˈpaɪlət] Pilot/in
pink [pɪŋk] rosa I
pirate [ˈpaɪrət] Pirat/in II
°**piss off** [pɪs ˈɒf] *(taboo)* sich verpissen
pitch [pɪtʃ] werfen, schlagen *(Ball)* IV
pity [ˈpɪti]: **That's a pity.** Das ist schade. I
pizza [ˈpiːtsə] Pizza I
place [pleɪs] Ort, Platz I **take place** stattfinden III
°**placemat** [ˈpleɪsmæt] Platzdeckchen
plan [plæn]:
1. Plan I
2. planen III
plane [pleɪn] Flugzeug III
plant [plɑːnt]:
1. Pflanze V 1 (15)
2. pflanzen V 1 (15)
plastic [ˈplæstɪk] Plastik, Kunststoff II **plastic bag** Plastiktüte II
plate [pleɪt] Teller IV
platform [ˈplætfɔːm] Bahnsteig II **at platform 4** auf Gleis 4 II
play [pleɪ]:
1. spielen I
play it cool *(infml)* sich cool geben IV **play the guitar/the drums** Gitarre/Schlagzeug spielen I
°2. (Theater-)Stück
player [ˈpleɪə] Spieler/in III
playground [ˈpleɪgraʊnd] Spielplatz IV
please [pliːz] bitte I
pleased [pliːzd] froh, erfreut, zufrieden V 2 (49) **Pleased to meet you.** Freut mich Sie kennenzulernen. V 2 (49)
plot [plɒt] Handlung(sverlauf) *(z.B. Film/Geschichte)* V 2 (47)
plough [plaʊ] pflügen IV
plow [plaʊ] *(AE)* pflügen IV
plus [plʌs] plus, (und) außerdem IV
pm [piːˈem]: **5 pm/5 p.m.** 5 Uhr nachmittags/abends, 17 Uhr I
pocket [ˈpɒkɪt] Tasche *(an Kleidungsstücken)* II
pocket money [ˈpɒkɪt mʌni] Taschengeld II
poem [ˈpəʊɪm] Gedicht I
°**poetry** [ˈpəʊətri] Dichtung, Lyrik, Poesie
point [pɔɪnt]:
1. Punkt III
point of view Standpunkt III
2. Argument V 4 (96)
make a point ein Argument vortragen V 4 (96) **make your point** sagen, wie du darüber denkst V 4 (96)
3. **2.5 million** 2,5 Millionen IV
point (at/to) [pɔɪnt] zeigen, deuten (auf) II **point a knife/gun at sb.** ein Messer/eine Waffe auf jn. richten V 4 (93)
°**poison** [ˈpɔɪzn] Gift
police *(pl)* [pəˈliːs] Polizei II
police officer [pəˈliːs ɒfɪsə] Polizeibeamter/-beamtin III
police station [pəˈliːs steɪʃn] Polizeiwache I
policy [ˈpɒləsi] Politik, Richtlinie(n), Bestimmung(en) III
polish [ˈpɒlɪʃ] Lack; Politur V 1 (22)
polite [pəˈlaɪt] höflich IV
°**politics** [ˈpɒlətɪks] Politik
pond [pɒnd] Teich I
pony [ˈpəʊni] Pony I
ponytail [ˈpəʊniteɪl] Pferdeschwanz *(Frisur)* V 1 (20)
pool [puːl] *(= swimming pool)* Schwimmbad IV
poor [pɔː], [pʊə] arm II **poor Ellie** (die) arme Ellie II
pop (music) [ˈpɒp mjuːzɪk] Pop(musik) III
°**pop** [pɒp] *(infml)* Papa, Vati
pop star [ˈpɒp stɑː] Popstar IV
popcorn [ˈpɒpkɔːn] Popcorn II
popular [ˈpɒpjələ] beliebt, populär II
populate [ˈpɒpjuleɪt] bevölkern, besiedeln IV
population [pɒpjuˈleɪʃn] Bevölkerung, Einwohner(zahl) IV
porch [pɔːtʃ] *(AE)* Veranda IV
port [pɔːt] Hafen(stadt) III
portrait [ˈpɔːtreɪt] Porträt V 4 (85)
self-portrait Selbstporträt V 4 (85)
position [pəˈzɪʃn] Position, (Arbeits-)Stelle, Platz IV
positive [ˈpɒzətɪv] positiv I
possible [ˈpɒsəbl] möglich IV
post [pəʊst]:
1. Post II
2. posten *(im Internet veröffentlichen)* IV
posted by gepostet von *(= in ein Blog gestellt)* IV
3. **Keep me posted!** Halt mich auf dem Laufenden! III
post office [ˈpəʊst ɒfɪs] Post(amt) II
postcard [ˈpəʊstkɑːd] Postkarte II
poster [ˈpəʊstə] Poster I
postman/-woman [ˈpəʊstmən, -wʊmən] Briefträger/in III
pot [pɒt] Topf III
potato, *pl* potatoes [pəˈteɪtəʊ] Kartoffel II
potato chips [pəˈteɪtəʊ tʃɪps] *(pl, AE)* (Kartoffel-)Chips IV
pottery [ˈpɒtəri] Töpferware(n), Töpferei, Töpfer- IV
pound [paʊnd] hämmern, schlagen, pochen IV
pound (£) [paʊnd] Pfund *(britische Währung)* I
powerful [ˈpaʊəfl] kräftig, stark, mächtig IV
practice [ˈpræktɪs]:
1. Übung; Training IV
2. Probe *(Band, Chor)* IV
practice [ˈpræktɪs] *(AE)* üben IV
practise [ˈpræktɪs] üben I
prefer sth. to sth. [prɪˈfɜː] etwas einer Sache vorziehen, etwas lieber tun/haben als etwas III **I'd prefer …** ich würde … vorziehen I
prejudice [ˈpredʒudɪs] Vorurteil, Voreingenommenheit V 2 (37)

prepare (for) [prɪ'peə] vorbereiten; sich vorbereiten (auf) II
present ['preznt]:
1. Gegenwart II
2. Geschenk I
°3. vorhanden; anwesend
present sth. (to sb.) [prɪ'zent] (jm.) etwas präsentieren, (jm.) etwas vorstellen III
presentation [prezn'teɪʃn] Referat, Präsentation III
presenter [prɪ'zentə] Referent/in V 1 (24)
president ['prezɪdənt] Präsident/in IV
press [pres] drücken V 1 (22)
pressure ['preʃə] Druck V 2 (34)
pretend (to be sth.) [prɪ'tend] so tun, als ob (man etwas wäre) V 3 (68)
pretty ['prɪti] hübsch III
price [praɪs] (Kauf-)Preis I
pride (in) [praɪd] Stolz (auf) III
°**primary school** ['praɪməri sku:l] Grundschule
prime minister [praɪm 'mɪnɪstə] Premierminister/in III
prince [prɪns] Prinz III
princess [prɪn'ses] Prinzessin III
principal ['prɪnsəpl] Rektor/in, Schulleiter/in I
prison ['prɪzn] Gefängnis IV **put sb. in prison** jn. ins Gefängnis sperren V 1 (15)
°**prisoner** ['prɪznə] Gefangene/r, Häftling
private ['praɪvət] privat; persönlich III
prize [praɪz] Preis, Gewinn II
probably ['prɒbəbli] wahrscheinlich III
problem ['prɒbləm] Problem I
product ['prɒdʌkt] Produkt III
professional [prə'feʃənl] professionell, Profi-; Profi IV
profile ['prəʊfaɪl] Profil; Beschreibung, Portrait V 4 (84)
profit ['prɒfɪt] Gewinn *(Profit)* III
program ['prəʊgræm] *(AE)* Programm V 3 (68)
programme ['prəʊgræm] (Fernseh-)Sendung I
project ['prɒdʒekt] Projekt II
prom [prɒm] *(AE)* Schulball IV
promise ['prɒmɪs]:
1. Versprechen IV
2. versprechen IV
°**properly** ['prɒpəli] richtig, ordentlich, korrekt
pros [prəʊz]: **the pros and cons** *(pl)* das Pro und Kontra; das Für und Wider V 4 (82)
°**prosthetic leg** [prɒs'θetɪk] Beinprothese
protect (from) [prə'tekt] (be)schützen (vor) IV
protest [prə'test] protestieren IV
Protestant ['prɒtɪstənt] Protestant/in; protestantisch, evangelisch II
proud (of) [praʊd] stolz (auf) I
PS (= postscript) [pi: 'es] PS, Postskript *(Nachschrift unter Briefen)* IV

pub [pʌb] Kneipe III
public ['pʌblɪk] öffentlich III
public transport [pʌblɪk 'trænspɔ:t] öffentlicher Personenverkehr III
pull [pʊl] ziehen II **pull back** sich zurückziehen, zurückweichen V 3 (70) **pull back your hair** sich die Haare zusammenbinden V 3 (70) **pull in** an den Straßenrand fahren, anhalten IV **pull over** anhalten, an den Straßenrand fahren V 1 (21)
pullover ['pʊləʊvə] Pullover I
pumps *(pl)* [pʌmps] Pumps *(elegante Damenschuhe)* V 3 (69)
punctual ['pʌŋktʃuəl] pünktlich V 3 (58)
puppet ['pʌpɪt] Puppe *(Handpuppe, Marionette)* II
purple ['pɜ:pl] violett, lila I
push [pʊʃ]:
1. schieben I
2. stoßen, schubsen IV
push sb. around jn. herumkommandieren IV
pushchair ['pʊʃtʃeə] (Kinder-)Sportwagen, Buggy II
put [pʊt], **put, put** *(etwas wohin)* tun, legen, stellen, stecken I **put down** hinlegen IV **put sth. on** etwas anziehen *(Kleidung)*; etwas aufsetzen *(Hut)* II **put sth. up (on social media)** etwas (in soziale Medien) (ein)stellen V 4 (84) **put up your hand** sich melden III
puzzled ['pʌzld] verwirrt, verwundert III
pyjamas *(pl)* [pə'dʒɑ:məz] Schlafanzug II

Q

quad [kwɒd] Quad *(vierrädriges Motorrad)* IV
qualification [kwɒlɪfɪ'keɪʃn] (Schul-)Abschluss, Qualifikation V 3 (60)
qualified ['kwɒlɪfaɪd] qualifiziert; ausgebildet, mit Abschluss V 3 (60)
qualify ['kwɒlɪfaɪ] (sich) qualifizieren V 3 (60)
quarter ['kwɔ:tə] Viertel I **quarter past 6** viertel nach 6 I **quarter to 7** viertel vor 7 I
queen [kwi:n] Königin III
question ['kwestʃən] Frage I **ask questions** Fragen stellen I
°**question mark** ['kwestʃən mɑ:k] Fragezeichen
queue [kju:] (Warte-)Schlange II
quick [kwɪk] schnell I
quiet ['kwaɪət] ruhig, still, leise I
quite [kwaɪt] ziemlich II
quiz [kwɪz] Quiz I
°**quote** [kwəʊt] Zitat

R

rabbit ['ræbɪt] Kaninchen I
raccoon [rə'ku:n] Waschbär IV

race [reɪs]:
1. (Wett-)Rennen V 1 (18)
2. rasen, schnell fahren V 1 (18)
racer ['reɪsə] Rennfahrer/in V 1 (18)
racing ['reɪsɪŋ] Rennsport V 1 (18)
racism ['reɪsɪzəm] Rassismus IV
racist ['reɪsɪst] Rassist/in; rassistisch V 2 (37)
radio ['reɪdiəʊ] Radio IV
rain [reɪn]:
1. Regen II
2. regnen II
rainforest ['reɪnfɒrɪst] Regenwald V 3 (64)
rainy ['reɪni] regnerisch II
raise (money) [reɪz] (Geld für gute Zwecke) sammeln IV
ran [ræn] *siehe* **run**
ranch [rɑ:ntʃ] Ranch, Viehfarm IV
rang [ræŋ] *siehe* **ring**
ranger ['reɪndʒə] *Aufseher/in in einem Nationalpark* II
°**rank** [ræŋk] einstufen, anordnen
rap [ræp]:
1. Rap I
2. rappen I
rapper ['ræpə] Rapper/in I
°**rare** [reə] selten
rat [ræt] Ratte I
°**rather** ['rɑ:ðə] ziemlich **rather than** anstelle von, (an)statt
reach (sb./a place) [ri:tʃ] (jn./einen Ort) erreichen V 4 (88)
react (to) [ri'ækt] reagieren (auf) III
°**reaction (to)** [ri'ækʃn] Reaktion (auf)
read [red] *siehe* **read**
read [ri:d], **read, read** lesen I
reader ['ri:də] Leser/in III
ready ['redi] fertig, bereit I **get ready (for)** sich fertig machen (für), sich vorbereiten (auf) I
real [rɪəl] echt, wirklich I
realistic [ri:ə'lɪstɪk] realistisch V 4 (90)
reality [ri'æləti] Realität, Wirklichkeit II **reality show** Realityshow II
realize sth. ['ri:əlaɪz] etwas erkennen, sich einer Sache bewusst werden V 3 (68)
really ['ri:əli], ['rɪəli] wirklich I
reason ['ri:zn] Grund, Begründung III **for lots of reasons** aus vielen Gründen III
recent ['ri:snt] aktuell, jüngst III
recently ['ri:sntli] in letzter Zeit; vor Kurzem III
receptionist [rɪ'sepʃənɪst] Empfangschef/in III
recipe ['resəpi] (Koch-)Rezept I
°**recommend sth. (to sb.)** [rekə'mend] (jm.) etwas empfehlen
recommendation [rekəmən'deɪʃn] Empfehlung IV
°**record** [rɪ'kɔ:d] aufnehmen, aufzeichnen

recycle [riːˈsaɪkl] recyceln, wiederverwerten II
red [red] rot I
redial [riːˈdaɪəl] die Wahlwiederholung betätigen V 1 (22)
redness [ˈrednəs] Rötung, Röte V 1 (13)
reduce (by) [rɪˈdjuːs] reduzieren, verringern (um) V 4 (86)
reef [riːf] Riff V 1 (9)
reference [ˈrefrəns] Referenz, Empfehlung; jd., der eine Referenz erteilt V 3 (62)
°**refresh** [rɪˈfreʃ] (sich) erfrischen
reggae [ˈregeɪ] Reggae(musik) II
°**regret** [rɪˈgret] bedauern, bereuen
regular [ˈregjələ] regelmäßig, normal V 1 (19)
relationship [rɪˈleɪʃnʃɪp] Beziehung, Verhältnis IV
relative [ˈrelətɪv] Verwandte/r IV
relax [rɪˈlæks] sich entspannen II
relaxing [rɪˈlæksɪŋ] entspannend, beruhigend II
reliable [rɪˈlaɪəbl] zuverlässig, verlässlich V 3 (58)
remember [rɪˈmembə]:
1. sich erinnern (an) I
2. daran denken, nicht vergessen I
remind sb. of sth. [rɪˈmaɪnd] jn. an etwas erinnern IV
remote [rɪˈməʊt] entlegen, abgelegen V 1 (18)
rent [rent] mieten, leihen IV
repair [rɪˈpeə] reparieren IV
repeat [rɪˈpiːt] wiederholen V 4 (86)
°**rephrase** [riːˈfreɪz] umformulieren, anders ausdrücken
°**replace (with)** [rɪˈpleɪs] ersetzen, austauschen
report [rɪˈpɔːt]:
1. Bericht IV
2. **report (on)** berichten (über) IV
°**report to sb.** jm. berichten
reporter [rɪˈpɔːtə] Reporter/in III
request [rɪˈkwest] Wunsch, Bitte; Anfrage V 2 (41)
requirement [rɪˈkwaɪəmənt] Voraussetzung, Anforderung V 3 (63)
rescue [ˈreskjuː] Rettung(sdienst) IV
research [rɪˈsɜːtʃ]:
1. erforschen, untersuchen, recherchieren II
°2. Forschung(en), Recherche(n)
°**do research** recherchieren
reservation [rezəˈveɪʃn]:
1. Reservierung, Buchung III
2. Reservat *(Gebiet)* IV
reserve [rɪˈzɜːv] Schutzgebiet V 3 (64)
resident [ˈrezɪdənt] Anwohner/in, Bewohner/in III
resort [rɪˈzɔːt] Urlaubsort V 3 (62)
°**resource** [rɪˈsɔːs] (Hilfs-)Mittel, Ressource

respect [rɪˈspekt]:
1. Respekt III
2. respektieren, achten III
respectable [rɪˈspektəbl] anständig, angesehen, ehrbar V 2 (44)
respectful (to) [rɪˈspektfl] respektvoll (gegenüber) V 4 (97)
°**response** [rɪˈspɒns] Reaktion, Antwort
responsibility [rɪspɒnsəˈbɪləti] Aufgabe, Zuständigkeit V 3 (63)
responsible (for) [rɪˈspɒnsəbl] verantwortlich (für); verantwortungsbewusst IV
rest [rest]:
1. sich ausruhen III
2. Pause, Rast I
°**take a rest** Pause machen
restaurant [ˈrestrɒnt] Restaurant I
restroom [ˈrestruːm] *(AE)* Toilette *(in öffentlichen Gebäuden)* IV
result [rɪˈzʌlt] Ergebnis, Resultat III
return [rɪˈtɜːn] zurückkehren, zurückkommen V 4 (90)
review [rɪˈvjuː] Besprechung, Rezension, Kritik IV
reviewer [rɪˈvjuːə] Rezensent/in, Kritiker/in IV
°**revision** [rɪˈvɪʃn] Wiederholung *(von Lernstoff)*
rhyme [raɪm]:
1. (sich) reimen II
2. Reim II
rice [raɪs] Reis III
rich [rɪtʃ] reich V 4 (91)
rid [rɪd]: **get rid of sth.** etwas loswerden II
ridden [ˈrɪdn] *siehe* **ride**
ride [raɪd] Fahrt; Fahrgeschäft *(auf Volksfest, in Vergnügungspark)* III
ride [raɪd], **rode, ridden**:
1. reiten I
2. fahren I
ride a bike/a BMX mit dem Fahrrad/dem BMX-Rad fahren I
right [raɪt]:
1. richtig I
be right Recht haben I
2. rechts; nach rechts I
on the right rechts, auf der rechten Seite I
3. **right now** gerade jetzt, genau jetzt III
right [raɪt] Recht IV **civil rights** *(pl)* Bürgerrechte IV **have every right to do sth.** guten Grund / das Recht haben, etwas zu tun V 2 (44)
ring [rɪŋ], **rang, rung**:
1. läuten, klingeln I
2. anrufen III
ringtone [ˈrɪŋtəʊn] Klingelton III
°**rip current** [ˈrɪp kʌrənt] Brandungsrückstrom *(gefährliche Strömung an Küsten)*
rise (by) [raɪz], **rose, risen** (an)steigen (um) IV

risen [ˈrɪzən] *siehe* **rise**
risk [rɪsk]:
1. riskieren, wagen V 1 (21)
2. Risiko IV
take a risk ein Risiko eingehen IV
°**at (your) own risk** auf eigene Gefahr
°**risky** [ˈrɪski] riskant
river [ˈrɪvə] Fluss II
road [rəʊd] Straße *(Landstraße zwischen Orten; Straße in Orten)* I
road trip [ˈrəʊd trɪp] Autoreise V 1 (9)
°**roadside** [ˈrəʊdsaɪd] (am) Straßenrand
rock [rɒk]:
1. Fels(en) I
2. Rock(musik) II
3. **Sydney rocks.** *(infml)* Sydney bringt's. / In Sydney geht die Post ab. V 1 (16)
rock climbing [ˈrɒk klaɪmɪŋ] Felsklettern II
°**rocket** [ˈrɒkɪt] rasen, schießen
rocking chair [ˈrɒkɪŋ tʃeə] Schaukelstuhl IV
rode [rəʊd] *siehe* **ride**
role [rəʊl] Rolle IV
role model [ˈrəʊl mɒdl] Vorbild III
role-play [ˈrəʊl pleɪ] Rollenspiel IV
roll [rəʊl]:
1. rollen; (sich) verdrehen *(Augen)* III
2. schaukeln, schwanken *(Schiff)* IV
°**roll as one** gemeinsam vorankommen
°**roller skating** [ˈrəʊlə skeɪtɪŋ] Rollschuhlaufen
Roman [ˈrəʊmən] Römer/in; römisch II
romance [rəʊˈmæns] Romanze; Romantik IV
romantic [rəʊˈmæntɪk] romantisch IV
roof [ruːf] Dach IV
room [ruːm], [rʊm] Raum, Zimmer I
rose [rəʊz] *siehe* **rise**
°**rose** [rəʊz] Rose
round [raʊnd]:
1. rund II
2. **do a paper round** Zeitungen austragen II
route [ruːt] Route, Weg III
routine [ruːˈtiːn] Routine IV
rubber [ˈrʌbə]:
1. Radiergummi I
2. Gummi IV
rubbish [ˈrʌbɪʃ]:
1. (Haus-)Müll, Abfall II
2. *(infml)* Unsinn, Quatsch III
That's rubbish. Das ist Unsinn. / Das ist Quatsch. III
rucksack [ˈrʌksæk] Rucksack II
rude [ruːd] unhöflich, frech III
rug [rʌg] Teppich, Läufer I
rugby [ˈrʌgbi] Rugby II
ruins *(pl)* [ˈruːɪnz] Ruine II
rule [ruːl] Regel II
ruler [ˈruːlə] Lineal I

run [rʌn], **ran, run** rennen, laufen II **run a business/a hotel** eine Firma/ein Hotel leiten, führen III **run out** knapp werden V 3 (56) **I often run out of money.** Mir geht oft das Geld aus. / Bei mir wird oft das Geld knapp. V 3 (56) °**run (a program)** (ein Programm) anbieten, abhalten

rung [rʌŋ] *siehe* **ring**

runner ['rʌnə] Läufer/in III

rural ['rʊərəl] ländlich IV

rustler ['rʌslə] Viehdieb/in IV

S

°**sacred** ['seɪkrɪd] heilig

sad [sæd] traurig I

sadness ['sædnəs] Traurigkeit V 1 (13)

safe [seɪf] sicher *(gefahrlos)* IV

safety ['seɪfti] Sicherheit II

said [sed] *siehe* **say**

sail [seɪl] segeln, *(mit dem Schiff)* fahren II

sailor ['seɪlə] Seemann; Matrose/Matrosin II

salad ['sæləd] Salat *(als Gericht oder Beilage)* I

salami [sə'lɑːmi] Salami II

salary ['sæləri] Lohn, Gehalt V 3 (60)

sale [seɪl] Verkauf; Schlussverkauf I

salesperson ['seɪlzpɜːsn] Verkäufer/in III

salt [sɔːlt] Salz III

same [seɪm]: **the same** derselbe/dieselbe/dasselbe; dieselben I

sample ['sɑːmpl] Muster, Probe(exemplar) V 4 (86)

sand [sænd] Sand I

sandals *(pl)* ['sændlz] Sandalen V 3 (70)

sandwich ['sænwɪtʃ], ['sænwɪdʒ] Sandwich I

°**sandy** ['sændi] sandig, Sand-

sang [sæŋ] *siehe* **sing**

sank [sæŋk] *siehe* **sink**

sat [sæt] *siehe* **sit**

Saturday ['sætədeɪ], ['sætədi] Samstag I

sauce [sɔːs] Sauce V 3 (56)

sausage ['sɒsɪdʒ] Wurst, Würstchen I

save [seɪv]:
1. retten III
2. sparen *(Geld, Zeit)* II
3. **God save the Queen.** Gott (be)schütze die Königin. III

savvy ['sævi] *(infml)* versiert, gewieft, erfahren V 4 (86)

saw [sɔː] *siehe* **see**

saw [sɔː] Säge IV

°**saxophone** ['sæksəfəʊn] Saxofon

say [seɪ], **said, said** sagen I **Say hi to everybody.** Grüß alle. I **say sorry** sich entschuldigen V 1 (15)

scan (a text for) [skæn] (einenText) überfliegen (nach), absuchen (nach) IV

scarecrow ['skeəkrəʊ] Vogelscheuche II

scared [skeəd]: **be scared (of)** Angst haben (vor) II

scarf, *pl* **scarves** [skɑːf], [skɑːvz] Schal II

scary ['skeəri] unheimlich, beängstigend, gruselig I

scene [siːn] Szene I

school [skuːl] Schule I **school is out** die Schule ist aus/vorbei I **at school** in der Schule I

school bag ['skuːl bæg] Schultasche I

science ['saɪəns] Naturwissenschaft I

science fiction, *infml auch* **sci-fi** [saɪəns 'fɪkʃn], ['saɪ faɪ] Sciencefiction III

scissors *(pl)* ['sɪzəz] Schere I

scone [skɒn] Milchbrötchen *(leicht süß, oft mit Rosinen)* I

score [skɔː] *(Punkt/Tor/Treffer)* erzielen IV

Scot [skɒt] Schotte/Schottin III

Scotland ['skɒtlənd] Schottland III

Scottish ['skɒtɪʃ] schottisch, aus Schottland III

scrambled eggs *(pl)* [skræmbld 'egz] Rührei IV

scream [skriːm] schreien II

screen [skriːn] Leinwand; Bildschirm V 1 (25)

screenager ['skriːneɪdʒə] Screenager *(Jugendliche/r, der/die sehr viel Zeit vor dem Bildschirm verbringt)* V 4 (82)

screenshot ['skriːnʃɒt] Screenshot *(Bildschirmabbild)* V 4 (87)

sea [siː] Meer, (die) See I **the sea's coming in** die Flut kommt; das Wasser steigt I

sea lion ['siː laɪən] Seelöwe IV

seagull ['siːgʌl] Möwe I

search [sɜːtʃ]:
1. Suche IV
2. **search (for sth.)** (etwas/nach etwas) suchen IV

seasick ['siːsɪk] seekrank IV

season ['siːzn] Jahreszeit II

°**seasonal** ['siːzənl] Saison-, saisonal

seat [siːt] (Sitz-)Platz I

second ['sekənd]:
1. zweite(r, s) I
2. Sekunde IV

second-hand [sekənd 'hænd] second-hand, aus zweiter Hand II **second-hand shop** Second-Hand-Laden II

Secondly, … ['sekəndli] Zweitens … III

secret ['siːkrət]:
1. Geheimnis II
2. geheim II

°**security** [sɪ'kjʊərəti] Sicherheit

see [siː], **saw, seen** sehen I **See for yourself.** Sieh selbst! / Sehen Sie selbst! V 2 (43) **See you around.** Bis dann. V 2 (49) **See you later.** Bis später. I **I see.** Ach so. / Aha. / Verstehe. II

°**seek shade** [siːk], **sought, sought** Schatten (auf)suchen

seem (to be/do) [siːm] erscheinen; (zu sein/zu tun) scheinen IV

seen [siːn] *siehe* **see**

segregate ['segrɪgeɪt] trennen IV

segregation [segrɪ'geɪʃn] Trennung *(nach Rasse/Religion/Geschlecht)* IV

°**self-confident** [self 'kɒnfɪdənt] selbstbewusst, selbstsicher

selfie ['selfi] Selfie *(Schnappschuss von sich selbst)* V 4 (85)

self-portrait [self 'pɔːtreɪt] Selbstporträt V 4 (85)

sell [sel], **sold, sold**:
1. verkaufen III
°2. sich verkaufen (lassen)

send [send], **sent, sent** senden, schicken I

sent [sent] *siehe* **send**

sentence ['sentəns] Satz II

separate ['seprət] getrennt, separat IV

September [sep'tembə] September I

serious ['sɪəriəs] ernst(haft) III

seriously ['sɪəriəsli] im Ernst III

servant ['sɜːvənt] Diener/in, Bedienstete/r IV

serve [sɜːv] servieren *(Essen, Getränke)*; bedienen *(Kundschaft)* III **serve sb. (with sth.)** jn. betreuen, (mit etwas) versorgen, jm. behilflich sein V 3 (61)

service ['sɜːvɪs] Dienst II **emergency services** *(pl)* Rettungsdienste II

set [set]: **(film) set** Bühnenbild, (Film-)Kulisse IV

set, set, set [set]: **set the table** den Tisch decken I °**set sth. up** etwas einrichten, aufbauen

setting ['setɪŋ] Schauplatz *(z.B. Film/Geschichte)* V 2 (47)

settler ['setlə] Siedler/in IV

seven ['sevn] sieben I

several ['sevrəl] mehrere, einige IV

shack [ʃæk] Baracke, Hütte IV

shade [ʃeɪd] Schatten *(vor der Sonne geschützt)* V 1 (12)

shadow ['ʃædəʊ] Schatten *(Umriss)* V 1 (12)

shake [ʃeɪk], **shook, shaken** schütteln III **shake sb.'s hand** jm. die Hand schütteln III

shaken ['ʃeɪkən] *siehe* **shake**

Shall I …? [ʃæl], [ʃəl] Soll ich …? IV

shame [ʃeɪm]: **a shame** eine Schande; schade V 2 (37)

shampoo [ʃæm'puː] Shampoo IV

share [ʃeə] teilen I **share a room with …** sich ein Zimmer mit … teilen I

shark [ʃɑːk] Hai V 1 (11)

sharpener ['ʃɑːpnə] Anspitzer I

she [ʃiː] sie *(weibliche Person)* I

sheep, *pl* **sheep** [ʃiːp] Schaf I

°**sheep station** ['ʃiːp steɪʃn] Schaffarm *(in Australien)*

sheepdog ['ʃiːpdɒg] Hütehund *(zum Hüten von Schafen)* III

sheet [ʃiːt] Blatt *(Papier)* V 4 (97)

shelf, *pl* **shelves** [ʃelf], [ʃelvz] Regal I

sheriff ['ʃerɪf] *(AE)* Sheriff IV
shift [ʃɪft] Schicht *(bei der Arbeit)* V 3 (61) **work shifts** im Schichtdienst arbeiten V 3 (61)
shine [ʃaɪn], **shone, shone** scheinen *(Sonne)*; leuchten, strahlen, glänzen III
ship [ʃɪp] Schiff II
shirt [ʃɜːt] Hemd I
shock [ʃɒk]:
1. Schock III
2. schockieren V 4 (96)
shocked [ʃɒkt] schockiert III
shocking ['ʃɒkɪŋ] schockierend V 4 (96)
shoe [ʃuː] Schuh I
shoestring ['ʃuːstrɪŋ]: **on a shoestring** *(infml)* mit ganz wenig Geld IV
shone [ʃɒn] *siehe* **shine**
shook [ʃʊk] *siehe* **shake**
shoot [ʃuːt], **shot, shot** schießen; anschießen, erschießen IV
shop [ʃɒp]:
1. Laden, Geschäft I
2. einkaufen, „shoppen" III
shopper ['ʃɒpə] Käufer/in IV
shopping ['ʃɒpɪŋ]: **shopping centre** Einkaufszentrum I **shopping list** Einkaufsliste V 3 (56) **shopping mall** Einkaufszentrum III **do the shopping** Einkäufe erledigen, einkaufen gehen V 3 (56) **go shopping** einkaufen gehen I
short [ʃɔːt]:
1. kurz II
2. klein *(Person)* II
short cut [ʃɔːt 'kʌt] Abkürzung V 4 (92)
short story [ʃɔːt 'stɔːri] Kurzgeschichte V 3 (68)
shorts *(pl)* [ʃɔːts] kurze Hose I
shot [ʃɒt]:
1. Schuss III
2. *siehe* **shoot**
should [ʃʊd]: **What should I do?** Was sollte ich tun? II **You shouldn't have.** Das wäre doch nicht nötig gewesen. III
shoulder ['ʃəʊldə] Schulter I
shout [ʃaʊt] rufen II
show [ʃəʊ] Show, Vorführung, Aufführung II
show [ʃəʊ], **showed, shown**:
1. zeigen I
2. sich zeigen, sichtbar sein V 2 (38)
shower ['ʃaʊə]:
1. Dusche; Schauer III
°2. (sich) duschen
shown [ʃəʊn] *siehe* **show**
Shut up! [ʃʌt 'ʌp] *(infml)* Halt den Mund! I
shy [ʃaɪ] scheu, schüchtern II
sick [sɪk] krank IV **I'm/I feel sick.** Mir ist schlecht/übel. IV
side [saɪd] Seite *(z.B. Straßenseite)* III **side by side** Seite an Seite IV
sidewalk ['saɪdwɔːk] *(AE)* Gehweg, Bürgersteig IV
sight [saɪt]:
1. Anblick, Bild I
2. Sehenswürdigkeit III
°3. sichten
°**sightseeing** ['saɪtsiːɪŋ] Besichtigung (von Sehenswürdigkeiten)
sign [saɪn]:
1. Schild; Zeichen I
2. unterschreiben IV
signal ['sɪgnəl] Signal III
silence ['saɪləns] Stille IV
°**silent** ['saɪlənt] still, lautlos
silly ['sɪli] dumm, blöd; albern II
similar (to sb./sth.) ['sɪmələ] (jm./einer Sache) ähnlich IV
simple ['sɪmpl] einfach, simpel V 1 (19)
since August [sɪns] seit August III
sincerely [sɪn'sɪəli]: **Sincerely ...** *(AE)* Mit freundlichen Grüßen *(Briefschluss)* IV **Sincerely yours** *(AE)* Mit freundlichen Grüßen *(Briefschluss)* V 3 (63) **Yours sincerely** Mit freundlichen Grüßen *(Briefschluss)* III
sing [sɪŋ], **sang, sung** singen I
singer ['sɪŋə] Sänger/in I
single ['sɪŋgl] ledig, alleinstehend II **single parent** Alleinerziehende/r IV
sink [sɪŋk], **sank, sunk** sinken V 1 (22) **sink down in your seat** auf dem Sitz zusammensinken, nach unten rutschen V 1 (22)
sir [sɜː]:
1. mein Herr *(höfliche Anrede z.B. für einen Kunden oder Vorgesetzten)* II
2. (gnädiger) Herr V 3 (63)
Dear Sir/Madam Sehr geehrte Damen und Herren V 3 (63)
°**sis** [sɪs] *(infml)* Schwester *(kurz für: sister)*
sister ['sɪstə] Schwester I
sit [sɪt], **sat, sat** sitzen; sich setzen I **sit up** sich aufsetzen, sich gerade hinsetzen V 1 (22)
site [saɪt] Stelle, Platz, Stätte III
situation [sɪtʃu'eɪʃn] Situation II
six [sɪks] sechs I
size [saɪz] Größe IV **What size do you take?** Welche Größe hast du? IV
skateboard ['skeɪtbɔːd]:
1. Skateboard fahren I
2. Skateboard I
skating ['skeɪtɪŋ] *(= ice skating)* Schlittschuhlaufen; *(= roller skating)* Rollschuhlaufen V 2 (42)
skewer ['skjuːə] (Grill-)Spieß IV
ski [skiː]:
1. Ski laufen, Ski fahren II
2. Ski(-) V 3 (60)
skier ['skiːə] Skiläufer/in III
skill [skɪl] Fähigkeit, Fertigkeit V 3 (57)
skim a text [skɪm] einen Text überfliegen *(um den Inhalt grob zu erfassen)* III
skin [skɪn]:
1. Haut; Schale *(z.B. Banane)* IV
2. häuten IV
skinny ['skɪni] *(infml)* mager, dürr III
skipping ['skɪpɪŋ] Seilspringen III
skirt [skɜːt] Rock I
skive [skaɪv] *(infml)* *(Schule)* schwänzen II
sky [skaɪ] Himmel II
skyline ['skaɪlaɪn] Skyline *(Silhouette einer Stadt)* IV
skyscraper ['skaɪskreɪpə] Wolkenkratzer IV
slam [slæm] (zu-, hin)knallen V 3 (69) **slam down the phone** den Hörer aufknallen V 3 (69)
°**slap on a hat** [slæp] *(infml)* einen Hut/eine Mütze aufsetzen
slave [sleɪv] Sklave, Sklavin IV
slavery ['sleɪvəri] Sklaverei III
sleep [sliːp]:
1. Schlaf II
Go to sleep! Schlaf jetzt! I
2. **sleep, slept, slept** schlafen I
sleeping bag ['sliːpɪŋ bæg] Schlafsack I
sleepover ['sliːpəʊvə] Schlafparty I
sleepy ['sliːpi] müde, verschlafen III
slept [slept] *siehe* **sleep**
°**slid** [slɪd] *siehe* **slide**
°**slide on some sunglasses** [slaɪd], **slid, slid** eine Sonnenbrille aufsetzen
°**slip on a T-Shirt** [slɪp] ein T-Shirt überziehen
slogan ['sləʊgən] Slogan V 4 (90)
°**slop on some suncream** [slɒp] *(infml)* Sonnencreme auftragen
slow [sləʊ] langsam I
small [smɔːl] klein I
smart [smɑːt] schick, smart; schlau, clever IV
smartphone ['smɑːtfəʊn] Smartphone V 4 (82)
smell [smel]:
1. riechen II
2. Geruch IV
smelly ['smeli]: **be smelly** stinken II
smile [smaɪl]:
1. lächeln II
2. *(ein)* Lächeln II
smoke [sməʊk] rauchen IV
smoothie ['smuːði] Smoothie *(Getränk aus Fruchtpüree, evtl. mit Milchprodukten)* II
smoothie maker ['smuːði meɪkə] Smoothie-Maker III
smuggler ['smʌglə] Schmuggler/in I
snack [snæk] Snack, kleine Mahlzeit II
snake [sneɪk] Schlange I
sneakers ['sniːkəz] *(pl, AE)* Sportschuhe IV
sniff (at) [snɪf] schnüffeln, schnuppern (an) II
snow [snəʊ] Schnee II
°**snowboard** ['snəʊbɔːd] Snowboard fahren

snowy ['snəʊi] schneebedeckt; verschneit II
so [səʊ]:
1. also, daher I
2. so II
so far bis jetzt, bis hierher II **so that** sodass, damit IV
3. I don't think so. Das glaube/denke ich nicht. III
I think so. Ich glaube ja. III
soap [səʊp] Seife; *(infml auch:)* Seifenoper II
soccer ['sɒkə] Fußball IV
social ['səʊʃl] gesellschaftlich, sozial; gesellig V 3 (62)
social media *(pl)* [səʊʃl 'mi:diə] soziale Medien/Dienste V 3 (62)
social skills *(pl)* [səʊʃl 'skɪlz] Sozialkompetenz V 3 (62)
sock [sɒk] Socke I
sofa ['səʊfə] Sofa I
°**soft drink** ['sɒft drɪŋk] alkoholfreies Getränk
sold [səʊld] *siehe* **sell**
soldier ['səʊldʒə] Soldat/in IV
solution (to a problem) [sə'lu:ʃn] Lösung (eines Problems) V 2 (36)
solve [sɒlv] lösen *(Rätsel, Problem)*, lüften *(Geheimnis)* III
some [sʌm], [səm] einige, ein paar; etwas, ein wenig I **Would you like some tea/chips?** Möchtest du (etwas) Tee / (ein paar) Pommes frites? II
somebody ['sʌmbədi] jemand II
someone ['sʌmwʌn] jemand II
someplace ['sʌmpleɪs] *(AE)* irgendwo(hin) IV
something ['sʌmθɪŋ] etwas I **... or something** ... oder so was III
sometime ['sʌmtaɪm] irgendwann V 2 (49)
sometimes ['sʌmtaɪmz] manchmal I
somewhere ['sʌmweə] irgendwo(hin) III
son [sʌn] Sohn III
song [sɒŋ] Lied I
soon [su:n] bald I **as soon as** sobald; so bald wie V 1 (12)
sore [sɔ:] schmerzhaft II **a sore throat** Halsschmerzen II **I have a sore leg.** Mein Bein tut weh. I
Sorry. / I'm sorry. ['sɒri] Tut mir leid. / Entschuldigung. I **say sorry** sich entschuldigen V 1 (15)
°**sought** [sɔ:t] *siehe* **seek**
sound [saʊnd]:
1. klingen III
2. Geräusch; Klang, Laut I
°**3.** Ton *(Fernseher, Radio)*
soup [su:p] Suppe I
south [saʊθ] Süden; nach Süden II **south-east** Südosten; nach Südosten II **south-west** Südwesten; nach Südwesten II

southbound ['saʊθbaʊnd] in Richtung Süden III
southern ['sʌðən] südlich, Süd- IV
souvenir [su:və'nɪə] Souvenir III
space [speɪs] Platz I
°**spare room** [speə 'ru:m] Gästezimmer
speak [spi:k], **spoke, spoken** sprechen I **speak to sb.** sprechen mit jm. III
speaker ['spi:kə]:
1. Lautsprecher I
2. Sprecher/in; Redner/in V 4 (97)
special ['speʃl]:
1. besondere(r, s) I
2. Special; Sondersendung; besonderes Angebot V 3 (64)
special effects *(pl)* [speʃl ɪ'fekts] Special Effects *(in Filmen)* IV
special offer [speʃl 'ɒfə] Sonderangebot I
°**speculate** ['spekjuleɪt] spekulieren
speech [spi:tʃ] Rede, Ansprache III
°**speech bubble** ['spi:tʃ bʌbl] Sprechblase
spell [spel] buchstabieren I
spelling ['spelɪŋ] Rechtschreibung, Schreibweise IV
spend time/money (on) [spend], **spent, spent** Geld ausgeben (für); Zeit verbringen (mit) II
spent [spent] *siehe* **spend**
spider ['spaɪdə] Spinne V 1 (11)
spinach ['spɪnɪtʃ], ['spɪnɪdʒ] Spinat III
spirit ['spɪrɪt] Geist, Stimmung IV **spirit of the times** Zeitgeist IV **be in good spirits** in guter Stimmung sein, guter Dinge sein IV **community spirit** Gemeinschaftssinn IV **school spirit** Schulklima, Gemeinschaftsgefühl IV **team spirit** Teamgeist IV
spoke [spəʊk] *siehe* **speak**
spoken ['spəʊkən] *siehe* **speak**
sponsor ['spɒnsə]:
1. sponsern V 4 (90)
2. Sponsor/in *(Geldgeber/in)* V 4 (90)
spook [spu:k] *(infml)* Gespenst, Geist V 2 (43)
spooky ['spu:ki] unheimlich, gruselig V 2 (43)
sport [spɔ:t] Sport; Sportart I **do sport** Sport treiben I
sports hall ['spɔ:ts hɔ:l] Sporthalle I
sportsman/-woman ['spɔ:tsmən, -wʊmən] Sportler/in III
sporty ['spɔ:ti] sportlich II
spot [spɒt]:
1. entdecken IV
2. Fleck, Pickel IV
3. Stelle, Ort V 1 (11)
spray-paint ['spreɪ peɪnt] mit Farbe besprühen IV
spread (sth.) [spred], **spread, spread** etwas verbreiten *(Virus, Krankheit)*; sich ausbreiten V 4 (90)

spring [sprɪŋ] Frühling II
square [skweə] Platz *(in der Stadt)* I
squat [skwɒt] (ein Haus/Grundstück) besetzen V 2 (43)
squatter ['skwɒtə] Hausbesetzer/in V 2 (43)
stadium ['steɪdiəm] Stadion III
staff [stɑ:f] Personal, Belegschaft III
stairs *(pl)* [steəz] Treppe; (Treppen-)Stufen II
stall [stɔ:l] (Markt-)Stand, Bude III
stamp [stæmp] Stempel; Briefmarke II
stand [stænd], **stood, stood** stehen; sich (hin)stellen II **stand up** aufstehen IV °**stand tall** aufrecht stehen, den Kopf hoch tragen
standard ['stændəd]:
1. Norm, Standard V 4 (84)
2. normal, üblich, Standard- V 4 (84)
stank [stæŋk] *siehe* **stink**
star [stɑ:]:
1. Star III
2. Stern IV
stare (at) [steə] (an)starren IV
start [stɑ:t]:
1. Anfang, Start II
2. beginnen, anfangen I
start off (as) anfangen (als) IV
To start with, ... Erstens ..., Zuerst (mal) ..., Zunächst ... IV
°**start-up** ['stɑ:t ʌp] Start-up, Jungunternehmen
state [steɪt] (Bundes-)Staat IV
statement ['steɪtmənt] Aussage(satz) III **personal statement** persönliche Beschreibung, Selbstbeschreibung V 3 (62)
station ['steɪʃn] Bahnhof II
statue ['stætʃu:] Statue II
stay [steɪ]:
1. bleiben I
2. Aufenthalt III
steak [steɪk] Steak III
steal [sti:l], **stole, stolen** stehlen IV
step [step]:
1. Schritt; Stufe II
step by step Schritt für Schritt V 2 (49)
2. treten *(einen Schritt tun)* V 4 (91)
step closer näher treten, näher (heran)kommen IV
stepbrother ['stepbrʌðə] Stiefbruder I
stepdad ['stepdæd] Stiefvater I
step-dancing ['step dɑ:nsɪŋ] Step Dancing *(irischer Tanz)* IV
stepfather ['stepfɑ:ðə] Stiefvater I
stepmother ['stepmʌðə] Stiefmutter I
stepmum ['stepmʌm] Stiefmutter I
stepsister ['stepsɪstə] Stiefschwester I
stick [stɪk] Stock IV
stick, stuck, stuck [stɪk]: **stick together** zusammenhalten III **stick with sth.** bei etwas bleiben V 1 (18)
still [stɪl] (immer) noch; trotzdem II

sting [stɪŋ]:
1. (Insekten-)Stich V 1 (11)
2. **sting, stung, stung** stechen *(Insekt)*; brennen V 1 (11)
°**stinger** ['stɪŋə] Würfelqualle *(giftige Qualle)*
stink [stɪŋk], **stank, stunk** stinken IV
stole [stəʊl] *siehe* **steal**
stolen ['stəʊlən] *siehe* **steal**
stomach ['stʌmək] Bauch; Magen II
stomach ache Bauchschmerzen II
stone [stəʊn] Stein II
stood [stʊd] *siehe* **stand**
stoop [stu:p] *(AE)* kleine Terrasse vor der Tür, Treppe/Aufgang zum Hauseingang IV
stop [stɒp]:
1. Haltestelle II
2. (an)halten; stoppen; aufhören (mit) I
stop by vorbeischauen (in/bei/an) II
°**It stops with me.** Es hört bei mir auf. / Ich mache da nicht mit.
store [stɔ:] Geschäft, Laden III
storey ['stɔ:ri] *(BE)* Stock, Stockwerk, Etage V 3 (69)
storm [stɔ:m] Sturm; Gewitter IV
story ['stɔ:ri]:
1. Geschichte I
2. *(AE)* Stock, Stockwerk, Etage V 3 (69)
straight [streɪt]:
1. gerade; *(Haare)* glatt II
2. **straight on** geradeaus (weiter) II
°3. **straight away** sofort
strange [streɪndʒ] seltsam, sonderbar II
°**strategy** ['strætədʒi] Strategie
strawberry ['strɔ:bəri] Erdbeere IV
street [stri:t] Straße *(in Ortschaften)* I
streetball ['stri:tbɔ:l] Streetball *(Variante des Basketballs)* IV
streetballer ['stri:tbɔ:lə] Streetball-Spieler/in IV
strength [streŋθ] Stärke, Kraft V 3 (58)
stress [stres] Stress, Belastung V 1 (12)
heat stress Hitzestress, Wärmebelastung des Körpers V 1 (12)
stressed [strest] gestresst III
strict [strɪkt] streng I
°**strike** [straɪk] streiken
stripe [straɪp] Streifen V 1 (21)
stroke [strəʊk] streicheln I
strong [strɒŋ] stark III
structure ['strʌktʃə]:
1. strukturieren, gliedern III
2. Struktur V 1 (24)
stuck [stʌk] *siehe* **stick**
stud [stʌd] (Ohr-/Nasen-)Stecker V 1 (22)
student ['stju:dnt] Schüler/in; Student/in I
studio ['stju:diəʊ] Studio I
study ['stʌdi] studieren; lernen V 3 (59)
stuff [stʌf] *(infml)* Zeug, Kram II
stung [stʌŋ] *siehe* **sting**
stunk [stʌŋk] *siehe* **stink**
stupid ['stju:pɪd] dumm, blöd I
style [staɪl] Stil(richtung); Art IV
stylist ['staɪlɪst] Friseur/in; (Mode-)Stylist/in V 3 (60)
subject ['sʌbdʒɪkt] Thema; *(in E-Mails)* Betreff II
subway ['sʌbweɪ] *(AE)* U-Bahn IV
success [sək'ses] Erfolg IV
successful [sək'sesfl] erfolgreich III
such (a) [sʌtʃ] so(lch) (ein/e) III
there's no such thing as ... es gibt kein/e ... III
suck [sʌk]: **It sucks!** Es nervt! / Es ist Mist! III
suddenly ['sʌdənli] plötzlich, auf einmal II
suffer (from) ['sʌfə] leiden (an), erleiden V 1 (12)
sugar ['ʃʊgə] Zucker II
sugary ['ʃʊgəri] süß(lich), zuckerhaltig II
suggest sth. (to sb.) [sə'dʒest] (jm.) etwas vorschlagen III
suggestion [sə'dʒestʃən] Vorschlag V 2 (36)
suitable ['su:təbl] geeignet, passend V 3 (61)
°**sum** [sʌm] Summe, Betrag
sum sth. up [sʌm 'ʌp] etwas zusammenfassen III
summarize ['sʌməraɪz] zusammenfassen III
summary ['sʌməri] Zusammenfassung III
summer ['sʌmə] Sommer I
summer camp ['sʌmə kæmp] (Sommer-)Ferienlager II
sun [sʌn] Sonne I
suncream ['sʌnkri:m] Sonnencreme I
Sunday ['sʌndeɪ], ['sʌndi] Sonntag I
sung [sʌŋ] *siehe* **sing**
sunglasses *(pl)* ['sʌnglɑ:sɪz] *(eine)* Sonnenbrille I
sunk [sʌŋk] *siehe* **sink**
sunlight ['sʌnlaɪt] Sonnenlicht IV
sunny ['sʌni] sonnig II
°**sunscreen** ['sʌnskri:n] Sonnenschutzcreme
sunshine ['sʌnʃaɪn] Sonnenschein IV
°**suntan** ['sʌntæn] Sonnenbräune
supermarket ['su:pəmɑ:kɪt] Supermarkt I
supplies *(pl)* [sə'plaɪz] Verbrauchsgüter, Vorrat/Vorräte IV
support [sə'pɔ:t] Unterstützung V 2 (37)
°**suppose** [sə'pəʊz] glauben, denken, annehmen **I suppose** ich denke, ich glaube, ich nehme an
sure [ʃʊə], [ʃɔ:] sicher I **for sure** ganz sicher, ganz bestimmt V 3 (66)
make sure that ... darauf achten, dass ...; dafür sorgen, dass ... V 1 (24)
surf [sɜ:f] surfen (über) IV
surfer ['sɜ:fə] Surfer/in IV
surprise [sə'praɪz]:
1. überraschen IV
2. Überraschung I
surprised [sə'praɪzd] überrascht II
surprising [sə'praɪzɪŋ] überraschend IV **surprisingly** überraschenderweise IV
°**surroundings** *(pl)* [sə'raʊndɪŋz] Umgebung
survey ['sɜ:veɪ] Umfrage II
°**survive** [sə'vaɪv] überleben
survivor [sə'vaɪvə] Überlebende/r IV
suspend (sb. from sth.) [sə'spend] (jn. von etwas) suspendieren, zwangsbeurlauben III
suspension bridge [sə'spenʃn brɪdʒ] Hängebrücke IV
suspicious (of) [sə'spɪʃəs] verdächtig; misstrauisch (gegenüber) IV
swam [swæm] *siehe* **swim**
swamp [swɒmp] Sumpf IV
swap (for) [swɒp] (aus-, um)tauschen (gegen) IV
sweat [swet] Schweiß IV
sweatshirt ['swetʃɜ:t] Sweatshirt I
sweets *(pl)* [swi:ts] Bonbons, Süßigkeiten I
swerve [swɜ:v] *(das Auto/Steuer)* herumreißen, *(mit dem Auto)* ausweichen V 1 (20)
swim [swɪm], **swam, swum** schwimmen I **go swimming** schwimmen gehen I
swimmer ['swɪmə] Schwimmer/in III
swimming pool ['swɪmɪŋ pu:l] Schwimmbad I
swimming trunks *(pl)* ['swɪmɪŋ trʌŋks] Badehose I
swimsuit ['swɪmsu:t] Badeanzug I
swing [swɪŋ], **swung, swung** schwingen; *(zum Schlag)* ausholen IV
switch sth. on/off [swɪtʃ 'ɒn], [swɪtʃ 'ɒf] etwas einschalten / ausschalten II
sword [sɔ:d] Schwert II
swum [swʌm] *siehe* **swim**
swung [swʌŋ] *siehe* **swing**
symbol ['sɪmbl] Symbol III
system ['sɪstəm] System V 3 (64)

T

table ['teɪbl]:
1. Tisch I
set the table den Tisch decken I
°2. Tabelle
tablet ['tæblət] Tablet(-PC) V 4 (82)
tae kwon do [taɪ kwɒn 'dəʊ] Taekwondo I
tag line ['tæg laɪn] (Werbe-)Slogan IV
tail [teɪl] Schwanz II
take [teɪk], **took, taken**:
1. (mit)nehmen; bringen II
2. dauern, *(Zeit)* brauchen, in Anspruch nehmen III
take me to the theatre mit mir ins

Theater gehen I **take notes** sich Notizen machen II **take over** die Macht übernehmen V 4 (90) **take photos** Fotos machen II **take place** stattfinden III **take sth. on** etwas annehmen, übernehmen V 1 (15) **take sth. up** mit etwas (neu) anfangen III **take the time to do sth.** sich die Zeit nehmen, etwas zu tun IV **take the train** dem Zug nehmen II **I'll take it.** Ich nehme es (ihn, sie). *(beim Einkaufen)* I **She can take a joke.** Sie versteht Spaß. III

takeaway ['teɪkəweɪ] Essen zum Mitnehmen V 3 (56)

taken ['teɪkən] *siehe* **take**

°**take-off** ['teɪk ɒf] Start *(Flugzeug)*

talent ['tælənt] Talent, Begabung III

talk [tɔːk]:
1. **talk (to)** sprechen, reden (mit) I
2. Vortrag, Rede; Gespräch II
give a talk einen Vortrag halten II

talker ['tɔːkə] Redner/in III

tall [tɔːl] groß *(Person)*; hoch *(Gebäude)* II °**stand tall** aufrecht stehen, den Kopf hoch tragen

tan [tæn] bräunen; braun werden *(in der Sonne)* IV

tap sth. [tæp] (leise) klopfen, tippen an etwas IV

target ['tɑːgɪt]:
1. Ziel V 3 (64)
2. **target sb.** auf jn. zielen *(jn. als Zielgruppe haben/wählen)*, jn. ins Visier nehmen V 4 (86)

tart [tɑːt] (Obst-)Törtchen III

task [tɑːsk] Aufgabe II

taste [teɪst] schmecken; kosten *(probieren)* III

tattoo [tə'tuː] Tattoo, Tätowierung II

taught [tɔːt] *siehe* **teach**

°**taunt** [tɔːnt] Spott, höhnische Bemerkung

taxi ['tæksi] Taxi II

tea [tiː] Tee I

teach [tiːtʃ], **taught, taught** jn. unterrichten; jm. etwas beibringen III **teach sb. a lesson** jm. eine Lektion erteilen V 1 (22)

teacher ['tiːtʃə] Lehrer/in I

team [tiːm] Team, Mannschaft I

teammate ['tiːmmeɪt] Mannschaftskamerad/in V 2 (37)

teamwork ['tiːmwɜːk] Teamwork, Teamarbeit III

tear [tɪə] Träne IV

tease sb. [tiːz] jn. hänseln, sich über jn. lustig machen V 2 (34)

technician [tek'nɪʃn] Techniker/in II

°**technique** [tek'niːk] Methode, Technik

techno ['teknəʊ] Techno *(Musik)* III

technology [tek'nɒlədʒi] Technik(unterricht); Technologie I

teen [tiːn] Teenager II

teen talk ['tiːn tɔːk] Teenagergespräche II

teenage kids ['tiːneɪdʒ] Kinder im Teenageralter III

teenager ['tiːneɪdʒə] Teenager III

teeth [tiːθ] *Plural von* tooth IV

telephone ['telɪfəʊn] Telefon III

tell (about) [tel], **told, told** erzählen (von), berichten (über) II **tell sb. (not) to do sth.** jn. auffordern, etwas (nicht) zu tun; jm. sagen, dass er/sie etwas (nicht) tun soll IV

temperature ['temprətʃə] Temperatur; Fieber II **have a temperature** Fieber haben II **take sb.'s temperature** (bei jm.) Fieber messen V 1 (13)

ten [ten] zehn I

tennis ['tenɪs] Tennis I

tent [tent] Zelt II

term [tɜːm] Trimester III

terrible ['terəbl] schrecklich, fürchterlich I

territory ['terətri] Gebiet, Territorium IV

test [test]:
1. testen III
2. Klassenarbeit, Test II
3. *(kurz für:* **driving test)** Fahrprüfung, Führerscheinprüfung IV

tester ['testə] Tester/in V 4 (93)

text [tekst]:
1. SMS; Text I
2. **text sb.** jm. eine SMS schicken I

text message ['tekst mesɪdʒ] SMS I

textbook ['tekstbʊk] Schulbuch, Lehrbuch I

than [ðən]: **older than me** älter als ich II

thank sb. [θæŋk] sich bei jm. bedanken II

thank you ['θæŋk juː] danke (schön) I

°**thankful** ['θæŋkfl] dankbar

thanks [θæŋks] danke (schön) I

Thanksgiving [θæŋks'gɪvɪŋ] Erntedankfest *(amerikanischer Feiertag am vierten Donnerstag im November)* IV

that [ðæt]:
1. das (dort) I
that field das Feld (dort), jenes Feld I **That's £ 159.** Das macht 159 Pfund. I
2. **that bad** so schlecht/schlimm V 2 (45)
3. der, die, das *(Relativpronomen)* II
a dog that could be Buster ein Hund, der Buster sein könnte II
4. dass II
the good news is that ... die gute Nachricht ist, dass ... II

the [ðə] der, die, das I

theatre ['θɪətə] Theater I

their [ðeə] ihr/e *(Plural)* I

theirs [ðeəz] ihre/r, ihrs *(zu „they")* V 1 (21)

them [ðem], [ðəm] sie, ihnen I **It wasn't them.** Sie waren es nicht. II

°**theme** [θiːm] Thema

theme park ['θiːm pɑːk] Themenpark *(Freizeitpark mit Attraktionen zu einem bestimmten Thema)* I

themselves [ðəm'selvz] sie/sich selbst *(Plural)* III

then [ðen] dann, danach I

°**theory** ['θɪəri] Theorie

there [ðeə] da, dort; dahin, dorthin I **there are** es sind / es gibt I **there's (= there is)** es ist / es gibt I

these [ðiːz] die, diese (hier) I

they [ðeɪ] sie *(Plural)* I

thin [θɪn] dünn IV

thing [θɪŋ] Ding, Sache I

think [θɪŋk], **thought, thought** denken, meinen, glauben I **think about** nachdenken über V 1 (21) **think of sth.** denken an etwas; sich etwas überlegen, ausdenken III **What do you think?** Was meinst du? / Was denkst du? I

thinker ['θɪŋkə] Denker/in V 3 (61)

third [θɜːd] dritte(r, s) I

Thirdly, ... ['θɜːdli] Drittens ... III

thirsty ['θɜːsti]: **be thirsty** durstig sein, Durst haben II

this [ðɪs]:
1. dies; diese(r, s) I
This is Rob Blake. Hier spricht Rob Blake. *(am Telefon)* III **this morning/afternoon/evening** heute Morgen/Nachmittag/Abend II
2. **this bad** so schlecht/schlimm V 2 (45)

those boys [ðəʊz] die Jungen dort, jene Jungen II

though [ðəʊ]:
1. obwohl V 4 (85)
°**even though** auch wenn, obwohl *(betont)*
2. **... though.** ... aber ..., ... trotzdem ... V 3 (66)

thought [θɔːt]:
1. *siehe* **think**
°2. Gedanke

thousand ['θaʊznd] tausend III

threaten ['θretn] (be)drohen V 1 (20)

three [θriː] drei I

threw [θruː] *siehe* **throw**

throat [θrəʊt] Hals II **a sore throat** Halsschmerzen II

through [θruː] durch I

throw [θrəʊ], **threw, thrown** werfen III

thrown [θrəʊn] *siehe* **throw**

thumb [θʌm] Daumen IV **give sb. the thumbs down** jm. Ablehnung zeigen IV **give sb. the thumbs up** jm. Zustimmung zeigen IV

thunderstorm ['θʌndəstɔːm] Gewitter IV

Thursday ['θɜːzdeɪ], ['θɜːzdi] Donnerstag I

ticket ['tɪkɪt] Eintrittskarte, Fahrkarte I

ticket office ['tɪkɪt ɒfɪs] Kartenschalter II
tidy ['taɪdi]:
1. aufräumen II
2. ordentlich II
tie [taɪ] Krawatte I
tiger ['taɪgə] Tiger I
tights *(pl)* [taɪts] Strumpfhose I
till [tɪl] bis V 4 (91)
time [taɪm]:
1. Zeit; Uhrzeit I
at all times jederzeit, ständig V 3 (61) **on time** pünktlich II **take the time to do sth.** sich die Zeit nehmen, etwas zu tun IV **What's the time?** Wie spät ist es? I
2. Mal I
this time dieses Mal I
timeline ['taɪmlaɪn] Zeitstrahl, Zeitachse, Chronik IV
timetable ['taɪmteɪbl] Stundenplan I
tip [tɪp] Tipp II
tired ['taɪəd] müde I
title ['taɪtl] Titel, Überschrift IV
to [tu], [tə]:
1. zu, nach I
to the cinema ins Kino I **Have you ever been to …?** Bist du schon mal in … gewesen? III **the most interesting information to me** die interessanteste Information für mich II
2. (um) zu I
how to do sth. wie man etwas tut / tun kann / tun soll III **she didn't know what to say** sie wusste nicht, was sie sagen sollte II **things to do** Dinge, die man tun kann III **time to eat** Zeit zu essen I
3. bis I
from Monday to Friday von Montag bis Freitag I
4. vor *(Uhrzeiten)* I
quarter to 7 viertel vor 7 I
toast [təʊst]:
1. Toast I
2. toasten IV
today [tə'deɪ] heute I
together [tə'geðə] zusammen I
toilet ['tɔɪlət] Toilette I
toilet roll ['tɔɪlət rəʊl] Rolle Toilettenpapier II
told [təʊld] *siehe* **tell**
tomato, *pl* **tomatoes** [tə'mɑːtəʊ] Tomate III
tomorrow [tə'mɒrəʊ] morgen II
tongue [tʌŋ] Zunge; Sprache IV **Has the cat got his tongue?** Hat's ihm die Sprache verschlagen? IV
tonight [tə'naɪt] heute Nacht, heute Abend III
too [tuː]:
1. auch I
from Berlin too auch aus Berlin I
2. too old zu alt I
took [tʊk] *siehe* **take**

tool [tuːl] Werkzeug IV
tooth, *pl* **teeth** [tuːθ], [tiːθ] Zahn IV
through my teeth mit zusammengebissenen Zähnen IV
toothpaste ['tuːθpeɪst] Zahnpasta IV
top [tɒp] Spitze, oberes Ende I **at the top** oben, am oberen Ende; an der Spitze I
topic ['tɒpɪk] Thema II
torch [tɔːtʃ] Taschenlampe; Fackel V 1 (12) **flash a torch** mit einer Taschenlampe leuchten/blinken V 4 (93)
tornado, *pl* **tornadoes** [tɔː'neɪdəʊ] Tornado *(Wirbelsturm)* IV
torture ['tɔːtʃə]:
1. Folter V 4 (90)
2. foltern V 4 (90)
total ['təʊtl] total II
touch [tʌtʃ] anfassen, berühren III
tough [tʌf] (knall-)hart; zäh, robust IV
tour [tʊə] Tour, Reise III **a tour of the school** ein Rundgang durch die Schule I
tour guide ['tʊə gaɪd] Reiseleiter/in, Fremdenführer/in III
tourism ['tʊərɪzəm] Tourismus V 1 (17)
tourist ['tʊərɪst] Tourist/in I
tourist office ['tʊərɪst ɒfɪs] Touristeninformation, Fremdenverkehrsbüro III
toward [tə'wɔːd] *(AE)* nach, auf … zu, in Richtung (von) IV
towards [tə'wɔːdz] nach, auf … zu, in Richtung (von) IV
towel ['taʊəl] Handtuch I
tower ['taʊə] Turm III
town [taʊn] Stadt I
toy [tɔɪ] Spielzeug II
track [træk] Pfad, (Feld-)Weg III
°**stay on track** auf dem richtigen Weg bleiben
tractor ['træktə] Traktor III
trade [treɪd] Handel V 1 (17)
tradition [trə'dɪʃn] Tradition IV
traditional [trə'dɪʃənl] traditionell III
traffic ['træfɪk] (Straßen-)Verkehr III
traffic lights *(pl)* ['træfɪk laɪts] (eine) Ampel II
trail [treɪl] Weg, Pfad IV
train [treɪn] Zug, Eisenbahn II
train sb. [treɪn] jn. trainieren, ausbilden III
train station ['treɪn steɪʃn] Bahnhof II
trainee [treɪ'niː] Auszubildende/r, Trainee V 3 (60)
trainers *(pl)* ['treɪnəz] Sportschuhe I
training ['treɪnɪŋ]:
1. Training III
2. Ausbildung V 3 (56)
tramp [træmp] Obdachlose/r, Stadtstreicher/in V 2 (44)
trampoline ['træmpəliːn] Trampolin I
transport ['trænspɔːt] *(no pl)* Fortbewegungsmittel; Beförderung II
°**transportation** [trænspɔː'teɪʃn] Deportation, Zwangsverschickung

trap [træp] einschließen, fangen *(mit einer Falle)* IV **be trapped** gefangen sein, in der Falle sitzen IV
trash [træʃ] *(AE)* Abfall, Müll IV
travel ['trævl] *(das)* Reisen V 3 (60)
°**travel agency** ['trævl eɪdʒənsi] Reisebüro
travel costs *(pl)* ['trævl kɒsts] Reisekosten V 3 (60)
Travelcard ['trævlkɑːd] *Ein- oder Mehrtagesfahrkarte (London)* III
treasure ['treʒə] Schatz IV
tree [triː] Baum I **Money doesn't grow on trees.** Das Geld liegt nicht auf der Straße. *(Redewendung)* II
trek [trek] Wanderung, Treck V 3 (65)
trend [trend] Trend V 4 (86)
trendy ['trendi] modisch, „angesagt" III
tribe [traɪb] (Volks-)Stamm IV
trick [trɪk] Trick, Kunststück V 4 (86)
°**tricky** ['trɪki] knifflig, schwierig
trip [trɪp] Ausflug; Reise I
tropical ['trɒpɪkl] tropisch, Tropen- V 3 (64)
trouble ['trʌbl] Ärger, Schwierigkeiten I **be in trouble** Ärger haben, in Schwierigkeiten sein I
trousers *(pl)* ['traʊzəz] Hose I
truck [trʌk] Last(kraft)wagen, LKW IV
true [truː] wahr, richtig I **come true** wahr werden V 4 (95)
truly ['truːli] *(AE)*: **Yours truly** Mit freundlichen Grüßen *(Briefschluss)* IV
trust [trʌst] (ver)trauen IV
truth [truːθ] Wahrheit IV
try [traɪ] probieren, ausprobieren I
try hard sich (sehr) bemühen, sich anstrengen IV **try to do sth.** versuchen, etwas zu tun III
T-shirt ['tiː ʃɜːt] T-Shirt II
tsunami [tsuː'nɑːmi] Tsunami IV
tube [tjuːb] Schwimmreifen I **the Tube** *(infml)* die Londoner U-Bahn III
tuck your shirt in [tʌk 'ɪn] das/dein Hemd in den Rock/die Hose stecken IV
Tuesday ['tjuːzdeɪ], ['tjuːzdi] Dienstag I
°**turbocharged engine** ['tɜːbəʊtʃɑːdʒd] Turbomotor
Turkey ['tɜːki] (die) Türkei I
turn [tɜːn] sich umdrehen IV **turn around** sich umdrehen IV **turn away** sich abwenden, sich wegdrehen V 4 (90) **turn over** (sich) umdrehen III **turn right/left** (nach) rechts/links abbiegen II **turn sth.** etwas umdrehen V 3 (68) **turn up** auftauchen, erscheinen V 1 (20)
turn [tɜːn]: **It's your turn.** Du bist dran. / Du bist an der Reihe. I
°**take turns** sich abwechseln
°**turtle** ['tɜːtl] (Wasser-)Schildkröte
TV [tiː'viː] Fernseher I
twelve [twelv] zwölf I
twice [twaɪs] zweimal III

twig [twɪg] (kleiner) Zweig IV
twin [twɪn]: **twin sister/brother** Zwillingsschwester/-bruder IV **twins** Zwillinge IV
twin room [twɪn 'ru:m] Zweibettzimmer III
two [tu:] zwei I
type (of) [taɪp] Art, Sorte, Typ (von) V 4 (89)
typical (of) ['tɪpɪkl] typisch (für) III
tyre ['taɪə] Reifen V 1 (18)

U

ugly ['ʌgli] hässlich I
umbrella [ʌm'brelə] (Regen-)Schirm I
unable to do sth. [ʌn'eɪbl] unfähig / nicht in der Lage, etwas zu tun III
unattractive [ʌnə'træktɪv] unattraktiv V 3 (69)
uncle ['ʌŋkl] Onkel I
uncomfortable [ʌn'kʌmftəbl] unbequem, ungemütlich III °**be/feel uncomfortable** sich unbehaglich fühlen
uncool [ʌn'ku:l] uncool II
under ['ʌndə] unter I
underage disco [ʌndər'eɪdʒ] Disco für Minderjährige III
underground ['ʌndəgraʊnd] U-Bahn III
°**underline** [ʌndə'laɪn] unterstreichen
understand [ʌndə'stænd], **understood, understood** verstehen I
understood [ʌndə'stʊd] *siehe* **understand**
unemployed [ʌnɪm'plɔɪd] arbeitslos III
unfair [ʌn'feə] unfair III
°**unfenced** [ʌn'fenst] nicht eingezäunt
unfit [ʌn'fɪt] nicht fit II
unfriendly [ʌn'frendli] unfreundlich II
unhappy [ʌn'hæpi] unglücklich I
unhealthy [ʌn'helθi] ungesund II
uniform ['ju:nɪfɔ:m] Uniform I
uninteresting [ʌn'ɪntrəstɪŋ] uninteressant II
unit ['ju:nɪt] Lektion, Kapitel I
United [ju'naɪtɪd]: **United Nations, UN** Vereinte Nationen V 3 (66) **the United Kingdom (the UK)** das Vereinigte Königreich III
°**unity** ['ju:nəti] Einheit, (innere) Geschlossenheit
university [ju:nɪ'vɜ:səti] Universität V 3 (59)
unless [ən'les] es sei denn; außer (wenn) IV
unlike [ʌn'laɪk] anders als, im Gegensatz zu V 4 (95)
unnatural [ʌn'nætʃrəl] unnatürlich V 4 (86)
unsure [ʌn'ʃʊə], [ʌn'ʃɔ:] unsicher II
until [ən'tɪl] bis *(zeitlich)* II
untuck your shirt [ʌn'tʌk] das/dein Hemd aus dem Rock/der Hose (heraus)ziehen IV
unusual [ʌn'ju:ʒʊəl] ungewöhnlich III
unwanted [ʌn'wɒntɪd] unerwünscht V 4 (90)
unwelcome [ʌn'welkəm] unerwünscht, unwillkommen II
unwell [ʌn'wel] unwohl, krank III
up [ʌp] hinauf, hoch II **be up for sth.** *(infml)* bei etwas dabei sein, mitmachen V 1 (21)
up to ['ʌp tə] bis (zu) V 3 (60)
upside ['ʌpsaɪd] Vorteil, gute Seite III
upside down [ʌpsaɪd 'daʊn] verkehrt herum, auf dem/den Kopf V 1 (18)
upstairs [ʌp'steəz] (nach) oben *(die Treppe hoch)* I
uptown [ʌp'taʊn] *(AE)* außerhalb des (Stadt-)Zentrums, am Stadtrand IV
us [ʌs], [əs] uns I
use [ju:z] benutzen, verwenden I
used to [ju:st]:
1. **be used to** gewöhnt sein an IV **get used to** sich gewöhnen an IV
2. **where he used to play** wo er früher (immer) gespielt hat IV
useful ['ju:sfl] nützlich, hilfreich II
user ['ju:zə] (Be-)Nutzer/in V 3 (61)
usual ['ju:ʒʊəl] üblich, gewöhnlich III
usually ['ju:ʒuəli] normalerweise, meistens I

V

vacation [və'keɪʃn] *(AE)* Urlaub IV
vacuum cleaner ['vækjuəm kli:nə] Staubsauger V 3 (56)
vain [veɪn] eitel V 4 (85)
valid ['vælɪd] aktuell, gültig V 3 (64)
valley ['væli] Tal IV
value ['vælju:] Wert I **It's good value.** Es ist sein Geld wert. / Es ist preiswert. I
vamping ['væmpɪŋ] *spät in der Nacht noch aktiv sein* V 4 (96)
vampire ['væmpaɪə] Vampir V 4 (96)
van [væn] Transporter, Lieferwagen III
vegetables, *infml auch* **veg** ['vedʒtəblz], [vedʒ] Gemüse I
vehicle ['vi:əkl] Fahrzeug V 1 (12)
°**venom** ['venəm] Gift
°**verse** [vɜ:s] Vers, Strophe *(Lied)*
°**version** ['vɜ:ʃn] Version
very ['veri] sehr I **Thanks very much.** Vielen Dank. II
°**vicinity** [və'sɪnəti] Umgebung
victim ['vɪktɪm] Opfer V 2 (33)
video ['vɪdiəʊ] Video II
video chat ['vɪdiəʊ tʃæt] Videochat *(Telefongespräch per Videokonferenz)* II
video-chat ['vɪdiəʊ tʃæt] sich per Videokonferenz unterhalten V 4 (82)
view [vju:] (An-)Blick, (Aus-)Sicht II **point of view** Standpunkt III
°**viewpoint** ['vju:pɔɪnt] Standpunkt, Blickwinkel
village ['vɪlɪdʒ] Dorf I
vinegar ['vɪnɪgə] Essig III
violence ['vaɪələns] Gewalt; Gewalttätigkeit IV
violent ['vaɪələnt] gewalttätig; gewaltsam III
°**violet** ['vaɪələt] Veilchen *(Blume)*
virtual ['vɜ:tʃʊəl] virtuell V 4 (90)
virus, *pl* **viruses** ['vaɪrəs], ['vaɪrəsɪz] Virus V 4 (90)
visa ['vi:zə] Visum IV
visit ['vɪzɪt] besuchen I
visitor ['vɪzɪtə] Besucher/in; Gast I
visitor pass ['vɪzɪtə pɑ:s] Besucherausweis IV
visual ['vɪʒuəl] optisch, Seh- IV
visually impaired sehbehindert IV
visuals *(pl) (kurz für:* **visual materials***)* ['vɪʒuəlz] visuelle Materialien/Hilfsmittel V 1 (24)
vitamin ['vɪtəmɪn] Vitamin II
vlog [vlɒg] VLog *(Video-Blog)* V 4 (86)
vlogger ['vlɒgə] Vlogger/in *(Video-Blogger/in)* V 4 (86)
°**vocabulary** [və'kæbjələri] Wortschatz, Vokabular
voice [vɔɪs] Stimme II
°**voice-over** ['vɔɪs əʊvə] Filmkommentar, Off-Stimme
volleyball ['vɒlibɔ:l] Volleyball II
volunteer [vɒlən'tɪə]:
1. freiwillig/ehrenamtlich arbeiten *(unbezahlt)* IV
2. Freiwillige/r, Ehrenamtliche/r IV **volunteer work** freiwillige/ehrenamtliche Arbeit IV
volunteering [vɒlən'tɪərɪŋ] Freiwilligentätigkeit, ehrenamtliches Arbeiten IV
vote [vəʊt] abstimmen V 2 (47) **vote for sb.** für jn. stimmen II
voyage ['vɔɪɪdʒ] (See-)Reise IV

W

wagon ['wægən] Planwagen, (Pferde-)Fuhrwerk IV
waistcoat ['weɪskəʊt] Weste V 1 (20)
wait (for) [weɪt] warten (auf) I **wait and see** abwarten I **you can't wait** du kannst es kaum erwarten III
waiter ['weɪtə] Kellner III
waitress ['weɪtrəs] Kellnerin III
wake [weɪk], **woke, woken** wecken I **wake up** aufwachen I
°**wake-up call** ['weɪk ʌp kɔ:l] Weckruf
walk [wɔ:k]:
1. wandern, (zu Fuß) gehen I **walk around** umhergehen II **walk sb. home** jn. zu Fuß nach Hause begleiten V 2 (40)
2. Spaziergang II **go for a walk** einen Spaziergang machen, spazieren gehen II
walker ['wɔ:kə] Wanderer/Wanderin, Spaziergänger/in III
walking boots *(pl)* ['wɔ:kɪŋ bu:ts] Wanderstiefel II

wall [wɔːl] Wand, Mauer III
°**wander** ['wɒndə] (umher)wandern
want [wɒnt] wollen I **want sb. to do sth.** wollen, dass jd. etwas tut III **want to be** *(etwas)* sein wollen I
war [wɔː] Krieg IV
wardrobe ['wɔːdrəʊb] Kleiderschrank I
warm [wɔːm] warm II
warn sb. (about/against/of sth.) [wɔːn] jn. warnen (vor etwas / davor, etwas zu tun) V 2 (43)
warning (of/against) ['wɔːnɪŋ] Warnung (vor) IV
was [wɒz], [wəz]: **I/he/she/it was** *siehe* **be**
wash [wɒʃ] waschen; sauber machen II **wash up** abwaschen I
washing machine ['wɒʃɪŋ məʃiːn] Waschmaschine V 3 (56)
waste [weɪst] Verschwendung V 4 (96)
watch [wɒtʃ] *(sich etwas)* anschauen; beobachten I **watch for** Ausschau halten nach III **watch sb. do sth.** (zu)sehen, wie jemand etwas tut II **watch TV** fernsehen I
water ['wɔːtə] Wasser I
waterproof ['wɔːtəpruːf] wasserdicht, wasserfest, wasserundurchlässig V 1 (18)
wave [weɪv] Welle IV
wave (to sb.) [weɪv] (jm. zu)winken I
way [weɪ]:
1. Weg I
ask sb. the way jn. nach dem Weg fragen II **on the way to ...** auf dem Weg zu/nach ... I **tell sb. the way** jm. den Weg beschreiben II
2. Art und Weise II
way of life Lebensweise V 1 (15) **by the way** übrigens V 2 (49) **in some ways** in mancher Hinsicht IV **No way!** Auf keinen Fall! III **the way you live** deine Lebensweise (die Art, wie du lebst) II
3. **way cooler** *(infml)* viel cooler, weit(aus) cooler IV
we [wi], [wiː] wir I
weak [wiːk] schwach III
weakness ['wiːknəs] Schwäche V 1 (13)
weapon ['wepən] Waffe V 4 (91)
wear [weə], **wore, worn** tragen, anhaben *(Kleidung)* II
weather ['weðə] Wetter II
weather forecast ['fɔːkɑːst] Wettervorhersage II
website ['websaɪt] Website II
wedding ['wedɪŋ] Hochzeit IV **wedding present** Hochzeitsgeschenk IV
Wednesday ['wenzdeɪ], ['wenzdi] Mittwoch I
weed [wiːd] (Un-)Kraut V 2 (43)
week [wiːk] Woche I
weekday ['wiːkdeɪ] Werktag, Wochentag III
weekend [wiːk'end] Wochenende I **at the weekend** am Wochenende I
weeper ['wiːpə]: **Finders keepers, losers weepers.** Was man findet, darf man behalten. *(Redensart)* V 4 (91)
weigh [weɪ] wiegen V 2 (34)
weight [weɪt] Gewicht V 2 (34) **lose weight** abnehmen *(Gewicht)*, dünner werden V 2 (34)
°**weightlifting** ['weɪtlɪftɪŋ] Gewichtheben
weird [wɪəd] seltsam, komisch III
welcome ['welkəm]:
1. **welcome sb. (to)** jn. begrüßen (in), jn. willkommen heißen (in) III **Welcome to Plymouth.** Willkommen in Plymouth. I
2. **You're welcome.** Bitte, gern geschehen. / Nichts zu danken. I
Well, ... [wel] Nun, ... / Also, ... / Na ja, ... I
well [wel]: **Well done.** Gut gemacht! I **I hope you are well.** Ich hoffe, es geht euch gut. / Ich hoffe, ihr seid gesund/wohlauf. IV **I'm not feeling well.** Ich fühle mich nicht gut. II **it doesn't pay very well** es wird nicht besonders gut bezahlt IV **work/speak well** gut funktionieren/sprechen I
well-built [wel 'bɪlt] gut gebaut, kräftig IV
well-known [wel 'nəʊn] bekannt V 1 (10)
went [went] *siehe* **go**
were [wɜː], [wə]: **we/you/they were** *siehe* **be**
west [west] Westen; nach Westen II
westbound ['westbaʊnd] in Richtung Westen III
western ['westən] westlich, West- IV
wet [wet] nass I
whale [weɪl] Wal IV
what [wɒt]:
1. was I
2. welche(r, s) I
What about you? Und du? / Was ist mit dir? I **What are ...?** Was sind ...? I **What is it?** Was ist los? I **What page is it?** Auf welcher Seite sind wir? / Auf welcher Seite steht das? I **What's the time?** Wie spät ist es? I **What's your name?** Wie heißt du? I
Whatever. [wɒt'evə] *(infml)* Ach, egal. / Was soll's. IV
wheel [wiːl] Rad I
wheelchair ['wiːltʃeə] Rollstuhl I
when [wen]:
1. als II
2. wann I
When's your birthday? Wann hast du Geburtstag? I
3. wenn I
where [weə] wo; wohin I **Where are you from?** Wo kommst du her? I
which [wɪtʃ]:
1. **Which club?** Welcher Klub? II
2. der, die, das; die *(Relativpronomen)* V 1 (11)
while [waɪl]:
1. Weile IV
2. während IV
whisper ['wɪspə] flüstern II
whistle ['wɪsl] (Triller-)Pfeife II
white [waɪt] weiß I
who [huː]:
1. wer I
Who are you? Wer bist du? / Wer seid ihr? I
2. wen; wem II
Who did Adam meet? Wen hat Adam getroffen? / Wen traf Adam? II
3. der, die *(Relativpronomen, Person)* I
a person who ... eine Person, die ... I
whole [həʊl] ganze(r, s) II
whose [huːz] wessen V 1 (21) **Whose are these?** Wem gehören die (hier)? V 1 (21)
why [waɪ] warum I **that's why** deshalb, darum II
wide [waɪd] breit, weit V 1 (14)
wife, *pl* **wives** [waɪf], [waɪvz] (Ehe-)Frau IV
Wi-fi ['waɪ faɪ] WLAN, kabellose Datenübertragung III
wild [waɪld] wild I
will [wɪl]: **it won't rain (= it will not rain)** es wird nicht regnen II **the weather will be good** das Wetter wird gut sein II **We'll (= we will) find him.** Wir werden ihn finden. II
win [wɪn], **won, won** gewinnen I
wind [wɪnd] Wind II
winding ['waɪndɪŋ] kurvenreich III
window ['wɪndəʊ] Fenster I
windscreen ['wɪndskriːn] Windschutzscheibe *(Auto)* III
windscreen wipers *(pl)* ['wɪndskriːn waɪpəz] Scheibenwischer III
windy ['wɪndi] windig II
winner ['wɪnə] Gewinner/in II
winter ['wɪntə] Winter II
°**wise** [waɪz] weise, klug
wish [wɪʃ] wünschen IV **I wish I could tell you ...** Ich wünschte, ich könnte dir erzählen, ... IV
wishes ['wɪʃɪz]: **Best wishes** Viele Grüße ... *(Briefschluss)* I
witch [wɪtʃ] Hexe II
with [wɪð] mit I **with Ellie** bei Ellie I
°**within** [wɪ'ðɪn] innerhalb (von), in
without [wɪ'ðaʊt] ohne II
woke [wəʊk] *siehe* **wake**
woken ['wəʊkən] *siehe* **wake**
woman, *pl* **women** ['wʊmən], ['wɪmɪn] Frau I
won [wʌn] *siehe* **win**
wonder ['wʌndə] sich fragen; gern wissen wollen III
wonderful ['wʌndəfl] wunderbar III
won't [wəʊnt]: **it won't rain (= it will not rain)** es wird nicht regnen II
wood [wʊd] Holz; Wald III
wooden ['wʊdn] hölzern, Holz- IV

woodwork(ing) ['wʊdwɜːk] Holzbearbeitung IV **woodworking tools** *(pl)* Holzbearbeitungswerkzeuge IV
word [wɜːd] Wort I **word building** das Bilden von Wörtern II
°**wordbank** ['wɜːdbæŋk] Wortbank *(Sammlung von Wörtern zu einem Thema)*
wore [wɔː] *siehe* **wear**
work [wɜːk]:
1. Arbeit I
work on sth. arbeiten an etwas V 1 (24) **at work** bei der Arbeit, am Arbeitsplatz I
2. arbeiten I
work sth. out etwas herausfinden, etwas herausarbeiten IV
3. funktionieren I
work experience ['wɜːk ɪkspɪəriəns] Praktikum/Praktika; Arbeitserfahrung(en) V 3 (58)
°**work placement** ['wɜːk pleɪsmənt] Praktikum
workday ['wɜːkdeɪ] Arbeitstag I
worker ['wɜːkə] Arbeiter/in III
working hours *(pl)* [wɜːkɪŋ 'aʊəz] Arbeitszeit(en) V 3 (60)
workshop ['wɜːkʃɒp] Workshop *(Kurs)* I
world [wɜːld] Welt I **the best of both worlds** das Beste von beidem I
worn [wɔːn] *siehe* **wear**
worried (about) ['wʌrid] beunruhigt, besorgt (wegen) I
worry (about) ['wʌri] sich Sorgen machen (wegen, um) I **Don't worry.** Mach dir keine Sorgen. I
worse [wɜːs] schlechter, schlimmer II
worst [wɜːst] der/die/das schlechteste, schlimmste; am schlechtesten, am schlimmsten II
worth [wɜːθ] wert IV **The film is worth watching.** Es lohnt sich, den Film anzuschauen. IV
would [wʊd]: **I'd (= I would) like ...** Ich hätte gern ... / Ich möchte ... I **I'd (= I would) love to come.** Ich komme sehr gern. / Ich würde sehr gern kommen. I
wrestling ['reslɪŋ] Ringen IV
write [raɪt], **wrote, written** schreiben I **write sth. down** etwas aufschreiben III
writer ['raɪtə] Autor/in, Verfasser/in III
written ['rɪtn] *siehe* **write**
wrong [rɒŋ] falsch I **be wrong** Unrecht haben I
wrote [rəʊt] *siehe* **write**

Y

yard [jɑːd]:
1. Gelände III
2. *(AE)* Garten IV
3. Hof *(Innenhof)* III
4. **school yard** Schulhof II
yeah [jeə] *(infml)* ja I
year [jɪə] Jahr(gang) I **a 16-year-old** ein/e Sechzehnjährige/r III
yellow ['jeləʊ] gelb I
yes [jes] ja I
yesterday ['jestədeɪ] gestern II
yet [jet]: **... yet?** ... schon ...? IV **not ... yet** noch nicht II
Yippee! [jɪ'piː] Hurra! I
you [ju], [juː] du; dich; dir; ihr; euch; Sie; Ihnen I
young [jʌŋ] jung I
your [jɔː], [jə] dein/e; euer/eure; Ihr/e I
yours [jɔːz] deine, deiner, deins I
yourself [jɔː'self], [jə'self] du/dir/dich selbst I **See for yourself.** Sieh selbst! / Sehen Sie selbst! V 2 (43)
yourselves [jɔː'selvz], [jə'selvz] ihr/euch selbst III
youth [juːθ] Jugend, Jugend- III
Yuck! [jʌk] Igitt! III
yum [jʌm] *(infml)* lecker I
yummy ['jʌmi] *(infml)* lecker II

Z

°**Zap off.** [zæp 'ɒf] *(infml)* Hau ab!
zip up sth. [zɪp 'ʌp] den Reißverschluss von etwas zumachen IV
zip wire ['zɪp waɪə] Seilrutsche I
zone [zəʊn] Zone III
zoo [zuː] Zoo I

English sounds

[iː]	**gree**n, h**e**, s**ea**
[ɑː]	**a**sk, cl**a**ss, c**ar**, p**ar**k
[ɔː]	**or**, b**a**ll, d**oor**, f**our**, m**or**ning
[uː]	r**u**ler, bl**ue**, t**oo**, tw**o**, y**ou**
[ɜː]	**ear**ly, h**er**, g**ir**l, w**or**k, T-sh**ir**t
[ɪ]	**i**n, b**i**g, expens**i**ve
[e]	y**e**s, b**e**d, ag**ai**n, br**ea**kfast
[æ]	**a**nimal, **a**pple, bl**a**ck, c**a**t
[ʌ]	m**u**m, b**u**s, c**o**lour
[ɒ]	s**o**ng, **o**n, d**o**g, wh**a**t
[ʊ]	b**oo**k, g**oo**d, p**u**llover
[ə]	**a**gain, t**o**day, **a** sist**er**
[i]	happ**y**, monk**ey**
[eɪ]	n**a**me, **eigh**t, pl**ay**, gr**ea**t
[aɪ]	**I**, t**i**me, r**igh**t, m**y**
[ɔɪ]	b**oy**, t**oi**let, n**oi**se
[əʊ]	**o**ld, n**o**, r**oa**d, yell**ow**
[aʊ]	n**ow**, h**ou**se
[eə]	wh**ere**, p**air**, sh**are**, th**eir**
[ɪə]	h**ere**, d**ear**
[ʊə]	t**our**
[b]	**b**ike, ta**b**le, ver**b**
[p]	**p**en, **p**a**p**er, sho**p**
[d]	**d**ay, win**d**ow, goo**d**
[t]	**t**en, le**tt**er, a**t**
[g]	**g**o, a**g**ain, ba**g**
[k]	**k**itchen, **c**ar, ba**ck**
[m]	**m**an, re**m**e**m**ber, **m**u**m**
[n]	**n**o, o**n**e, te**n**
[ŋ]	wro**ng**, you**ng**, u**n**cle, tha**n**ks
[l]	**l**ike, o**l**d, sma**ll**
[r]	**r**uler, f**r**iend, so**rr**y
[w]	**w**e, **wh**ere, **o**ne
[j]	**y**es, **y**ou, **u**niform
[f]	**f**amily, a**f**ter, lau**gh**
[v]	**v**ery, se**v**en, ha**ve**
[s]	**s**ix, po**s**ter, ye**s**
[z]	**z**oo, qui**z**, hi**s**, mu**s**ic, plea**se**
[ʃ]	**sh**e, sta**t**ion, Engli**sh**
[ʒ]	u**s**ually, revi**s**ion, gara**ge**
[tʃ]	**ch**ild, tea**ch**er, wa**tch**
[dʒ]	**j**ob, **G**erman, pro**j**ect, oran**ge**
[θ]	**th**ing, **th**ree, ba**th**room, bo**th**
[ð]	**th**e, fa**th**er, wi**th**
[h]	**h**ouse, **wh**o, be**h**ind
[x]	*a**ch**, do**ch***

The English alphabet

a [eɪ]	**e** [iː]	**i** [aɪ]	**m** [em]	**q** [kjuː]	**u** [juː]	**y** [waɪ]
b [biː]	**f** [ef]	**j** [dʒeɪ]	**n** [en]	**r** [ɑː]	**v** [viː]	**z** [zed]
c [siː]	**g** [dʒiː]	**k** [keɪ]	**o** [əʊ]	**s** [es]	**w** ['dʌbljuː]	
d [diː]	**h** [eɪtʃ]	**l** [el]	**p** [piː]	**t** [tiː]	**x** [eks]	

infinitive	simple past	past participle	
be	*I/he/she/it* **was**; *you/we/you/they* **were**	**been**	sein
beat	**beat**	**beaten**	schlagen, besiegen
become	**became**	**become**	werden
begin	**began**	**begun**	beginnen, anfangen
bite [aɪ]	**bit** [ɪ]	**bitten** [ɪ]	beißen
bleed	**bled**	**bled**	bluten
blow	**blew**	**blown**	blasen (in); wehen *(Wind)*
break	**broke**	**broken**	brechen; zerbrechen
bring	**brought**	**brought**	bringen, mitbringen
build	**built**	**built**	bauen
buy	**bought**	**bought**	kaufen
catch	**caught**	**caught**	fangen, erwischen
choose [uː]	**chose** [əʊ]	**chosen** [əʊ]	(sich) aussuchen, (aus)wählen
come	**came**	**come**	kommen
cost	**cost**	**cost**	kosten
creep up (on)	**crept**	**crept**	sich heranschleichen (an)
cut	**cut**	**cut**	schneiden; *(Rasen)* mähen
deal with	**dealt** [e]	**dealt** [e]	umgehen mit, fertigwerden/klarkommen mit
dig	**dug**	**dug**	graben
do	**did**	**done** [ʌ]	tun, machen
drink	**drank**	**drunk**	trinken
drive [aɪ]	**drove**	**driven** [ɪ]	*(mit dem Auto)* fahren; (an)treiben
eat	**ate** [et, eɪt]	**eaten**	essen
fall	**fell**	**fallen**	fallen, hinfallen
feed	**fed**	**fed**	füttern
feel	**felt**	**felt**	fühlen; sich fühlen
fight	**fought**	**fought**	kämpfen; bekämpfen
find	**found**	**found**	finden
fly	**flew**	**flown**	fliegen
forget	**forgot**	**forgotten**	vergessen
freeze	**froze** [əʊ]	**frozen** [əʊ]	(ge)frieren; erstarren
get	**got**	**got**	bekommen; holen, besorgen; werden; gelangen, (hin)kommen
give	**gave**	**given**	geben
go	**went**	**gone** [ɒ]	gehen
grow	**grew**	**grown**	wachsen; anbauen, anpflanzen; (allmählich) werden
hang	**hung**	**hung**	hängen
have	**had**	**had**	haben
hear [ɪə]	**heard** [ɜː]	**heard** [ɜː]	hören
hide [aɪ]	**hid** [ɪ]	**hidden** [ɪ]	verstecken; sich verstecken
hit	**hit**	**hit**	schlagen; treffen; prallen/stoßen gegen/auf
hold	**held**	**held**	halten
hurt	**hurt**	**hurt**	verletzen; wehtun
keep	**kept**	**kept**	behalten; halten; aufbewahren
know [nəʊ]	**knew** [njuː]	**known** [nəʊn]	wissen; kennen
lay	**laid**	**laid**	legen
lead	**led**	**led**	führen, leiten
leave	**left**	**left**	abfahren; (weg)gehen; verlassen; zurücklassen
lend sb. sth.	**lent**	**lent**	jm. etwas leihen

infinitive	simple past	past participle	
let	**let**	**let**	lassen
lie [aɪ]	**lay**	**lain**	liegen
light	**lit**	**lit**	anzünden
lose [uː]	**lost** [ɒ]	**lost** [ɒ]	verlieren
make	**made**	**made**	machen
mean [iː]	**meant** [e]	**meant** [e]	bedeuten; meinen, sagen wollen
meet	**met**	**met**	treffen; sich treffen; kennenlernen
overspend (on)	**overspent**	**overspent**	zu viel Geld ausgeben (für)
overtake	**overtook**	**overtaken**	überholen
pay	**paid**	**paid**	bezahlen
put	**put**	**put**	*(etwas wohin)* tun, legen, stellen
read [iː]	**read** [e]	**read** [e]	lesen
retell	**retold**	**retold**	nacherzählen
ride [aɪ]	**rode**	**ridden** [ɪ]	reiten; *(Rad)* fahren
ring	**rang**	**rung**	läuten, klingeln; anrufen
run	**ran**	**run**	rennen, laufen
say [eɪ]	**said** [e]	**said** [e]	sagen
see	**saw**	**seen**	sehen
sell	**sold**	**sold**	verkaufen
send	**sent**	**sent**	schicken, senden
set the table	**set**	**set**	den Tisch decken
shake	**shook**	**shaken** [eɪ]	schütteln
shine	**shone** [ɒ]	**shone** [ɒ]	scheinen *(Sonne)*
show	**showed**	**shown**	zeigen
shut up	**shut**	**shut**	den Mund halten
sing	**sang**	**sung**	singen
sink	**sank**	**sunk**	sinken
sit	**sat**	**sat**	sitzen
sleep	**slept**	**slept**	schlafen
speak	**spoke**	**spoken**	sprechen
spend	**spent**	**spent**	ausgeben *(Geld)*; verbringen *(Zeit)*
spread	**spread**	**spread**	verbreiten *(z.B. Krankheit)*
stand	**stood**	**stood**	stehen; sich (hin)stellen
steal	**stole**	**stolen**	stehlen
stick together	**stuck**	**stuck**	zusammenhalten
sting	**stung**	**stung**	stechen *(Insekt)*; brennen
stink	**stank**	**stunk**	stinken
swim	**swam**	**swum**	schwimmen
take	**took**	**taken**	nehmen; mitnehmen; (weg-, hin)bringen; dauern, *(Zeit)* brauchen
teach	**taught**	**taught**	unterrichten, lehren
tell	**told**	**told**	erzählen, berichten
think	**thought**	**thought**	denken
throw	**threw**	**thrown**	werfen
understand	**understood**	**understood**	verstehen
wake	**woke**	**woken**	wecken
wear [eə]	**wore** [ɔː]	**worn** [ɔː]	tragen, anhaben *(Kleidung)*
win	**won** [ʌ]	**won** [ʌ]	gewinnen
write	**wrote**	**written**	schreiben

First names (Vornamen)
Aaron ['eərən]
Akira [ə'ki:rə]
Alex ['ælɪks]
Amanda [ə'mændə]
Amelia [ə'mi:liə]
Amy ['eɪmi]
Andi ['ændi]
Andrew ['ændru:]
Angie ['ændʒi]
Ant [ænt]
Ava ['ɑ:və], ['eɪvə]
Bella ['belə]
Ben [ben]
Bibi ['bɪbi]
Billie ['bɪli]
Brooke [brʊk]
Cal [kæl]
Cara ['kɑ:rə]
Carol ['kærəl]
Catherine ['kæθrɪn]
Charlotte ['ʃɑ:lət]
Chloe ['kləʊi]
Chris [krɪs]
Cindy ['sɪndi]
Claire [kleə]
Clay [kleɪ]
Cody ['kəʊdi]
Cynthia ['sɪnθiə]
Daisy ['deɪzi]
Dan [dæn]
Dana ['dɑ:nə], ['deɪnə]
Daniel ['dænjəl]
Danny ['dæni]
David ['deɪvɪd]
Devon ['devən]
Dominic ['dɒmɪnɪk]
Don [dɒn]
Dylan ['dɪlən]
Elias [ɪ'laɪəs]
Ella ['elə]
Elli ['eli]
Emily ['emɪli]
Emma ['emə]
Eric ['erɪk]
Ethan ['i:θən]
Gemma, Gem ['dʒemə], [dʒem]
Geoff [dʒef]
Grace [greɪs]
Harry ['hæri]
Hermione [hɜ:'maɪəni]
Hugh [hju:]
Jack [dʒæk]
Jacob ['dʒeɪkəb]
Jake [dʒeɪk]
Jamaal [dʒə'mɑ:l]
Jamie ['dʒeɪmi]
Jane [dʒeɪn]
Janine [dʒe'ni:n]
Jay [dʒeɪ]
Jess [dʒes]
Jessa [dʒesə]
Jessie [dʒesi]
Jimmy ['dʒɪmi]
Jon [dʒɒn]
Josh [dʒɒʃ]
Julia ['dʒu:liə]
Julie ['dʒu:li]
Justin ['dʒʌstɪn]
Kai [kaɪ]
Kat [kæt]
Kat-Anna [kæt'ænə]
Kate [keɪt]
Kathryn ['kæθrɪn]
Kirsty ['kɜ:sti]
Kumar [kʊ'mɑ:r]
Kyle [kaɪl]
Leah ['li:ə]
Leo ['li:əʊ]
Lily ['lɪli]
Lois ['ləʊɪs]
Lynn [lɪn]
Maggie ['mægi]
Marek ['mɑ:rek]
Mark [mɑ:k]
Marla ['mɑ:lʌ]
Matt [mæt]
Max [mæks]
Megan ['megən]
Megan, Meg ['megən], [meg]
Mel [mel]
Michael ['maɪkl]
Michelle [mɪ'ʃel]
Mike [maɪk]
Milly ['mɪli]
Mohammed [məʊ'hæmɪd]
Munny ['mʌni]
Natasha, Tasha [nə'tæʃə], ['tæʃə]
Neil [ni:l]
Nellie ['neli]
Nikki ['nɪki]
Niko ['ni:kəʊ]
Nuala ['nʊələ]
Ollie ['ɒli]
Oscar ['ɒskə]
Patrick ['pætrɪk]
Paul [pɔ:l]
Phillip ['fɪlɪp]
Poppy ['pɒpi]
Rani ['rɑ:ni]
Ratib ['rɑ:tɪb], ['reɪtɪb]
Reeko ['ri:kəʊ]
Riya ['raɪə]
Rob [rɒb]
Robert ['rɒbət]
Ron [rɒn]
Rosie ['rəʊzi]
Ruby ['ru:bi]
Scarlett ['skɑ:lət]
Scott [skɒt]
Serena [sə'ri:nə]
Shaz [ʃæz]
Simon ['saɪmən]
Simone [sɪ'məʊn]
Sophie ['səʊfi]
Steve [sti:v]
Sue [su:]
Tammy ['tæmi]
Thomas ['tɒməs]
Tia ['ti:ə]
Todd [tɒd]
Tommy ['tɒmi]
Zee [zi:]

Family names / Surnames (Familiennamen)
Backshall ['bækshɔ:l]
Blake [bleɪk]
Bradford ['brædfəd]
Chamberlain ['tʃeɪmbəlɪn]
Davis ['deɪvɪs]
Duggan ['dʌgən]
Eyers ['eɪəz]
Fermer ['fɜ:mə]
Fisher ['fɪʃə]
Forbes [fɔ:bz]
Gwynne [gwɪn]
Hughes [hju:z]
Jones [dʒəʊnz]
Karpinsky [kɑ:r'pɪnski]
Li [li:]
McCarthy [mə'kɑ:θi]
Metzger ['metsgə]
Moffat ['mɒfət]
Nolan ['nəʊlən]
Potter ['pɒtə]
Radcliffe ['rædklɪf]
Rayban ['reɪbən]
Smalley ['smɔ:li]
Smith [smɪθ]
Thomson ['tɒmpsən]
Twycross ['twaɪkrɒs]
Watson ['wɒtsən]
Winslow ['wɪnzləʊ]

Place names (Ortsnamen)
Adelaide ['ædəleɪd]
Alice Springs [ælɪs 'sprɪŋz]
Arctic Avenue [ɑ:ktɪk 'ævənju:]
Atlantic City [ətlæntɪk 'sɪti]
Ayr [eə]
Bondi Beach [bɒndaɪ 'bi:tʃ]
Brain [breɪn]
Brisbane ['brɪzbən]
Broadwater Farm Estate [brɔ:dwɔ:tə fɑ:m ɪ'steɪt]
Broken Hill [brəʊkən 'hɪl]
Brooklyn ['brʊklɪn]
Broome [bru:m]
Burdekin ['bɜ:dəkɪn]
California [kælə'fɔ:niə]
Canberra ['kænbərə]
Chester ['tʃestə]
Chicago [ʃɪ'kɑ:gəʊ]
Coober Pedy [ku:bə 'pi:di]
Crocosaurus Cove [krɒkə'sɔ:rəs 'kəʊv]
Darwin ['dɑ:wɪn]
down under [daʊn 'ʌndə]
Dublin ['dʌblɪn]
Frenshaw Avenue [frenʃɔ: 'ævənju:]
Great Barrier Reef [greɪt bæriə 'ri:f]
Heron Island [herən 'aɪlənd]
Hollywood ['hɒliwʊd]
Hong Kong [hɒŋ 'kɒŋ]
Kakadu National Park [kækədu næʃnəl 'pɑ:k]
Kalbarri [kæl'bɑ:ri]
Kimberley ['kɪmbəli]
Los Angeles [lɒs 'ændʒəli:z]
Louisiana [lui:zi'ænə]
Melbourne ['melbən]
Milan [mɪ'læn]
Mindil Beach [mɪndl 'bi:tʃ], [maɪndɪl 'bi:tʃ]
Muloorina Station [mʌlʊ'ri:nə steɪʃn]
New Jersey [nju: 'dʒɜ:zi]
New South Wales [nju: saʊθ 'weɪlz]
Oz [ɒz]
Paris ['pærɪs]
Perth [pɜ:θ]
Port Augusta [pɔ:t ɔ:'gʌstə]
Queensland ['kwi:nzlənd]
Regent's Park [ri:dʒənts 'pɑ:k]
Santa Monica [sæntə 'mɒnɪkə]
Seashell Motel [si:ʃel məʊ'tel]
Skillman ['skɪlmən]
Stroud [straʊd]
Sun Peaks Resort [sʌn pi:ks rɪ'zɔ:t]
Sydney ['sɪdni]

Tasmania [tæz'meɪnɪə]
Tottenham ['tɒtnəm]
West Thames College [west temz 'kɒlɪdʒ]
Yulara [jʊ'lɑːrə]
Yunta ['jʊntə]

Other names
(Andere Namen)

Anangu ['ʌnʌŋu]
Brothablack [brʌðə'blæk]
Darling ['dɑːlɪŋ]
Elite Stylists [eɪliːt 'staɪlɪsts], [ɪliːt 'staɪlɪsts]
Ghan [gæn], [gɑːn]
Hogwarts ['hɒgwɔːts]
Holden Monaro [həʊldən mə'nɑːrəʊ]
Incredible Hulk [ɪnkredəbl 'hʌlk]
Melburnian [mel'bɜːniən]
Royal Flying Doctor Service [rɔɪəl flaɪɪŋ 'dɒktə sɜːvɪs]
Snowbird Ski Hire [snəʊbɜːd 'skiː haɪə]
Stuart Highway [stjuːət 'haɪweɪ]
Sydneysider ['sɪdnisaɪdə]
Synapse ['saɪnæps], ['sɪnæps]
Terra nullius [terə 'nʊliəs]
Thunderbolt ['θʌndəbəʊlt]
Typhoon [taɪ'fuːn]
Uluru ['uːləru]
Zing [zɪŋ]

ENGLISH-SPEAKING COUNTRIES

English spoken as a first language
English used as an official language

General	Allgemein
You now have 60 seconds to read the tasks.	Du hast ab jetzt 60 Sekunden zum Lesen der Aufgaben.
Tick the right statements. (There's only one possible answer per statement.)	Setze ein ✓ bei den korrekten Aussagen. (Pro Aussage ist nur eine Antwort möglich.)
Complete the sentences (with not more than three words per gap / … than two words each).	Vervollständige die Sätze (mit bis zu drei Wörtern pro Lücke / mit je bis zu zwei Wörtern).
Fill in suitable words / the correct numbers.	Füge passende Wörter / die korrekten Zahlen ein.
Choose the correct options and fill in the blanks.	Wähle die korrekten Varianten und fülle die Lücken aus.
There is an example at the beginning.	Am Anfang steht ein Beispiel.
Listening	**Hörverstehen**
You are going to hear a story / an interview about …	Du wirst eine Geschichte / ein Interview über … hören.
Listen to these people talking about … Who thinks what? Tick the correct letters.	Höre dem Gespräch dieser Personen über … zu. Wer denkt was? Setze ein ✓ bei den korrekten Buchstaben.
You will hear each conversation twice.	Du wirst jedes Gespräch zweimal hören.
While you are listening, tick the correct box / …	Während du zuhörst, setze ein ✓ in das richtige Kästchen.
Mark the correct option to complete the sentences.	Markiere die jeweils korrekte Vervollständigung der Sätze.
Reading and Writing	**Leseverstehen und Schreiben**
First read the information about the people, then look at the job / holiday / … offers. In each case find two options the person could choose.	Lies zuerst die Informationen über die Personen, dann schau dir die Job-/ Ferien-/ …-Angebote an. Finde für jede Person zwei Möglichkeiten, die sie wählen könnte.
Match each of these headings with a suitable paragraph from the text. (Some paragraphs don't match.)	Ordne jede dieser Überschriften einem passenden Textabsatz zu. (Zu einigen Absätzen passt keine Überschrift.)
You can't find the answers to the following questions directly in the text.	Du wirst auf die folgenden Fragen keine direkten Antworten im Text finden.
The following words have more than one meaning. Which of the meanings is the one used in the text?	Die folgenden Wörter haben mehr als eine Bedeutung. Welche Bedeutung ist im Text gemeint?
Complete the following sentences with suitable phrases from the text (with not more than five to seven words per gap).	Vervollständige die folgenden Sätze mit passenden Wendungen aus dem Text (max. fünf bis sieben Wörter pro Lücke).
Decide whether the following statements are right or wrong.	Entscheide, ob die folgenden Aussagen wahr oder falsch sind.
Scan paragraph A. Name two examples …	Scanne Absatz A. Nenne zwei Beispiele …
Find words or expressions that mean more or less the same.	Finde bedeutungsähnliche Wörter oder Wendungen.
Include the following points: …	Berücksichtige die folgenden Punkte: …
Make sure to write about all the aspects presented in each task.	Achte darauf, dass du über alle Aspekte jeder Aufgabe schreibst.
Write your introductory letter.	Schreibe einen Brief, in dem du dich vorstellst.
Explain Susan's opinion of … and how she feels about …	Erkläre Susans Meinung über … und wie sie zu … steht.
Comment on the statement (from your point of view).	Kommentiere die Aussage (aus deiner Sicht).
Write about your own experience.	Schreibe über deine eigenen Erfahrungen.
Give your personal opinion about / of / on …	Schreibe dein persönliche Meinung über / zu …
Write a conclusion and state …	Schreibe eine Schlussfolgerung und lege … dar.
Write a diary entry / a letter of complaint / a suitable ending (in the way the story is told).	Schreibe einen Tagebucheintrag / eine Beschwerde / ein passendes Ende (im Stil der Geschichte).
Write a reply to the blog entry / email and include at least four of these aspects: …	Schreibe eine Antwort auf den Blog-Eintrag / die E-Mail und berücksichtige mindestens vier dieser Aspekte: …
Choose one topic and mark it. Write a text of about 180 words. Count your words and write the number at the end of the text.	Wähle ein Thema aus und markiere es. Schreibe etwa 180 Wörter. Zähle die Wörter und schreibe die Summe ans Ende deines Texts.
Complete the questionnaire below. Write keywords or short sentences.	Vervollständige den untenstehenden Fragebogen. Schreibe Stichwörter oder kurze Sätze.
What is the story behind the picture? Imagine you're one of the people. Write a text and include at least four of the following aspects: …	Was ist die Geschichte hinter dem Bild? Stell dir vor, eine der abgebildeten Personen zu sein. Schreibe einen Text und berücksichtige mindestens vier dieser Aspekte: …
Speaking	**Sprechen**
Discuss the advantages and disadvantages of …	Erörtere / Diskutiere die Vor- und Nachteile von …
Explain which … you would choose and why.	Erläutere, welche/n/s … du wählen würdest und warum.
Explain the positive and negative aspects / the pros and cons of …	Erläutere die positiven und negativen Aspekte von / die Pro- und Contra-Argumente zu …
Ask four different questions about … Use four different question forms.	Stelle vier verschiedene Fragen zu … Verwende vier unterschiedliche Frageformen.
Mediation	**Sprachmittlung**
Read the information and write down the main ideas in German.	Lies die Informationen und notiere die Hauptgedanken auf Deutsch.
Summarize the article in complete German sentences.	Fasse den Artikel in vollständigen deutschen Sätzen zusammen.

Titelbild
Shutterstock/Ralph Loesche

Illustrationen
Carlos Borrell, Berlin (Umschlaginnenseite 1, Umschlaginnenseite 3); **Michael Fleischmann**, Waldegg (S. 56; S. 57; S. 87; S. 207; S. 210; S. 211; S. 215; S. 222 oben, unten); **Jeongsook Lee**, Heidelberg (More challenge icon); **David Norman**, Meerbusch (S. 13 C (u. 30); S. 14; S. 20; S. 21 Mitte u. unten; S. 22 (u. 160); S. 35; S. 36; S. 40; S. 41; S. 42; S. 43; S. 44; S. 45; S. 46; S. 55 unten; S. 70; S. 90; S. 91; S. 92; S. 93; S. 94; S. 104 unten (u. 118); S. 118; S. 142; S. 143; S. 146; S. 178); **Dorina Teßmann**, Berlin (S. 13 unten; S. 28; S. 30; S. 39; S. 49; S. 55 A–C; S. 104 oben; S. 112)

Bildquellen
action press, Hamburg (S. 29 can regatta: REX FEATURES LTD.; S. 66 1. von oben: EVERETT COLLECTION/Warner Bros, 2. v. oben: REX FEATURES LTD.; S. 81 I: Everett Collection, K: Everett Collection, O: Rex Features; S. 85 A: NASA/REX; S. 148 oben: theoceancleanup/Exclusivepix Medaction press; S. 149 oben: theoceancleanup/Exclusivepix Medaction press); **akg-images**, Berlin (S. 141 Founding of Australia: Erich Lessing); **Bridgeman Art Library**, Berlin (S. 85 C: BRIDGEMANART.COM); **The Burdekin Crew, Smugglers of Light Foundation, Desert Pea Media** (S. 4 oben li.; S. 14 oben u. unten); **Clip Dealer** (S. 31 unten: Wavebreak Media LTD); **Corbis**, Düsseldorf (S. 6 unten li.: Hero Images; S. 10 A: Jim Holmes/Design Pics; S. 54 A: Ted Horowitz; S. 64 Mitte li.: Glowimages/Canopy; S. 66 unten: Johns PKI/Splash News; S. 82: Hero Images; S. 88 unten: I Love Images; S. 89: I Love Images; S. 98 oben: Ricardo Maynard/Demotix, unten re.: Mike Kemp; S. 150 oben re.: Corbis/Paul Martinka/Splash News); **www.colourbox.com** (S. 103 oben: Monkey Business Images); **dpa Picture Alliance**, Frankfurt/Main (S. 66 3. v. oben: AP Photo; S. 79: dpa; S. 99: dpa; S. 141 unten: dpa); **Frank Donoghue**, Nenagh (S. 154 oben li., Mitte, Mitte li. u. re.); **F1 Online**, Frankfurt/Main (S. 6 unten re. (u. 101): Maskot); **Fotofinder.com** (S. 13 A: images.de/Robert Harding; S. 31 1: images.de/Robert Harding); **Glow Images**, München (S. 8 B: imagebroker.com; S. 15 oben: Heritage Images RM; S. 54 B: CulturaRF); **Fotolia** (S. 6 oben re. 3. v. li.: olgavolodina; S. 10 B passport: Bernd Leitner; S. 16 oben girl: leonlester; S. 18 D: cirkoglu; S. 27: liza5450; S. 31 2: Mingis; S. 42 tablet (M): koosen; S. 51: Robert Elias; S. 52 Mitte: olly, unten: djtaylor; S. 53: hyunsuss; S. 54 C: VadimGuzhva; S. 59 Summer: olgavolodina; S. 60 1: Petro Feketa, 4: Wojciech Gajda, apply logo: valentint; S. 68 li.: Alexander Raths; S. 77 (u. 128): hartphotography; S. 78: Marcin Sadlowski; S. 80 A: Yevhenii Kukulka; S. 80 D: Chrispo, G: BlueSkyImages, H: Jurijs Korjakins, like/dislike: bahram7; S. 81 J: danr13, L: Axel Bueckert, M: berc, R: underworld; S. 84 S. 78 2. v. oben: lev dolgachov, 3. v. oben: szefei, 4. v. oben: Waldemar Dabrow, 5. v. oben: virinaflora, 6. v. oben: Vitalinka 17762, 7. v. oben: Jenifoto1; S. 85 B: loreanto; S. 86 unten: stockasso; S. 100: Hagen111; S. 102 A: Texelart, B: Leksiy Mark, C: Cobalt, D: sdecoret, F: sdecoret; S. 102 unten: Pavel Pecherskii; S. 103 unten li.: kotoyamagami; S. 139 working abroad: gustavofrazao, laboratory: Alexander Raths, factory: industrieblick, hospital: Robert Kneschke; S. 140 map (orange), opera, kangaroo, flag, currency, population, government: a7880ss; S. 150 oben li.: Eléonore H; S. 152 oben li. Bild A: Maksimchuk Vitaly, re. Bild B: Andrey Kiselev, brush: euthymia; S. 153 oben: Antonioguillem, unten: pixelliebe; S. 154 oben re.: cybrflower; S. 155 oben: Mark Higgins; S. 156 oben: TONO BALAGUER; S. 166: Monkey Business; S. 167: lev dolgachov; S. 170: JPC-PROD; S. 208 unten: spiders: Henrik Larsson; S. 210: Coka; S. 215: timonko; S. 216 vacuum cleaner: Nikolai Sorokin); **Imago Sportfotodienst**, Berlin (S. 37 unten); **Image Source**, Köln (S. 69: Rick Becker-Leckrone; S. 88 oben: Rick Becker-Leckrone; S. 106: Stefano Gilera; S. 130: Rick Becker-Leckrone; S. 155 unten: Image Source/Haris Artemis); **Indigineous Advisory Council/Australian Human Rights Commission** (S. 38); **klein und halm**, Berlin (S. 4 signs (u. 48): Steffen Schönbrunn); **LAIF**, Köln (S. 8 C (u. 166): COLIN Matthieu/Hemispheres Images; S. 9 G: Jean-Daniel Sudres/hemis.fr; S. 64 oben: Sven Torfinn); **Lyon Photography 2012** (S. 50 unten); **mauritius images**, Mittenwald (S. 8 D: Alamy/Marc Anderson; S. 9 E: Steffan Hill/Alamy, F li.: Bluegreen Pictures, re.: Diversion; S. 11 oben: Christine Osborne Pictures; S. 12 unten: Simon Grosset/Alamy; S. 15 Mitte: Susie Bennett/Alamy; S. 16 Bondi Beach: World Pictures; S. 17 oben boy: Novarc, unten street art: Ozimages/Alamy; S. 18 C: doug steley/Alamy; S. 20 (u. 160): martin berry/Alamy; S. 29 turtle watching: Gerry Pearce/Alamy, train journey: iconotec; S. 61 6: Greg Bajor; S. 65: Andrew Watson/Alamy; S. 68 re.: Ian Dagnall/Alamy; S. 70: PFMIX/Alamy; S. 80 B: Alvey & Towers Picture Library/Alamy, E: incamerastock/Alamy; S. 81 P: Fancy, Q: AKP Photos/Alamy; S. 86 oben billboard (M): Jeff Morgan 15/Alamy; S. 150 unten: Tom Hanley/Alamy; S. 156 unten: Stephen Barnes/Public Transport/Alamy; S. 169 unten: Image Source; S. 179: Onoky; S. 181 oben: UrbanImages/Alamy); **Reuters**, Berlin (S. 80 F: Brendan McDermi); **Rockfinch/Claire Cunningham**, Dublin (S. 24; S. 32 1–4 (u. 180); S. 33; S. 48; S. 58; S. 72 Mitte li. u. re., unten li. u. re.; S. 96; S. 134); **Royal Flying Doctor Service**, Brisbane, Australia (S. 12 oben u. RFDS logo); **Shutterstock** (S. 4 unten li. teenagers (u. 37): SpeedKingz; S. 6 oben li. (u. 75): AeChan, oben re. 1. v. li.: Golden Pixels LLC, oben re. 2. v. li.: Monkey Business Images; S. 8/) road (M): Totajla; S. 10 B flag: Steve Allen, girl: tmcphotos; S. 11 unten: Ethan Daniels; S. 13 B: Chet Mitchell; S. 18 A: Niels Quist, B: Martin Smith; S. 21 oben map (M) (u. 29): alison1414; S. 29 sandboarding: Lev Kropotov; S. 31 3 u. 5: Michael Leslie, 4: Visual society; S. 34 oben: michaeljung, unten: Hugo Felix; S. 42 unten: CREATISTA; S. 50 oben: Stokkete; S. 52 oben: Vikulin; S. 59 Charlotte: Monkey Business Images, Tom: Volt Collection, Max: Golden Pixels LLC, Ruby: Monkey Business Images; S. 60 2: Falcon Eyes, 3: CandyBox Images; S. 64 Mitte re.: Ioan Florin Cnejevici, unten li.: senee sriyota, unten re.: Riccardo Mayer; S. 72 oben: leungchopan; S. 74 A: Stephane Bidouze, C: Featureflash; S. 84 S. 78 1. v. oben: Helga Esteb; S. 86 oben boy (M): Kamenetskiy Konstantin; S. 97 oben: VIGE.CO; S. 98 unten li.: GTS Productions; S. 102: E: RealVector; S. 103 unten re.: mypokcik; S. 129: Benjavisa Ruang-

varee; S. 136: Monkey Business Images; S. 137: Path-Doc; S. 140 map (climate) of Australia: Rainer Lesniewski, plane icon: Dmitry Fokin, weather icon: bluelela; S. 141 A: Filipe Frazao, B: Stanislav Fosenbauer, C: Bildagentur Zoonar GmbH, D: Photo Image, E: Taras Vyshnya; S. 148/149 background plastic: archetype, plastic bottle caps: cici_2012, plastic bottle: Picsfive; S. 149 oben plastic bottle: Picsfive, plastic bag: photka, buoy: BW Folsom, bottle: Mariyana M, fishing line: Ad Oculos, cup: M. Unal Ozmen, drink holder: You Touch Pix of EuToch; S. 151 oben: Dana Nalbandian, unten: JStone; S. 152: computer, icons (M): WonderfulPixel, cursor: MSSAMSSA; S. 159: Paul Vasarhelyi; S. 165: Lorelyn Medina; S. 169 oben: Jesus Sanz; S. 171: Tharakorn; S. 174: Monkey Business Images; S. 206 oben: Anan Kaewkhammul, Mitte: annalisa e marina durante; S. 207: saraporn; S. 209: eddo; S. 216 washing machine: Sashkin, iron: Chimpinski; S. 222 lips: Trifonenko Ivan. Orsk, lipstick: Picsfive, kids: ostill; S. 223: Adisa; S. 224 oben: suns07butterfly, unten: NikoNomad; S. 225: Laura Gangi Pond; S. 226 li.: Crevis, re.: nanami7; S. 227 oben: Petr Malyshev, unten: Volt Collection; S. 228 oben: mkkmc, dog: Annette Shaff, hands: ags1973, unten: Sam Aronov; S. 230 li.: nanD_Phanuwat, re.: lynea; S. 231 oben: Arcady, unten: Ricardo Reitmeyer; S. 232: Anna Jedynak; S. 233: elenovsky); **TOPICMedia Service**, Putzbrunn (S. 16/17 skyline: Ingo Schulz); **vario images**, Bonn (S. 15 unten: RHPL); **Silvia Wiedemann**, Berlin (S. 154 unten)

Textquellen

S. 18 A *Living in the Kimberley*, reproduced with minor modification by permission of the Australian Broadcasting Corporation - Library Sales © ABC - Joanna Koeyers; **S. 18 B** *I'm a mud racer*, reproduced with minor modification by permission of the Australian Broadcasting Corporation - Library Sales © ABC - Ashlee Modr; **S. 20–22** *Swerve* adapted from Phillip Gwynne: Swerve, Penguin Australia, used by permission; **S. 26–27** The Spare Room from Kathryn Lomer © Kathryn Lomer, 2004, reproduced with minor modification by permission of University of Queensland Press; **S. 43–44** *Natasha's side of the story* and **S. 45–46** *Matt's side of the story* adapted from Chloe Rayban: Watching You, Watching Me, Harper Collins Publishers, London 1999, used by permission; **S. 50** *The kid in a wheelchair*, reproduced with permission of Teen Ink and TeenInk.com © Britain R. All rights reserved; A fashion model and a role model from Theo Merz: Jack Eyers: My dream is to be seen as a good model, not a sob story, in: The Telegraph, used by permission; **S. 68–70** *Seashell Motel* adapted from Lois Metzger: Working dayS. Short stories about teenagers at work, Persea Books; **S. 90–93** *Gamer* adapted from Chris Bradford: Gamer, Barrington Stoke Ltd., used by permission; **S. 142–147** *Riot* from David Fermer, Cornelsen English Library, used by permission; **S. 158** *My first real job* excerpt from 'Climbing the Golden Arches' by Marissa Nunez reprinted with permission from 'Starting With I' (Persea Books) © 1997 by Youth Communication / New York Center, Inc. (www.youthcomm.org)